DOING FIELDWORK IN JAPAN

CONTRIBUTORS

David M. Arase

Theodore C. Bestor

Victoria Lyon Bestor

Mary C. Brinton

John Creighton Campbell

Samuel Coleman

Suzanne Culter

Andrew Gordon

Helen Hardacre

Joy Hendry

David T. Johnson

Ellis S. Krauss

David L. McConnell

Ian Reader

Glenda S. Roberts

Joshua Hotaka Roth

Robert J. Smith

Sheila A. Smith

Patricia G. Steinhoff

Merry Isaacs White

Christine R. Yano

THEODORE C. BESTOR

PATRICIA G. STEINHOFF

VICTORIA LYON BESTOR

Doing Fieldwork in Japan

University of Hawai'i Press | Honolulu

© 2003 University of Hawaiʻi Press

All rights reserved

Printed in the United States of America

08 07 06 05 04 03   6 5 4 3 2 1

Library of Congress Cataloging-in-Publication Data

Doing fieldwork in Japan / [edited by] Theodore C. Bestor,
Patricia G. Steinhoff, and Victoria Lyon Bestor.

   p. cm.

Includes bibliographical references and index.

ISBN 0–8248–2525–X (hardcover : alk. paper) —

ISBN 0–8248–2525–1 (pbk. : alk. paper)

1. Ethnology—Japan—Field work. 2. Anthropologists—Japan.
3. Japan—Social life and customs. I. Bestor, Theodore C.
II. Steinhoff, Patricia G. III. Lyon-Bestor, Victoria.

GN635.J2 D65 2003

305.8ʹ007ʹ23—dc21

                     2003002472

University of Hawaiʻi Press books are printed on acid-free
paper and meet the guidelines for permanence and durability
of the Council on Library Resources.

Designed by April Leidig-Higgins

Printed by Maple-Vail Book Manufacturing Group

Andō Yoshifumi

(1936–2001)

College basketball star, kimono dyer,
community leader, bon vivant, and
family man. A wise mentor, good friend,
and close confidant of Ted and Vickey
Bestor for an all-too-brief two decades.

Takazawa Kōji

(1947–)

Student activist, editor, dog lover, chronicler
of the New Left, and prize-winning author.
Transformed over two decades from cautious
informant to research colleague and good
friend of Pat Steinhoff.

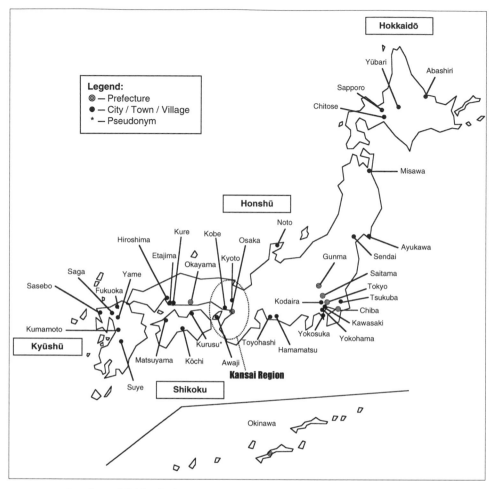

Legend:
◎ — Prefecture
● — City / Town / Village
* — Pseudonym

Hokkaidō

Yūbari
Abashiri
Sapporo
Chitose

Misawa

Honshū

Noto

Hiroshima
Kure
Kobe
Osaka
Ayukawa
Etajima
Kyoto
Gunma
Sendai
Okayama
Saitama
Saga
Yame
Tokyo
Sasebo
Fukuoka
Kodaira
Tsukuba
Chiba
Kawasaki
Kumamoto
Yokosuka
Yokohama

Kyūshū

Matsuyama
Kōchi
Kurusu*
Toyohashi
Hamamatsu
Awaji

Kansai Region

Suye

Shikoku

Okinawa

Contributors' Fieldwork Sites

CONTENTS

THEODORE C. BESTOR, PATRICIA G. STEINHOFF,
AND VICTORIA LYON BESTOR

Introduction: Doing Fieldwork in Japan

"You can observe a lot just by watching."
—attributed to Yogi Berra

This book brings together the experiences and reflections of twenty-one foreign scholars whose research in Japan has relied on talking to ordinary people (and extraordinary ones as well) about their lives and experiences; participating in everyday events; reading and listening to Japanese media, both popular and highly specialized; slogging through archives and bureaucratic records; and piecing together analyses and interpretations of contemporary Japanese life through the direct experiences of fieldwork. The book is certainly not a step-by-step how-to manual, but it does offer many insights and suggestions about doing research in Japan. We hope that it will be useful and accessible to various audiences concerned with information about Japan: graduate students and advanced researchers; Japan specialists and comparativists; academic scholars and people who use academic research for business or policy goals; journalists and businesspeople; students and instructors in courses about contemporary Japan. All of these audiences are concerned in one way or another with how field research in Japan is accomplished, if only to evaluate the usefulness of its results.

We also hope that the book offers models for social scientists planning research in other modern, complex societies; this book is focused on Japan and necessarily involves content and context specific to Japan, but it is our point that fieldwork in any society involves careful attention to cultural specificity. Many social scientists have written books on fieldwork and methodology, but we know of no other collection of research essays that explores such a range of research topics and methodologies with cultural context in clear focus. The fact that our contributors tackle such a wide variety of topical issues in their research should enable researchers planning fieldwork in other cultural contexts to draw inspiration, or at least insight, for their own projects elsewhere.

On a practical level, researchers encounter many issues as they plan for and engage in field research in Japan. Graduate students often struggle to identify appropriate methods for conducting their first fieldwork in Japan, sometimes because of a lack of detailed familiarity with either field research or with Japan, at other times because adapting general research methods to a specifically Japanese context presents unexpected problems. Non-Japan specialists doing short-term comparative research in Japan (with or without Japanese collaborators) face other challenges of reworking familiar techniques to unfamiliar settings. Still other questions about fieldwork in Japan, often raised by people who are interested in Japan but have little or no exposure to social science research methods, revolve around how a field researcher can "penetrate" the supposedly "closed" world of Japanese information and emerge with any useful, informed observations.

Through this book, we hope those who actually conduct fieldwork will gain a better understanding of some successful, concrete strategies for such research. We hope that the interdisciplinary insights made by our contributors will broaden understanding of the ways fieldwork can provide important data that are not easily found through other means. And we hope that general readers with an interest in Japan will find in these accounts of fieldwork a wide spectrum of illustrations of the grassroots realities of everyday life in contemporary Japanese communities, companies, institutions, and social movements.

If field research is regarded as a distinctive methodological approach, some academic disciplines such as anthropology and sociology that rely heavily on this technique are the obvious focus of attention. But in this volume we have defined fieldwork as gathering information in situ: on site, non-experimentally, from and about human informants. Framed in this way, researchers in many fields including history, political science, literature, religion, theater and performance studies, linguistics, organizational behavior, art history, legal studies, media studies, geography, management, architecture, and economics also rely to a greater or lesser extent on field research, even if "fieldwork" as such is not defined as part of a particular discipline's methodological canon.

As we worked on this volume, we were aware, of course, that many scholars of Japan have written excellent accounts of their own field research experiences. Some of these are extended examinations of both personal experience and Japanese society. Daniel I. Okimoto's *American in Disguise* (1971) and Dorinne K. Kondo's *Crafting Selves* (1990) both recount the refractions of multiple identities as researcher/American/Japanese American that occurred in their relationships with family, friends, mentors, and fieldwork contacts. In *Okubo Diary,* Brian Moeran reflects on the eventually bittersweet dissolution of formerly close ties between him and his family and their friends and neighbors in a Kyushu pottery community (Moeran 1985). And Joy Hendry has written a biographical account of her research career spanning many different periods of research in Japan (Hendry 1999a). Some studies, including Kondo's, as well as Anne Allison's ethnography of bar hostesses and male sexual fantasies (Allison 1994), Edward Fowler's account of life on skid row in Tokyo (Fowler 1997), Robin LeBlanc's ethnography of women and local politics (LeBlanc 1999), and Gail Lee Bernstein's life history of a rural woman (Bernstein 1985), place the researcher's role and interactions methodologically and rhetorically as a centerpiece and touchstone for the analysis. In a similar vein, the Media Production Group, founded by the late Jackson H. Bailey and David W. Plath, has produced an extended series of documentary videos focused on fieldwork in Japan by anthropologists and historians.[1]

Other researchers have written about much more specific aspects of their fieldwork, often in an introduction or as a theme running throughout a larger work. Yuko Ogasawara, for example, discusses the question of academic credentials and entry to the field in office settings (Ogasawara 1998); Christena Turner reflects on issues of gender and social class in her research on Japanese factory workers (Turner 1995); Michael Ashkenazi has written about the interrelationships among networks of informants and the anthropologists with whom they are engaged (Ashkenazi 1997); Matthews Hamabata examines how his status as an unmarried, male, Japanese-American student shaped his relationships quite differently with male and female elite contacts as he studied kinship and family businesses (Hamabata 1990). Still other scholars have written short essays, much like those in this volume, that examine a particular facet of fieldwork experience: Fran Markowitz and Michael Ashkenazi explore questions about sexuality in fieldwork in Japan and elsewhere (Markowitz and Ashkenazi 1999); Takeyuki Tsuda discusses his interactions as a Japanese American among other foreign workers in an electronics factory (Tsuda 1998); and both David W. Plath and Robert J. Smith have written about their use of fieldnotes as a key methodological element of their research (Plath 1990; Smith 1990). And there exist in various disciplines reviews of the development of scholarship on Japan that have discussed methodological as well as topical or interpretive issues: William W. Kelly (1991) and Jennifer Robertson (1998) on anthropological research; Mariko Tamanoi (1990) on gender studies in Japan; and Andrew Gordon (1998b) on Japanese studies as an area studies field. In addition, the field of Japanese studies has been analyzed in the context of national academic cultures, including Helen Hardacre's volume (1998) on Japanese studies in the United States, and the collection edited by Harumi Befu and Josef Kreiner (1992) that compares perspectives on Japan in the scholarship of ten countries, in which David W. Plath and Robert J. Smith (1992) specifically examine American studies of Japan.

Against this backdrop, we knew that this volume could not be encyclopedic. There were many difficult decisions about what to include and exclude. A first decision was to limit ourselves to contributions from nonnative fieldworkers—that is, people for whom the cultural and social experience of operating in Japanese society is itself an important source of data for their analyses. Many distinguished scholars whose native language and culture are Japanese have done excellent fieldwork and have contributed widely to the English-language scholarship on Japanese society and culture, including Hiroshi Ishida, Takie S. Lebra, Hiroshi Wagatsuma, and Emiko Ohnuki-Tierney, to mention just a few who have spent considerable portions of their scholarly careers engaged with Japanese studies outside Japan. Of course, many of the topics our contributors have examined are the same or similar to topics studied by Japanese researchers, but clearly the methodological implications of immersion in a foreign cultural setting make the conduct of fieldwork very different for natives and nonnatives.

Another decision was to try to focus on specific lessons that can be drawn from research experiences. Although our contributors convey much of their wider personal experiences in Japan, we asked them to focus on techniques, puzzles, problems, and solutions that they encountered while doing research. Also, we restricted ourselves to authors who have carried out *academic* rather than journalistic, market, or personal research in Japan. There are, of course, many very interesting and informative accounts by foreigners of their experiences in Japan, including those of a sumo wrestler (Kuhaulua with Wheeler 1973), a schoolteacher (Feiler 1991), and a wanderer (Booth 1997) among many, many others, but we decided to focus exclusively on academic research experiences.

And finally, we did not seek out polemics about the openness of Japanese institutions to critical external scrutiny. This is not to deny that such problems exist (and some of our contributors discuss their own encounters with bureaucratic secrecy and suspicion). In the field of Japanese studies, some scholars have written about the intellectual constraints inherent in the political culture of area studies, particularly as research focuses on issues of national interest (Samuels 1992, 1994). Other criticisms of Japanese intellectual and bureaucratic circles, like Ivan P. Hall's *Cartels of the Mind* (1998), argue that Japan maintains an intellectual isolationism that renders much research impossible and restricts discourse to "approved" topics. Still other critiques, like Pat Choate's *Agents of Influence* (1990), argue that Japanese cultural, social, and political elites have effectively channeled avenues of foreign research on Japan into noncritical arenas.

This book does not directly address these kinds of macrocritiques of the openness of Japanese society. At least implicitly, however, the research experiences of the contributors to this volume suggest that stereotypes of Japan as a society that is impenetrable to outsiders, able to deflect critical inquiry, and able to shape outsiders' perspectives into propagandistically positive directions are overdrawn. Our premise is that there are many ways researchers can develop independent, critical interpretations of Japanese society and culture that take into account elite perspectives, radical counterviews, or the outlook of ordinary members of society.

Although we did not set out with geographical criteria in mind, the chapters of this book demonstrate the accessibility of Japanese communities and institutions of many different kinds and in many different parts of the nation. Certainly, Tokyo has been the major center of research on Japan by foreign scholars, particularly and understandably for those with a focus on national institutions of politics and policy-making. This book contains many accounts of research in and around Tokyo, both in the halls of power and in the back alleys of daily life. But the book also includes examples of research in other major cities, such as Osaka, Kyoto, and Kobe, as well as in rural, suburban, and urban communities in Okinawa, Kyushu, Shikoku, Hokkaido, and various parts of the main island of Honshu. The map at the front of this book shows the locations of the significant research sites discussed in the following chapters (places that are mentioned simply in passing are not included).

The practice of fieldwork does not have a specific set of well-defined rules of engagement or strategies that apply across all research settings. The twenty essays in this volume recount the challenges faced by scholars from a range of disciplines—anthropology, history, political science, international relations, religious studies, and sociology—examining dozens of different facets of Japanese society. We asked our contributors to tell some of their favorite fieldwork stories and to reflect on what they have learned from these experiences. We encouraged them to focus not only on how these incidents affected their own research, but also on how their insights might help others. We hope their ability to laugh at themselves as they recount their mistakes will lend courage to others taking their first plunge into fieldwork in Japan.

The lessons from these fieldwork accounts are twofold. Most directly, accounts of field research experiences and techniques are useful within the field of Japanese studies to help students and others learn how to conduct independent research in Japan. At a more general, analytic level, descriptions of field research undertaken in Japan focus attention on how disciplinary research problems and techniques are inevitably situated in specific cultural, historical, and social contexts. This is a topic not only of great immediate relevance to Japanese studies, but it also helps to stimulate the kind of reflective consideration of research methods in context that contributes to a more sophisticated understanding of the relationship between area studies and social science disciplines.

Area and Method

This book began on a day of torrential rain in June 1990, when Theodore C. Bestor and Patricia G. Steinhoff both decided not to venture out to their respective research sites and instead spent the day—inside and dry—talking about fieldwork methods. Steinhoff's former doctoral student, Suzanne

Culter, had already suggested the need for a book to help new researchers with their first project in Japan, and they had discussed what it might include. Bestor had been thinking along similar lines while teaching methods courses to graduate students. The conversation—and the shape of the book—developed over the next several years in various venues, including a miniworkshop attended by Bestor, Mary C. Brinton, Takie S. Lebra, and Steinhoff that was held under the auspices of the Social Science Research Council (SSRC). At the time, SSRC's Joint Committee on Japanese Studies was struggling with the council's efforts to redefine area studies vis-à-vis disciplinary knowledge. The workshop, held in Honolulu in 1995, discussed the ways in which research methods in Japanese studies link the work of scholars in adjacent disciplines. After the workshop, Bestor and Steinhoff extended invitations to about two dozen researchers to write essays about their fieldwork experiences. Some invitees were unable to participate, and others regrettably had to withdraw along the way because of competing obligations. The editors have added other scholars, especially younger researchers, along the way.

In 1996, Victoria Lyon Bestor joined the editorial team. She became the organizational ramrod and provided critical insights based on her many years of participant observation of fieldwork (fieldwork on fieldwork, perhaps), her own experience doing research on Japanese philanthropy and civil society, and her long familiarity with the field of Japanese studies as a whole. Her expertise on library resources, especially electronic ones, in Japanese studies has also contributed to this volume. In her own words, she became the editorial "sheepdog" for the project, setting deadlines, nipping at the heels of contributors, and nagging her coeditors when necessary. The final product has been an intense collaboration of the three editors, largely carried out electronically, but punctuated by brief editorial conferences at Association for Asian Studies (AAS) meetings, at International House in Tokyo, and in hotel lobbies here and there—in short, completed on the run, rather like some of the fieldwork described in the following chapters.

From a methodological perspective, this volume grows out of discussions about the complicated dynamic of field research, poised between standardized disciplinary research methodologies and the challenges of doing research within a particular culture. Japanese society has highly developed patterns for conveying or restricting social information and has been the focus of a great deal of interdisciplinary research under the rubric of area studies. We would argue that area studies researchers develop a mediated research technique or methodology that draws upon the cultural specificity of the research setting and uses that local insight as a means to modify general, standardized disciplinary research methods. The results of good fieldwork, in turn, inform both area studies and the general academic disciplines. In addition, their interdisciplinary training encourages area studies researchers to borrow methods from adjacent disciplines that may be more fruitful in the Japanese context than the mainstream methodologies of their own disciplines, which were devised in other cultural contexts.

Simultaneous with the decade-long gestation of this volume there has been an intensive debate within academic circles about the relationship between and the relative merits of area studies training and theoretical disciplinary training. The approaches have been set in opposition to one another in a variety of ways. Global versus local knowledge is one such rubric. In his presidential address for the AAS in 1997, James Scott defended area studies as a necessary antidote to what he referred to as the "thin formalizations of high altitude, low oxygen theory." This volume was inspired in part by a desire to explore the tension between area studies and social science disciplines through the methodological problems that arise in the course of doing fieldwork. Andrew Gordon has suggested that some scholars view area studies as "an artisanal craft akin to bricklaying" and theory as "a grander pursuit akin to architecture." In this perspective, the cathedrals of learning are the creations of architects (theoreticians), not of craftspeople (area specialists). In contrast, Gordon proposes the metaphor of "think[ing] of theory and discipline as the lens and camera, the scholar as a photographer and the area the object or subject being examined." Suggesting that theory and method in area studies and the social sciences are integrally complementary, Gordon observes that "usually the best photographers pay attention to their lenses, and the top lens makers know something about taking pictures" (Gordon 1998b: 387–405). Gordon's perspective reflects an ideal that is easier to achieve in disciplines such as history and anthropology, which acknowledge the geographic or cultural basis of much knowledge. His view is less persuasive in social science disciplines such as sociology and economics, which are often more interested in grinding perfect lenses than in taking beautiful pictures. We hope that this volume may help some in those disciplines to think more about how adjusting the lens to the scene may improve the sharpness and depth of the picture.

The essays in this volume address these broad questions through the immediate, firsthand experiences of Japan specialists from a range of disciplines that vary in their stance toward research methods. Our authors have used a broad array of research techniques and interpretive approaches in an extremely diverse set of research environments, from fish markets to the radical underground, from coal mining towns in Hokkaido to anti-U.S. protests in Okinawa, from prosecutors' offices to junior high schools, from bioengineering labs to the newsroom of NHK television. Each essay draws on the author's own field research experiences and highlights some of the challenges faced and solutions discovered to the tasks of collecting data. The essays are necessarily selective: neither the topics about which the authors have done research nor the methodological techniques and interpretive frameworks they have used are covered in full. Yet through the juxtaposition of these glimpses of different topics and techniques, as well as the discovery of issues that crosscut different fieldwork situations, a broad picture of the possibilities of fieldwork in Japan emerges.

Many of the chapters raise the question of Japanese language ability. Certainly the linguistic levels expected of researchers keep rising as each succeeding generation of fieldworkers has access to more systematic language study earlier and earlier in their academic training. All of the authors of these essays speak Japanese well and use the language fully in their field research. But it is important to note that the ability to do fieldwork and linguistic fluency are by no means the same thing. One challenge of fieldwork is evaluating the fit among research topic, research techniques, and the linguistic requirements of the project. Even the most fluent researcher—foreign or native speaker of Japanese—must learn to evaluate the linguistic environment of a particular topic. The collective point of the chapters here is *not* that there is an absolute standard for language ability nor that linguistic competence is the be-all and end-all of research. Rather, any research project requires careful attention to feasibility in light of the linguistic abilities required by the project and the interpretation of data.

First-time researchers with limited Japanese language skills may need to tailor their research ambitions to fit their language limitations. Yet doing fieldwork is in itself a powerful language-learning opportunity, which can be readily assessed by reflecting on the improvement in one's language facility from the beginning to the end of the field research. What seemed impossible at the beginning of a research experience may become much more feasible just a few months later. Moreover, as a project gets underway, even a researcher with the highest levels of language training will find it necessary to master new terminological terrain; indeed, the specialized vocabularies and semantic domains of any Japanese institution or setting provide an enormous amount of basic social and cultural data that a fieldworker will need to master in order to understand the ethnographic site and the phenomenon under study.

Ethnographers and other field researchers, Clifford Geertz suggests, establish their authority in part by telling their readers how they found their field site and how they came to be accepted by the people among whom they conducted research (Geertz 1988). This trope of discovering one's way into a field site and a research topic is taken up in many of the chapters that follow. They illustrate something of the very human qualities of fieldwork and the motivation to use fieldwork as a means to tell the stories of other people, to bring "their" stories back with "us." Beyond this, these accounts also address the very practical questions that first-time researchers agonize over. We hope that reading about the experiences of other researchers in Japan, presented more frankly and in more detail than is usually possible in formal research monographs, will help new researchers gain the confidence to find their own way.

Successful completion of a fieldwork enterprise is another common feature of the essays in this volume. However, as several authors note, the process of writing up one's research is often subject to delays that unexpectedly enrich and broaden the final product. Other avenues of research may also serendipitously present themselves, diverting the researcher's path. These discoveries may redirect the original research project or lead to research topics that are picked up later in one's career. Our authors express twinges of guilt about how long it took to bring their projects to completion—just as the editors wish that this volume had been completed much, much sooner—but they (and we) are unanimous in feeling that the ultimate results are much better for these unanticipated delays.

The chapters in *Doing Fieldwork in Japan* are grouped loosely around several themes, including getting started, gaining access to a fieldwork site, and making contacts; navigating bureaucratic institutions; surveying and interviewing techniques as well as getting access to statistical and archival data; and building and maintaining networks over time and among different research sites and cultural groups. Of course, this arrangement represents only one partial way of organizing the chapters, and any reader will find innumerable other themes that link the fieldwork experiences and techniques of the contributors.

Merry Isaacs White leads off by providing insights into how a researcher of a certain age gains the confidence of teenagers to get them to reveal their own understandings of their lives and the impact of popular culture on them. Patricia G. Steinhoff writes about her research among progressive social movements and underground political groups through fieldwork at demonstrations, courtrooms, and prisons. Joy Hendry explores the complex and often unpredictable networks of introductions and chance encounters that serendipitously draw a researcher and a research site together. Helen Hardacre and Ian Reader both study religion in contemporary Japan, and their two chapters present different approaches to fieldwork, including various modes of participating in religious life, maintaining contact without becoming a target for conversion, and the role of chance in determining the directions of one's research.

Research among more highly structured bureaucracies is the focus of the next group of chapters, in widely varying ways. Samuel Coleman's research was conducted inside the laboratories of biogenetic research groups, and he discusses issues of access and accountability in doing research on scientific institutions. David L. McConnell did fieldwork on the Japan Exchange and Teaching (JET) Program for English-language teaching, and his chapter talks about gaining entrée to schools, to teachers, and most importantly to the bureaucratic guardians of the program at the national level of the Ministry of Education. David T. Johnson focuses on fieldwork in a public prosecutors office, in which issues of professional, legal confidentiality and the bureaucratic structure of the organization framed his fieldwork. Sheila A. Smith's research examines Japanese defense policy and cooperation between Japan and the United States on security issues; her chapter discusses getting access to bureaucrats, uniformed personnel, policy analysts, and academic specialists concerned with security issues, and also learning to interpret the semantics of Japanese discourse on security as a key element of understanding its political context. Ellis S. Krauss explains his multifaceted fieldwork on political journalism and NHK television news broadcasting, which involved extensive interviewing on the production of news programs and detailed content analysis, including cross-national comparisons of news broadcasts.

National agencies and the mass media in Japan sponsor enormous amounts of large-scale social survey research, and the published results are widely used by foreign researchers. Mary C. Brinton discusses the creation of national surveys, some of the limitations of such data, problems of gaining direct access to data sets for further analysis, and how she conducted her own survey concerning labor, education, and gender equality with samples drawn from several regions of Japan. On a different scale, Suzanne Culter discusses the process of designing and conducting qualitative, structured interviews through her own experiences both in a rural community, where she studied local responses to the painful restructuring of the coal mining industry, and in an urban setting, where she studied local social policies directed toward foreign migrants. John Creighton Campbell draws on his extensive research on budget politics in the national bureaucracy and on health and welfare policies at both the national and local levels to illustrate techniques for systematically getting information, including statistical data, from working bureaucrats involved in the policy process. David M. Arase recounts how he abandoned his prior plans of conducting formal interviews with bureaucrats and adapted new strategies for observing and synthesizing data in the midst of his research in order to discover how foreign-aid policy is actually made and implemented. Historians often do not regard what they do as fieldwork, but Andrew Gordon's research on labor history and the interactions of companies, unions, and the government demonstrates the delicate field research skills that are required to identify, locate, and finally negotiate access to historical archives held in institutional hands.

The final cluster of chapters addresses issues of tracing networks and locating the researcher in relation to them, in the short term as well as over the longer haul, sometimes across multiple sites and sometimes across generations. Through her research on popular singers of *enka* ballads, and particularly the communities of fans and professional marketing people who surround them, Christine R. Yano shows how she created contacts and juggled multiple identities of student, fan, and parent in the field. Glenda S. Roberts reflects on a variety of different fieldwork experiences working alongside factory workers, studying government social welfare programs, and analyzing corporate employment policies to show how unpredictable opportunities affect the researcher's ability to explore a subject from various perspectives, and how research interactions can suddenly develop a personal dimension. Drawing on research in urban neighborhoods and wholesale markets, Theodore C. Bestor's chapter focuses on the ways in which he developed networks as he engaged in "inquisitive observation" and how various techniques of social mapping and reading signposts on the local landscape enabled him to sketch out large, complex institutions. In a very different setting, Joshua Hotaka Roth explores networks of Brazilian Japanese workers in Hamamatsu and discusses how fluid definitions of identity among and between local residents, *Nikkeijin* (foreigners of Japanese descent), and himself shaped his research experiences. And finally, Robert J. Smith draws on his experiences of over fifty years of research in Japan to reflect on changing relationships with community members and friends and changing perspectives on Japanese society.

The appendix on digital resources and fieldwork, by Victoria Lyon Bestor, provides an overview of some of the key tools for accessing on-line information, along with the caveat that—as other chapters also emphasize—successful use of web sites and other electronic media also depends on fundamental fieldwork techniques: interviewing experts and understanding documents in their social contexts.

Fieldwork and the Ethics of Research

Researchers at American universities are bound both by the ethical codes of their own disciplines and by their institutions' compliance with federal research requirements to maintain ethical standards that reflect the three principles of respect for persons, beneficence, and justice. For most social science research that does not involve physically or psychologically invasive procedures and entails little risk of harm to the subjects, the primary concerns are to ensure that subjects have given their informed consent to participate in the research and that their privacy is protected by the way the research materials are maintained and the results are publicized. The current regulations also provide additional requirements when the research involves minors, prisoners, or other vulnerable populations who may not be able to give informed consent.

Researchers going into the field in Japan today as graduate students or postdoctoral scholars will most likely be required to obtain formal approval from their institution's Committee on Human Subjects or institutional review board before they may begin their research. (Specific procedures vary from university to university, and researchers should check with their local university research administrators.)

Our contributors discuss, both explicitly and implicitly, many of the key issues of fieldwork ethics in research on human subjects. Even though much of the fieldwork described in this volume was carried out before these formal requirements were applied to social science research conducted outside the United States and not funded by federal agencies, it is clear from their accounts that our authors have maintained high ethical standards. Their experiences in applying standards appropriately within the Japanese cultural context may also suggest ways to present or explain field research that will be useful to researchers whose institutional review board for human-subjects research may not understand the research environment in other countries.

Most of the authors in this volume emphasize the need for introductions from a third party in order to obtain research access. Whether the introductions are for permission to conduct participant observation or to interview individuals, they ensure that the human subjects of the research understand its purpose and range and have given their informed consent to participate, even if the researcher does not return home from Japan with a folder of legalistic signed documents of consent. In a society where the careful cultivation of interpersonal trust is given far greater weight than formal contracts and where written contracts often are viewed with distrust, there are many research situations in which American-style legalistic consent requirements would not only be culturally unfamiliar, but would call into question the researcher's cultural understanding and trustworthiness. And no one who has done any interviewing in Japan doubts for a minute that a respondent who does not want to answer a question knows how to avoid a substantive response, even if he or she is too polite to throw the researcher out the door.

There are many descriptions in this volume of how well-placed Japanese provided the introductions that opened doors for a young, foreign researcher. What these accounts do not convey is the understanding that such introductions involve the standard Japanese cultural practice of borrowing trust from other people in order to gain access to a new situation, which carries complex obligations to act responsibly and not misuse or damage the trust. The researcher must understand that his or her behavior in the research situation not only affects the relationship between researcher and research subjects, but also reflects directly on the person who made the introduction. The person providing an introduction is—in a very real cultural sense—accepting a role as social guarantor. The social networks many contributors to this volume describe in detail cannot be changed or disregarded at the researcher's whim; they are very real, constraining social facts that bind the researcher to his or her introducer and to the group of people among whom she or he is doing research. If difficulties arise, the research subject will most likely complain directly to the go-between who introduced the researcher, with long-lasting negative consequences for both the researcher and his or her erstwhile sponsor.

Several chapters in this volume describe how researchers obtained informed consent from their interview subjects in Japan and how they protect their subjects both during the interview and in their subsequent use of the material. White describes her procedures for obtaining parental consent before doing research with minors, and Steinhoff explains how she gained prisoners' informed consent to interview them. (Both of these projects involve research populations to which the regulations for human-subjects protection are specifically pertinent.) Even in less sensitive settings, there is often a lengthy process of obtaining institutional access for participant observation or interviews, as both Johnson's and Culter's chapters demonstrate. Roberts and Coleman each describe situations in which access was denied and the ways in which they were able to reorient their research projects around other field sites. Still other authors discuss their lengthy searches and the chains of introductions sometimes required to find research sites that would accept them. All of these examples demonstrate how ethical research standards can be applied appropriately in the Japanese context, and we encourage researchers new to Japan to pay particular attention to them.

Other perennial issues for social science research are questions of objectivity and how field researchers can ensure the validity and reliability of their findings. There are some fundamental divisions within the social sciences about how this can be accomplished, and to some extent the expectations vary with the discipline and topic. Field researchers generally fall into the camp that argues for the value of depth and understanding of context over those who insist upon statistical significance based on scientific sampling methods as the only acceptable standard. Several of our contributors explicitly discuss the ways in which methodological models of research design in their disciplines cannot be taken for granted in the field. Brinton and Culter describe their efforts to produce research that would meet rigorous sampling and statistical standards within the constraints of Japanese research conditions. Arase describes how he abandoned the formal research plan that his American advisors had approved when he discovered it would not help him learn how policy was really made in Japan.

Most of our authors are less constrained by a statistical or hypothesis-testing model of social science research, but their accounts reveal how they attend to the underlying principles of reliability and validity. They tell us how they have expanded their research to different sites or settings, explored the research problem at different levels, or utilized multiple methods to gain a fuller understanding and to cross-check their findings. Many emphasize the value of returning to the same research site or maintaining long-term contact with the same research subjects as ways of correcting early misconceptions, deepening their understanding, and observing stability and change over time.

Several researchers also speak frankly about how they manage problems of objectivity in their relations with their subjects or with persons who have provided institutional access. Hardacre describes strategies for dealing with religious organizations seeking converts, while Steinhoff notes the choices she has made in order to do research with radical political groups. McConnell and Roberts both acknowledge the pressure from bureaucratic organizations to produce only favorable reports and describe how they avoid these demands. Bestor describes the suspicions he encounters that an American studying Japanese seafood consumption must be an agent for environmental activists bent on disrupting Japanese markets. Many researchers also describe their strong sense of gratitude and obligation to the informants and organizations that have made their research possible and discuss how they try to reciprocate in small ways without compromising their position as objective researchers. There is no single correct approach to these difficult issues of access, obligation, and reciprocity, but we hope that reading about how other researchers have dealt with them will raise awareness and stimulate further discussion.

The chapters that follow provide many examples of how scholars have done fieldwork in Japan. While the essays stand on their own as methodological studies, we believe they may be most instructive when they are read in conjunction with what the same scholars have produced from their fieldwork. To make it easier to match up the fieldwork essay with the research that resulted from it, we have asked each author to suggest a few of their own publications for the list of related readings that appears at the end of the chapter. (Citations of other work on the topic are included in the comprehensive bibliography that appears at the end of the volume.) Reading the fieldwork chapter alongside an example of the research product will illuminate how researchers incorporate the results of participant observation and interviews into their publications and how different methodical strategies may be related to different ways of presenting the results.

Together these chapters demonstrate that with proper training, patience, and ingenuity field researchers can find Japanese society to be an incredibly open, diverse, and multivocal society in which they can "observe a lot just by watching" (and listening and asking).

Notes

The editors are very grateful to Makoto Kuroda and Elissa Sato, both undergraduates at Harvard University, for their care in cross-checking translations and bibliographic citations, and to Ryoko Yamamoto, a graduate student at the University of Hawai'i, for her assistance in creating the map and the final glossary. Dawn Grimes-MacLellan made many useful comments on early drafts of several chapters.

1. The Media Production Group's (MPG) series, "Voices of Experience," includes six videos of extended interviews about fieldwork with Jackson H. Bailey, Theodore C. Bestor, L. Keith Brown, William W. Kelly, Margaret Lock, and Takie S. Lebra. These interviews are also summarized in a single video titled *What's an Anthropologist Doing in Japan?* (MPG 1992b). Other documentary videos in the series include *The Language of My Teachers*, which follows the research of Robert J. Smith from Japanese-language training during World War II through fieldwork in Japan during the Occupation era and subsequent research through the late 1990s (MPG 1996b); *Ella's Journal*, focused on the fieldwork of John Embree and Ella Lury Wiswell in Suye Mura in the 1930s and Wiswell's return to the village on the fiftieth anniversary of their research (MPG 1996a); and *Times of Witness: Fieldwork in Japan*, featuring Smith and Wiswell discussing social change in Japan during their research careers (MPG 1996c). Videos produced by the MPG are distributed by the Asian Educational Media Service at the University of Illinois. Its website includes an extensive catalogue of audio-visual materials on Japan, in addition to listings of these MPG productions: www.aems.uiuc.edu/.

STARTING OUT

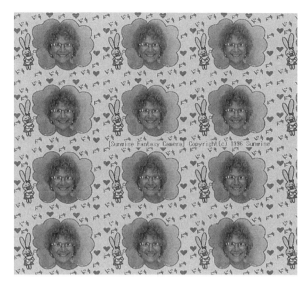

Merry Isaacs White's *purikura*, or photographic stickers exchanged among friends, especially adolescents.

MERRY ISAACS WHITE

Taking Note of Teen Culture in Japan:
Dear Diary, Dear Fieldworker

The fieldwork researcher expects to encounter both the predictable and the surprising, to confirm expectations and to confound them. In ticket lines for a pop music concert in Tokyo, on the subway going to a high school, sitting in a coffee shop with three middle-school girls with brown-striped hair, the American anthropologist sees the familiar but comes to understand that contexts and meaning may differ from her preconceptions: objects in the mirror may be farther away than they appear. Of course, that adjustment of vision and understanding is what she came to Japan for, and for its natural corollary, the fine-tuning of preconceptions and a reconsideration of the universalisms of the Western behavioral and social sciences.

In the study of adolescence some preconceptions come easy: I assumed, for example, that access and communication with informants would be hard for a foreign, middle-aged female researcher and that the "nature" of adolescence would be part of the problem. I assumed that teenagers in Japan are suspicious of adults, are uncommunicative and clique-ish, and that they would be dismissive of the goals of the study. My assumptions that they would be inaccessible or hostile were unfounded, however, and emanated from assumptions about American youth, which, I discovered by interviewing at home as well, were similarly unfounded: discovering Japanese teens, then, was an eye-opener for me in two societies.

Interviewing grandmothers in Japan is said to be a very satisfying experience: older people often do not have younger ones interested in hearing their stories, and they are grateful for the researcher's attentions. Young people, too, are glad of an ear—especially one attached to a person who is not critical of them and who is not associated with the institutional goals of their educational and occupational futures. Adults in their lives see their futures as guiding their present, and, like their parents and teachers, they also see themselves as people under construction. The young, however, are more likely to focus on friendship and communication and relationship-tied self-development—and on the material culture that guides and parallels that development—than on examinations and tracks to occupational security as sources of identity. There is no perfect fit, then, with mainstream adult notions of who they are or should be, and they like telling nonmainstream stories about themselves, especially to someone who does not represent the institutions and relationships of *their* adult society. Still, a problem of communication remained: how would I be able to maintain an open line when the prime focus of youth is youth?

Communication itself is the essence of relationships, and relationships are the very stuff of teen life. While hanging out and engaging directly in *machikomi* (street-corner communication) and using ephemeral teen argot were not in my repertory of field skills or possibilities, other modes of teen-generated linkage were. Finding the medium, the conveyancer of information and interactions teens themselves used was critical, a means for validating my access as well as a chance for "participation" in teen culture of the time without losing my valuable outsider "place." One prime medium, the *kōkan nikki,* or "exchange diary," was only one of several modes of communication I used, but it is, as I will show later, a good example of how discovering the local medium can enhance greatly the message.

Map-Making and a "Sociography" of Youth

Walking in Harajuku, a district of Tokyo noted for its lively youth scene, and scanning the throngs of teenagers among whom I hoped I would find prospective informants in the late 1980s, I wondered what hubris had brought me there. What could they possibly want to say to me, a postadolescent advanced in age and backward in the lore that identifies and accredits members of the *zoku* ("tribe" or members of a scene; participants in a subculture)? And knowing my own children's reluctance to share their lives with adults unknown to them, indeed (as parents often bemoan) sometimes even with familiar adults, I figured this would be a bigger challenge than I had encountered in the twenty-some years I had been conducting research in Japan. I seemed to be walking without a map and without cultural competency in a subcultural zone where preconceptions and experiences were sure to fail me. Beginning fieldwork is always a jumpy business: research begins with questions, a classic review of the literature, and a dance between the desire to predict, control, and know and the need for openness and flexibility in face of the unknowns and surprises a good plan of action somewhat paradoxically anticipates. And this "subcultural zone"—the communities of adolescents outside schools and families—is as notoriously hard to locate as a floating craps game, always one hangout ahead.

My earlier experiences in the social sciences did not completely prepare me for the weightlessness, the complicated issues of gravity, involved in landing on Planet Teen. My training in anthropology had been neither classical nor postmodern. My previous research projects in education, family, and organizational cultures in Japan engaged both participant-observation techniques embedded in ethnography and broader sociological surveys. This combination was the result of an interesting historical accident bringing me into both fields as disciplinary homes for Japanese studies changed between the late 1950s and mid-1970s. My study of Japan began before the economic boom of the mid-1960s put Japan into Western consciousness as more than an exotic Oriental outpost or a defeated war remnant under reconstruction. At the time, Japan seemed to belong to anthropology, where, at least at my university, the study of "premodern" or "less developed" societies was located. By the time I entered graduate school after several years as a journalist, Japan had a new position in the world and in the social sciences. I was encouraged to study Japan even more at that time, but I was now encouraged to join a sociology department, where Japan's "sudden modernity" seemed to place it. Though the frames were different, my predilection for ground-up perspectives and tacked-down detail, together with wider societal implications, remained. What a "sociological" hypothesis might have to say to guide my work did not to me seem vastly different from a framing question as a point of entry into anthropological fieldwork. I used very small samples of informants but tried to place them (families, workers, students) in a comprehensive "surround" including demographic, social, and historical detail. Collecting data, however, still remained a question, for although the analytic possibilities were open, gathering material that was both broad enough to answer the questions posed by sociological hypotheses and detailed enough to allow for ethnographic stories to "sing" the tale was still difficult.

I decided that what I was doing was building "sociographies"—broad, grounded frames and analytic structures epitomized in detailed narratives, located in the "communities" the phenomena seemed to indicate. My field sites were less concrete and geographic than classical anthropological locations and were more abstract communities and conceptual neighborhoods created by phenomena like "internationalization" and "educational reform." These communities were "imagined" and ideological, given shape by ideas as well as by the people who participate in the particular common experiences and activities that mark their membership.

In the mid-1970s I had designed this sort of study on the effects of internationalization on Japanese families and organizations. In this study I looked at how the marginalization of "opened" people returning to a "closed" society created a kind of placeless community of otherwise unrelated people sharing the markings of their overseas experiences. In this period the unprecedentedly large numbers of overseas workers faced what came to be known as "reverse culture shock," a more profound lack of fit on return to Japan than they had experienced overseas. Their changed (and to employers, unpredictable) work style and behavior were perceived as a problem for organizations and individuals. As in my later study of adolescence, I was interested in the problem both as framed and as experienced and needed perspectives from both framers and the principals themselves.

Teenagers may inhabit this kind of space, marked as a "community" by media and marketing in ways different from the organization of their lives by official institutions. On the face of it, Japanese teens still belonged primarily to home and school. They were still referred to in "official" culture by their year in secondary school and in traditional family settings by their place in the sibling order, while in America a teenager was defined by a collection of traits and behaviors attached to an age stage more independent of these institutions. It was the apparent lack in Japan of such a generic notion of the teen that had begun my fascination with the potential differences between "our" and "their" teens. In Thomas Rohlen's ethnography of Japanese high schools (Rohlen 1983), he noted that the word "kodomo" (child) was appropriate to use with reference to a high schooler in Japan. I was struck by this simple statement as I was all too aware of the sometimes prickly sensitivity of American teens to the language adults used about them, and I wondered if indeed a Japanese young person was differently situated or differently conscious. With this remark as catalyst, I sought historical, linguistic, cultural, and ideological explanations and further explorations of change in the various niches teens filled besides those of student and child. It became clear that studying an age cohort meant giving the notion of cohort itself some context and fine tuning: to whom and how did "teens" seem a relevant category? And what subcategories did the notion of youth itself contain, recognizable to themselves and perhaps invisible to others?

A popular nonschool, nonfamily image of adolescence was clearly emerging—not Western or American exactly, but definitely "modern"—casting teens into categories apart from the institutions earlier identifying them in postwar Japan or, as some developmental psychologists in the West would say, masking the symptoms of adolescence understood to be "universal." The emerging image was recognizable in the West but still different: it was that of a trend-driven consumer rather than of a hormone-driven rebel. Those in the ages roughly delineated by biological maturation to be "adolescent" did not exhibit all of the signs of "hormonally driven" stage-related development; as Margaret Mead had noted in Samoa, youth is defined more by culture than by nature (and in any case, "nature" is culturally defined as well) (Mead 1928).

Learning from the Market

Studying an emerging phenomenon means starting at the source apparently driving it, and so I began with experts in media and advertising and conducted interviews with these fingers-on-the-pulse observers of the changing social scene as I also observed and met with young people themselves. My first contacts in this aspect of the study were made through my university connections, who helped me set up interviews with researchers working for consumer-marketing think tanks and, later and through their connections, with social commentators and journalists and the advertisers and producers of goods themselves. I asked the question that is their raison d'être: who were the objects of their attentions and how did they guide them to purchase and engage in their products? I found that even more than the astute and thorough academic researchers in university settings, "commercial" researchers were in tune with the present and the future. This is, after all, their stock in trade; to serve their corporate masters they pinpoint the audience and market for goods and create the moods and trends that sell them.

Discussions of consumer industries, especially those focused on youth, emphasize their control over their audience, their manipulations in extracting the pocket money of young innocents. Their research is indeed profit driven and "applied," but it is thorough and accurate, as they need to know their market in great detail and because manufacturers spend large amounts of money on their youth-marketing manuals. Marketing think tanks engage in solidly empirical work and are quite open to learning from adolescents themselves. Preconceptions do not sell teen gear. They collect information of all kinds, from (of course) the amounts of ready cash young people have to less obvious data, such as how a thirteen-year-old feels about her mother, what a fifteen-year-old thinks the government should do about the environment while not neglecting how she feels about baring her midriff, and how many close friends she has.

One example of the use of such information by the highly interrelated pop-star industries came when I interviewed an editor at one of the leading pop-star magazines targeted to junior high school girls. He told me of the research they had conducted that showed girls of this age tending to form friendship groups consisting of about five to seven girls. This led the promotion agency to which their magazine was "affiliated" to seek out (and create) boy pop-star singing groups of this number. Their rationale was that if there were about the same number of boys in the idolized group as in the group of friends most important to a girl, then there would be harmonious adoration without competition: each one could idolize a different performer in the group. Their strategies, and the close and sensitive relationship between media and "manufacturers," seemed based on a nice use of applied social science.

Such sensitivity includes attention to socioeconomic differences beyond the usual framing by academic research. Advertising agencies understand from their surveys and from the young people themselves that Japan is not all middle class nor in other ways homogeneous and that children in Kyushu, Okinawa, Tohoku, and Shikoku may desire or be able to afford different goods. Knowing these things makes them better able to do two important things: create products and trends aimed at different subsegments of the youth market and, at the same time, create products and trends that are able to cut across the differences and "mass-ify" the audience for efficiency and profit. These experts were also in a position to mobilize the young themselves to create new goods. By employing teen focus groups located in different areas in Japan, they were in touch with savvy insiders who were encouraged to express themselves and suggest new products. At the other end of the hot-lines in Tokyo were marketers ready to create instant trends by accommo-dating the teens who suggested them. This interactivity between the young people as informants and as research and development experts and those defining them makes it hard to determine where the prime mover in the construction of the adolescent market really lies. During the four years in which I gathered data, I continually went back and forth between these observers (and, interactively, creators) of youth and the young people them-selves, interviewing and testing my own ideas about the sources of "teenager culture."

Learning from the Experts

I began with the researchers in universities and think tanks because I wanted to know what else there was to know about the years of "adolescence" (a term I was keeping in quotation marks until I understood it better in con-text) beyond school and home—or, if I found nothing, to confirm the com-mon conception that school and home was all there was to know and that somehow Japanese schools and families had avoided the whole teen prob-lematique so emphasized by Western social and behavioral scientists, the popular media, psychologists, and law enforcement authorities. If there was no idea in the air that young people were predisposed to confrontations with adults, sexual experimentation, reckless lifestyles, thoughtless materialism, and other perceived ills of adolescence, and if there were no popular social theories to give shape to teens' lives beyond the approved institutions in which they were prepared for adult life, well, either way I would have to start from the teens themselves to understand their lives, and here, too, I encoun-tered a Western preconception. If indeed they would open up to me about their lives, this openness was itself "data." Open access in itself might mean that they were different. Western experiences and constructions of youth were based on the stereotype that had emerged in 1950s America: that teens (a new term then) were social pathologies and that nasty, brutish behavior was stage driven and inevitable (and thus located them in a period of high risk to themselves and others).

As it turned out, there was in Japan a strong problematique associated with youth, but it was not what an American might imagine. And what the teens themselves had to say about their lives was far more interesting, far more complex, nuanced, and various than we would have imagined of them *or* of ourselves.

Teens themselves, like grandmothers who have time and few people to listen to them, are avid storytellers and are mostly pleased to be asked. I wanted stories, narratives of their involvement in friendships, their concerns for the future, consumer culture—all the things they wanted most to talk about, including sex. School and family were of course on the list, but what they most wanted to talk about were their lives in the worlds of friends and things. They came up with what were to me surprisingly Big Thoughts to share, surprising revelations about their sex lives, their families, and their capacity to subvert the myths of Japan's homogeneity and classlessness.

Guided by the street wisdom of market researchers, I first worked the locations where young people congregated, but this did not necessarily lead to deep, introspective interviews. I usually had at least one and often two or three young people with me as we explored shopping streets and pop-idol souvenir stands or went to rehearsal and recording studios to watch for the emergence of a star.

Obviously I was obvious: in no sense was I "going native" with teens. Unlike Michael Moffatt, who passed as an undergraduate while conducting a study of adolescence in New Jersey (Moffatt 1989), and unlike those who engage in an occupation or training alongside their informants in a Japanese bank (Rohlen 1974), a confections factory (Kondo 1990), a hostess club (Allison 1994), or a Kyoto geisha house (Dalby 1983), or the many others who are able to engage in an activity shared by Japanese colleagues, I could not take on the activities let alone the age-stage definitions and identities of the young. Studying an age rather than a place or a job was different.

I was in the very useful position of a neophyte, someone needing instruction. I was a foreign woman interested in teens' lives, an oddity of course, but an enthusiastic one who was refreshingly *not* focused on their lives in school and study, one who tried to "get it" without being *too* embarrassing to have along, and someone who needed their expertise. What made me an acceptable adult was in part my foreignness, for I was someone outside the world that judged them, someone desperately needing instruction. They were teachers on the street in a reversal of their usual institutionalized roles as students in school. I also wanted to know about things they wanted to talk about in the categories of meaningful, random chatter and gossip that shapes their membership in teen society: Tell me what you wear to be *shibu-kaji* ("Shibuya-casual" style)? What magazine should I read to find out about SMAP (a pop-idol boy group)? What's so *kakko-ii* (trendy or in) about that boy? What are you doing Saturday afternoon? How old were you when you first . . . ? Would you . . . ? Do you know anyone who . . . ? Streets and shops were not my only locales; I worked with families and the teens themselves in more intimate locations, from coffee shops (where permitted—some secondary-school regulations prohibit "children" from going to coffee shops) to park benches to homes.

With many good sit-down interviews behind me in the first year of the study, I began to be more organized, and I decided I would work with teenagers from a wide variety of backgrounds—not to pretend to representativeness of all teens through this means, but to give witness to diversity of at least regional and educational backgrounds. Since I would be working for three or more years on this study, and since I wanted to follow a core cohort through their "teen" years (a period that was unmarked culturally in Japan and so remained quite fluid in my study), I chose a small group of fifty to interview. I managed to interview most of them several times over the term of the study. I found this core group of teens through a "networked" sample: I first contacted schools, parents, and others with whom I had worked on earlier studies and asked them each to recommend to me two or three other families with children from the ages of twelve to twenty, roughly. Personal introductions are very important in Japan, but to ensure that there was no "proximity" effect diluting differences I already knew were in the population, I interviewed these young people and then asked each of them to introduce to me three or four others. In this case, I did not ask the parents, as I felt they might connect me more with people similar to themselves, while young people often have a broader acquaintance in schools. Parents helped by giving me introductions to families in other parts of Japan, where I followed the same network procedures. By the fourth removal from the initial contact, the sample became quite diverse.

In addition to individual interviews, I followed the marketers' strategy of establishing "focus groups" of teens for group discussions in several parts of Japan, and they proved to be lively events. I learned about the effects, for example, of being geographically "marginalized." In one group in Hiroshima a young girl moaned over the fact that they were "three weeks from Tokyo"—meaning that it took a full three weeks for a trend in Tokyo to become current in Hiroshima, a definite hindrance to coolness.

Tokyo culture is a magnet for youth, and the teens I spoke with measured their own cool by their proximity to this hub of media and marketing. Thus in my multisited ethnography, I charged myself both with finding the effects of this overwhelmingly assertive core youth culture and with assessing the regional and local influences that shape young people. Looking at core and peripheries in Japan is especially important because Tokyo-based observers may not take local reception of the "core" culture into consideration. But youth—particularly sensitized to fitting in to this culture of cool-centricity—are a good indicator both of its spread and of local priorities and resistance. Marketers rarely consider if a product will fly in the Japanese equivalent of "Peoria," that is, someplace outside the orbit of metropolitan culture, where the cachet of the big city doesn't count for very much. For youth, there is no such place. Things will sell precisely because they come from Tokyo. A regional center like Sendai has been compared to Minneapolis—a northern outlier but a city of energy and industry. Sendai youth, however, will not admit to local energy since their magazines and media (based in Tokyo) simply reiterate that *Tokyo is the only place.* One young woman I interviewed in Sendai even asked me whether sunflower-printed clothing was popular in Tokyo, since she liked it and didn't want to be *dasai* (gauche). Like her counterpart in Hiroshima in the south, she measured things, even her anxieties, by what she wanted to imagine was a Tokyo standard. Even in the Kansai, which prides itself as an alternative center of Japan, kids in Osaka attempted defiance of the Tokyo monopoly on teen status by developing their own styles but still confessed that they were reacting to Tokyo.

The groups I met often discussed "Tokyo" and "not Tokyo" and what marked the "hinterlands" or the "core" in either positive or negative stylistic terms. The groups included five to seven people each and met usually on Saturday afternoons or Sundays for about two hours out of their busy schedules, which also included study, tutoring, classes, and for some, sports activities. Some not attending college preparatory "academic" high schools had part-time jobs on weekends, and some assisted in their families' shops or other trade. Discussion of school and family was not of greatest interest, perhaps, in the case of school, because competition or comparisons of aspirations might be implied, which made people uncomfortable. The topics of greatest interest were friendship, media, and, above all, goods and clothing: they were "material children," but not for their acquisitiveness alone. It was the power of knowledge about trends and goods that made the material world so important. As the members of these groups got to know each other better (rarely were they already acquainted with all of the others, and often the group consisted of teens of mixed ages), their tastes bounced off each other and they began to be known by their favorite music or activity or magazine. These groups were not naturally formed teen communities, but they were taking on some of the qualities of a "crowd" for the time the young people were in the same room together. What was missing was the critical importance of the intimate and spontaneous "friendship group," the ultimate source of social value and identity.

Face-to-Face at a Distance

The names and introductions obtained through my networks of teachers and families from earlier studies included young people from Hiroshima, Kyoto, Osaka, Gunma, Chiba, Sendai, and Tokyo, with some in Saitama and Yokohama as well. Because I could not always meet face-to-face with the same people in the same order with the same intervals of time between, I decided that I would need several modes of communication with them.

In the second year of the study (which engaged me in Japan for nine months the first year, three months during the second and third years, and outside Japan for the times in-between) I began a supplementary system of data collection, in addition to face-to-face interviews and street and family observations. This new source of information began as a serendipitous finding in my exploration of the novelty industry, which includes the manufacture and sale of vaguely school-related items such as bobbles and key chains to attach to school bags, pencils and other paraphernalia decorated with trendy cartoon characters, and notebooks and small diaries. One representative of a novelty company told me that the very old Japanese tradition of diary keeping included the custom of "kōkan nikki," or exchange diaries. In its manifestation in the 1990s, junior high schoolers, especially girls, would write their semiprivate dreams, confessions, and now, shopping lists, fashion commentary, sketches of rooms and wardrobes, and caricatures of friends and beaux, and would exchange them with friends for their comments, in a kind of cooperative journal. The novelty company had capitalized on this trend and produced preformatted exchange diaries in which different categories were given special spaces, such as "What I am wearing to school tomorrow, how about you?" or "How I will redecorate my room," or "My best friends' birthdays." (It should be noted that the same novelty company produces preformatted notes to pass to friends in class, saying things like "See you after school" or "Isn't X cute!"—notepads encouraging directly a communication usually forbidden in school.)

My informants and I worked out a system in which I gave them college-insignia notebooks from the United States (would this become a trend, I wondered?) in which they would keep notes on various aspects of their lives to be sent to me at home at set times. We would mail them back and forth at least twice during the months I was away from Japan (I paid postage costs). In these diaries, as it turned out, the richest material appeared: more than even the relatively open discussion groups provided. I realized that this intimacy came about because I had already met with them, because they trusted me, and because of the accepted nature of the medium. While this of course took valuable time from other activities, the young people seemed to think it was novel and interesting enough as an activity to pursue. Only in two or three instances did a young person (boys and girls both participated) ask me to preserve his or her confidentiality, although of course I had already assured all of them that anything they said would be made quite anonymous in my published work. The material they included in their exchange diaries and on which I would comment, asking more questions, sometimes including some lore or recipes of my own to keep the reciprocity intact, was, as I said, rich, various, and individual. Sometimes an entry had items taped or pasted in for illustration; sometimes the author illustrated it with cartoons of his/her own devising, or with charts and maps (such as diagrams of the author's room plan). A few included "friendship charts" in which the relationships with close friends were diagrammed and functions and strengths of certain friends indicated. Occasionally an unpleasant episode with a friend or family member would be included in which the narrator would expostulate dramatically: in one case discolored patches in the page were circled and identified as tear stains resulting from the writer's misery. Diaries also showcased the influences of other teen media: some girls particularly included brief fantasy scenarios about romance and dreams of the future that were reminiscent of the romantic fantasies in girls' magazine fiction. Cartoons drawn by girls and boys were highly influenced by the illustrations of popular *manga* (comic books or magazines).

I did not create the exchange diary as a mode of communication; its presence as a minor fad within the peer group antedated my study and served the study well. It supplemented and enhanced interviews; much of the writing exchanged extended other discussions and at the same time followed the form of more typical diaries focused on friends and trends. My earlier background survey conducted to provide a baseline profile of young people included a written questionnaire and a short interview, conducted by myself and two Japanese research assistants in different parts of Japan. This was much less successful in obtaining answers to open-ended questions, or even in gaining information in brief, focused questions. Many times the questionnaires would be returned with only a few questions treated and most left blank. There are clearly two factors in the failure of such questionnaires, at least with this age group: the lack of prior engagement and face-to-face encounters to provide a "relationship" in which the responses would figure, and the resemblance of the form itself to "official" documents associated with formal institutions. The exchange diary method was employed only after face-to-face meetings, and its style suited the off-duty (away from school and family) context of the study and its informants.

Another convention I employed that was already familiar to my informants is the *sakubun,* or short composition, an assignment frequently used in school. We called it a *jiyū sakubun,* or "free composition," for which I only lightly sketched the theme. I asked informants before I visited with them to write a one-page essay (and provided the special paper) on the theme of "Who I think I will be in ten years" or "What I want with all my heart to do when I finish school," or the like. As in the diary entries, many *sakubun* seemed spontaneous, written in a stream-of-consciousness mode, and were illustrated with cartoonlike drawings or occasional photographs. Even though the models for such compositions were set for students in school, they were able to deviate from the more formal exposition required in secondary schools in this informal way. Though young people might at first associate the writing of a *sakubun* with boring schoolwork, the responses revealed playful self-examination and even rebelliousness. In fact, it might be that the informants were engaged in this way because of earlier presecondary school experiences in which students use essays to explore issues rather than to confine them (White 1986). Whatever the explanation for the apparently sincere, spontaneous reflections recorded in these *sakubun,* it was clear that there is a benefit in using existing (if not traditional) modes of communication in fieldwork.

Virtual Interviews and the Future of Youth Studies?

This study was conducted before the widespread use in Japan of the Internet, cell phones, and beepers. These new communications media give opportunities for teens to develop and maintain friendships in new ways. They also have greater potential for dissemination of information among what marketers call "info-maniacs"—the avid, media-targeted middle schoolers. Such modes of communication thus serve marketers even more in amplifying teen culture and providing a wider circle of opportunities for connection and new potential for those sometimes now anonymous communications. Now most teens have access to a cell phone or at least to a beeper, putting them in constant touch with their friends—in some cases with clients as new telephone clubs enlist female teens in the business of teleporn. Teens vie with each other for the longest list of virtual-friend callers and callees, with Internet web sites offering teens long lists of anonymous potential phone pals. When you join a telephone club or add yourself to a caller list, you can also take on a new identity along with the nickname you may give yourself. You can exit a list and leave behind all your fictive friends as easily as you entered it, raising questions about the difference these virtual friendships make in a young person's code of relationships. Internet access is rapidly spreading among teenagers after a relatively slow start in Japan, and e-mail and chat rooms make access to friends, virtual and otherwise, an easy matter, even in the middle of a long night of study, isolated in one's home. Those children who, like the teens of Hiroshima, find their distance from the media and fashion center of Tokyo damaging to their cool, will find that the new means of communication shrink distances and time. All are equal in the virtual geography of the Internet, and the gap in trends and goods, which now include the even more ephemeral media messages, will diminish. The rising number of *hitorikko,* or only children, means a larger percentage of children are sibling-free at home and, engaged in long hours of homework to satisfy their own and their parents' ambitions for academic success, find it even more important to communicate through the media.

What these new media may provide as vehicles for future research, both in themselves as objects of inquiry and as mediating devices for communication with informants, remains to be seen. It is obvious that they are becoming institutionalized in the lives of young people and that engagement in them may provide researchers with yet another "culturally appropriate" mode of interactive data gathering. Mihaly Csikszentmihalyi anticipated by at least a decade the moment when teens would "naturally" incorporate beepers into their lives by conducting a study of teens' lives in the Chicago area. This study aimed at capturing random moments in their lives through the means of "beeping" young people and asking them to record what they were doing at the moment of the beep (Csikszentmihalyi and Larson 1984). While such a study would, in Japan, be seen in "official" institutions as inappropriate—that is, as interrupting the work of adolescence—other uses of the media may be seen by teens themselves at least as quite "relevant" to their lives. The interviewer of the future relying on these faceless means alone will miss out on the still palpable connections in real time and space important to teens. While using such technologies does to some degree replicate the teen's own experience of media life, thus producing a second-level, virtual "participant-observer" situation, the full "sociography" of adolescence must also include the street wisdom, the smell of the coffee shops, and the parade of fashion and styles teens will continue to experience as they map their own identities including and beyond the web sites, chat rooms, and places given them by school and home.

Note

I want to thank Hidetada Shimizu, who served as research assistant and colleague during this project. Thanks also go to Mariko Fujiwara of Hakuhodo Institute of Life and Leisure and to Sumio Kondo of the Children's Research Institute, both of whom helped locate me in the world of material children. The study was funded by several grants from the American Council of Learned Societies, the Social Science Research Council, and the Japan Foundation.

Related Readings

White, Merry Isaacs. 1986. *The Japanese Educational Challenge: A Commitment to Children*. New York: Free Press.

———. 1993. *The Material Child: Coming of Age in Japan and America*. New York: Free Press. (Paperback edition: Berkeley: University of California Press, 1995.)

———. 1995a. "The Marketing of Adolescence in Japan: Buying and Dreaming." In Brian Moeran and Lise Skov, eds., *Women, Media and Consumption in Japan*. London: Curzon Press.

White, Merry Isaacs, and Robert A. LeVine. 1986. "What Is an *Ii Ko?*" In Harold W. Stevenson, Hiroshi Azuma, and Kenji Hakuta, eds., *Child Development and Education in Japan*. New York: W. H. Freeman.

Patricia G. Steinhoff
(third from left,
holding the orange
juice) being toasted
on the publication of
her Japanese book,
*Nihon Sekigunha:
Sono shakaigakuteki
monogatari*, 1992.

PATRICIA G. STEINHOFF

New Notes from the Underground:
Doing Fieldwork without a Site

I study radical social movements and their conflicts with the state. Although some of my work has been historical, I use participant observation and interviews to study the social movements that arose from the great protest wave of the late 1960s. A fieldworker normally begins by finding a site—a community, an office, a school, a work site—and then settling down to observe and interview people in their natural setting. However, the groups I want to study do not have a regular place of business; indeed, they attract a crowd of plainclothes police whenever their members gather.

In order to do fieldwork without a fixed site, I have to find the trails that lead to my invisible subjects and then work out ways to talk to them and observe their activities intermittently, in scattered locations. I have found four different strategies for tapping into the social networks of the people I want to study, each of which leads eventually to all of the others. They include entering through network portals, monitoring communications networks and publications, observing gatherings, and following individual cases. To emphasize how unsystematic and serendipitous the process of discovering these pathways to the underground has been, I will first narrate some of my early experiences and then take a more general, analytic look at the four strategies.

Serendipitous Beginning

If I had started the field research a few years earlier, I could have found my subjects on any college campus or clashing with the police in violent street demonstrations. In fact, I was in Tokyo, based right at the University of Tokyo, when the massive protest wave of the late 1960s began rising in 1967 and early 1968, but I was busy then studying the conflict between the Japanese communist movement and the state in prewar Japan, and I paid very little attention to the new protests that were beginning to swirl around me.

By the time I was ready to examine how protest and its social control by the state had changed in postwar Japan, the protest wave of the late 1960s had already peaked and the people I was most interested in had been driven underground, surfacing only in occasional bursts of violence that splashed across the front pages of the newspapers. It was no longer an easy matter to find the postwar principals, let alone to observe their activities. And I was no longer in Japan.

It turned out that the easiest and safest place to find my subjects was in jail, but that raised its own set of access problems. I found my first one in Israel, a Japanese college student named Okamoto Kōzō who had been captured after a devastating attack on Lod (now Ben Gurion) Airport in 1972. Just after his military trial had concluded, I obtained permission from the Israeli government to interview their high-profile Japanese prisoner, with their caution that he might not be willing to talk to me.

My working hypothesis was that both the constitutional changes and educational reforms of the early postwar period might have given this generation of young activists better resources for standing up to the overwhelming power of the state than their prewar counterparts had possessed. I wanted to study this, as I had the prewar communist movement, by looking very closely at the experiences of individuals who had chosen to confront the state out of personal ideological commitment. Since organizations, even more than individuals, become the targets of the state, my larger goal was to understand the group that had sent him on his deadly mission.

Israel is quite literally halfway around the world from Hawai'i, so I decided to go by way of Japan. In addition to collecting some background material, I thought that if I could make contact with Okamoto's family, I could offer to take something from them to their son. I naively imagined walking into the interview and handing him a gift from his parents, which would set us up for a standard Japanese interview. I did not know the prisoner's family, but I knew the direct approach I had used to get permission for the interview from the Israeli authorities would certainly not work with his parents in Japan. With another stroke of luck, I was able to use a connection to an editor at a major Japanese newspaper to move very rapidly through a series of introductions to the journalists who had been covering the case. Three days later I found myself on the doorstep of the Okamoto family home in Kumamoto. I had a cordial and productive interview with the family members, then set off for Israel carrying the genetics textbooks that Okamoto had asked his father to send him.

On the day of the interview I met first with the prison director, who quickly deflated my naive expectations about how the interview would proceed. He took the textbooks and explained that they would be delivered to Okamoto, but only after they had gone through a censorship process that might take as long as two weeks. I would have to go into the interview empty-handed. The prison director then laid down two further conditions. First, I could not take any recording device, not even pencil and paper, into the interview room. Second, afterward I would have to return to the director's office and write out a full report of what had transpired in the interview.

The first condition was not a problem, as that was how I always did interviews. In preparation for my earlier dissertation research I had trained myself to conduct interviews without taking notes and without using a tape recorder. After an interview I would retire immediately to a quiet place to jot down quick notes, then expand the notes into a full narrative record of the interview. As with any interviewing method there is a trade-off; with this method of interviewing I end up with many pages of field notes rather than a transcript suitable for verbatim quotes. The advantages are that I can concentrate completely on the interviewee's words and body language and that I can turn any situation into an interview without being dependent on such visible props as pencil and paper or a tape recorder. In retrospect, my years of research on radical and underground social movements would not have been possible with any other interviewing method. At the time, I was simply relieved that I was prepared on such short notice to conduct my first prison interview without using a tape recorder or taking notes.

Although the restriction on all recording devices was not a barrier, the sticking point was the demand that I write out my notes in the director's office and hand over a copy. I felt uncomfortable about violating the confidentiality of a research interview, but there were obviously security considerations from their point of view. I had come too far to jeopardize the opportunity, so I swallowed hard, accepted the conditions, and went on to have an intense, two-hour interview in the most rapid-fire Japanese I had ever heard. I later found that the interview conditions in Israel had been relatively generous compared to those in Japanese prisons, which also do not permit any note taking or tape recorders, but in addition station a guard next to the prisoner to take notes on the conversation.

After one successful prison interview with a Japanese radical activist in Israel, I had a specific group to focus on, the various branches of the Red Army, but I was not any closer to doing fieldwork in Japan. The subject was simply too sensitive to pursue in Japan at that moment. For several years I followed the overseas exploits of the Japanese Red Army through the news media and read whatever other background materials I could find. A decade later I was ready to pick up the threads of the research in Japan and fortunately was able to obtain strong institutional sponsorship. Without such legitimacy the project would have been much riskier for me, and entree to my subjects might have been more difficult as well.

Normally when I go to Japan to begin a new project, I begin by collecting things to read and asking everyone I know for leads to the people I want to interview, and then I read for a month or two while I wait for the inquiries to ripen into introductions. In this case the channels between the respectable "aboveground" world of academics and professionals and the underground world of former student radicals were quite restricted. Several people offered me the same introduction as their only link to this hidden world, a journalist who had covered the student protests of the late 1960s for a major newspaper. As it happened, I already knew him from my whirlwind of introductions to the Okamoto family ten years earlier. Fortunately, my research assistant had more direct channels into the movement. She had participated in the student conflict at the University of Tokyo as a first-year graduate student, and later her husband had been arrested for a protest act and had spent a year and a half in jail.

She took me to Kyūen Renraku Sentā (Relief Contact Center), which since 1969 has operated a hotline for arrested New Left students and served as a resource center and contact point for their supporters. In addition to subscribing to the monthly newspaper, I bought a reduced-print, republished edition of earlier issues, which has proven to be an invaluable reference source (Kyūen Shukusatsuban Kankō Iinkai 1977, 1984). The center's staff filled me in on current trials, encouraged me to observe trial sessions, and helped me begin the process of snowball interviewing with people who had been involved in the movement in various capacities. This led fairly quickly to the fringes of the Red Army.

My main concern initially was to try to understand the origins of the group and what its attraction had been for certain students within the broader array of protest groups. My curiosity may have been a bit less threatening because initially I was asking about events of ten to fifteen years earlier, rather than what might have been going on underground at that moment. I also traded freely on my own personal experiences, first as a student and student newspaper reporter at the University of Michigan during the early years of New Left student protest in the United States, and then as a scholar who had gone to Israel to interview Okamoto Kōzō shortly after the Lod Airport attack. My earlier research on the prewar Japanese communist movement also helped to establish my credibility.

A number of Red Army activists were in prison on various charges. Through my fellowship sponsors I could have obtained official permission from the prison authorities for some interviews, but my assistant and the center staff advised against it. They thought I would have a much better response if I simply used the regular visiting system for prisoners in unconvicted detention, who are permitted one visit of twenty to thirty minutes per day. That excellent advice has made all of my subsequent years of research possible. If I had used special permission from the prison authorities to get interviews, not only would my motives have been suspect to the prisoners, but the interviews would have been restricted to the prisoners the authorities selected for me, and I would not have been able to see them more than once or twice. Using the normal visiting system sharply limited the time for each interview, but I have been able to return again and again, to correspond with prisoners even after I left Japan, and to develop contacts with new prisoners as they entered the criminal justice system

To use the prison visiting system, I first had to get an introduction to a particular prisoner. Although it was ten years after the event, the major trial in the complex United Red Army purge case had just ended, and the defendants were preparing their appeals. Even though two of the three defendants had received death sentences, they would remain in Tokyo House of Detention for the duration of their appeals, with all the communications privileges of prisoners in unconvicted detention. My first prison interview in Japan was with Nagata Hiroko, the leading woman in the case. I prepared for the interview by reading her recently published two-volume autobiography. After I had been formally introduced in absentia by someone who knew her, I wrote her a letter introducing myself and asking if I could visit her. She sent back a postcard specifying the day that I should come.

My research assistant prepared me carefully for the visiting procedures at the prison. She told me where to go and what to write on the visitor's form, explained the two different waiting rooms in which I would wait for my number to be called, and even warned me not to confuse the suffix for room number (*XXgō-shitsu*) with the room number five (*gogō-shitsu*) when my visiting cubicle number was announced on the loudspeaker. As I waited in the inner waiting room for that first interview, I was called over to a special window, where a prison official grilled me briefly about my purpose and my connection to Nagata, with the warning that they had to protect her from journalists. I said I was a professor, not a journalist, and produced my name card and the postcard from Nagata, which settled the matter. In retrospect, I think they were primarily checking whether I could conduct the interview in Japanese, but the prison administration also prohibits visits by journalists. At any rate, I passed muster and was escorted to the women's section for the first of many interviews with Nagata Hiroko.

Since that first year of field research in the early 1980s, I have gone back to Japan nearly every year for two to four weeks and have spent two additional yearlong periods of fieldwork studying other aspects of postwar Japanese social movements. I continue to build on the contacts and strategies I developed in that first year. As this narrative has revealed, I began the research with some credentials and general background, but with no direct connections or assured entree to the people I hoped to study. I was able to find them by tapping into their social networks, just as one would do for most any kind of fieldwork in Japan. The only difference was that these networks were not as visible to the mainstream of Japanese society, both because they did not converge in regular sites of daily interaction and because the network ties were often deliberately obscured from public view. I stumbled into those networks from several different angles, which we can now examine as potential strategies for doing research on social movements and other hidden groups in Japanese society.

Portals to Hidden Social Networks

Outer-Ring Professionals

Probably the easiest source of entree for foreign researchers is the professionals who work more or less in the mainstream of Japanese society, but whose work brings them into contact with social movement participants. In my case, everyone seemed to know one mainstream journalist who had such ties. Lawyers who handle movement-related legal cases can be useful sources of information as well as potential sources of introductions to other people involved in the cases. Like journalists, they know the people and the details, but they take a relatively objective, intellectual view of the case or movement in question and can discuss it in broader context. These mainstream journalists and lawyers are outsiders to the movement itself. Talking to them can be enlightening, but it is definitely not the same thing as talking to actual participants in social movements and getting their view of the world. For some movements, there may be Japanese academics who have ties, either because of their research or their personal interests.

There are others who straddle the line between the mainstream and the social movements by virtue of their occupation, but who are more closely identified with the movements. These include small publishers and editors who publish books and magazines by and about the movement and the freelance writers who provide them with material. These people tend to be well-educated former student activists who were marginalized out of mainstream employment by their youthful political activity. The outer ring also encompasses certain Japanese Christian ministers and priests who advocate a liberal social agenda and whose churches provide meeting space for some social movement activities as part of their social service mission. The ministers know the participants and sometimes sit in on the sessions or join the parties afterward. For some social causes, these religious professionals might offer direct access to a church-related group engaged in social service activities; in other cases they might be willing to provide introductions to activists they know.

Central Contact Points

Although the individual social movement organizations that I study rarely have anything resembling a regularly staffed office, there are certain contact points with addresses and telephone numbers that can provide information about or access to a wide range of other organizations. Often, because of the links between social movements and the universal need to economize, one such office may serve as a mail drop for other, seemingly unrelated organizations.

One type of central contact point is the meta-organization or association whose purpose is to help unify specific organizations that are working for a common cause. Some take the form of a hierarchical central organization or a formal coalition committee to which other organizations belong. Such meta-organizations often serve as the organizing agency for major social movement campaigns that mobilize various groups to participate.

In other cases the contact point is simply a clearinghouse and resource center with informal ties to other organizations. Kyūen Renraku Sentā is a clearinghouse organization that operates a twenty-four-hour hotline for arrested activists, but equally important is its function as a clearinghouse for information that is published in the monthly newspaper, much of which is contributed by the support groups for individual legal cases. A Christian organization in Tokyo operates an informational clearinghouse for the anti-emperor movement and publishes a newsletter that reports on the upcoming meetings and demonstrations of many groups. Similar clearinghouse organizations no doubt exist for other social movements. The local office or affiliate of an international social movement organization may also serve as a contact point for other local organizations interested in the same issues.

Bookstores that distribute the small-scale publications *(mini-komi)* of social movement organizations comprise a third type of central contact point. During the early 1970s there were quite a number of such *mini-komi* distributors, but today there are just two or three general ones left in Japan. The most famous and most accessible is the Mosakusha Bookstore in Shin-juku San-chōme. It carries a wide range of hard-to-find books and magazines on various social movements and social issues, as well as a vast assortment of the newsletters, newspapers, and other publications produced by social movement organizations. Since Mosakusha obtains these materials directly from the publishers and *mini-komi* producers on consignment, it carries materials long after they have disappeared from circulation.

Mosakusha should certainly be part of the rounds of anyone studying any kind of social issue or social movement in contemporary Japan, along with whatever central clearinghouse organization is most relevant. These central contact points are useful when one is just getting into a research topic, but they become even more important over time, as places where you can catch up on what has happened since you left Japan, collect all the new publications, and find out what other issues are now current.

Communications Networks and Publications

Commercial Publications

One essential way to begin fieldwork on a new topic is to read what has already been written about the subject. For social movements other than local environmental or citizens' movements, very little can be found in academic publications in either English or Japanese. However, there is usually quite a bit of nonacademic material available in Japanese if you know where to look. Even if academics in Japan are not studying a social movement, there are usually plenty of books about it written by journalists and participants. Some of these are published by mainstream presses and can be found in most large bookstores designated as "nonfiction" or contemporary issues, but do not expect to find much on these subjects in your neighborhood bookstore.

Weekly magazines and small press monthlies are good sources of information about current happenings in social movements, but unless you know the freelance journalists who produce most of these articles, it is hard to find them. Some small press monthlies carry social movement material regularly, while the weeklies only occasionally will have a single story or a series on some current incident or trial. Certain small magazines are published explicitly to present antiestablishment views and commentary, and their owner-editors give prominent coverage to social movements with which they sympathize, including special issues and retrospectives. Mosakusha carries most such sympathetic monthlies, including back issues, and a few of the more general ones can be found even in local bookstores, usually back in an obscure corner. For the weeklies, the best strategy is to do what everyone else does: stand at a magazine rack and flip through the table of contents to see if there is anything interesting.

Except for first-person accounts by movement participants and occasional collections of real documents (as opposed to journalistic accounts called *"dokyumento"* to indicate the reporter's direct involvement), the materials described thus far are secondary accounts of social movement activity by journalists. Since the authors and publishers are not academics, there is always a question of how reliable the secondary material is and whether it is appropriate to use it for academic research. The only way that question can be answered is through careful consideration of who wrote the material and how well it is corroborated by other sources. Still, the fact that a lot of journalists are repeating the same thing does not make it true, since they may simply be repeating the same completely wrong information from a standard source.

There is also material produced by government agencies about certain social movements. If the social movement in question is a target of state surveillance and social control, reports about it will appear in regular police and security agency publications as well as in special reports. When dealing with marginal social movements that are targets of state social control, it is safe to assume that most of the mainstream mass media, particularly the major newspapers, are publishing information provided by police sources to the reporters' club without much independent confirmation. It may be factually correct, but it reflects a particular point of view and in some cases a conscious public relations campaign. Weekly and monthly magazines that do not participate in the reporters' club system are more likely to publish material produced by investigative reporting, but some of that may also be wildly off the mark. If the writer is someone close to the movement with access to inside information, most of the facts are probably correct, although the writer's sympathetic bias must be taken into consideration.

What is most important is simply to recognize that the reliability of secondary print sources is an issue, and that the kinds of secondary materials that are going to be available will not have the same authority as the academic sources one normally would use for background information. It makes no sense to reject all such material, but it cannot be accepted uncritically as factual. There is also a fair amount of fiction based on social movements, much of which is written by people who participated in them to some degree. While such work must be recognized as fiction and not fact, it can be useful for capturing the mood of the times, the emotions of participants, and the details of contemporary lifestyles.

Primary Materials Produced by the Movement

Serious research on social movements requires access to the primary materials that the movement itself produces. These may have their own distortions, particularly in their interpretations of external events, but they at least represent accurately how the movement views the world and communicates with its own members. Virtually any social movement organization in Japan, regardless of its size, produces at least a desktop-published newsletter. Many produce regular newspapers and magazines and issue pamphlets on special topics. Most of these publications are only available by subscription to members and friends or in places like Mosakusha that specialize in the distribution of *mini-komi* materials. They are also sold at information tables around the edges of rallies and public meetings.

One of the first things I do when I make contact with a new social movement organization is to ask if I can subscribe to their newsletter. While many small groups would be happy to provide free copies at least for a while, they all operate on a shoestring and should not have to subsidize a foreign scholar's research expenses. Outsiders are not expected to pay the regular monthly membership dues of the organization, which may be quite substantial, but you can usually get a year's subscription to the newsletter for two thousand to three thousand yen. It is well worth it, particularly as the collection accumulates over time. While I am in Japan, the newsletter alerts me to events I should attend, and if I remember to give them a change of address and some extra money before I leave, it becomes an important way to keep abreast of the organization's activities after I return home. It is also usually possible to buy copies of back issues from the person who produces them, although a few key issues such as the first one may no longer be available.

The newsletter or newspaper carries current news about what the organization is doing and presents opinions about relevant current events in the organization's own ideological language. More extended discussions of the organization's philosophy are likely to appear in pamphlets, books by the leader, or in some other organizational publication such as a monthly magazine. The leaders of social movement organizations are prolific writers, and many have published books about their philosophy as well as autobiographies or collections of other writings. My personal view of social movements is that the activities and perspectives of ordinary members are just as important as the abstract ideas of the leader and may reveal a great deal more about how the organization actually functions. Still, reading what the leader has written helps to demonstrate the sincerity of my interest in the group.

Web Sites

Nowadays, a growing number of social movement organizations have established web sites. With a web browser that can handle Japanese, it is easy enough to access many of the organization's documents and perhaps even develop a dialogue with the person maintaining the site. These sites are often a personal labor of love by one individual, so they may not stay up-to-date and may even disappear if the person in charge cannot pay his or her bills or drifts away from the organization. Do not expect that the person running the web site can or will communicate in English. To really develop interactive communication through these sites, it is essential to be able to send and receive e-mail messages in Japanese. (See the appendix to this volume for more information on this.) The University of Hawai'i also maintains a bilingual web site catalog of its Takazawa Collection of Japanese Social Movement Materials, which contains links to some social movement sites in Japan along with descriptions of the primary and secondary materials in the collection: www.takazawa.hawaii.edu (Steinhoff 2001).

Periodic and Occasional Gatherings

Social movement participants come together occasionally for various types of gatherings, each of which has a standard format. Although it takes some work to track down these events, they offer good opportunities for fieldwork both during the gathering and through follow-up with participants.

Shūkai

Shūkai are meetings or rallies held in a fixed location, either indoors or out, which often bring together members of several different organizations to highlight an issue. At the ones I attend, there are invariably knots of plainclothes police standing around outside in their conspicuously inconspicuous casual dress. I always count the number of plainclothes police and write it down in my notes, since I know they are also putting my presence into their notes. Indoor *shūkai* generally have a table by the door where attendees are supposed to sign in and pay a small attendance fee, receiving in exchange a program and other handouts. There are often some tables set up nearby at which various groups display and sell their publications.

Large *shūkai* may be all-day affairs with an endless succession of speakers. The audience comes and goes rather freely, especially during the long series of greeting speeches by supporting organizations that precede or follow the main attraction. These ancillary speeches provide an opportunity for other organizations to promote their own causes and often are only marginally connected to the main theme, but they offer important clues to the ideological connections among social movements. Shorter rallies in a meeting hall or a public park also precede street demonstrations. They provide an opportunity for the demonstrators to gather, build some momentum, and get organized into marching groups before the street procession begins under careful police guard. At the end of the street demonstration each participating group often holds a short, closing rally at another small park before the demonstrators disperse.

Demonstrations

Street demonstrations are highly organized affairs that require police permits and extensive advance planning. They often involve a large number of separate groups that demonstrate under a permit issued to one lead organization, which negotiates the march route and makes basic support arrangements for the demonstrators. Mild demonstrations involve only uniformed police directing traffic around the demonstrators, but more serious ones are accompanied by uniformed traffic police, riot police in full regalia, plainclothes police in their own distinctive casual outfits, and a host of odd-shaped, unmarked, gray police vehicles.

Committee Meetings

Once I have developed good access to an organization, a more important type of small gathering is the periodic committee meetings at which the organization's key members conduct the routine business of the group. Sometimes I get invited to such a meeting for the purpose of explaining my research and asking for the members' cooperation. Once a relationship has been established, I may simply be permitted to attend the meetings regularly and observe what goes on. Typically there will be some reports of recent events and ongoing activities, discussion of what will go into the next newsletter, and planning for the next event. I have most often attended the committee meetings of support groups for persons involved in legal cases that arise out of social movement activity. At these meetings movement activists interact informally with lawyers, and the broad range of support activity becomes visible.

Because these sessions are small and informal, the observing academic is sometimes unexpectedly drawn into the activity. I have on occasion been asked to explain the behavior and motives of a third party whom I knew better than the group members did, to help translate English letters or documents, to explain American laws or legal procedures, or to contribute a short item to the newsletter. I do not volunteer for anything except occasional translation assistance, but I generally do whatever is requested unless it seems to compromise my position as an observer. Such sessions often end with food and socializing, either at the meeting site or at a nearby bar or snack shop. These are valuable opportunities for informal interviews and to observe interaction, but they are also opportunities for the group members to ask challenging questions about American foreign policy or social practices, especially after a certain amount of alcohol has been consumed. I always stay for as long as my presence seems appropriate, even though I know that I still have hours of writing up fieldnotes ahead of me.

Shūkai, demonstrations, and committee meetings are important occasions for fieldwork, but unless I just happen onto one by chance, I have to know in advance when and where it will occur. The best source of such information is the organization's own newsletter or newspaper, or the newsletter of the clearinghouse organization most closely associated with it. These are the sources the movement's own members use to find out about the events. If I do not have a personal invitation, I try to arrange to go to indoor events with someone who is known to the group and can introduce me to at least a few people. Once some people in the movement know who I am, it is perfectly all right to turn up alone. The social movement networks are so interconnected that even at a gathering for an unrelated issue, I will usually see at least one or two people whom I already know.

Sidewalk Activities

There are also occasional gatherings that one might happen onto or find out about from more general public sources. Social movement organizations often conduct small-scale leafleting and petition signature campaigns outside train stations or on busy shopping streets. In the late 1960s student activists frequently collected donations in their organization helmets outside train stations, but street solicitation of donations is less common today. More focused leafleting or even picketing sometimes takes place outside the offices where protested activities are taking place. These settings offer opportunities to observe casual interaction between social movement activists and ordinary passersby, but they generally are not very productive as fieldwork sites. However, engaging in conversation with the participants might offer an opening to meet more people, attend other events, or obtain more formal interviews.

Individual Legal Cases

A final way that I do fieldwork on invisible groups is through the individual legal cases that form a prominent part of social movement activity in contemporary Japan. These cases come about in several different ways, but they are pursued through organized support groups as a form of social movement activity (Steinhoff 1999). The first cases that I followed involved criminal charges against people associated with the Red Army, and later I began following some civil cases related to social movements. I subsequently became interested in the support groups themselves as a form of social movement activity. There are three aspects to following individual cases as a strategy for studying invisible groups: meeting the individuals actually being charged or bringing suit and learning the specifics of the case; utilizing the trial sessions as a fieldwork site; and making contact with the support groups that can usually be found working closely with the lawyers to facilitate the case.

The Principals in the Case

The people directly involved in a legal case are prime subjects for interviews or, if it is a criminal case and they are being held in unconvicted detention, for prison visits. They are usually eager to tell their stories to a sympathetic listener, and they put a human face onto abstract issues and movements. Depending on the case, there may also be a lot of written background material from legal documents or the person's own writings that can be used to prepare for the interview. Even if it seems that everything one would ever want to know is in these written materials, the face-to-face interview is still invaluable for getting a sense of the living and feeling individual behind the case, for following up on details and discrepancies in the record, for finding differences between the public persona and the private person, and for following personal changes over time (Steinhoff 1976, 1992, 1996).

Trial Sessions

Trials in Japan do not run continuously. They usually meet once or twice a month for half a day, and they may even recess for several months at a time. Both sides can appeal, and trials with any sort of social movement implications or support will generally be appealed at least once. This makes it difficult for a researcher to attend all the trial sessions of one case without living in Japan for years at a time, but conversely, it becomes much easier to attend an occasional trial session and then make arrangements to keep tabs on the course of the case.

Trial sessions are open to the public, but courtrooms are small, some seats are reserved for designated press corps representatives, and the number of seats for ordinary observers is limited. This is not a problem except for sensational cases that attract a lot of additional news media and general observers and the early sessions of social movement trials with large support groups. Tokyo District Court has two systems for managing the limited seats for trial sessions, particularly criminal trials. One is to have people line up in a designated waiting area outside the court building to obtain *bōchōken,* or observation passes, which are handed out fifteen minutes before the trial session is set to begin. For a trial that is likely to run out of seats, it is sometimes necessary to arrive an hour in advance to get a place near the front of the line. When a large overflow crowd is expected, court personnel set an earlier time on the day of the trial when people can come to the court and obtain a lottery number for the session. The results are later posted, and people with winning numbers can exchange them for observation passes.

Tape recorders, cameras, and cell phones are not permitted in the courtroom; however, thanks to a suit brought by an American lawyer (Repeta et al. 1991), observers may now take notes during trials. Guards strictly enforce proper decorum and silence in the gallery, but at the first session of social movement trials the supporters traditionally cause a loud disruption that ends in a brawl with court guards and the supporters' ejection from the courtroom. Many social movement trials are assigned to high-security courtrooms, in which case observers must pass through a metal detector or undergo hand screening before entering the courtroom area and are permitted to take only one handbag into the courtroom.

The content of a trial session can range from riveting drama to mind-numbing detail. Still, the sessions are useful on several counts. In a criminal trial it is an opportunity to watch and be seen by the defendant, which may be useful for later contact. Even more important, trial sessions offer an opportunity to meet support group members and lawyers while waiting for the session to begin or during the break, to learn about other activities related to the case, to obtain newsletters and trial documents, and to arrange for prison visits and interviews. To make the most of these opportunities, I try to observe the same trial for more than one session so that people come to know me as a person who is genuinely interested in the case.

Support Groups

Sometimes a legal case is precipitated directly by the actions of a social movement organization, but in other cases social movement organizations either find or form around individual cases that they can support. Researchers pursuing a social issue or social movement often stumble onto the support organization for a legal case and find it a rich resource of knowledgeable activists eager to share materials and promote their cause. Such groups, often called the *"shienkai"* or *"kyūenkai"* for a particular case, invariably publish a newsletter about the trial and usually produce other related documents. They work closely with the trial lawyers and in some cases may even have been organized by the lawyers to handle some of the paralegal work and to help keep up the spirits of the principals in the case. Often the support group members who attend trial sessions meet informally with the lawyers after the session, and a regular observer can tag along to these meetings and learn a great deal about both the support group and the progress of the case.

Research Ethics, Values, and Risks

By now it should be apparent that all of the research strategies I have outlined interlock. Social movement participants produce communications materials, organize gatherings, stay in touch through contact points, and interact with both outer-ring professionals and the principals in individual legal cases. This hidden world can be entered through many secret doorways, but once inside there are well-traveled corridors linking them all together. The same pathways also link movements together and tie individual activists into multiple movements and organizations.

Once contact has been made with these invisible networks, it becomes relatively easy to move along them, but by the same token, the researcher becomes highly visible within them, and his or her behavior is scrutinized as closely as it would be in a village. There are ethics involved in any kind of social research, but working with underground groups and social movements poses a special set of issues. Early on in this research, I realized that I could not play both sides of the street. If the strength of my research was to be my ability to understand the movements and their members from the inside, then I could not in good conscience maintain close ties to law enforcement agencies that wanted to know about them for their own purposes. In addition to maintaining a polite distance from the police, over the years I have said no to inquiries and requests from the Japanese Security Research Agency (the agency charged with investigating matters of national security and subversion) and the FBI and CIA in the United States. There are undoubtedly some Japanese in the movement who suspect that I am connected to these agencies, but my own conscience is clear. By the same token, I sometimes have to turn down requests or maintain some distance from the movements I study in order to protect both my data and my reputation as a legitimate, reasonably objective scholar.

Every researcher has to make up his or her own mind on these issues, but I take a very conservative position about the importance of maintaining my position as a scholar of and not an activist with or apologist for the groups I study. This approach is underscored by the fact that I conduct research in a country where I am a visitor, and the conditions of my visa preclude any participation in domestic politics. I never sign petitions, and I never join the organizations I study, although I do pay for subscriptions to their publications and admission fees to events for research purposes. While I attend *shūkai* as a member of the audience, at demonstrations I do not march with the demonstrators but observe from the sidewalk. All of the various police and security agencies that conduct surveillance of political and social movements are well aware of my presence, just as I am aware of theirs. I have never felt in any danger of arrest, although at the end of one memorable anti-emperor demonstration in 1990 I spent two hours sealed off by the riot police in a cul-de-sac along with a couple thousand demonstrators until the emperor's coronation parade was safely over. Much more than by my own behavioral circumspection, I am protected by the strong legalistic orientation of the Japanese authorities, by their perception that I pose no real threat, and by the prevailing norms regarding academic research by foreign scholars.

In the course of my research I have published two books and several articles in Japanese that many of my informants have read (Steinhoff 1991; Steinhoff and Itoh 1996). They have seen from these writings that I do not intend to harm or expose them, but that I am genuinely trying to understand their motives and to analyze the social dynamics underlying some of their most sensational acts. They do not always agree with my interpretations, and their critiques and subsequent explanations have greatly enriched my understanding. It has been difficult to achieve closure in some of my research because the people are still active and there is always more to learn. Yet at the same time, what I am able to write now has benefited immeasurably from my long and patient fieldwork in the underground. It has led me into topics, personal relations, publications, and research collaborations that I would never have dreamed of when I started.

Note

This research has been supported by three Fulbright Senior Research Fellowships to Japan in 1982–1983, 1990–1991, and 1998–1999, and a fellowship in 1990–1992 from the Harry Frank Guggenheim Foundation, plus additional support from the Japan Studies Endowment, Center for Japanese Studies, University of Hawai'i. During my stays in Japan I have been affiliated with the Institute of Social Science, University of Tokyo, thanks to the generous sponsorship of Professors Ishida Takeshi, Toshitani Nobuyoshi, and Ishida Hiroshi. I am also indebted to the many social movement activists who have so generously shared their life experiences, their thoughts, and their social movement materials with me.

Related Readings

Steinhoff, Patricia. G. 1989. "Hijackers, Bombers and Bank Robbers: Managerial Style in the Japanese Red Army." *Journal of Asian Studies* 48(4):724–740.
———. 1991. *Nihon Sekigunha: Sono shakaigakuteki monogatari* [Japan Red Army faction: A sociological tale]. Tokyo: Kawade Shobō Shinsha.
———. 1992. "Death by Defeatism and Other Fables: The Social Dynamics of the Rengo Sekigun Purge." In Takie S. Lebra, ed., *Japanese Social Organization*. Honolulu: University of Hawai'i Press, 195–224.
———. 1996. "Three Women Who Loved the Left: Radical Woman Leaders in the Japanese Red Army Movement." In Anne E. Imamura, ed., *Re-Imaging Japanese Women*. Berkeley: University of California Press, 301–323.
———. 1999. "Doing the Defendant's Laundry: Support Groups as Social Movement Organizations in Contemporary Japan." *Japanstudien, Jährbuch des Deutschen Instituts für Japanstudien* 11:55–78.
Zwerman, Gilda, Patricia G. Steinhoff, and Donatella della Porta. 2000. "Disappearing Social Movements: Clandestinity in the Cycle of New Left Protest in the United States, Japan, Germany, and Italy." *Mobilization* 5(1):85–104.

Joy Hendry writing fieldnotes in the pre-laptop era, at her desk in Kyushu.

JOY HENDRY

From Scrambled Messages to an Impromptu Dip: Serendipity in Finding a Field Location

When I was in Tokyo setting about finding a suitable location for my first fieldwork, an eminent American anthropologist, who for diplomatic reasons shall remain nameless, told me that British anthropologists are far more concerned with their own egos than with the study of science. Since I had a degree in general science, which I subsequently discovered bore little relation to the subject of social anthropology, I was not too concerned with this apparent put-down. I mention the incident at the start of this chapter for three reasons. First, like a government health warning on cigarette packets, I advise that my approach may possibly interfere with the anthropological health of an American reader. Second, I wish immediately to make clear that my cultural background may have influenced the proceedings. And third, I hope that by introducing some of the more controversial aspects of my early anthropological experience, I might encourage a new student to see that there may be more than one way to solve a problem.

Life was in fact very different for students setting out to work in Japan in 1975, when I made my first foray into the world of anthropological fieldwork. First, there were only a very small number of anthropological ancestors. For a British student, these were almost all foreign, and they had a somewhat different idea of the subject. However, I did find that when I wrote to them, each replied in some way or other offering to help, and I am still grateful to them all. Even the one who made the above comment did it in frustration because I was unwilling to join a team revisiting the site of a big previous study. I had no training in the apparently American science of anthropology, and I set out with the possibly romantic idea that I wanted to find my own village and do a relatively bounded study there.

This approach is now out-of-date, but it was at the time what many anthropology students setting out from Oxford (and other British universities) did. Moreover, we had very little preparation before going to the field. Courses in research methods had yet to be invented in the UK, and the difficulties of life in the field were regarded as an appropriate *rite de passage* for future professional life. Qualified with a diploma in social anthropology, some Japanese language, and background reading on the area of my choice, I was dispatched to the field with a grant obtained by outlining a general plan for the study of marriage practices. I set off with little more than a letter of recommendation from a senior professor (a China specialist), a very basic grant, and a few names and telephone numbers.

Preparation for fieldwork is now much more available, and there are several personal accounts of the experience and many more ancestors to shine a light along the path. Formal arrangements with Japanese universities also help new fieldworkers to orient themselves once they arrive. What follows may be surprising to the neophyte of the early twenty-first century, then, but I believe that the serendipitous events that occur during the endeavor are often where the best lines of inquiry emerge. I therefore hope that the details I recount here of my first taste of fieldwork may prove, if strange, as useful to the new reader now as they were to me then.

One advantage I had when I set out for fieldwork was prior experience of Japan, a benefit often shared by today's anthropology students. My first visit had been largely to study Japanese, when I was fortunate to find accommodation in a house with ten young Japanese who, though keen to practice their English over dinner, also provided excellent role models for speaking Japanese during the rest of the day. It was here also that the seeds of inquiry for my first project were sown, for particularly the young women with whom I found myself living spent much of their time discussing the subject of marriage. Their chief concern was to compare the relative merits of love matches versus arrangements initiated with a meeting called a *miai*, and this seemed so to absorb everyone who joined the circle that I decided to make it the main focus of my study. I felt that anything that sparked such a range of views and opinions must lead me to a greater understanding of the society in which I was staying. It was also a stage of life on which I was just myself embarking.

Some of these housemates were to become lifelong friends, and several were helpful when I returned to do fieldwork. One of them, Kyoko, had also taken the plunge and had acquired not only a husband, but also a small child, whose impending arrival seemed to have precipitated the wedding. Another of the girls had gone to work in Finland and looked likely to marry a Finn. Both were clearly love matches. A third former housemate, this one a man, became a guinea pig for participant observation as I played go-between and introduced him to the (unmarried and aging) secretary of an Englishman I happened to meet. The rest offered to help in other ways, so I did not arrive without Japanese contacts. It is just that they were friends, rather than academic advisors, and the first part of my fieldwork experience was not only to find a field location, but also to enlist some local academic support. Herein lies the first piece of serendipity.

Finding a Japanese Supervisor

One of the names I had been given to contact was a sociologist, a Professor Aoi, but unfortunately I had not been given his telephone number. I was staying with a Japanese friend when I returned for fieldwork, so I asked her to help me to find it. The telephone book proved useless with such a common name, so she called another professor for advice. He was away, but his wife offered the name of a third person who might know it, and eventually a number was procured. I called this number myself, gave my name, and explained the situation. In response, I received a warm reception and an appointment to meet.

There was a student strike at the professor's university on the day I arrived, so we were at first forced to converse through the bars of a fence surrounding the closed campus. We managed to make contact, however, and eventually met in a nearby café. It had not really occurred to me to wonder how the professor knew who I was as I approached the campus. Once we were in the café, however, it became clear rather quickly that he knew me already and assumed that I knew him; moreover, he was quite willing and happy to help me. I had never met Professor Aoi, and as far as I knew he had not heard of me before, so I had not expected such immediate support.

I tried to adjust my conversation as best I could to the emerging circumstances, and I must have done reasonably well, for another meeting was soon arranged. This time I would encounter some more anthropologists (not sociologists) who might be of practical help. Fortunately, at this stage, a name card was forthcoming, and the name of my interlocutor was revealed as a young man by the name of Aoki, not Aoi at all. I did subsequently meet Professor Aoi, who proved to be of very little help, but Mr. Aoki, who had been a student in Oxford where we had apparently met and who is now a well-known professor of anthropology in his own right, was the one who really set me on my way. Although I could hardly have known it that day, my first really useful contact was made through a misheard name, a scrambled message.

The next few weeks were spent meeting a number of other new people who played roles of more or less significance in my future research, but serendipity had hardly begun. Aoki's first suggestion for my research had interesting consequences, but he also introduced me to the professor of anthropology who became my immediate advisor in Tokyo and with whom I have had very strong connections ever since. This professor, Yoshida Teigo, suggested that I become a research student *(kenkyūsei)* at Tokyo University, and I had to set about writing out my plans in Japanese. A minor panic arose when they found I had no proof of my British degree, and I also needed to check with England that my grant would cover the fees, but eventually all hurdles were crossed and I was offered a place. I had secured myself not only a local supervisor, but also a prestigious university to write on my name card.

Seeking a Field Location

Next, I needed to find a place to carry out my study. I had set off six weeks in advance of my husband Dennis, who would join me for about half of the year I would spend in Japan. I hoped to settle on a place for us to stay before he arrived. I wanted to find a community where we could live alongside people working and thus place my study of marriage in the context of everyday life. Everyone had ideas. Aoki suggested that I go up to the Noto Peninsula, a popular site for Japanese field research at the time, where he had a friend who would help. Yoshida thought Kyushu or Shikoku might be good, because there were still thriving local communities in a time of rural depopulation, and he gave me the name of a professor at Fukuoka University. My old friends from English House also offered contacts, one in Tokushima, another in Uwajima (both Shikoku), and a third in northern Kyushu.

I decided to set off and visit each of the places in turn, talk to people locally, and settle on the one that seemed most promising for a study of contemporary marriage practices. My grant was limited and my husband was also a graduate student, so it was important to find somewhere we could afford, and the country seemed more promising than cities in this respect. The train journeys I would make were expensive even in those days, but I saved overnight costs by staying in youth hostels or with friends, and it seemed worthwhile making a thorough investigation before deciding where to spend a whole year in close contact with people. I felt I might intuitively know when I had found the right place—another example of romantic idealism, perhaps?

The Saturday evening before I was to leave for Kanazawa (on the Noto Peninsula), I had a telephone call from Aoki, who said that his friend there was coming to Tokyo for a meeting the following Tuesday, and why didn't I wait to see him there? I tossed and turned through the night wondering what to do, but eventually decided to travel anyway, since I would lose 30 percent of the quite substantial ticket price if I canceled, and I wanted to see what the place was like. It was a splendid journey through the mountains of Gunma Prefecture, and the people with whom I spoke in Kanazawa were delightfully friendly. I liked the place at once and felt greatly encouraged.

I spent the night in a youth hostel up in the mountains, planning to call Aoki's friend before he left in the morning and then see a bit of the Noto Peninsula. Unfortunately the day dawned dreary, and the pouring rain made the latter plan seem less attractive. Aoki's friend was in a rush for the train and so couldn't spend much time speaking, though he sounded pleasant. I made a rapid and rather risky decision to take the *shinkansen* (bullet train) back to Maibara, where I would pick up a connection to my next port of call in Shikoku and possibly also meet the elusive professor on the train. Japanese communication skills came through with flying colors on this occasion, for I just managed to catch the next fast train, and the conductor agreed to announce the professor's name, together with my seat number. Sure enough, the professor soon appeared, smiling, by my side.

He would indeed help me if I decided to go for the Noto Peninsula, he said, but he actually thought that Shikoku or Kyushu might be better. This was mostly because Noto was such a popular choice for Japanese researchers, who had therefore published a lot of material that I would need to read, but also as we talked we began to realize that I was after something less unusual and specific. He gave me another piece of advice that was to prove helpful as I continued my search for a suitable location, and that was to contact the offices of local boards of education *(kyōiku iinkai)* when looking for accommodation. They keep a list of houses available for teachers as they move around the country, and there may be an empty one I could rent out.

I was running a day early for my next appointment in Tokushima, so I left the train at Akashi and took a boat to Awaji Island, where I again found myself a youth hostel for the night. This place was most attractive, too, and quite appealed to me as another possible site for fieldwork, although my sole traveling companion said that Awaji Island was more like the Kansai region than like Shikoku. On impulse, however, I called at the local education office, where I was received kindly, though my request for possible accommodation could not be dealt with at once, and I left them the forwarding address of my former housemate's family in Kyushu.

Tokushima looked very industrial from the approaching boat, and my heart sank initially, but this visit was to prove another exciting and serendipitous experience. First, I met the local English teacher (in those days there was rarely more than one) who had been introduced to me by my friend Kyoko, from English House. He promised to take the following day off and drive me around to see possible locations. I then went on to the prefectural office, where I found myself surrounded by a number of helpful and excited people. They produced maps, made calls, and generally came up with ideas and possible locations for my work. I was to appear again the next day, and they would tell me exactly where to go.

True to their word, they sent me off to visit two possible fieldwork sites. The first was in the district of Hiwasa, a charming bay surrounded by mountains, where turtles clamber annually out of the sea to lay their eggs on the beach. Here, I was greeted by the entire education office staff of five individuals, who seemed delighted to put all other work on hold to attend to my needs in the interests of "international goodwill." After some considerable discussion and a very reasonable lunch, the office was abandoned and we were taken up into the mountains to see some possible houses. The location was charm itself: quiet, peaceful, and incredibly beautiful, with an appealing smell of wood smoke hanging in the fresh mountain air.

The houses were various. One was clearly too low ceilinged, as I walked in and immediately bumped my head. Another was a little isolated but in such a perfect spot that I felt inclined to move there for the rest of my life. A third was more convenient, though with a less spectacular view. When we returned to the office, there was much further discussion, and a local newspaper reporter came to take my photograph. Nothing could be decided immediately, and although the place was magnificent, I had to admit that I was forcing myself to ignore information I had gleaned about the relative lack of young people and the high rate of migration to the cities. I might be lucky even to find a wedding to attend in this area, one of the party sighed sadly.

After another couple of Shikoku visits, I sailed from Yawatahama to Beppu, where I boarded a train for Hakata. Here I was met by the family of my closest friend from English House, a young man by the name of Yasuro, whose brother had also (by chance) spent some time in Oxford, where he had received a small amount of help from me. This was quite enough for royal treatment from his mother in return, however, and nothing was too much trouble. I stayed with the family for some ten days, taking time twice to visit the professor in Fukuoka to whom I had been introduced by Professor Yoshida. I also went sight-seeing with Yasuro, visiting possible locations and generally becoming confused and frustrated that nothing quite right seemed to be turning up.

Professor Matsunaga, my newfound local advisor, was kind and serious, but he seemed unwilling to understand how keen I was to settle down and get started. He kept telling me about things that might come up the following month, while my husband's date of arrival was now only a few days away. Yasuro and I visited a couple of the possible places he mentioned on our own, and we did all eventually visit the district of Yame in the south of Fukuoka Prefecture, where the professor had himself done fieldwork. We met a local member of parliament named Nishie, who had been the prime mover behind a big, collective tea-growing enterprise, a thriving concern that ensured work for young people in the area and increased the likelihood of finding new marriages to observe. Some efforts were made to find suitable housing for a strange foreign couple, but nothing was definitely forthcoming before I had to leave for Tokyo to meet the flight from London.

I seemed to have been traveling for weeks, explaining my project for months, and visiting houses for even longer, but still I had settled on nothing. I didn't really have any definite offers, though I rang the offices in Awaji Island and Hiwasa regularly for news. Professor Matsunaga was confident I would find something eventually, and he encouraged me to return to Kyushu. On the way back, I called in again to Hiwasa and Awaji to impress on everyone the seriousness of my purpose and to see if I could secure some real possibilities for settling down for a year. It continued to be frustrating, however, as people would show me places that looked fine, and then check with the higher education office to find these apparently empty houses weren't available after all. I don't think it occurred to me at the time, but knowing Japan better now, I suspect that people were nervous about having a couple of foreigners living in their midst. They probably weren't sure they would have all we needed in the area, and they may have worried that we would not know how to treat a Japanese house. My Japanese probably wasn't good enough to pick up nonverbal indications of concern, so I wasn't ready enough with reassurance, and I was probably given the negative answers to some of my requests long before I realized their significance.

In the end I faced up to the unlikelihood of Hiwasa as a good location for a study of contemporary marriage. It was just too isolated, though heartachingly beautiful. Awaji seemed to be more appropriate, with plenty of young people who returned after a few years even if they left for a while to sample the city. There was also clear evidence of the practice of *miai*. However, the only possible accommodation I had seen was cramped and very damp. Kyushu had a professor willing if not yet clearly able to help, a family of very pleasant friends, and some support from a dynamic local politician. Altogether the last seemed the best option, though I had as yet nowhere specific to go.

Back in Tokyo, there was something of a break in the proceedings as I met Dennis off the plane from England and took him around to meet my friends. This, in the long run, was probably another piece of serendipity, for Professor Yoshida returned from a field trip so I could consult him about my various experiences, and he agreed with the tentative decision I had made. He felt sure that Matsunaga would be able to help me, given time, and this is what I was now able to do. By the time we were ready to leave for Kyushu again, news had come through of a house he had found in Yame, right on the periphery of the tea-growing area. An English couple leaving for Britain offered us their futons for our new Japanese home, and we gave them their first airing on the ferry bound for Kokura. Our sojourn in Kyushu was about to begin.

Our Japanese Home

I suppose I should have been prepared for further delays, but I couldn't help being a little disappointed when we arrived in Kyushu two days later to find that we still had to wait another day before we could even visit our new home. Matsunaga did turn out to help us with our luggage, and we deposited it at Kurume Station, where we could also change to the line heading back to Yasuro's family in Saga. They didn't seem too surprised to see us again, and Yasuro's mother had even prepared various household utensils for us to use in our new kitchen. It would have been expensive and time-consuming to go out and find these items for ourselves, so her generosity was another great boon. We also later bought a full set of bowls and dishes at the annual sale of seconds in Arita.

The next day, we duly took the train back up the line to Yame, meeting Professor Matsunaga on the way in Kurume and going on to the house of the politician we had met the first time, who had clearly taken up our cause with a vengeance. He bustled us all into his car and drove ceremoniously a short distance down the road to one of the most opulent houses I had ever seen in Japan. We were ushered in, and the four of us sat in a row along one side of a long, low table in a room furnished in an expensive Western decor. The owner, whom Dennis immediately nicknamed "The Mogul," appeared through a sliding door and sat, alone, at the other side.

This was the owner of a local paper mill who had bought a piece of land for a warehouse that also just happened to have on it a large, empty house, apparently abandoned by a bankrupt who had done a "midnight flit." The Mogul was clearly well off, portly, and prosperous, and he greeted Nishie warmly, exchanged name cards with Professor Matsunaga, and largely ignored the pair of us. He did, however, soon lead us all out to his sumptuous black Mercedes car and personally drove us back an equally short distance to the plot of land in question. The house had two stories, several large rooms with tatami mats and beautiful wooden carvings *(ranma)* above the sliding doors *(fusuma)* that ran between the rooms, and a large kitchen and bathroom. It was, however, pretty dirty.

We could borrow it for nothing, he declared magnanimously, as long as we would pay for a pump to bring water from the well, the connection of electricity, and gas facilities to replace the old wood stove in the kitchen. A man was summoned immediately to give us an estimate of the total cost of all this, and the figure sounded most alarming, although it was explained that we could pay it in two installments, the second one after I had received my next check from England. As I set about calculating how all this would work out over the period we were planning to stay, Matsunaga and Nishie began to tell me about the community only a few minutes' walk away where they envisaged I might focus my work. It had about sixty houses, mostly farmers growing the new and successful crops of flowers and tea, and it was bristling with young people on the verge of marriage.

It was disappointing to me at first that the house was not in this perfect-sounding village; on the other hand, it was only a few steps from a small branch line of the local railway system (as the level-crossing bells reminded us six times a day for the whole of our stay), it was rather pleasantly isolated from main roads and industrial clutter (except for the warehouse), and my immediate neighbors were very friendly. In fact, these neighbors turned out to be another example of a most serendipitous encounter. They started by offering the use of their telephone until I could arrange to be connected up, explaining how to dispose of waste, and instructing me on the best way to get to know the wider neighborhood. By the time I left, they had also become excellent friends and good informants to boot. The husband had many old classmates in the village where I did indeed choose to work, but as an outsider he was better able than they were to help me disentangle valuable information from excessive politeness and derogatory gossip. The wife, who was from Yokohama, revealed much about local society by confiding many of her difficulties with adjusting to this distant part of Japan. And as the two older daughters came to Dennis for English conversation, we could offer some reciprocity.

We did, of course, decide to move in, and when we returned with our luggage, we were pleasantly surprised. There were two desks and a veritable stack of chairs awaiting us, as well as enough toilet paper for our whole stay, a crate of beer, and, for some curious reason, a supply of butter. The Mogul clearly intended to make us welcome, and he also sent round a gardener to tidy up the once quite pleasant surrounds to the house and a carpenter to make sure that our sliding *fusuma* and paper screens (shōji) ran smoothly. We had barely deposited our luggage inside, deciding to buy some cleaning materials before unpacking properly, when Matsunaga (or as my witty husband now renamed him, "Ace") arrived on the doorstep to take us on a round of introductions.

Meeting the People

We met, first, the head of the community where I had been assured it would be acceptable for me to make a case study, and he was a wonderful man. He made some statements about love matches and arranged marriages that, together with truths I later learned about him and his views, still provide good fodder for lectures touching on Japanese arts of diplomacy (see Hendry 1999b, 5–6, for further details). He revealed that his son, who lives in Kyoto, was due to return the following week to get married, and I resolved to ask him later if I might attend the wedding. We then went on to meet, in turn, the head of the community in which our house was located, the local policemen, and the mayor of the administrative district of Yame, which incorporated both communities.

All these formalities seemed somewhat tedious at the time, especially as much of the conversation tended apparently to exclude us, but I think, with hindsight, that Matsunaga was truly an Ace to arrange it all. Due to his efforts, we ended up having completed all the vital procedures for foreign residence in Japan, knowing where to go for maps and statistics, and having all the appropriate local people aware of who these two strange (and at that pre-JET time), unique aliens were. We didn't need to see many of these people again, but they were the ones through whom word filtered out, and it only remained for me to try endlessly to explain exactly what it was that I, and not my husband, was doing there.

An introduction that was particularly useful almost immediately was the one to the local policeman in the area of my chosen village. He and his wife were extremely friendly, explaining that he kept a house map for the communities within his district, and he knew the names of the people in each of the houses, as well as any significant property, vehicles, and other valuables they owned. I spent several days sitting in his house copying down information about the occupants of all the houses in the village, and his wife, who did piecework at home, would help me to read the characters *(kanji)* I could not manage. She also explained much about the usual arrangements with regard to the occupation of houses, inheritance, and other details required in order to fill in the policeman's registration form.

This information was brilliant for getting to know people, for once I had the complete list from the police box, as well as a detailed map, I could go round house to house introducing myself. I felt a little uncomfortable at first already having acquired the names of the occupants of the houses, but I introduced myself as interested to learn as much as I could about the community and keen to check the policeman's rather sketchy record. At only one household did the people seem a bit disconcerted that I had transcribed the policeman's list, but even this was a transitory concern, and they eventually became as friendly as anyone else. One of their teenage sons was in some kind of trouble at the time, a fact they may have wanted to hide. In any case, most people had already heard about the strange visitors, and they were only too pleased to invite me into their homes, where they could question me directly.

In fact, for many, these visits were not the first opportunity we had had to meet face-to-face, for when I returned to the community head's house to ask if I might attend his son's wedding, I was made most welcome. There were several parts to the celebrations, but most interesting for me in my efforts to meet the local people were the celebrations that took place for the neighbors and, later, the friends of the bride and groom. By the time these took place, many of the participants had been drinking for several hours, and certainly the conversations were becoming most informal. Indeed, I was shocked by the degree of intimacy that seemed to be the order of the day. I was ready to explain much of my personal background, but I had not thought to be required, in exchange for local cooperation, to give quite such a full account of the details of my sex life. It was only later that I realized that the custom of talking so freely about this subject was particularly characteristic of wedding celebrations preceding the first night of marital union.

But then, my own behavior could also have been influenced by the alcohol, as I lost my footing and slipped into a fast-flowing stream on my way home and almost ended my fieldwork before it began. This impromptu dip, fortunately rapidly curtailed by Dennis, who unusually was with me on this occasion, taught me to pace my consumption at future weddings. However, the whole event was again most serendipitous, because I was never again so simultaneously relaxed and nervous that I answered innocently almost all the questions I was asked, thus apparently assuring the villagers that I was something of a good sort to whom cooperation should be given in abundance—as indeed it was for the whole of the year to come.

Lessons for the Neophyte

How, then, can this very personal, possibly quite British, and certainly well out-of-date experience help a graduate student setting out to Japan in the early years of the twenty-first century? Well, I think it can help in several ways and on several levels, and in this last section of the chapter I would like to tease some of them out.

First, in the choice of subject matter for research, I have said little more here than what the subject was, but I did mention how I came to choose it. This, I think, is a very important part of the procedure, for though village studies went out of fashion fairly soon after my work was complete, the study of marriage in Japan has been of continuing interest. Many students of Japanese today decide to take up a subject after living informally in Japan, or at least after having good Japanese friends, and I would like to encourage them to draw on this experience in the decision-making process. The views of young people in Japan change almost as often as the Scottish weather, and even a few months in friendly local circumstances can make a student aware of a new project that a staid old professor might never dream up.

Professors are also useful, however, and the second lesson I think can be learned from my somewhat haphazard discoveries is that the introduction of a Japanese scholar can be more valuable than I ever realized at the time. When looking for a quick decision on some suitable accommodation, it was frustrating to find myself continually waiting. In the end, however, I suspect that the chain of presentation from scholar to politician to local business tycoon was much more useful than a local teacher's house would have been, however cheap. My subsequent informants knew all the people who had helped me, and they were respected for their success in various fields. As I was later to learn in connection with weddings, association with success is thought to bode well for further success, and the unstinting cooperation of the villagers of Kurotsuchi may well have been related to this.

There were also several practical advantages to the way I ended up finding myself accommodated. First, the introduction of the business tycoon put me immediately in touch with all the necessary services for maintaining my house, not an insignificant benefit in a strange country with no compatriots to pass on advice about local circumstances. Second, as I mentioned, introductions through Nishie to members of the local bureaucracy not only ensured a smooth response to requests for information such as statistics and maps, but also enabled me to gain permission to read the *koseki* (family registers), which by law were confidential. It involved asking each of the families in the village if they would agree, but this in itself gave me a good excuse to see what people were doing during the summer *Obon* festival.

The value of my introduction to the local policeman became particularly clear many years later when I tried in another part of Japan to obtain the same kind of cooperation. On this occasion, my status as a university teacher with a visiting position at a prestigious private university in Tokyo was less impressive to the police than my previous experience in Kyushu, and a reference from their colleagues there was all they required. Staff in the education offices in the various other places I visited were friendly enough, but in the end they didn't actually find me a suitable house, and even if they had, I would probably have had to spend a lot more time and effort to gain the same degree of trust and cooperation from the people living and working around me.

Foreigners are much more prevalent in all parts of Japan now, and I suppose that the importance of a chain of connection will depend to some extent on prior experience. In another place where I later did fieldwork, the local bureaucracy was deeply suspicious of all foreigners after particularly bad encounters with two successive JET teachers, and people were relieved to find that I could speak Japanese and had some idea about how things worked. My first situation may (inadvertently) have benefited from the relative lack of previous contact, and also perhaps from Japanese folk ideas about foreigners, later so ably analyzed by Professor Yoshida (Yoshida 1981). I am convinced, however, that the formal introductions were also extremely important.

On the subject of language, I was clearly less than perfectly prepared for this visit, as my inability to pick up negative answers from people probably makes clear. There is also a fairly strong dialect in Yame, and this would certainly have required some further study even if I had spent years living in another part of Japan. The shortcomings of my language ability I actually feel worked to my advantage, however, since I was forced to clarify new words and usage that I continued (as in English House) to pick up in their social and cultural context. This mechanism is, I feel, vital for a deep understanding of the local system of classification, which I worried for a few years after my first fieldwork could have been quite particular to rural Kyushu.

With twenty-five years of hindsight, however, and further fieldwork experience in other parts of Japan, I feel confident that the only problem with learning so much of my Japanese language in an area with a strong dialect is that the shortened vowels used there may have interfered with my pronunciation. This also makes it difficult for me always to identify where macrons should be placed. As for the system of classification, I think that this village view of the world actually laid a strong foundation for understanding other aspects of urban Japan and Japanese that may otherwise have been more difficult to interpret. I think, therefore, that "total immersion" in a village was a very appropriate first fieldwork experience, *rite de passage* or not, and though the village is not a vital part of the package, I still strongly encourage students to immerse themselves as far as possible in a Japanese situation.

Maurice Bloch has analyzed the cognitive development of an anthropologist working in the field, and he describes the knowledge acquired, often intuitively, as "chunked mental models" that allow for post hoc interpretation. This "nonlinguistic" learning he compares to the acquisition of the skills to drive a car. Once absorbed, one no longer needs to think about every stage of the procedure. An anthropologist picks up a huge amount of knowledge and information simply to cope with daily life, and this is subsequently available not only for social interaction in the field, but also for analysis and writing up. On these grounds Bloch also encourages anthropologists to have confidence in their new cognitive constructs (Bloch 1991).

I have said very little here about the specifics of my investigation into the marriage practices of people living in Japan in 1975, although this was the subject matter of my thesis and the monograph I published (Hendry 1981). Both did also detail much about village life, but that part of the work is rarely referred to. This essay goes a little way toward redressing that balance, then, in the hope that students will be more patient than I was in making sure that their initial arrangements are carefully made. It may seem frustrating at the time, but people helping out have their own lives to lead, and I think it is worth holding out for the best introductions you can manage in order to establish total acceptability within the field community, where the important detailed work will take place. In the end, the frustrations will undoubtedly contribute to a long-term understanding of the people with whom you are planning to work.

As for serendipity, the strange chain of connection that brought me to the village in which I worked proved to introduce an essential part of my long-term understanding of marriage in Japan, as well as another reason for good relations in the village. The reaction my story of a scrambled message provoked in informants to whom I recounted it was usually to describe it as *en,* a kind of karmic destiny also thought to underpin a good marriage. As well as learning this, then, I found that people in the village felt positive about the way we had been brought together, as if we, too, had made a good marriage in my choosing them for my research. Thus whether your subject matter is marriage or not, I hope that your own serendipity may have a similar effect.

To return to the put-down I recounted in my opening paragraph, I have to say that the most interesting aspect of the exchange for me—then and with hindsight even more so—was that it took place during a lunch with several Japanese scholars who remained blissfully unaware that any kind of disagreement had taken place. It was a good early lesson in a communication style I would later come to absorb so well that I found I had temporarily lost my nonverbal skills when I returned to live in a village in England. I may still not be a very good American "scientist," but I do hope that this essentially egotistical analysis may be helpful to my successors in a broader Japanese field.

Note

Fieldwork supported by the Social Science Research Council (UK) and the writing up by the Japan Foundation Endowment Committee (UK) and the Henrietta Jex-Blake Research Scholarship, Lady Margaret Hall, Oxford.

Related Readings

Hendry, Joy. 1979–1980. "Is Science Maintaining Tradition in Japan?" *Bulletin of the British Association of Orientalists* NS11:24–34.

———. 1981a. *Marriage in Changing Japan: Community and Society.* London and New York: Croom-Helm and St. Martins Press. (Republished version: Tokyo and Rutland, Vt.: Charles Tuttle, 1986.)

———. 1981b. "*Tomodachi ko:* Age-Mate Groups in Northern Kyushu." *Proceedings of the British Association for Japanese Studies* 6(2):43–56.

———. 1981c. "The Modification of Tradition in Modern Japanese Weddings and Some Implications for the Social Structure." In P. G. O'Neill, ed., *Tradition in Modern Japan.* Tenterden, Kent: Paul Norbury Publications.

———. 1987. *Understanding Japanese Society.* London and New York: Routledge.

———. 1999a. *An Anthropologist in Japan: Glimpses of Life in the Field.* London and New York: Routledge.

Helen Hardacre as unobtrusive observer (back of head in foreground) during the Kurayami Matsuri of the Ōkunitama Shrine, 2001.

HELEN HARDACRE

Fieldwork with Japanese Religious Groups

The opportunity of doing fieldwork with Japanese religious groups has provided, without a doubt, the most important experiences of my professional life. Fieldwork is essential to reaching an understanding of religion as a lived and living tradition, as opposed to a body of doctrine or an abstract statement of creed. No competent study of modern religious life can emerge without it, and each such study is richer in proportion to the depth of field experience. Undertaking fieldwork among religious people in Japan requires an understanding of the relation between observable realities and historical religious tradition, as well as a commitment to a lifetime of learning from people. Fieldwork on religion inevitably requires close and sustained contact with people in a variety of settings, calling on the researcher for endurance and perseverance, as well as for such skills as the use of honorific language and the formal seated posture, *seiza*. The researcher will generally be viewed by the hosting religious association as a learner, someone who has come to learn what the group believes and how it seeks to implement or actualize its beliefs. This means that the researcher's role is often seen by the host as child-like, uninformed, and in need of instruction. It is vital to accept this role sincerely; if one does, all doors can open. Refuse it or dispute it, and all doors close.

Nothing is more characteristic of fieldwork with religious people in Japan than to receive repeated sermons and exhortations, a barrage of concepts, deities, and ritual practices that are entirely alien and frequently uncongenial to one's own religious or philosophical orientation. The academic challenge is to understand how these form a coherent system of meaning for one's hosts and teachers in the field and how they fit within the longer flow of Japanese religious history. The personal challenge is to respect one's hosts for the sincerity of their beliefs, no matter what your assessment of them on philosophical or theological grounds, and to sustain a relationship through the sincerity of your own desire to learn from them, without holding out the false hope that you will convert and become a proselytizer for the religion. Successful fieldwork with religious people can establish friendships that last a lifetime, enriching each subsequent fieldwork project and one's understanding of Japanese religions and shaping one's own character. In this chapter I will illustrate these points by drawing on experiences gained from 1976 to the present, among a variety of new religious movements and in the religious practices of Japan's Korean minority.

The Experience of Fieldwork with Religious Groups

Explaining One's Purpose

A researcher on religion faces a dilemma in explaining one's aims and intentions to the host religion and its members. Ethically it is completely unacceptable to withhold this information from one's hosts, and it is vital to explain as fully as possible what one wants to know and how the information will be disseminated. My experience has always been that religions understand what academic research is and are generally accepting of it. At the same time, however, it is characteristic for religious people to say that academic study is inevitably thin, partial, and incomplete by comparison with religious practice, urging the researcher to gain a fuller understanding by study and ritual participation. Religions may express a general acceptance of academic research yet be reluctant to discuss such touchy subjects as political activity, political campaign contributions, and finances generally. Nevertheless, if there is a prospect that a book (or a dissertation) about the religion will be written in English, that is taken as a possibility for good publicity, which the religion does not need to fear and which it will generally support. It is useful to prepare an explanation of each stage and aspect of one's research, so that it can be repeated to new contacts in possession of needed information. In twenty years of field research on a variety of religious associations in Japan, I have never been refused permission to conduct research by a religious organization, and while individual adherents may show greater or less willingness to talk about their religious lives, nearly everyone one encounters has a story to tell and rather eagerly anticipates the opportunity to tell it to a foreign researcher. The challenge for the researcher is to communicate empathy, to come across as someone the believer trusts who will receive their experiences with respect and a sincere desire to understand.

At the same time, however, it is nearly always the case that religious groups understand the practice of religion better than the academic study of it and that key hosts will fervently hope that the researcher will "see the light" and convert to become a believer, leaving research behind. To religious people this possibility seems more realistic the younger the researcher, and the researcher can become the object of sustained campaigns of proselytization. The resulting position is a difficult one, because it is unethical to falsify one's real intentions and simply let the hosts think they have made a convert, though this might seem the easiest way out. And yet if one prefaces each encounter by saying, in effect, "You know, of course, that I am here purely for academic research," then the hosts quite understandably become discouraged, less interested in explaining their beliefs and practices. The challenge for the researcher is to convey the desire to write the most accurate and sensitive portrait possible, to show by one's actions and demeanor as well as in verbal protestations that one is uninterested in making value judgments about the religion or in conveying any sort of exposé. In the end this comes down to convincing the hosts that one is in sympathy with them even if not a convert and that the commitment to academic research requires one to portray the organization fairly and with respect.

Means of Access

The best way to grasp the religious life of a group of people is to live with its members, but the choices one makes about how to contact the group initially shape the resulting association in ways that both create important research options and exclude other possibilities. The academic researcher will generally form an affiliation at a university in Japan where the faculty can give advice and provide crucial introductions. While academic introductions can be very useful in some aspects of field research, it can be helpful to supplement these with personal contacts. Especially if the researcher is still a student, and hence under the age of thirty or so, the broadest access can be secured not by trading on one's academic credentials but by meeting members of the religion and telling them directly of one's desire to study the group and learn more about it. The people met in this way may not be well positioned to give official approval for fieldwork or assistance in setting up such an arrangement in its details, but they can quickly help the researcher meet other members of the same age group and establish informal, "uncensored" associations, and they can eventually produce necessary connections to the organization's headquarters and leadership.

In researching the new religion Reiyūkai as a student of twenty-six in 1976, I knew both that I wanted a period of fieldwork with the group and that it would eventually be necessary to adopt a more formal approach, relying on professorial introductions. I knew that the largest branch of the organization was located in Osaka, while the headquarters was in Tokyo, and I was also aware of a certain division between the Eighth Branch in Osaka, led by older, direct disciples of Kotani Kimi, and the younger leadership represented in Tokyo by the new president, Kubo Tsugunari, who was educated in Buddhology at the University of Tokyo. Proselytization and devoted practice under a leader's supervision were characteristic of the Eighth Branch, whereas the Tokyo headquarters was establishing a practice emphasizing more study, discussion, and consideration of Buddhism's social contributions. I wanted to collect data on Reiyūkai organization, daily activities, and religious framework through the Eighth Branch, but I also wanted to carry out a large-scale survey of the membership and collect nationwide statistical data, which only the headquarters would have. My solution was to establish myself first through the Eighth Branch and later move to Tokyo to design and administer the survey through the headquarters.

I had begun my first contacts with Reiyūkai by visiting the Los Angeles branch, which was headed by the son-in-law of the Eighth Branch leaders. I found him very open to my desire to research the religion, and he arranged for me to live with office employees of the Eighth Branch in the house he had vacated when he moved to the United States. I was met at Osaka Airport by his relatives and taken to live with three Eighth Branch office employees and a housekeeper. Life at the Eighth Branch was very rich in personal contacts and varied experiences. Date Katsuko, a young woman employee of the

Eighth Branch also living in my residence, was put "in charge" of me, and it was her job to help me get acquainted with the office routine and others working there. She and the other young woman living at the Eighth Branch became good friends and invaluable to my efforts to learn about Reiyūkai. We were together nearly continuously, sharing a bedroom, rising at the same time, reciting the sutra as the first act of the day, traveling to the office together, and attending after-work meetings in the city as a group. It was these two who fielded the initial, inevitably "dumb" questions a fieldworker must ask: Why do you recite the sutra? How do you feel when you are reciting it? Wouldn't it be just as good to record a recitation and play that before the altar instead of getting up so early? And so on.

From the point of view of Reiyūkai as a religious organization, an unmarried female of twenty-six who does not know the answers to such questions is someone deeply in need of religious instruction. Older leaders asked incredulously whether I had no previous instruction in the nature and existence of the ancestors, how so fine a religion as Christianity (they presumed that I must be a Christian) could have failed to teach me such fundamental religious truths, and they were horrified to learn that in my family it was traditional not to build gravesites. My first months living at the Eighth Branch were largely made up of instructional sessions on basic points of the religion's beliefs and participation in ritual based on these beliefs. In the process, I also learned a great deal about the etiquette expected of unmarried women: how to bow deeply and correctly; how to greet branch leaders politely; how to sit properly (not with one's arms folded, but with hands together on the lap); how one should not walk and eat or drink at the same time; and myriad other niceties expressing the humility and subordination appropriate to the group into which I had been slotted.

It goes without saying that this regimen was both extremely informative and highly taxing. Information seemed to pour in like a waterfall, and I was hard-pressed to keep my resolution to write up my fieldnotes by the end of each day, no matter what. Everyone had a story about how their lives had been improved by Reiyūkai, about the blessings of the sutra, and about the virtues of the Eighth Branch leaders. My modest ability in spoken Japanese improved rapidly as I struggled to keep up with people's stories and questions. For several months I met no one who spoke English. For virtually the first time, I experienced language learning as a real joy and could acquire new vocabulary and grammatical patterns easily. This was a period of tremendous excitement for me, in which I was living in a state of high stimulation nearly every waking moment. Ostensibly my job at the Eighth Branch was to assist Reiyūkai in translating some of its literature into English, and this activity offered innumerable opportunities to discuss fine points of belief and practice with a variety of people. I was also reading the autobiographical writings of the founder Kotani Kimi (1901–1971), and since these were not well known to the other young women, I could occasionally come up with an incident unknown to them and ask for their interpretations. These sessions were tremendously helpful to me in learning how members' thinking was channeled into the patterns approved by the organization. At the same time, however, the regimen was physically demanding in its requirements of group living, which meant early rising, intensive interaction for many hours each day, and little time in privacy even to record one's experiences. Reiyūkai did not observe weekends as holidays, and office workers had only a couple of days' leisure per month.

The lack of privacy and time away from the fieldwork produced a problem for me in sorting out distinctions between patterns I observed in Reiyūkai and similar phenomena that I took to be characteristic of Japanese society generally. I was not yet sufficiently experienced at life in Japan to draw clear lines between what I observed about Reiyūkai members and general, Japanese cultural patterns. I knew, for example, that both the religion and the society I was studying assumed that women would be subordinate to men and that youth would be subordinate to their elders. I observed behavior of Reiyūkai women that seemed all out of proportion to what I had learned about Japan in general—bows repeated more times and at greater angles than anything I saw elsewhere, kneeling to approach a seated leader, and convoluted patterns of speech indicating humility and self-effacement that proved to be greatly exaggerated versions of patterns common in much of Japan as a whole. It took time to understand that what I saw in Reiyūkai was mostly a heightened expression of more general phenomena, not a radical departure from general cultural patterns.

Fieldwork is well understood by students to have an initiatory character, indicating, the student hopes, a death of student status followed by the acquisition of some modicum of authority based on knowledge uniquely acquired in a liminal period, involving a quest, ordeals, and difficulty. My fieldwork experience in Reiyūkai was overwhelmingly positive and stimulating, but because its overall meaning for me was structured as a path toward more confidence and self-assertion, I initially felt great resistance to using honorific language, or *keigo*. As a feminist, the self-effacement and subordination expressed through honorific language's many passive and causative expressions expected in female speech grated on me for a long time. I hated even to pronounce the answers expected of me as a young woman in Reiyūkai to such simple questions as "Will you go?" *Hai, mairasete itadakimasu* (Yes, I will be caused-to-be-allowed-to go [humble]). The pronounced emphasis on young women's use of honorific language was both characteristic of Reiyūkai at that branch at that time and representative of members' sincere efforts to instruct me fully in the attitudes expected of me as someone learning about their religion. Compared with the simple forms in use in nonreligious contexts, the group's expectations about women's use of honorific language were distinctive—even extreme sometimes—but language use was also an important aid to me in sorting out the various roles of men and women, young and old, in Reiyūkai and in understanding the full spectrum of relationships among them.

Eventually I came to a much more pragmatic, utilitarian approach to language. It was made clear to me that young women were expected to use honorific language correctly and with alacrity. I observed that once I got those "suffering passives" to roll smoothly off the tongue, people would open up to me much more, would regard me as teachable and worth spending time with. In other words, honorific language began to enrich the data I could collect and to expose me to people I could not be introduced to without it. I began to see language not as key to my personal identity, but as a tool that I must use according to the expectations of the people around me. At the same time, I began to see the postures and gestures that young Reiyūkai women encouraged me to adopt (*seiza* when seated on straw mats at home; head down while walking, arms pressed to the sides; hands clasped and ankles together when standing; not looking people in the eye; etc.) as similar to language in constituting crucial props that could assist me in learning about this religion and the behavioral and intellectual patterns it sought to instill in its members. Language, posture, gesture, and demeanor were taken as the outward indicators of a person's sincerity; with the right ones nearly anything was possible, but without them, the researcher has little chance of being let into people's confidence. These are some of the performative aspects of fieldwork on religions in Japan, and while they occasionally produce a schizophrenic feeling, they are very valuable in acquiring necessary information.

I have frequently been asked whether it is a disadvantage in fieldwork on Japanese religions to be a woman. I have always found quite the opposite: that as long as one can exhibit the culturally accepted patterns of speech, an attitude of respect for the religion, and a sincere desire to learn about it, being a woman is a significant advantage. This may be because I have concentrated on new religious movements, in which women predominate as grass-roots leaders and activists and which have a special focus on problems rooted in the family, a subject about which, in Japan, women are presumed to know more than men. It is a simple matter for a female researcher to visit female members of such a religion in their homes, to interact with their children and relatives, and to ask relatively personal questions without discomfort. By contrast, interaction with senior men can easily become stiff and formal, though the adept researcher also learns techniques for dealing with this, humor and persistence being the most effective in my experience. A potentially more difficult issue in researching religious groups is the understandable reluctance to admit a novice to higher levels of teaching than that for which one has qualified by demonstrations of religious practice. For example, I was eager to attend monthly meetings for Reiyūkai women leaders from surrounding prefectures, as I wanted to meet these women and get a sense of the range of their activities. But my hosts found it inappropriate that I attend such meetings, as I was not qualified for the requisite leadership rank. I could compensate for this denial of access to a certain degree by meeting these women during their lunch and tea breaks throughout the day. Because the sermons and lectures were actually broadcast in the office where I was working, I could record these. Whenever my sex or status denied me access to some occasion I wanted to document, I tried to find some compensating measure. While I did not always succeed, I usually did.

I assume that male researchers would find it correspondingly difficult to gain access to female members, but also that techniques for coping with the problem would be found. It seems to me that if I were studying instead a male priestly order, one of the Buddhist sects, for example, being female might present more challenges in getting information or in being taken with any seriousness. Against that, however, stands my experience since beginning a teaching career, in which one's institution and academic rank are taken as defining how a person should be treated, and sex then becomes a secondary consideration that only rarely makes a significant difference. For the researcher contemplating fieldwork, it is desirable to have a realistic idea of how one's sex is likely to make it seem natural to the organization to put one together with others of the same sex and roughly the same age and to develop strategies for gaining access to others beyond that group.

Shifting Gears

At a certain point in my fieldwork on Reiyūkai I had collected as much data as I could on the Eighth Branch and the beliefs and attitudes of its membership, and I decided to move to Tokyo and do survey and statistical work at the organization's headquarters. I established an affiliation as a visiting student at the Religious Studies Department of the University of Tokyo, and a senior faculty member introduced me to the president of Reiyūkai, who gave me permission and assistance in this second phase of my research. Inevitably, however, my hosts at the Eighth Branch saw this move as a defection on my part, and their unexpressed hopes about my becoming a convert left them disappointed with me. They saw themselves as rivals of the Tokyo headquarters, and they could not but regret my decision to move. They did not regard my plans about undertaking a survey as very important, not putting much faith in such measures. I was not able to secure their consent to this move, and my relationships with them were unfortunately damaged by the evolving needs of my research. While I have tried in the ensuing years to seek a reconciliation, it is probably unrealistic to imagine that host and researcher will always be able to part harmoniously. As one grows older, however, it becomes easier to assert oneself.

When I moved to Tokyo in 1978, I began a new phase of fieldwork with Reiyūkai. I was no longer living with group members, and because I had come with professorial mediation, I was on rather more formal terms with my hosts. I was allowed to attend virtually all public worship ceremonies at the headquarters, and this gave me the opportunity to meet members from all over the country, a broader section of the membership than I had been able to contact through living at the Eighth Branch. I soon grew to miss the opportunities for sustained contact with individual members that I had enjoyed in Osaka, but I was very glad to have more time to think, absorb what I saw, and record and analyze things with more leisure. I was able to design my survey, have access to historical records, and to talk with the people administering various aspects of the religion's management. These activities were essential to my overall understanding of the religion, and I believe that the earlier period of living with members in Osaka greatly enriched my understanding of what I learned in Tokyo.

In designing my survey of the membership, I was guided by various handbooks for sociological research in Japan, and wherever possible I phrased my questions exactly as previous surveys had so that I could be confident in comparing results from the past or from the general population. In order to secure Reiyūkai's assistance in distributing the survey, I had to have my schedule of questions approved by the leadership. I had been put in the charge of a young section head of the Overseas Proselytization Bureau, a rather officious young man, and he eventually required that I delete one or two questions having to do with the emperor and his religious status. In truth, I had guessed that a couple of changes would be requested, whatever I submitted, so I had included a couple of "red flags" not really essential to my research design specifically to be deleted. This strategy seems to have worked.

I would have preferred to have administered my survey personally, traveling to various branches for the purpose, but I lacked the funds to support this method. In the end, I decided upon a mail survey, even knowing that the return rate on such instruments is generally low. This is an example of the kind of compromise one must sometimes make because of funding limitations. Having made this decision, however, I could only assume that the branch leaders who received the questionnaire packets would distribute them to the members they believed best represented Reiyūkai's ideals and that a secondary selection of respondents would take place that I could neither control nor observe. This meant that I had to shape my understanding of the results accordingly, believing that what I received back from the mail represented in large part "approved answers" and that there might be more variation in members' beliefs than I could access.

When You Don't Like What You Learn

While working with Reiyūkai, I occasionally met another American researcher working on another new religion nearby. He and I would exchange experiences and strategies, and this contact helped me put my own fieldwork in some perspective. One problem we shared was a conflict between our own, individual religious or (in my case) philosophical beliefs and those of our hosts. My friend and I both sometimes had to struggle with a feeling of resistance to the beliefs we were learning about. His reaction was particularly negative, and he eventually swore off fieldwork as a result of this problem. In my case the issue was feminism, though at the time I could probably not have articulated it in that way.

The dilemma I faced resulted from an encounter with the idea, current in Reiyūkai's Eighth Branch in the late 1970s, that women have a greater karmic burden than men and face greater obstacles to salvation than men do. Women were regarded in no uncertain terms as inferior beings, based in part on the supposed pollution of the female body deriving from menstruation, and the idea of the greater karmic burden was advanced as the explanation for every form of sex discrimination against women advocated by the religion: lower wages, the expectation of subordination, exclusion from the labor force after marriage, and the requirement of repenting to husbands and elders (to me) ad nauseum.

It troubled me greatly to learn that this was Reiyūkai's view of women, and I found it deeply disturbing that women were the loudest voices in favor of this ideology, calling on married women to quit their jobs, devote their lives to support of the husband, sequester themselves in the domestic sphere, and train their daughters in this same vein. One of the most difficult interviews I had during my fieldwork was with the woman in charge of day care at the Tokyo headquarters, who was particularly vociferous in taking this line and who was ideally placed to communicate it to young girls. I remember vividly writing an anguished letter to my mother after this interview, and her writing back that it must be truly "soul killing" to have to confront this repeatedly. That was precisely how I experienced it.

My dilemma arose because, at the same time that I truly hated what these women were saying, I could see clearly that they personally were some of the strongest and most independent women I had ever met. Many of them had created post-child care careers in the religion on the basis of this sexist ideology, traveling all over the country to instruct other people in it and the rest of Reiyūkai's ideas. They were entirely committed to the religion, unswerving in their loyalty, and they acted with complete emotional independence. I could see that their sexism also communicated a variety of strategies for managing men and for providing support to other women. It was clear to me that these women leaders were in fact able to marshal members of both sexes to assist women involved in some confrontation with an abusive husband, and I understood that this unspoken provision of support and strategy was one of the religion's strongest appeals to women members. How should I interpret what I saw?

The interpretative frameworks of gender studies were clearly what I needed in order to understand what I saw in Reiyūkai, but these were just coming into academic vernacular in English, and I had had no opportunity to acquire relevant training in my prior education. My teachers, both in Japan and in the United States, could not assist me. Friends and fellow students pointed me toward portrayals of women in popular media, especially television, or toward Japanese proverbs to the effect that "women are their own worst enemies," *(onna no teki wa onna),* but these forays yielded vague inklings at best. As a result, I groped for appropriate vocabulary and a way to relate what I saw in the religion to more general patterns in Japanese society. This process took several years, but the result for me was the discovery of a lifelong problem: religions' paradoxical and multivalent relations to gender, an intellectual focus that has continued to shape each new project.

In the course of my field research at the time, however, I realized that I would need a concentrated period of archival research on such topics as the "problem" of women's salvation in Japanese Buddhism; I needed to go back to the writings of medieval religious figures like Nichiren on this topic in order to understand basic concepts and terminology, and I needed to read commentarial literature on the Lotus Sutra's motif of females needing to be reborn as males in order to attain a final salvation. I spent weeks in the National Diet Library nonplussed by the "how-to" manuals penned by Buddhist savants instructing their female adherents on how to conduct themselves in order to be reborn as men. The common thread in their recommendations was that women should conceive a great hatred for the female body. I could see a direct relation between this doctrinal casuistry and the pained statements of living members of Reiyūkai, who frequently said to me that they wished they had been born as men or that they hoped they would be male in the next life.

This experience of confronting the limitations of my previous training has been repeated many times, and I think it must frequently be the case that the fieldworker cannot proceed further without interrupting participant observation for archival research or academic consultations. It is very helpful to establish academic affiliations in Japan for access to libraries and in order to consult colleagues about one's research. It is not usually realistic for students to expect that an advising professor in Japan can frequently spare the time to assist in the basic design and planning of field research, but they can be very helpful in suggesting relevant archival sources or in suggesting the meaning and historical derivation of practices observed in the field. If it is possible for students to attend seminars with graduate students of their own age, they will find that these contacts become some of their most valuable associations over a lifetime of teaching and research, for they, or their students, will probably later be the advisors to whom you eventually send your own students, and likewise, they will look to you for help in arranging affiliations for their students in your country.

It cannot be expected, however, that one's academic colleagues in Japan will always approve of your methods or conclusions, and it is important to maintain an independent perspective. The single experience that best illustrates this dilemma for me came during research on the religious practices of Japan's Korean minority, conducted in and around Osaka in the summer of 1982. During this time, I was affiliated with Osaka University and had secured housing there. I located and documented some fifty temples maintained by Koreans in the Ikoma Mountains east of the city. Over the course of the summer, I was able to discern patterns in ritual practice and general religious orientation that departed significantly from anything I had observed elsewhere in Japan. Becoming friends with Koreans in Japan completely changed the understanding I had had up to that time of such basic cultural values as the supposed homogeneity of the Japanese people, harmony, and consensus. Koreans spoke bitterly of living fifty years in Japan and never entering the house of ethnically Japanese families. They told stories of Japanese shrinking from them in distaste of the smell of garlic or from fear that because they were Korean they might be criminals. Koreans whom I met expressed considerable alienation from Japanese society, and they saw that the values I had been taught to believe were positive and constructive in character could, when exercised against a marginal group, become techniques of exclusion and discrimination. This is no longer a very contentious point in Japanese studies, but at the time it came to me like a thunderbolt, and I felt the scales fall away from my eyes. Suddenly I realized that a great variety of perspectives on Japanese cultural values are possible and that these values have no fixed meaning, but rather can be "deployed" differently in varying circumstances with consequences that vary by such qualities as sex, age, and ethnicity. I got the point through fieldwork, with an immediacy and unforgettable impact that could never be duplicated by theoretical study.

In return for the hospitality I received at Osaka University, I was expected to give a presentation on my research after the conclusion of my fieldwork. Faculty and students from the university attended, as did Koreans in the area not connected with the religious practices I had been documenting. While I had not intended to make a controversial presentation, the occasion came close to a brawl, with Japanese scholars offended by my portrayal of treasured values seen through the eyes of Koreans, and the Koreans offended that any non-Korean would have the audacity to speak about the life of the minority. It was difficult to know whether they were more angry at me or at each other. The confrontation itself was marvelous grist for my mill, though difficult to contend with at the time. It made me realize that it is vital to maintain independence in one's analysis and a great mistake to hope for approval from others.

Fieldwork with Japan's Korean minority convinced me of the importance of cultivating field experience outside the social mainstream. Stereotypes of Japan are deployed so continuously by Japanese themselves and they so pervade most of what has been written on the society that it is vital to understand how such stereotypes appear to those on the margins and outside cultural norms. This is the basic prerequisite for developing an independent perspective based on a full understanding of stereotypes about cultural homogeneity.

Long-Term, Cumulative Field Experience

Fieldwork is not necessarily a "one-off," never-to-be-repeated experience with a particular group of people. Instead, contacts and friendships formed in the field can and should be carefully preserved in order to maintain openness to future researchers, who may include one's own students or oneself in pursuit of a "restudy." If these pragmatic reasons were not sufficient, it has usually been my experience that genuine friendships arise spontaneously in the course of fieldwork, and that it is one of life's greatest satisfactions to go through life together with those who have provided one the opportunity to study living religions. In the course of fieldwork one enters a matrix of relations with people that carries a variety of privileges and obligations, and much of their continued receptivity to future researchers depends on how you carry through on these obligations once the period of initial fieldwork has ended.

So many aspects of Japanese society and culture remain virtual terra incognita that it is easy to imagine one's own study of a place, person, or organization as both the first and the last, but at least in the case of religion, that is not necessarily true. It is important to realize that after oneself will come not *le déluge,* but future researchers. And if you have not left the field in good condition, those future researchers may not find the welcome they need in order to continue further investigation of topics and questions you explored. In fact, there are cases in the history of the study of Japanese religious organizations in which the group had such a negative experience with foreign researchers that they effectively closed the door permanently for future researchers. Whether you contemplate a future restudy yourself or not, maintaining good relations in the long term is one of the obligations of fieldwork.

In the area of less formal expectations is the hope that when the fieldworker visits Japan, she will "come home." If you have received a fictive kinship designation, your hosts will not assume that the relationship has ended with the publication of your book based on the fieldwork they hosted, and neither should you. Part of your ongoing reception is based on your hosts' quite natural assumption that you will show respect to people important to them, that you will appear and perhaps speak formally on ceremonial occasions, and that if you are specially invited to an occasion of importance to them, that you will come, come hell or high water. If they have taught you how to offer incense or a *tamagushi* (sacred branch) formally, then it will reflect badly on them as well as you if you forget the proper etiquette. In part, you become part of your hosts' achievements, which they wish to show off to friends and followers. This means a reunion with many people who will be waiting with presents and who not unnaturally think that you may have something for them as well.

Gift giving can be a real financial burden, but it is important to follow through, if only with photos or a token piece of memorabilia from the university bookstore. Do not overlook financial accounting for these outlays, the costs of travel, film, photo processing, and any other research-related expenses, as they are tax deductible and should be claimed as legitimate expenses stemming from your research. Develop your own system of post-fieldwork bookkeeping so that no deductible stone is left unturned. Otherwise, you will quickly find that keeping up your field research on an annual basis becomes financially impossible, a problem that rapidly increases in magnitude if you acquire a mortgage, have children, or otherwise incur large, ongoing financial responsibilities.

Beware of Religions Bearing Gifts

Over the years, I have acquired a wide variety of obligations and debts to religious organizations that give me pleasure to acknowledge and attempt to repay. On the other hand, it is important to be very careful of the kind of debts one incurs to religious groups. There exist today any number of religions with "image problems" in Japan. They may seek to compensate for the poor impression believers inevitably get from, say, newspaper accounts of civil suits brought by disgruntled former followers with a bit of good news manufactured overseas. If you value your access to a variety of religious groups, and if the good opinion of your scholarly colleagues in Japan means anything to you, beware of unknown religious groups who come bearing gifts you have no reason to receive. You may be offered all-expenses-paid trips to Japan, high fees for translating their founders' works, expensive pens or jewelry, fat envelopes for a short lecture, and expensive nights on the town, and expensive gifts may arrive out of the blue at the summer and winter gift-giving seasons. If your instincts tell you that there will probably be "strings attached," or if it is made clear to you that the religion hopes to buy your patronage or good opinion, you must refuse the gift, sending it back at your own expense with an explanation that you cannot receive it. If it becomes known that you are on retainer to some specific religious organization, all others will perceive you as a spy for that organization and will be very reluctant to grant more than superficial access to you or your students.

It is not too difficult to refuse personal gifts (though it can be quite expensive to return heavy gifts even by sea mail), especially when you realize that if you have done nothing to deserve such a gift, then an attempt is being made to "buy you." It is common to receive a great deal of exaggerated praise and flattery in these situations, but beware. At the very least, such an approach is made with the expectation that pictures of you can be printed in the religion's publications and your and your university's names used to validate the group in a general way or to endorse the leader's character. More grandiose hopes may lead to requests that you assist the leader in receiving an honorary degree from your university, that a chair or program be named for the religion, and so on. Do not imagine that your conduct would be known only to the group in question—word gets around quickly that so-and-so has "sold out." Especially if your university or your students are badly in need of funds, overtures on this scale can be very difficult to refuse, and you may come under pressure from your university's administration to accept. But refuse you must, if you do not wish every other religious group in Japan to perceive from such a gift that you have become the property of the religion in question. You will forfeit your good name among scholars if you trade your name and your university's for such blandishments. And once you have lost their respect, you will never get it back, nor will your students be free of the suspicion that they, too, can be bought. Never do it.

A Friend in the Field

It has been my experience that religious thought and activity in Japan usually can be seen as extensions of or more pronounced forms of patterns seen in society at large. If this were not the case, we could not understand how religious organizations attract ordinary members of society to membership in the religion, or how religions could coexist with the rest of society. Continuities in values and general orientations seem to me to far outweigh the disjunctures between religions and ordinary society, even taking into account the internal variety and lack of homogeneity in Japanese society. Frequently the researcher on religion can be unsure how distinctive the religion in question is, how far it departs from patterns recognizable to the rest of society. In such cases, it is very useful to have a friend outside the religion who can act as a sounding board for puzzling data of observation or interaction. While fellow academics can play this role, it is also useful to be in contact with a friend outside the academic world, someone you regard as level-headed and sympathetic to the goals of your research even if not fully informed on all nuances of your project.

Because many people in Japan grow up without religious education but nevertheless understand that religion has played important roles in Japanese history, they are frequently quite interested to learn about what religious people do and how they think. They will say quite cheerfully that the foreign researcher is likely to know more about Japanese religions than they do, and in many cases this is true. Their curiosity about their fellow countrypeople can provide much needed perspective and encouragement for the researcher immersed in an intense period of fieldwork.

Note

I would like to thank the following for supporting my fieldwork over the years: Northeast Asia Council of the Association for Asian Studies; Australian Research Council; American Academy of Arts and Sciences; Japan Institute of Cetacean Research; Lilly Endowment; Social Science Research Council; Council on Research in the Social Sciences and Humanities, Princeton University; Fulbright-Hays Doctoral Dissertation Abroad Fellowship; Social Science Research Council Dissertation Fellowship; and Edwin O. Reischauer Institute of Japanese Studies.

Related Readings

Hardacre, Helen. 1984a. *The Religion of Japan's Korean Minority*. Berkeley: Center for Korean Studies, Institute of East Asian Studies, University of California.

———. 1984b. *Lay Buddhism in Contemporary Japan: Reiyūkai Kyōdan.* Princeton, N.J.: Princeton University Press.

———. 1986. *Kurozumikyō and the New Religions of Japan.* Princeton, N.J.: Princeton University Press.

———. 1997. *Marketing the Menacing Fetus in Japan.* Berkeley: University of California Press.

Ian Reader visiting a priest along the Shikoku pilgrimage route.

IAN READER

Chance, Fate, and Undisciplined Meanderings: A Pilgrimage through the Fieldwork Maze

"The Goddess of Fortune visits all researchers. The question is whether or not you let her escape. If you see the Goddess in front of you, you've got to hold on to her tightly." —Taniguchi Tadatsugi, Japanese molecular biologist, discoverer of the genetic structure of beta-interferon

Whether one believes in gods or goddesses is not the point for, after all, one does not have to believe in order to pray in Japan (Reader 1991; Tanabe 1998). The reason why this statement by a leading scientist about the importance of fortune appeals to me is because it emphasizes just how much chance and circumstance—and the willingness to make use of them—play a part in any endeavor we undertake. Indeed, what may well differentiate between those who succeed and those who do not is how they react to the chances and opportunities offered by fate and fortune. While Edison's dictum—inscribed on votive tablets at shrines in Japan that revere him (Reader and Tanabe 1998, 172–176)—that genius is 1 percent inspiration, 99 percent perspiration, may be a useful reminder of the importance of perseverance and hard work, it is not wholly accurate because it omits the importance of chance. Without the offerings of chance even the hardest working and most inspired researcher might struggle to succeed in his or her endeavors, a point Taniguchi recognized only too well. The willingness to seize such opportunities is important in the pursuit of research: it is, in my experience, critical in fieldwork.

This has certainly been my experience in my research on pilgrimage in Japan, which has developed haphazardly rather than through well-thought-out plans with periods in the field directed toward specific and predetermined research schemes. The purpose of this chapter is to outline some of the experiences I have had while undertaking this haphazard journey through the fieldwork maze and to illustrate how the workings of serendipity can, and should, affect and influence one's research. My discussion illustrates why I consider it important not to have too many preplanned schemes and schedules when approaching fieldwork, and how my own research has been conditioned by this apparently cavalier attitude to organization and planning.

Transience, Pilgrimage, and Research

I date the origins of my research on pilgrimage in Japan to the first months of 1984, though I cannot precisely ascertain when an interest that began as an antidote to work expanded into a research obsession. Being deeply fascinated by travel and transience, I had a natural interest in wanderers and pilgrims, an interest fueled by my first experiences of pilgrimage while walking around Kashmir in northern India in 1971. Since it was the time of the annual Hindu pilgrimage to the cave at Amarnath I soon found myself sharing mountain tracks with groups of pilgrims and ascetics heading to the cave. Interested in their goal, I decided to join in, walking for a couple of days with a group of sadhus whose constant refrain about the benefits of worshiping at such sacred sites alerted me to the meanings that religious travel had for them. Entering the sacred cave with them I felt the tremor of awe that pilgrims are supposed to feel when entering sacred realms: I learned what pilgrimage could mean for participants and developed a taste for the experience. I became hooked not just on travel but on pilgrimage, an addiction that subsequent visits to pilgrimage sites in other parts of the world intensified.

In my thirties, having given up the life of an itinerant, and failing to be much use at anything else, I decided to become an academic, went back to university to study Japanese, met Dorothy (my wife), and began a Ph.D. We both wanted to see as much of Japan as we could, and, since we liked old temples, enjoyed walking, and wanted to get away from the cities, we found ourselves naturally drawn to pilgrimage routes. Our earliest foray was around the thirty-four-temple Chichibu pilgrimage in Saitama, a wonderful five-day walk during which we met a variety of pilgrims. In talking to them, we heard a multiplicity of stories and reasons why they were undertaking this task. Then came Shikoku, a forty-day walk in late winter and early spring, during which the immense variety of experiences and levels of activity, faith, and commitment inherent in pilgrimages became apparent to us. We walked and talked with ascetic pilgrims sleeping rough, met devout pilgrims traveling comfortably by bus and car, and encountered people whose main interest was in sight-seeing and getting their pilgrimage scrolls stamped at the temples. We also met temple priests and their families, and talked to people who lived along the pilgrimage route, and heard what they had to say about the pilgrims.

Our Shikoku experience was the catalyst that turned an interest into a research topic. I got a job teaching English at a state university in Kobe and was told not only that I was supposed to research but that I had an annual research allocation to this end. Pilgrimage obviously fitted the bill, not least since it would provide an excuse for traveling round Japan—and through the research funds, the wherewithal to do it.

From these casual beginnings I began in earnest, digging in to the copious Japanese scholarship on the subject and beginning to see where my focus might turn. Noting the number of new pilgrimages that had developed in Japan in the 1980s, and seeing how such pilgrimages were publicized, led me to focus on the commercial aspects of pilgrimage and the ways in which they were being promoted. It was a topic I was still working on when we moved back to the UK in 1989.

Chance, Change, and Serendipity: Unforeseen Fieldwork in Shikoku

When, in September 1990, we (Dorothy and I plus Rosie, our eighteen-month-old daughter) returned to Japan for six months to examine the business of pilgrimage in Japan, I actually believed, or assumed, that I did not need to do much work on the topic. After all, I had over several years amassed a large amount of material on image construction in pilgrimages and on the role of temple priests and transport companies in the development of pilgrimages. The research trip was intended to enable me to gather final information on the subject and to tidy up a few loose ends before writing the impending book. It also allowed me time to look more closely at pilgrimage routes such as Shikoku, which I had largely neglected since our initial foray there. It was also to be the first period in which I was able to focus specifically on pilgrimage research, since all my previous fieldwork had been fitted in around my teaching and other academic duties in Japan.

The results were not what I had expected. Not only did I collect so much new data that I felt in danger of information overload, but the very focus of my research changed because of the chances that presented themselves. Indeed, my smug belief that I already knew enough to write a book on Japanese pilgrimages and that my fieldwork visit was thus almost superfluous was thoroughly undermined by my experiences back in Japan. It was not just that in this fieldwork I encountered new questions and issues that proved to be more interesting than the ones I had previously been looking at, but that the focus of my research and hence my subsequent writing project changed. I went to Japan in September 1990 largely interested in pilgrimage promotion and related topics: I returned intent on writing a detailed study of the Shikoku pilgrimage, having collected extensive material on pilgrims who had performed this pilgrimage many times, and on their aims, motivations, and activities.

This change occurred largely as a result of a visit I paid in October 1990 to Matsuyama in Shikoku. We had located ourselves in the Kansai region, within striking distance of Kyoto and Osaka and of the pilgrimage routes of that region, which I intended to make the main focus of my work. Having already visited various other pilgrimage sites and made field trips to various organizations involved in transporting pilgrims prior to visiting Shikoku, I felt that Shikoku was hardly a major aspect of my project: a book chapter maybe, but certainly not a book.

My aim in visiting Shikoku was to examine the commercial aspects of the pilgrimage by looking at the bus companies who transport the majority of Shikoku pilgrims. Thus, having arrived in Matsuyama in mid-October 1990 and intending to stay two or three nights in Shikoku, I made my first port of call the office of the Iyo Tetsu Bus Company, the single largest carrier of pilgrims on the island and also the publisher of a monthly newsletter about the pilgrimage. While I was interested in asking some questions about how the newsletter was used to promote the pilgrimage, I had given little thought to the recipients of the newspaper or their motivations. I had no idea that this would become a major theme of my research, or that it would alert me to an issue that is rarely discussed in anthropological literature on pilgrimages: that of people who perform the same pilgrimage over and over again. Much anthropological study of pilgrimage has been conducted at specific pilgrimage sites and, as such, deals with pilgrims in transit, performing what appears to be a singular and fleeting activity. As a result, little consideration has been given to the possibly more enduring results of pilgrimages and to the extent to which participants may continue to make or repeat their pilgrimages. Yet it transpired that the Iyo Tetsu newsletter was sent primarily to several thousand people who had performed the pilgrimage many times, and who had been awarded the title *sendatsu* (pilgrimage guide) by the temples as a result.

Though it had not been my intention to look at such issues, I came to do so because of a serendipitous encounter at the Iyo Tetsu office while pursuing my interests on the commercial nature of pilgrimage. This change of direction arose through discussions with an Iyo Tetsu official, who just happened to be the first person I encountered when I walked unannounced into the company's premises.

As is common with most of the visits I make to institutions in Japan— whether to bus companies, temples, shrines, or new religious movements— I had not made an appointment or called in advance to explain what my interests were and why I wanted to visit. I generally operate in this way both because I dislike advance planning and prefer getting up each day not knowing quite what I might be doing during it, and because I find it is an effective fieldwork strategy. For a start, one can keep to one's own schedule, and if a particular visit produces valuable results one can extend one's stay or interviewing time, rather than having to rush off to the next appointment. More importantly, unannounced arrivals mean that organizations are unprepared and hence unable to utilize avoidance tactics. Officials cannot conveniently get called out of the office or institution just before I arrive, an experience that has occurred on various occasions when I was trying to make appointments while investigating some delicate questions relating to a particular new religion. Nor (an alternative way of disarming the investigator) can they roll out the proverbial red carpet, deflect questions with generosity and kindness, or usher one into the presence of senior officials who can largely be relied on to provide a party line that one is already aware of.

One gets a good sense of what institutions and individuals are like (and who might be most receptive to intrusive requests) when one approaches them informally and without prior arrangement. It was, for example, the welcoming and open attitude of a particular Shikoku priest at whose temple office I appeared unannounced to ask some questions that made me feel he would be the right person to ask for assistance in a particular project mentioned later in this chapter. He had readily agreed to talk to me, had then invited me in for a beer (a surefire way to endear anyone to me) and dinner, and then suggested I should stay overnight so we could talk more. He might well have done all of this had I contacted him formally before visiting, but this way I felt that his interest was spontaneous and genuine.

Of course it does not always work, and one should be prepared for occasional rejections or (if visiting temples, for instance) for finding the priest unavailable or even hostile because one has not called in advance. Overall, however, it is my preferred modus operandi and it has produced excellent results.

It certainly worked in Matsuyama. The man I approached in the office turned out to be a middle-ranking company official who coordinated the company's scheduled monthly pilgrimage bus tours. Moreover he was, as he told me over several beers later that evening, intrigued by the fact that a foreigner appeared interested in the issues of pilgrimage promotion and commerce. He was equally interested in my casual and unscheduled approach, which suggested that I would be prepared to chase up any line of enquiry that turned up.

For a couple of hours he sat patiently in the office fielding my questions on commerce and the like. A number of interesting points had begun to emerge from the conversation, particularly in terms of how the company sought to demonstrate that its involvement in the pilgrimage, though based in commercial considerations, also was underwritten by concepts of service to the pilgrims and commitment to the religious traditions of the island. My interviewee had by this time assumed control over the discussion, telling me what was important and what I needed to look at. I am often content to allow interviews to take this form since it is a good tactic for elucidating information: by allowing informants/interviewees to set the agenda one can often discern what their areas of concern are and what issues they think need to be pursued. Since my interviewee/potential director of research was keen to emphasize the sincere role of the company in pilgrimages, it seemed a good idea for me to follow this point up.

Hence, when I answered that I had never experienced the type of service his bus company provided for pilgrims and had not met any ardent *sendatsu* who spent their lives guiding other pilgrims around the route, I realized he felt these were important gaps in my research. Moreover, it was clear that he wanted to—indeed was determined—to show me these things.

Here fortune played a hand. He checked his schedule and found that one of the company's buses, carrying thirty-three pilgrims, was scheduled to complete its ten-day circuit of the route within the next few hours. It would shortly reach its last stop, Ishiteji, a temple on the outskirts of Matsuyama, after which it would return to the company's office, from whence the pilgrims would make their way home. We leapt in his car and set out for Ishiteji, where he introduced me to the bus driver, the company's pilgrimage tour guide, and the pilgrims. Besides experiencing the last hour or so of this pilgrimage tour (including a "closing ceremony" for the tour) and seeing how the company officials catered to the pilgrims, I was able to interview several of the pilgrims about their experiences on the bus, and to talk to the driver and to the bus guide (that ubiquitous Japanese figure with the flag and whistle whom one encounters leading tour groups at every tourist location in Japan).

The bus guide was an ardent believer in the merits of the pilgrimage and in the grace of Kōbō Daishi (the central figure of worship for Shikoku pilgrims). He regaled me with miracle tales about the pilgrimage and assured me that it was as a result of working for the Iyo Tetsu company and spending much of his time in the company of pilgrims that he had turned into a devotee of Kōbō Daishi. Many years later I met him again in the Iyo Tetsu offices—by now promoted to a senior position in the company. After the guide and driver gave farewell talks to the pilgrims, the pilgrims took leave of each other, many vowing to meet up and do the pilgrimage again. I assumed this was simply said for the sake of politeness, but later found that this was not necessarily so: many pilgrims do return regularly and often plan to do future pilgrimages with people they had been on buses with in previous years. Indeed, all the people I later traveled with on an organized Shikoku pilgrimage tour had previously traveled together and were considering further joint pilgrimage ventures.

By the time the bus had returned to the Iyo Tetsu office, my contact there had arranged an interview for me with a *sendatsu,* an elderly man living just outside Matsuyama who had done numerous pilgrimages, including the Shikoku pilgrimage over seventy times. Mori Masamitsu was a retired farmer who had become the head of a *kō* (pilgrimage group) that regularly gathered people together to perform pilgrimages. His life since retirement had revolved around devotion to Kōbō Daishi and faith in the merits of performing pilgrimages. As is common in Japan, Mori's pilgrimage activities were not limited to one route or figure of worship but ranged across a whole spectrum. He was, in effect, what I have since come to describe as a "permanent pilgrim," someone who devotes a large part of his or her life to performing pilgrimages and spends much of the time when not on a pilgrimage either planning to do one or actively preaching the virtues of pilgrimage to others (see Reader 1993b for more details).

Mori was well known to the Iyo Tetsu company. As an ardent *sendatsu* with a talent for narrating miracle stories, he was occasionally asked by the company to lead the tour parties they organized. Because of this connection, and because it was clear that he loved to talk about pilgrimages, Mori was very amenable to being interviewed, and our talk lasted several hours, during which time he acted, as it were, as my guide through the various pilgrimages he knew. He spoke not just of Shikoku but of other smaller and more localized pilgrimages that he liked to perform and that took only a day to go around. He talked of the role and responsibility of the *sendatsu*—as a leader of pilgrim parties, as promoter of faith in Kōbō Daishi, and as a narrator of the miracle stories that abound in Shikoku, and which he viewed as evidence of Kōbō Daishi's grace.

Through our discussion I gained a picture of someone whose life was focused on pilgrimages, and for whom pilgrimage was a religion, a hobby, and a way of life. Through Mori's explanations of his role as *sendatsu* I began to get a clearer picture of the influence—and indeed the responsibilities—of those who had performed the pilgrimage a number of times, and to see how such pilgrims could acquire a certain form of holy status as a result. It was clear, too, that my Iyo Tetsu company contact regarded him as someone with special religious status. I was later to encounter other *sendatsu* who were regarded in similar or more exalted ways by their fellow pilgrims.

Besides providing me with a clear indication of the nature of *sendatsu* in Japan, Mori also showed me that pilgrimage could be a way of life in modern Japan and that people might spend much of their lives performing or preparing to perform pilgrimages. I had previously met people in Shikoku who had spent much of their lives following the pilgrimage circuit, but this was the first time I had been able to gather extensive testimony from such a person. As we talked I became aware that this would be a fascinating topic to study. If the encounter with the bus party had piqued my interest in the experiences of pilgrims in Shikoku and made me think of focusing some of my energies on this issue, it was through the interview with Mori that I came to realize I needed to know more about the *sendatsu* system, its origins, and its workings if I was going to understand the workings and dynamics of the Shikoku pilgrimage (in commercial or any other terms).

My Iyo Tetsu contact had not, however, finished. Not only did he insist that I stay overnight with his family so that we could continue talking about the pilgrimage, but the next day he took me to meet the editor of the company's monthly pilgrimage newsletter, which was routinely sent to all registered *sendatsu*. Naturally, too, the journalist decided that he had to insert an article about my research in the next issue along with a comment about how I was interested in pilgrims' experiences. It was an article that produced, in its wake, an enormous amount of further research materials, as a number of *sendatsu* contacted me, wanting to tell me their stories and sending copies of pilgrimage diaries they had written. In one case, a *sendatsu* living in Kyushu invited me to his hometown to take me on a special pilgrimage in the mountains nearby, and then proceeded to talk all night to me about his pilgrimage experiences.

Although I had not actively sought such publicity for my work, the newsletter article proved extremely valuable. Priests and pilgrims alike, having heard about me from this source, became readier to open their doors and talk. Two further articles and interviews followed as a result, one in a local Shikoku magazine, the other in a series the national newspaper, *Yomiuri Shinbun,* was running on Shikoku. These, too, produced further letters and contacts from pilgrims wanting (and even demanding) to be interviewed by me. Amongst those I was able to interview as a result were several elderly pilgrims who had first done the pilgrimage over sixty years before and had done it dozens or even hundreds of times since. From these interviews I was able to reconstruct a picture of what the pilgrimage was like in the immediate pre- and postwar years (eras for which virtually no accounts have been written) and to learn more about the feelings, experiences, and motivations of other "permanent pilgrims."

As a result of those two days in Matsuyama the focus of my research changed, primarily because a helpful official in a bus company had brought the question of *sendatsu* to my attention but also, and crucially, because when this chance came along I was ready and willing to go along with it. Thus I found myself rapidly homing in on issues related to Shikoku and the views and experiences of pilgrims and *sendatsu* there. While I cannot put this change of direction down solely to one friendly official in a bus company office, it was clear that his intervention and suggestions at that point had had a crucial effect on the direction of my research. Indeed, he assisted me further by suggesting the names of a couple of priests on the other side of the island whom I should talk to if I were serious about following up my interest in *sendatsu*. Abandoning my earlier plans to continue delving into the commercial activities of other Shikoku bus companies I did just this, boarding a train the next day for Tokushima and heading out to the temples concerned. At both temples I turned up without prior warning, and in both cases found myself spending many hours talking to the priest concerned. In both cases, too, I later spent a number of nights at the temple doing research, in one case trawling through the archives with the priest to work out when and how the *sendatsu* system developed, and with the other not only spending many hours talking about pilgrimage, but using his temple as the focus of the study of pilgrims' prayers, which will be mentioned later in this chapter.

Commerce, Faith, and an Unexpected Pilgrimage Tour

Before I did that particular piece of research on prayers, however, I took part in an organized pilgrimage tour of Shikoku, an experience that had not originally been part of my fieldwork plans. Indeed, it had not even been on my agenda when, three weeks after the above experiences in Shikoku, I walked into the office of a small travel company in Osaka specializing in pilgrimage tours. I was still intent on furthering my knowledge of the pilgrimage travel business while extending my understandings of the activities of *sendatsu*, and it seemed that this particular firm would be a good place to visit. It was a two-person company run by a husband and wife team. She ran the office while he was a *sendatsu*, the leader of a pilgrimage association, and president of the company, and they made their living from organizing pilgrimage tours. When I entered their office, unannounced, my intention was simply to seek information about how they ran their operations and promoted their pilgrimage tours, how they related the roles of *sendatsu* and travel company boss, and how they regarded the relationship between pilgrimage and commerce.

I was lucky because the office was not busy and I was able to talk to them uninterrupted. They were frank about their commercial role, making none of the pious remarks I had occasionally heard from others associated with the promotion and selling of religion. Both cheerfully agreed that, while being devotees of Kōbō Daishi, they were also commercial operators whose source of income derived from Kōbō Daishi worship. They were a mine of useful information about the types of people who were their clientele on the Shikoku and on other routes, and were affable in their responses. It was one of those days when getting information from an informant was pleasant and enjoyable and I was feeling rather complacently pleased with myself when, toward the end of the conversation, he asked, "Have you ever been on a package tour pilgrimage yourself?" When I responded negatively, he pointedly asked how I could spend so much time inquiring about pilgrimage tours and the activities of *sendatsu* without experiencing them firsthand.

My mumbled response that I hoped one day to have the opportunity to do so was cut abruptly short by his comment that if I were a serious researcher I would do it immediately. I parried again by saying that the problem with going on the normal-sized buses (as I knew from having traveled short distances on them) was that seat places are usually fixed so that one gets little chance to interact with more than the one or two pilgrims in adjacent seats. Why not go with a smaller party, then, he asked. I responded that this would be ideal, but where (given that most small parties are private groups) could one find one? I should have known the answer immediately, for I had walked straight into a trap woven by a master pilgrimage salesman. The very next evening they had a minibus leaving for Shikoku that had eight seats besides the driver's. There was one place left.

Later, as I left his office clutching not just my interview notes but also my tour reservation, I mentally congratulated him on his skill in selling the reluctant researcher a seat on his tour. I was grateful that he had, because the tour provided me with much information. The salesman who was leading the party, acting as its *sendatsu* and driving the bus, provided me with a constant demonstration of the interactions between the faith-driven and commercial aspects of pilgrimage. S-san (as I call him here) wore two hats. One related to his role as driver/commercial operator of the tour, in which capacity he managed to bring the party to various souvenir shops along the route, often whetting everyone's appetite in advance with skillfully told stories about the delights of certain types of sweetmeats available only at such-and-such a shop or the merits and miracles produced by the amulets sold at such-and-such a temple. Clearly he had arrangements for the bus to stop or linger long enough at certain temples and stores for the pilgrims to buy souvenirs and yet, although this was fairly evident to all of us in the party, his style of delivery and sales patter were so entertaining and captivating that most of the party were cheerfully ready to buy their souvenirs where he guided them to do so. Equally, as we were coming to the end of our pilgrimage, he managed to guide the conversation around to other interesting pilgrimages that everyone ought to do at least once in their lives (and of course, as luck would have it, his company was organizing a tour shortly . . .). Yet alongside the sales banter he kept up a fascinating narrative about miracles and salvation that had no discernible commercial motive and that displayed his ardent faith— a faith that manifested itself every time we arrived at a temple, when he would engage in prayers and carry out all the ritual actions of the pilgrim. S-san's performance was, in short, a demonstration of how commercialism and faith could operate together.

Even if his primary motive in getting me aboard appeared to have been economic, S-san proved to be completely right in enticing me into traveling with a small party. With only nine people in a minibus, it was far easier to get to know my fellow pilgrims, to listen to their stories, and to talk about their motives. At first my companions were a little reluctant to talk, since they were aware that my motives were not to venerate Kōbō Daishi but to do research, but they rapidly began to treat me as one of the group, especially after one of the older men in the party confessed that his real intention was to have a holiday away from his family, see some new parts of Japan, visit scenic places, and take photographs. That broke the ice and started a discussion regarding motives, after which it became less and less difficult for me to engage with my companions. Indeed, they began to volunteer information rather than waiting for me to extricate it. As this happened we developed as a social unit and began to think of ourselves as a party of pilgrims traveling together even though we were a motley group of individuals and couples, each with his or her own agenda and motivations (see Reader 1993a for more details).

I became aware of how the party began to include me as an integral member when we engaged in friendly discussion with another pilgrimage party. Often when pilgrimage groups come into contact with each other there is some friendly banter in which one group quietly seeks to establish its priority over another, perhaps by talking of how many times they or their *sendatsu* have done the pilgrimage. In this case, the pilgrims in my group had a distinctive feature that marked their party out: me, the foreign researcher. Yes, my fellow travelers remarked to the other group, he's with us. He's a professor from England doing research on pilgrimage. And he has chosen to travel with us. I was "their" researcher. In quietly boasting to the other group who, devoid of foreign researchers, were clearly of lesser status, they signaled their acceptance of me. My transition from external observer to party member was complete.

From then on gathering information became easier and easier, and the abiding memory I have of the tour, apart from the sheer exhaustion of it— getting up at 5:00 A.M. to attend early morning services, traveling all day, and talking late into the night—was how, as we crystallized as a social unit, the opportunities to dig out more information became easier. Indeed, since I was "their" researcher they became increasingly keen to provide me with information, constantly and repeatedly telling me fresh aspects of their stories and experiences. The result was a bulging fieldwork notebook that served further to focus my research interests onto the activities, beliefs, and experiences of pilgrims. Again, as with my initial entry into the *sendatsu* system and related matters, this opportunity had come about not through some planned action of my own but because an interviewee had pushed me toward a particular action, and because, when the chance had manifested itself, I was ready to take it.

Kōbō Daishi's Scottish Bonfire

Through talking with pilgrims I had begun to develop a picture of what types of prayer requests pilgrims made to Kōbō Daishi. However, I was keen to get some more concrete, quantitative data as well, and I saw a way to do so. Normally pilgrims write prayer requests (and often also their names, addresses, and other information) on prayer slips known as *osamefuda,* which are then left in offering boxes at the temples the pilgrims visit. The *osamefuda* appeared to be a potentially valuable source of information of the type I wanted. There was, however, a major problem. The prayer slips are sacred personal offerings from the pilgrim to Kōbō Daishi that are placed in the safekeeping of the temple. Moreover, they are ritually burnt by the temple at periodic intervals because, in popular belief, when they are incinerated the requests ascend to Kōbō Daishi.

It hardly seemed feasible, in such circumstances, that I could gain access to, sort through, and categorize a large quantity of what were effectively private prayer requests that would shortly be burned. However, there was only one way to find out, and if I did not try I would never have the chance to get the data. By this time, I had become friendly with one of the aforementioned priests who had welcomed an unannounced stranger appearing at his temple asking for an interview. We shared an interest in talking nonstop while drinking beer, and every time I visited we would sit until late downing bottles of Kirin beer and discussing everything from the pilgrimage to Islam and its relations with the West—a topic that fascinated him immensely. I felt he appreciated what I was trying to do in my research, and since he had already allowed me to examine various documents and historical records of the temple I decided to broach the subject with him.

I began by dropping comments about pilgrims' prayers and *osamefuda* into the conversation, eventually plucking up courage to tackle the issue in an indirect manner so as not to cause embarrassment. I wrote to him saying something along the lines of "if one could examine *osamefuda* I am sure they would yield interesting material." The next day he phoned, inviting me to study the *osamefuda* at his temple before they were burned. I spent a week there in a huge tatami room, surrounded by heaps of *osamefuda*, working through several hundred a day and categorizing into types of request (Reader and Tanabe 1998, 200–201). At around 5:30 each evening the door would open and in would walk the priest clutching two bottles of beer and telling me it was time to end my work for the day.

After several days of this I had to return to Osaka, largely because I missed Dorothy and Rosie (I can only manage very limited bursts of fieldwork away from home because of this). I had made inroads into, but not managed to work through, the mountain of prayer slips. I told the priest this as I thanked him for his help. The ones I had categorized were of immense help to my research, and it was a shame that, since we were shortly returning to Scotland, I would not be able to categorize any more. His response took me aback, pleasantly. Why not take a bag full back to Scotland? To me this seemed to be a breach of religious decorum and I expressed concern about the ritual burning process, which surely had to be done in Shikoku. Not at all, he said: Kōbō Daishi was transcendent and could therefore read them anywhere. "Burn them in Scotland. Kōbō Daishi can read them there."

A Japanese colleague researching on pilgrimage later told me he had wanted to do a similar study but had never felt able to ask for permission. It was the sort of thing that he felt, as a Japanese, he could not do. It would have been too much of a breach of etiquette (especially as he was himself a priest). Consequently he was restrained from certain forms of research because of cultural reservations. By contrast, my outsider position worked to my advantage, as my Japanese academic colleague recognized. I had been able to make a suggestion and get away with what could have been an indecorous request. If it had caused offense it would have been seen just as an example of ignorant foreign behavior. Because I stood outside the Japanese system, it was much easier for the priest concerned to grant my request. A distinct advantage for foreigners when doing fieldwork in Japan is that they can slide around normative rules of appropriate behavior—an advantage that should be used sparingly and with caution, but one that should never be disregarded.

Shortly afterward we flew back to Scotland with a sack of *osamefuda*, which I proceeded to catalogue before having a bonfire for Kōbō Daishi in our garden. By that point, the whole focus of my research on pilgrimage had changed. What had transformed it and taken it in different directions were a series of fortuitous encounters and opportunities, ranging from the help of a bus company official, to the example of a devout *sendatsu*, to the commercial skills of a tour operator-cum-*sendatsu*, to the interest of a temple priest. Of course, if I had clung to a fixed plan of research and studiously ignored the vagaries of chance and the opportunities that it presented me, I would have shut my eyes to these extraneous temptations and stayed on track with my work on pilgrimage promotion. I did not, of course, because it seemed far more interesting to seize the goddess and follow the paths of fortune and chance. It has meant much more work, since I put aside a lot of the material I had collected in the earlier phase of my pilgrimage research, but it has been more fun to do. It may even produce a more interesting book than I had originally planned.

Conclusions: Fate, Fortune, and Aum Shinrikyō

I must add a coda to this chapter, which will partially explain why the aforementioned book has yet to be finished and which emphasizes how our research can change because of the shifts and events in the world around us. I began to write my Shikoku book. I even finished a chapter—on March 19, 1995. As every student of religion in Japan knows, the next day saw quite possibly the most important event in postwar Japanese religious history: Aum Shinrikyō's attack on the Tokyo subway. The upshot was that my phone began to ring with calls from the media desperate for information—

any information—about this group. I had some Aum materials and books picked up in a previous visit to Japan, for future reference. Quickly leafing through them I was able to answer some immediate questions about Aum's teachings, with the result that, in a situation where few knew anything about Aum, even a little knowledge was enough to make one an "expert." Before I knew it, I experienced my fifteen minutes of fame as predicted by Andy Warhol and had become a media "Aum expert." As an "expert," though, I then needed to know more in order not just to satisfy my own curiosity but to answer the questions of my colleagues and students.

The rest was inevitable. I plunged headlong into Aum, each piece of information and apparent insight seemingly demanding that I go further. And each time I felt it was time to get back to earlier work, something new came along to make me continue. Contacts with Aum led to interviews with current and former disciples, and unpublished texts circulated inside Aum came into my hands. What followed has been a five-year immersion in the strange world of Aum Shinrikyō. The result, of course, has been that I have not managed to complete the intended book on Shikoku.

I am not annoyed at having become embroiled in research on Aum. It was a topic that so demanded attention it would have been impossible, indeed negligent, for me to have not taken it up. The Aum affair was simply the most dramatic, challenging, and foundation-shaking event in Japanese religion in my lifetime, and since my prime field is religion in the modern day, it was not something I could ignore. Chance had set the trap. Naturally I fell headlong into it.

My engagement with the study of Aum was fortuitous in nature. As a very contemporary Japanese religious phenomenon it clearly fell within my territory. By chance I happened to have some materials on hand that enabled me to comment on the movement and, before I knew it, the topic had found me. Likewise my engagement with the study of pilgrimage grew, as I have described, out of a casual interest and developed into an extensive yet changing project influenced by circumstances and fieldwork encounters. It was not so much a project that I deliberately chose as one into which I fell because of circumstances and interests, and that somehow, like Aum, found me. Five years later than intended, as I return to writing up my pilgrimage book I am fortified by my clear resolution not to get distracted until it is done. Naturally, too, I wonder what serendipity has in store for me next, and whether it will produce something enticing enough to distract me from my goal.

Note

I would like to thank the Leverhulme Trust and the Japan Foundation Endowment Committee (UK) for providing funds to partially support a fieldwork visit to Japan in 1990–1991 as part of this project.

Related Readings

The first article (1987), from my earliest period of fieldwork, provides an interesting comparison to later writings (such as 1993a) because one can see how my views have changed as a result of further fieldwork especially among pilgrims who travel by bus.

Reader, Ian. 1987. "From Asceticism to the Package Tour: The Pilgrim's Progress in Japan." *Religion* 17(2):133–148.

———. 1993a."Dead to the World: Pilgrims in Shikoku." In Ian Reader and Tony Walter, eds., *Pilgrimage in Popular Culture.* Basingstoke: Macmillan, 107–136. (Republished 2001, London: Palgrave.)

———. 1993b. Sendatsu *and the Development of Contemporary Japanese Pilgrimage.* Nissan Occasional Papers on Japan no. 17. Nissan Institute for Japanese Studies, University of Oxford.

———. 1996. "Creating Pilgrimages: Buddhist Priests and Popular Religion in Contemporary Japan." In *Proceedings of the Kyoto Conference on Japanese Studies,* vol. 3. International Research Center for Japanese Studies, Kyoto, 311–324.

———. 1996. "Pilgrimage as Cult: The Shikoku Pilgrimage as a Window on Japanese Religion." In P. F. Kornicki and I. J. McMullen, eds., *Religion in Japan: Arrows to Heaven and Earth.* Cambridge: Cambridge University Press, 267–286.

NAVIGATING BUREAUCRATIC MAZES

Samuel Coleman (top
row, third from right) at
the Osaka Bioscience
Institute, 1990.

SAMUEL COLEMAN

Getting Cooperation in Policy-Oriented Research

I have conducted two extensive fieldwork projects in Japan. The first, in the
mid-1970s, was a twenty-eight-month doctoral dissertation research stint to
study the birth control methods used by married couples (Coleman 1983
[1991]). The second, in the early 1990s, concerned the social organization of
laboratory scientists, and most of the data gathering took place in one year
in the field (Coleman 1999). The first project had no primary site. Research
committed to one spatial locus could not provide the kind of data I needed
because the behavior that concerned me most was taking place in bedrooms.
The latter fieldwork put me in the midst of Japanese bioscientists at work in
their laboratories; I wanted to see what was going on there, organizationally,
that would help explain Japan's lackluster performance in basic research
despite its affluence and technological sophistication. Since the laboratory
study has left details of methodology fresher in my memory, it will occupy
more of my discussion.

Despite their very different settings, both projects relied heavily on the
cooperation of concerned specialists in Japan. As all of the accounts in this
volume surely illustrate, access to resources—affiliations, introductions, and

sites for data gathering—requires negotiation, some of it extensive. In my own experience, two factors proved critical to getting the needed cooperation: Japanese-language study, both preparatory and ongoing in the field; and collaboration with Japanese whose concerns and goals had points in common with my own. The latter consideration stems from the policy-oriented nature of my research projects, so I do not anticipate it applying to more classically academic fieldwork. I do hope, though, that my observations are of some use to those preparing to conduct research in Japan in applied fields and the professions (such as law or social work).

Language Study

It would be hard for me to overstate how important a command of the Japanese language has been for my fieldwork. No Japanese would ever confuse me for a native speaker on the telephone, but I have attained enough Japanese-language proficiency to learn far more about my research subjects than I ever could have if I had to confine my inquiries to English-speaking informants or relied on someone else for translation and interpreting. I have also, with the help of educated native speakers, written statements of purpose in Japanese in the course of seeking cooperation, as well as statements in Japanese for informed consent for my subjects that have served to convey my methods and goals.

Like others who were not taught Japanese since childhood, I have been facing a formidable challenge in learning the language as a research tool. I began language study at the not so tender age of twenty-one in a university program run by a literature specialist who regarded introductory students in the social sciences as a necessary evil. (As consolation, for a long time afterward I used the experience as a plausible excuse for my faulty speaking and listening skills.) When I arrived in Japan for my dissertation fieldwork and called my first contact, I realized within seconds that I was hearing a phone message recording and I would have to leave a recorded response. My hands went clammy and I hung up at the beep. It took several weeks to get back on the phone again. On the same day of my abortive phone call I was unable to understand a representative from Tokyo Gas who came to my home to explain automatic bank payments.

At that point I thought that my goal of studying birth control in Japan was a delusion of grandeur. With some further thought, though, I realized that telephone chats with machines are one of the hardest situations for communicating, and if I were to just calm down and learn a few relevant words for banking and personal finance I could prevent having my utilities shut off. In the meantime, I gathered together everything I could in print literature in Japanese concerning sexuality and family planning and began learning vocabulary and expressions. Of course, more preparation in specialized Japanese terminology before entering the field would have been better, but at that time there was hardly any current vernacular literature on those subjects available to me in the United States.

Some twelve years later, when I was preparing for my laboratory research fieldwork, I was able to stock up on specialized literature in Japan thanks to a small grant for pilot work. The outlets for the Japanese government's printing office (Seifu Kankōbutsu Ryūtsū Sentā) in Tokyo's Kasumigaseki District and in a number of other major cities throughout Japan have always proved to be a good place to start for any policy-related topic, and the titles on their shelves reflect the country's major policy problems, from illegal immigrants to the aging of the population. The publications for sale also include aggregate statistics prepared under government auspices. When I was preparing for the laboratory study, "creativity" in science and engineering posed a major concern, so I could read up on the latest approaches to the problem while absorbing the appropriate terminology.

In the course of fieldwork for both my birth control and laboratory studies, I found I could unlock whole areas of discussion by learning the colloquial expressions that my informants used. Inserting the words and phrases in my questions sometimes inspired revealing soliloquies among my discussion partners. In my research on laboratory scientists, for example, words like "chores" (*zatsuyō*, nonresearch tasks) and "hitting walls" (*ikizumari*, unproductive, dead-end experiments) inspired a lot of out-loud reflection about work conditions and career aspirations.

In my birth control research, sensitivity to terminology in Japanese also proved critical to managing my image. When I began my stint in the field, I wrote up a business card that identified me as a foreign "research student" *(kenkyūsei)*, the official term for my status under the Japanese university that offered me an affiliation. It drew the comment that I was "rather young" (read: too young) to be studying such a serious and sensitive topic as birth control, even though I was then thirty years old and married. I promptly changed the title on my card to "research fellow" *(kenkyūin)*.

The Importance of Shared Concerns and Goals

I have experienced the best cooperation when collaborating with Japanese who have shared some or all of my concerns. That has meant studying *with* Japanese organizations and individuals to pursue issues in common, as well as studying them as objects of inquiry. It has also meant having to figure out not only who is doing what, but where I fit in and how both sides could mutually benefit while maintaining my independence as a researcher.

I first became acutely aware of the issue of shared concerns when I was seeking sites for my laboratory study. My prospective hosts' perception of the benefits of my research topic proved critical to my gaining access to laboratories. Our shared goals were, ultimately, to raise the quality of basic research in Japan and realize more research collaboration between Japanese and foreign researchers, particularly those from the United States. An increase in the latter depended ultimately on progress in the former. I had garnered some connections and visibility among a few concerned Japanese science administrators for my activities to promote more access to Japanese scientific and technical information in the United States. That included a high-profile fund-raising drive that memorialized Harry C. Kelly, chief science advisor to the Allied Occupation of Japan. Kelly was revered by his generation of Japanese scientists as an icon of international cooperation. The connection was a grand bit of serendipity (Kelly had gone on to become provost at the university whose Japan Center later hired me), and the fund-raising featured a documentary that appeared on Japanese television with a prominent role for me as "reporter." I had also conducted a survey among university faculty in the sciences and engineering on Japanese information sources, and that made for a piece of reportage that helped me establish some credentials for myself.

Ultimately, my three major participant observation sites in Japan for the bioscience organizational study were the Osaka Bioscience Institute (OBI), Protein Engineering Research Institute (PERI), and a private medical college, among which I divided a year of research. I was introduced to the directors of both OBI and PERI through a government science administrator with whom I had collaborated on the Kelly Fund. Both directors were acutely aware of the organizational problems ailing Japan's science community, and their research organizations were attempting to correct some of them— hence their interest in my research, and our shared goal: an understanding of the organizational features that would encourage more world-class scientific research in Japan. OBI and PERI were located literally next door to each other. They were at once the objects of my research and my collegial bases. In fact, my first grant for the project from the National Science Foundation (NSF) stipulated the director of OBI as co-investigator. In the course of our association, however, neither he nor I brought up the possibility of co-authoring publications. As a biochemist, he would not have gotten much professional mileage out of publishing in the social sciences anyway.

I may have benefited indirectly from an aura of American greatness in the sciences and technology, but my coming from the United States, a mecca of bioscience research, could have made me an ethnocentric critic. Also, the age of the devalued American dollar had arrived, and a perceived decline in the economic power and standard of living of the United States had become a staple of commentators' discussions. The OBI and PERI directors might have been hoping for some publicity, but they also surely recognized the risk that it could be negative, since every organization has its problems and its detractors, within and without. Japanese colleagues in the social study of science told me that they could not have gotten the access that I did. They may have had a point, but I know of no cases in which they had requested access and were denied. During my stay at OBI its administration allowed a Japanese organizational researcher from Hitotsubashi University to conduct interviews with twelve researchers.

Encountering Indifference

My laboratory science research project proposed a benchmark observational study for three months in an American laboratory before going to Japan. This portion of the research was a kind of ethnographic exercise through which I wanted to learn in an inductive fashion about workday rhythms, division of labor, and whatever else might pop up serendipitously. Contrary to my expectations, it proved much harder for me to get into an American laboratory than the ones I had targeted in Japan, despite the fact that I had the imprimatur of a research grant from NSF. I approached the heads of several laboratories in the university where I was then teaching, but their response was noncommittal, and the process dragged on until one lab chief whom I subsequently approached finally consented.

My American university laboratory and sites in Japan also contrasted sharply in the latitude afforded me in research methods. The director of the molecular biology institute where I studied in the United States informed me that questionnaires were verboten—flat out, before I even raised the possibility myself. When, near the end of my year of fieldwork, I proposed questionnaire surveys at OBI and PERI, I submitted drafts to their directors. Within a few days they had approved distribution without proposing revisions. Some of the questions dealt with sensitive issues like work hours, subsequent job placements (OBI), and relations between industry and academic researchers (PERI). I do not recall whether or to what extent the directors consulted with department heads before reaching their decisions, but in both cases department heads, like the directors, expressed ready agreement with my offer to report my results to an assembly of researchers and technicians.

Among the differences vis-à-vis the American scientists and the Japanese that could explain this contrast, I think the chief factor was the Americans' skepticism due to their lack of a stake in what I was trying to accomplish. They were perched at the top of the international status ladder, so they were not eager to hear about organizational innovations. Japan had no professional mystique for them, either. The Americans had their own share of organizational tensions, in particular sensitivity to sex discrimination and the plight of postdocs ("permadocs") treading water in an academic job market almost as grim as that of anthropology, my home discipline at the time.

The American scientists did not perceive me as someone who could help them solve these problems. Social scientists were an unknown commodity among them, and, unlike Japan, I had no professional introductions. The inductive nature of my study made matters worse—the goal that I presented to the American academic bioscientists was a vague sort of, "I want to see how you work and live." My presentations to the Japanese, in contrast, mentioned such specific issues as hierarchy, material resources, and professional mobility.

Institutional Affiliation in the Birth Control Research Project

My Japanese university affiliation during my birth control fieldwork provided a bureaucratic convenience for me (for my visa approval and as an impressive affiliation on my business card) but little more. I had no prior research track record in the subject area to create networks and promote myself as a resource. A sociologist on my home university's dissertation committee sent a letter of introduction to a colleague at the target university in order to establish the affiliation. The Japanese counterpart specialized in journalism and society. Like his fellow department members he had no interest in my research subject. If anything, research involving sexuality made them somewhat ill at ease, since it lacked academic legitimacy. The Japanese university's computer facilities proved helpful, but I had no office or desk, and not once did I make a presentation to the host department of my findings as they unfolded.

Introductions to knowledgeable colleagues came instead from several other sources, chief among them a prominent university-based obstetrician-gynecologist and the then director of the Population Problems Research Institute. There were several fault lines of opinion regarding birth control then, as there surely are now, but the most acute was the issue of whether or not to legalize oral contraceptives. Nearly everyone shared the perception that the country's induced abortion rate was excessively high, however, and there lay the shared problem orientation. Since my primary concern was to find out how married couples made their decisions regarding choice and use of contraceptive methods, most specialists in relevant fields such as maternal and child health, human sexuality—and even a few demographers—were interested in hearing my observations. Physicians, midwives, and counselors at eight health care-related facilities distributed 1,020 forms for a self-administered questionnaire study I devised. The questionnaire was unique because it sought a very thorough reproductive history and asked about frequency of sexual intercourse, along with information on social class and the quality of the conjugal relationship. Our effective return rate was a little over 60 percent. This kind of cooperation was, I believe, a classical example of shared collegial interest.

Sources of Informant / Interviewee Cooperation

When I entered OBI, the first of my laboratory field sites, I felt intensely insecure. I was not quite sure of how I would attack the issues I had in mind. Observing research group discussion meetings was one source of data, but the discussions were centered on projects that had begun well before my arrival, and the bulk of the discussion was of highly technical matters. I was also hoping that I would get data by osmosis, just by being around. Ultimately I did garner some very helpful observations that way, but for some weeks after beginning my stay there I felt I was getting absolutely nowhere. I had hoped that my introductory presentation to my new laboratory mates, in which I explained my goals, would inspire individuals to seek me out and chat with me. It did not. Lunchtime discussions were pretty thin on substance, too. I had soon exhausted my repertory of clever jokes in Japanese, and I realized that I would have to engage the people around me in serious, structured, one-on-one interviews.

I found the prospect of asking for interviews difficult. In retrospect, I think my repeated, ardent assurances to the lab chiefs that I would not cramp anyone's productivity had taken a toll on my self-confidence. I confided my fears about approaching researchers to a departmental secretary, who suggested I request an interview from a postdoc in another department who was a friend of hers. (That the postdoc was a woman fits with both fact and perception that women are more cooperative than men in survey research.) I am grateful to both the secretary and my first formal interviewee. The interview went well and gave me the courage to ask others. My informed consent statement helped also, I believe, because it outlined my interests and described the steps I would take to protect my interviewees' anonymity.

When I was first formulating my research strategy for the laboratory study, I had hoped that I could generate rapport through the classical "participant observation" route by performing routine laboratory tasks. My schedule before beginning fieldwork did not afford me the time for training, however, and my one attempt at helping by sterilizing pipette tips resulted in my being escorted out the laboratory door. My offer to provide English-language editing had far more gratifying results for both parties. I believe my repeated offers of assistance aided in establishing friendly feelings. Although they did not result in systematic use of my services, I would estimate that roughly four hours of every week, on average, went to helping researchers and administrators with translation and editing. I benefited by learning about such matters as authorship, the phrasing of scientific arguments, and the problems of dealing with international journal editors.

An important note here on logistics: having my own desk in the laboratory offices at both OBI and PERI was an immense help, since my prospective interviewees could come by at a time that fit with their bench schedules. Indeed, in a few cases when my request for an interview was met with a vague "maybe later," the researcher showed up at my desk three or four days afterward, ready to begin talking. I had assumed that I was getting a classical

Japanese-style rejection, but as it turned out my request had simply come at a particularly busy time.

Once I got my feet wet, the task of interviewing laboratory researchers became easier because I could craft my questions to target issues that made sense to both my interviewees and to me. I could also reformulate the sequence in which I asked the questions. I have found very effective a kind of rhythm to an interview, in which I ask first the easier to answer questions, shift gradually into the more potentially stressful topics, and then end with a lighter or even whimsical question. I soon had a very serviceable protocol. Since my population was highly educated and, for the most part, derived considerable satisfaction from their work, they tended to enjoy discussing profession-related questions in general and their own careers in particular. A few even went out of their way to thank me for the discussion afterward, saying it gave them a chance to rethink their professional priorities. I had a few indications that my interviewees shared information on their interview experience among themselves. It didn't exactly result in a line of bioscientists forming at my desk, but I suspect that word of positive experiences paved the way for more cooperation. The final score at my major research sites was 101 interviews out of 103 requests.

Interviewing for the birth control research project involved a very different set of circumstances, and the reasons for cooperating must have differed also. I was entering an ongoing controversy surrounding birth control methods when I approached obstetricians, midwives, and sex therapists and educators for interviews and discussions. I was not only a concerned colleague from the United States, but a vehicle for their take on the debate as well, particularly for those who were critical of the status quo. Some voiced a hope I also heard in my interviews with scientists, but far more rarely: that I, as an American, would draw attention to the situation in Japan and criticize it internationally as a lever for reform. I did also get a sample of twenty-two married couples for interviews; I interviewed the husbands, and a female Japanese collaborator interviewed their wives. Physicians, midwives, and the collaborator provided the introductions for more than half of the sample, and I think a large part of the interviewees' motivation to participate came from the nature of their relationship with the referring party—trust plus dispensing a favor as part of an ongoing web of mutual obligations. A few were eager to hear about contraception and abortion in the United States, but not as many as I had anticipated.

I think there were two factors influencing prospective interviewees that cross-canceled each other: the glamour of associating with an American versus the particularly strong taboos surrounding discussions of subjects having to do with sex. Both of these factors were far more influential then, in the mid-1970s, than now. Young Westerners complained then about being approached on the street by Japanese people for discussion, which often meant free English practice. No one fact or vignette could adequately summarize the extent of sexual repression, but suffice it to say that it was a subject that occasioned more stress than it would in most other urbanized cultures at the time.

I will admit, at risk of sounding like an eternal child, that I usually enjoyed the attention and the interaction when I was singled out in public places for conversation. Also, throughout my two-year, four-month research stint I was looking everywhere for first-person information on marital life and birth control. My eagerness in the first several months was fueled by the fear that I would end up coming home with no firsthand accounts of attitudes and behavior. Since I used my one-hour train commute to Tokyo to study materials in Japanese, curious fellow commuters surmised that I could converse in Japanese. On two or three occasions men engaged me in a chat when I was not high on the pure joy of exchanging pleasantries with the natives, so I ever so gradually moved the discussion to more personal subjects, figuring that if my partner was comfortable with the trend of the discussion I would gain some data, and if not I could get back to my reading.

I obtained both outcomes, but if I were to do it again I would not do it again. I would not recite an informed consent statement to new acquaintances as if I were reading them their Miranda rights; instead, early in the discussion I would have given them a written description of my research with an invitation to participate (including information required for human subjects protection), along with my points of contact, and then I would have gotten back to some pleasant chat. Perhaps this after-the-fact preference for a more professional, arm's-length approach comes from the reassuring knowledge that I ended up with a comfortable margin of data. Fortunately, too, while in the field I was expanding the variety of my data sources, from interviews with a wide range of specialists to treatment of relevant themes in the mass media, since advice columns and even popular comics had their own views of birth control.

The Virtue and Rewards of Reporting Results

Reporting results to those who cooperated in my research was a component of my work in Japan in both major fieldwork projects. Before leaving Japan after my laboratory study I presented my tentative results to audiences at both OBI and PERI. During fieldwork for both projects I eagerly accepted invitations to speak before professional groups, and on a few rare occasions the media aided me by devoting some attention to my research. When I conducted the interview and self-administered questionnaire studies for the birth control project, I provided participants with a self-addressed postcard to receive a report of survey results. Unfortunately I did not keep a count of the requests, but I recall responding to about twenty-five or thirty. After I returned to the United States from my fieldwork on laboratory organizations, I kept in contact with several dozen bioscience researchers and other specialists who had been particularly helpful, and in the course of correspondence offered them copies of publications in both English and Japanese that had resulted from my fieldwork.

The most difficult reporting task has always been writing up results in Japanese. I find it extremely time-consuming to write in Japanese, and writing a monograph-length report in Japanese is beyond my means in more ways than one. Nor would I ever attempt to write up information for distribution unless aided closely by a well-educated native speaker. My book on laboratory science has been translated by a small but reputable publisher in Tokyo who agreed to give me right of final review—something that is evidently hard to wrest from the bigger publishing houses. Fortunately, the editor understood my concerns, especially my fear that a ham-handed back-translation of the book's direct quotes from some prominent Japanese scientists would do them a disservice. It took several years to get out some serious reporting in Japanese of my birth control survey. A prominent obstetrician-gynecologist arranged for the Japan Family Planning Association to publish an English-language journal article of mine on condom use as a monograph in Japanese, and he did the translating. After my book based on the research finally came out, I found no takers among Japanese publishers for a Japanese edition.

I have long felt that the individuals in Japan who have gone out of their way to help me deserved some kind of reward, however modest. I was influenced by the wave of concern that rippled through the anthropology profession in the late 1960s and 1970s about how we should compensate the subjects of our research in exchange for the various ways in which we impose on them. One argument even claimed that native knowledge was a valuable commodity stolen from the locals by outsider ethnographers. The era's political ambience helped prompt attention to the issue, as did local insurgencies in Third World countries and Native American political movements. In any event, the "concern" never did translate into professional recognition for the conscientious fieldworker who shares his or her observations with the subjects of the research by publishing in the vernacular.

Those of us who work on policy-related problems do have the means for reciprocating our subjects' and colleagues' favors, however, by reporting our research results to the participants in our studies, and it has rewards beyond the intrinsic satisfaction of contributing to knowledge regarding a specific problem. My presentations to specialists invariably provided me with critiques and insights from the audience that helped me refine my arguments. The several dozen bioscience researchers and other specialists with whom I kept contact after leaving the field in 1991 provided me with more information that proved invaluable, including news of the professional fates of other members of their cohorts at OBI and PERI. By sending them copies of publications in both English and Japanese that had resulted from my fieldwork, I could show them I was still active and keep the channel open for requesting further information.

What's Japanese about All This?

If by now it looks as if there is nothing particularly unique about Japan in the dynamics I have discussed—minus the language issue—then my argument has succeeded. We should all marvel at the durability of that hoary refrain, "You'll never be truly accepted by the Japanese." The myth has probably survived because its proponents benefit from a view of Japan as impenetrably exotic, and the ambiguity of the expression "truly accepted" taps unrealistic expectations of instant intimacy. We Americans are particularly good at cultivating hopes like that. Let me instead address the specific fear that you will be denied access to the organization(s) that could help you most, or that you will be stonewalled or deceived even if you are formally admitted as a guest researcher.

No researcher is immune from such treatment in any foreign country, but I believe the danger of misunderstandings and deception decreases as a function of the congruency of goals that I believe is so important. Next in importance comes effective communication, especially foreign language skills. Strong communicative skills in Japanese are the single most important antidote for overcoming the feeling that the whole country is keeping critical information behind its back and snickering at you behind yours.

Transparency and fairness in the target organization's decision-making process play an important part as well. I have less firsthand experience with this issue than do some other Japan specialists, but I wanted to bring it up because here lies the dark side of many Japanese organizations. Ivan Hall's book catalogues and analyzes some of the worst offenders among knowledge-intensive institutions quite nicely (Hall 1998). In my own experience, OBI administrators from city hall refused to allow me to observe the institute's annual research presentation, evidently out of fear that I would leak potentially profitable information to American pharmaceutical firms. The academically oriented director and lab heads objected. I would like to believe that my allies responded out of a desire for open inquiry, but they probably also knew that my knowledge of bioscience was not extensive enough to communicate information of commercial value to anyone.

On a more serious note, the Japanese Biochemical Society tacitly refused to disclose to me the return rates on their elections that decided reviewers for government-funded research grant selection committees, despite my repeated requests. I had to content myself with published speculation about participation rates, but I also noted in print their tacit refusal to provide the information. The Ministry of Education also withheld important information regarding its track record in awarding grants.

As in any other country, such organizations will withhold information from us that they would want withheld from fellow citizens outside their cozy enclave. I can imagine some choice questions for representatives of the U.S. Department of Defense that would get you ushered briskly out of their presence. I believe that the Japanese Biochemical Society and the Ministry of Education were well aware of critical flaws in the administration of grants and were thus unwilling to divulge certain statistics to anyone, native or outsider. Such information would be available in the United States and, I would like to think, in most Western European countries also. Japanese institutions have more leeway in putting us off, but this may be changing. In 2001 the information disclosure law *(Gyōsei kikan no hoyū suru jōhō no kōkai ni kansuru hō)* came into effect. Its proponents want it to function much like the United States' Freedom of Information Act. Although bureaucrats will surely try to devise ways of blunting the new law's intent, the effort stands as a milestone in public attempts to question the status quo (Choy 1999).

The intensity of an organization's internal hierarchy will also discourage cooperation in the organization you enter for your fieldwork. First, who decides to let you in, and how? If it is an arrangement decided by fiat, underlings are going to have a hard time generating enthusiasm for the outside investigator's presence. I did not systematically reconstruct the process that went on at OBI and PERI, but I did learn that the directors consulted department heads before reaching their decisions. At the university in the United States where I conducted my three-month study, the lab director who let me in was proud of the democratic process through which he reached a decision: he submitted the issue to his postdocs and graduate students.

Lest I end this discussion of access and cooperation on a discouraging note, I also want to relate my recent very positive experience in the land of statuses and institutional affiliations. In 1995 I received a fifteen-month continuation grant from NSF to supplement and write up my laboratory ethnography. The grant gave me three months at the National Institute for Science and Technology Policy in Tokyo. In that year I also lost my academic position. Technically speaking, when I went to Tokyo the next year I was still an assistant professor in my lame duck year, but for a variety of reasons I did not want to continue using that affiliation in my dealings with Japanese colleagues. I told everyone in my professional radius that I was an independent researcher. My business card had no institutional affiliation, and I occasionally apologized when introducing myself for a card that looked like a CIA agent's. Although I was very concerned that I would fall out of everyone's radar screen, the momentum from my past activity and everyone's interest in my research topic were enough to get all the cooperation I needed and more. My colleagues and contacts were very much still there when I needed them, because they knew what my goals were, and those goals fit with their own.

A Word on Affiliation and Bias

Let me anticipate the worry that a shared orientation or overlapping goals with certain Japanese organizations will bias results. The accuracy and predictive power of our research results are insulated from such biases by rules and methods refined by generations of social scientists and by the professional consequences to us of calling the wrong shots. I have seen my own role as "telling it like it is" as a first and indispensable step toward policies for reform. My birth control research identified the obstacles to making available a broader range of contraceptive method choices to Japanese women and men, and the laboratory study identified the organizational obstacles to more creative basic research. There are scientific criteria for judging the value of my research independently of any program agenda. If Japan's induced abortion rate were to suddenly drop steeply without a change in contraceptive repertory, or remain unchanged despite the introduction of a broader range of effective contraceptive methods, my arguments would be discredited. Similarly, if a traditional, hierarchical university laboratory were to start popping out Nobel laureates, my laboratory organization studies would, deservedly, get filed in the trash can.

The hardest part for the policy-oriented researcher is threading his or her way through organizations that have minimal overlap of goals but control resources that are valuable, if not indispensable, to the research project. I cannot offer formulas for resolving those individual problems, but I do believe that dialogue on the subject among us as researchers will help us find solutions.

Note

I thank the editors of this volume and my colleague Eleanor Westney for comments and suggestions that greatly improved the quality of my contribution. A dissertation research grant from the Social Science Research Council (SSRC) supported the fieldwork for the birth control study; a Japan Foundation grant and a postdoctoral fellowship from the U.S. Public Health Service enabled write-up of the dissertation and book, respectively. NSF supported a year of fieldwork for the laboratory study, and grants from the NSF and SSRC funded follow-up visits to Japan. (My findings do not necessarily reflect the views of the NSF.)

Related Readings

Coleman, Samuel. 1983 (1991). *Family Planning in Japanese Society: Traditional Birth Control in a Modern Urban Culture.* Princeton, N.J.: Princeton University Press. (Expanded edition published 1991.)
———. 1996. "Obstacles and Opportunities in Access to Professional Work Organizations for Long-Term Fieldwork: The Case of Japanese Laboratories." *Human Organization* 55(3):334–343.
———. 1999. *Japanese Science: From the Inside.* London: Routledge. (Translated version: *Kenshō: Naze Nihon no kagakusha wa mukuwarenai no ka?* Tokyo: Bun-ichi Sōgō Shuppan, 2002.)

JETs and high school students at a school international festival with David L. McConnell (second from right).

DAVID L. MCCONNELL

JET Lag: Studying a Multilevel Program over Time

Most anthropologists of Japan have committed numerous mistakes during the course of their fieldwork. In my own case, I inadvertently committed a serious error before I even set foot in Japan, simply by writing a letter to an acquaintance in the organization I was hoping to study.

At the time I was a doctoral student in Stanford University's anthropology of education program, and my dissertation focus was the cultural form and meaning of internationalization in Japan. As a window on this topic, I chose the Japan Exchange and Teaching (JET) Program, a high-profile government attempt to "import diversity" in the form of thousands of college graduates from mostly English-speaking countries. Begun in 1987, with an annual budget of over $400 million by 1999, this program sends foreign youth to local offices of education and secondary schools throughout the country, where most serve as assistants to Japanese teachers of English. My overall goal was to assess the "closed system" image of Japanese society by examining how Japanese administrators, teachers, and students coped with these reform-minded foreigners at the level of face-to-face interaction (McConnell 2000).

From a methodological standpoint I had a lot going for me. For one, I had "team-taught" English for two years in junior high schools in rural Iwate Prefecture and thus knew my way around Japanese schools. My conversational Japanese, while not stellar, was adequate for interviewing. Moreover, I was extremely fortunate to have received a Fulbright grant, which provided an affiliation with the School of Education at Kyoto University and, more important, a mentor, Kobayashi Tetsuya. Finally, an acquaintance from college, Campbell,[1] had just been chosen as one of four foreigners to work in the arm of the Ministry of Home Affairs known as CLAIR (Council of Local Authorities for International Relations). This last development elated me, as CLAIR was the coordinating office for the entire JET Program! I dashed off a letter to Campbell asking how she and her office might assist in my project.

Arriving in Japan with my wife and two-year-old son about a month later, I asked the Fulbright office to arrange a courtesy call at CLAIR. Campbell was out of the office that day, but another American, Thompson, greeted me graciously. It was not long, however, before he raised the matter of the "smoking letter." As it turned out, Campbell had shown the letter to her boss, Fujisawa, who had categorically rejected the possibility of CLAIR's cooperation with my study. Worse still, they had fought over it, and Fujisawa had forbidden Campbell to contact me. Thompson went on to disclose that CLAIR staff members were extremely sensitive about "outside research." They felt the JET Program had already been unfairly criticized in both the Japanese and foreign media. Moreover, earlier in the year someone had passed out questionnaires at a JET conference without CLAIR's permission. While Thompson politely offered any assistance he could personally provide, the message was all too clear: CLAIR as an organization was off limits to outside researchers.[2]

My ill-advised letter only compounded the formidable methodological challenges I already faced. The sheer breadth and scope of the JET Program made the traditional anthropological practice of participant observation highly problematic. The JET Program could not be isolated in one geographic location. At the national level alone, the principal actors included three sponsoring ministries (home affairs, foreign affairs, and education), CLAIR, the embassies of participating countries, and the Japanese consulates abroad. To these structural complexities were added the realities of implementation as the JET Program unfolded in dozens of prefectures, hundreds of district boards of education, and thousands of secondary schools across the country. To make matters worse, my arrival in the fall of 1988 meant that I had missed the crucial first year of implementation and thus needed to reconstruct what had transpired. Yet I had just been told the one office that had any semblance of general control—over budget, counseling, the placement of participants in local governments, and program-wide policies— was not receptive to my project.

The next three months were frustrating in the extreme. My wife and I discovered firsthand the difficulties foreigners can face in finding affordable housing in urban markets, and my son's own culture shock and slow adjustment to Japan affected us all. I learned quickly that my own ability to focus on my research was to some extent dependent on the adjustment of my family. My mentor arranged an interview with a curriculum specialist in a local board of education, but his answers to my questions were guarded, and it was clear he did not want to talk again. I called a friend the curriculum specialist had recommended and was utterly embarrassed at my bumbling telephone Japanese. I approached a group of foreigners working privately in Kyoto as assistant language teachers (hereafter ALTs), but they flatly rejected my request to study their program, fearing that I might give the information gained to Japanese officials and jeopardize their jobs. Mostly, I fretted away in my office, rationalizing my time there as much needed for brushing up on Japanese and reading about my topic. Clearly, this was shaping up to be a much more difficult task than I had anticipated.

Finally, I did what most graduate students do when the going gets tough. I sought out one of my advisors, Thomas Rohlen, who had just arrived as director of the Stanford Center in Kyoto. Rohlen reminded me that when the goal of research is the elaboration of cultural meaning, as it was in my study, then every barrier is a potential insight. He pointed out that Tokyo bureaucrats were cautious about people like me precisely because the origins of the JET Program lay in foreign pressure on Japan to open up its society. The last thing they wanted was for some outside researcher to pronounce the JET Program a failure. He reminded me of the adage: anthropology is really nothing more than going to new cultures and getting headaches—but the key lies in keeping track of the headaches.

This advice at least made me feel better, and I resolved to keep careful notes about the fieldwork process itself. It still did not solve the practical problem of how to gain access to the Japanese administrators, teachers, and

126 | DAVID L. MCCONNELL

students involved in the JET Program. Only gradually did it dawn on me that there was no silver bullet. If my goal was to capture the multiple and competing ways in which Japanese coped with foreigners, I would have to use an eclectic approach. In fact, such a methodology would complement my theoretical approach, which stressed that implementing the JET Program was like playing a game of three-dimensional tic-tac-toe; it involved both horizontal and vertical tensions and cleavages.[3] In effect, I decided to turn the idea that bureaucracy is not a monolithic entity into a methodological advantage by trying to negotiate access to different levels of the JET Program independently. The rest of my essay describes this process.

National Level

Because the sponsoring ministries were not receptive to any type of participant observation, the biggest challenge at the national level was to get beyond the official, or *tatemae,* version of the JET Program. The Ministry of Foreign Affairs, which was in charge of recruiting JET participants abroad and emphasized the diplomatic goals of the program, proved to be almost impossible to crack during my initial period of fieldwork. Quite simply, I knew of no one who could provide a good introduction. I had applied to the JET Program as a backup in case my Fulbright application was rejected; thus I did have the experience of participating in the interview process and had even talked with a high-ranking official in the San Francisco consulate. But penetrating the Ministry of Foreign Affairs in Tokyo was a different matter. While I was able to arrange one interview with an official in the Second Cultural Affairs Division by calling "out of the blue," the interview was hurried and the answers to most of my questions were polite but evasive. After two years, I had very little firsthand information about this ministry's role in the JET Program.

Given the conservative reputation of the Ministry of Education, I expected a similar reception there. In an incredible stroke of luck, however, my mentor actually knew the very person, Wada Minoru, in the Ministry of Education who was in charge of the JET Program. Kobayashi made a personal visit to Kasumigaseki in Tokyo to ask Wada to help me out, and I soon received a letter inviting me to come and see him at the ministry. I met Wada in the crammed and very "public" space of the Upper Secondary School Division, and we talked for over an hour. Partly as a result of Kobayashi's introduction and partly due to Wada's personality, it was immediately clear to me that he was willing to offer his frank assessments of the program and that his knowledge of the program and its antecedents was extensive. I was able to interview him twice more before leaving Japan, and he put me in touch with several other Ministry of Education officials.

In a curious twist, as part of its campaign to encourage local governments to get on the bandwagon of internationalization, the Ministry of Home Affairs had taken over official control of the JET Program, even though 90 percent of JET participants worked in public schools. As a result, the cooperation of CLAIR was absolutely essential to my project. In some ways CLAIR was not at all akin to the tight-knit Japanese work groups described in much of the social science literature on Japan; instead, it better corresponded to what John Campbell has called "pseudo-*uchi* agencies" (that is, pseudo-insider agencies) that cut across ministerial lines (Campbell 1993a, 53). In 1988, CLAIR was staffed not only by Ministry of Home Affairs bureaucrats but also by representatives from local government, individuals from the private sector, and four foreigners called "program coordinators" who served as buffers and liaisons between the Japanese staff and the hundreds (soon to be thousands) of JET participants.

Because of my earlier faux pas, I knew I needed to get permission from Japanese officials at the very top. After consulting Rohlen, I finally settled on a "letter bombardment scheme" to try to bring as much pressure as possible to bear on the decision. I asked both the dean of the School of Education at Stanford University and the executive director of the Fulbright Association to send letters to the secretary-general of CLAIR; then, my mentor, Kobayashi, followed up with a phone call. This approach finally got CLAIR's attention, and I was asked to send a research proposal in Japanese along with a list of specific requests. A subsequent phone call by Kobayashi produced a negative reply to most of my requests for official documents (such as the percentage of participants who had left the program early) but an affirmative for being able to interview several CLAIR officials in Tokyo. To my relief, I also learned that Fujisawa had been transferred in April; his replacement, Noguchi, would serve as the gatekeeper for my visits.

This foot in the door was all I needed. Over the next eighteen months, I made three trips to CLAIR, and each time I was able to spend several hours on site, interviewing different persons and acquiring at least some program-related documents. By the last trip I had learned that it paid handsomely to ask if there was a quieter place to talk than the very public (and cramped) space in the office where casual guests are usually received (the reason I gave was that my Japanese was poor and the background noise made it hard to understand). Even so, I found that the Japanese staff members were quite cautious about what they said during my initial visit; on subsequent visits, however, the degree of disclosure increased. By contrast, once I was able to convince the "program coordinators" of the legitimacy of my research, they often divulged a great deal about the behind-the-scenes operations at CLAIR. In one instance I remember almost cringing as an American woman I interviewed at CLAIR blasted the Japanese staff in full view (but not earshot) of the entire office. By moving back and forth between details divulged by both Japanese officials and the program coordinators, I was able to painstakingly reconstruct events and policy decisions that had occurred during the first year of the program.

Having made contact with bureaucrats from both the Ministry of Education and the Ministry of Home Affairs, I was now ready to ask for another big favor: permission to attend several of the national-level conferences. I knew that the Tokyo Orientation, the Mid-Year Block Conferences, and the Renewers' Conference brought together all the major players in the JET Program (except students) for several intense days of seminars on topics such as team teaching, office relations, life in Japan, and the meaning of internationalization. My request, however, revealed the extent of ministerial compartmentalization. Wada would approve only the two days sponsored by the Ministry of Education; the same was true for the secretary-general of CLAIR. I was unable to attend the last day because it was sponsored by the Association of JET (AJET, a support group for JET participants that was initially viewed by the Japanese staff as a "quasi-union"), and polling all their members in order to give me permission simply was not feasible. After a long wait, approval came from the first two quarters with the stipulation that I could not take pictures nor interfere with those in charge of the program.

Once permission had been granted, however, I was free to roam around the hotel, attending the concurrent sessions and talking informally with people as I pleased. I cornered Japanese officials in the halls to ask for clarification on this or that point; I introduced myself to ALTs or to Japanese teachers in attendance and then hung out with them at lunch or in the evenings.

Mostly I remember my hand was sore from scribbling notes nonstop for hours on end. I remember, too, that these conferences were usually dominated by the JET participants, while Japanese teachers and administrators largely remained silent. Overall, I found I was getting plenty of material about the JET participants' reactions to their reception, but precious little about the private feelings, or *honne,* of Japanese teachers and local administrators.

Prefectural Level

Indeed, now that my momentum was increasing at the national level, my worries shifted full circle. I became increasingly afraid that I was missing the crucial realities of implementation in boards of education and local schools. If nothing else, an anthropological approach to social policy ought to be able to move beyond the plans and guidelines of policymakers to see how those ideas were supported, reinterpreted, or subverted by people downstream. I began to wonder if I would ever be able to produce a full-bodied account of local responses to the JET Program.

Once again I was saved by my mentor. Sensing that I was at an impasse, Kobayashi arranged for a meeting with the head *(buchō)* of the guidance division at a prefectural board of education in the Kansai region. He even accompanied me to the meeting, and of course I let him do all the talking. In turn, the *buchō* introduced me to Sato, the English curriculum specialist overseeing the JET Program, and Tanabe, a career civil servant. At the end of the meeting, Tanabe asked me for my wish list. I asked if I could visit some schools, attend prefectural activities connected with the program, and meet with Sato and Tanabe over coffee once a month for updates. They said they would be in touch with me soon.

Only later did I realize how perfect this introduction was. Not only was Kobayashi of higher status than any of us, but he knew both me and the *buchō* personally. In addition, the *buchō* was a level above Sato and Tanabe's boss, the section chief; he was someone whom they would not want to let down. Most important, I found out that Kobayashi was owed a huge favor by the board of education as a result of assistance he had provided in their campaign to make prefectural schools more competitive on university entrance exams.

It was as if the floodgates had suddenly opened. Tanabe called the following week to let me know he had made appointments at six prefectural schools and three district offices of education and to ask if I could meet him and Sato for dinner. Joined by a friend of theirs, Ueda, who taught English at a local high school, we met at a small but intimate drinking establishment.

Once seated in a semiprivate tatami room with beer and hot snacks, Tanabe and Sato warmed to the task of sharing recollections of their first year of coordinating the JET Program. I instinctively liked both of them and returned home on the late train that evening vowing to let them be my eyes and ears in understanding Japanese prefectural responses to the JET Program.

The school visitations proved to be fascinating, as the differences in the way I was received told me much about the makeup of each school and its approach to internationalization. At the first school I visited, a prefectural showpiece for internationalization, the principal himself guided me through the school, took me to both team-taught and solo-taught English classes, let me mingle with students, and arranged for me to interview the entire English faculty for an hour in English! At the next school, known for the high entrance exam scores of its students, I never met any teachers or students. I was introduced to the ALT by the vice-principal, and we were escorted to a private room to "talk as long as you like." At yet a third school, the teacher taking the call from Tanabe had forgotten to relay the message to the vice-principal. He had no idea I was coming! I just happened to arrive at the same time as two Japanese teachers from Aichi Prefecture who had come to receive advice on how to be a successful "base school" for an ALT! Clearly put out and muttering about having to accommodate a *tobikomi* (someone who just pops in unannounced), the vice-principal nevertheless let me stay and gave a fascinating talk geared primarily at the Japanese teachers on the pros and cons of hosting a foreigner.

These initial school visits allowed me to exchange phone numbers with a number of Japanese teachers and ALTs whom I was able to contact later for one-on-one interviews. In most cases I took the person to a coffee shop or a bar, treated them to a drink, and worked through an interview protocol I had constructed. In this way I was able to meet teachers of all stripes, from those who saw the ALTs as a virus to those who saw them as saviors. Similarly, I talked with ALTs who ran the gamut from those with strictly a "tourist mentality" to those who practically rejected their own culture in the rush to embrace Japan. In all cases, I promised anonymity to those whom I interviewed.

The monthly meetings with Sato and Tanabe at the coffee shop were invaluable as a chance to reconstruct "critical incidents" that had occurred prior to my arrival, such as a serious sexual harassment case and several premature departures of ALTs. I was also able to ask questions about prefectural policy that had arisen in previous conversations with Japanese teachers or ALTs. In the interest of trying to encourage candidness, I decided not to use a tape recorder, a decision I deeply regretted later. My notes were insufficient, and I quickly learned how fallible the human memory is.

Over the next eighteen months, then, I developed good rapport with Sato and Tanabe. They included me in all prefectural JET Program activities, including the initial orientation, the briefings for base schools and host institutions, special Japanese classes they taught for ALTs, and the team-teaching seminars held at local schools. These team-teaching seminars usually involved a "demonstration class" *(kenkyū jugyō)* followed by discussion among teachers and comments from the curriculum specialist. For the most part I was able to be a "fly on the wall" and then follow up in subsequent interviews with ALTs, Japanese teachers, or Sato himself.

After a while, I found it was easy to get access to events that involved the JET participants themselves. But I also wanted to see how prefectural officials described their expectations to representatives from schools and localities in an all-Japanese setting. I asked Sato and Tanabe for permission to attend such a meeting, and to my surprise they agreed. Their solution was to place me at the speakers' table next to them and to introduce me as a "consultant." While my presence may have changed the tone of the meeting, I did witness a somewhat icy exchange between Sato and a representative from a small village who felt the prefecture was being overly controlling.

Fieldwork in Japan, as elsewhere, often involves tension between juggling the role of researcher and that of friend since our research is not so easily separated from our lives (see Small 1997). Gradually, I became a confidante and even a sounding board for Sato and Tanabe, and on one occasion, after an especially late night drinking, Sato invited me to spend the night at his house. At the same time, I had become more than a casual acquaintance with a number of ALTs, and I sometimes joined them for informal get-togethers as well. Finally, I had befriended a number of Japanese teachers, including several who were union activists and opposed to the board of education. Obviously, my varied group of "friends" did not always see eye to eye, and I learned early the importance of remaining "officially" neutral on key points of contention while becoming a bit of a chameleon (i.e., lending a seemingly sympathetic ear to each individual) in private conversations.

To be sure, trying to juggle multiple friendships and multiple points of access did not always work out smoothly. For example, just after I had succeeded in gaining an invitation to attend the prefectural conference of the teachers' union, Sato called to invite me to travel to Tokyo with him to greet the new prefectural ALTs at the national-level orientation. To my dismay, I was forced to cancel my participation in the teachers' union conference. I was also totally unprepared for the suicide shortly after Christmas of one of the ALTs whom I had gotten to know quite well. Her death deeply shook everyone connected with the JET Program, and I felt quite guilty when I later asked questions of Sato and Tanabe about their handling of the event, as if I was somehow reducing her death to mere "data."

In addition, I struggled to introduce reciprocity into the relationship. When CLAIR was unable to supply Sato and Tanabe with their requested number of ALTs, I was able to introduce a friend of mine to the board of education. When a British museologist visited Kyoto, Tanabe asked me to serve as interpreter for the day, which I gladly did. But on balance I know I took more from the two of them than they received.

The School Level

While the one-shot school visits arranged by the board of education were useful, I still needed an extended, inside look at the "base school" experience from the point of view of both an ALT and Japanese teachers and students. I had a start on this angle by virtue of attending a professional conference for Japanese teachers of English. I was the only foreigner in attendance, and when I introduced myself to one of the speakers, a junior high school teacher from Osaka, he enthusiastically invited me to his school. As the head English teacher and head of the ninth-grade homeroom teachers, he provided wonderful access to the principal, to other teachers, and to students over the course of several visits. His school was particularly interesting to me because it had a significant problem with student violence; in fact, on my first visit, I encountered students setting off firecrackers in the language lab and letting the air out of the tires of the teachers' cars! In another case I joined a "research group" that had formed among high school teachers in the Osaka area to discuss team teaching. We met once a month at a school that hosted five ALTs and then adjourned for dinner and drinks.

As helpful as the above visits were, I finally asked Sato if he could arrange for me to visit on a regular basis a high school that hosted an ALT. He promised to look into it and called a few days later to ask if his old school, Nishikawa High School, would be all right. He had arranged a meeting for me with the principal. Elated at the good news, I hurried out to a prestigious department store and bought a big basket of expensive cookies to give to the teachers to share with each other.

The limits of board of education authority over local schools became clear to me, however, as soon as I arrived in the principal's office and offered the cookies, along with my profuse thanks. It turned out that I had misinterpreted Sato's words; the decision to admit me to the school had not yet been made. The vice-principal and principal were very reluctant to accept my presence in the school because they were worried about opposition from other teachers. They asked detailed questions about my project and my expectations. I assured them that I would only visit two or three days a week and would be as nonintrusive as possible. It would require much discussion, they said. They would get back to me soon. About a week later I received a call from the head English teacher, Hayano, saying that I had been allowed to enter the school, with the understanding that this was not a school-wide decision but had been arranged on an individual basis with him. In other words, I had to remain under his close supervision. Two weeks later I was introduced at the morning meeting, and much fuss was made over the cookies I had graciously brought for everyone. No one mentioned that they were now three weeks old!

In any event, I was given a desk used by part-time teachers and allowed free run of the school. I met McLain, the school's ALT from Scotland, explained my project, and was relieved to find that she was not at all upset about having a researcher watching over her shoulder. Such was not the case with the other English teachers, however. While several extended a blanket invitation to observe their classes, most kept a very low profile, and only over time was I able to gain their trust. Hayano went out of his way to include me in school-wide events, especially those involving the English teachers. I sat in on weekly curriculum meetings of the English teachers, attended their annual holiday party, graded the English entrance exam to Kyoto University with some of them, and attended a session on career guidance sponsored by a top-ranked *juku* (exam preparation or tutoring academy), to mention a few. I did make a point to visit Nishikawa on the two days a week McLain was scheduled to visit other schools. In this way, I was able to forge relationships with students and teachers that were independent of McLain. At the end of the year the English teachers even invited me to attend their "evaluation meeting" to discuss how team teaching with McLain was progressing.

In addition to interviews and participant observation, two other data collection strategies bear mentioning. First, I let many people know I was searching for newspaper articles on the JET Program and on internationalization. By the time I left Japan I had compiled an entire booklet of clippings from both English-language and Japanese newspapers. Second, I was also able to travel to a number of other prefectures—Kumamoto, Shiga, Hyogo, Iwate, and Toyama, among others—to conduct interviews with local administrators and teachers. While I did not enjoy the degree of access I had with Sato and Tanabe, I was able to learn something about the different structures for receiving ALTs (ukeirekata).

At some point in my fieldwork it suddenly dawned on me that my initial concerns were misplaced. Now, the JET Program seemed to be everywhere. The real danger lay in being overwhelmed with data and in keeping track and making sense of the multiple and competing points of view.

Assessing the Learning Curve

I returned to Stanford for a frantic year of writing and gained a new appreciation for the difficulty of sifting through fieldnotes. By now, I had thirty-four thick, yellow pads scribbled full of notes from interviews, team-teaching classes, after-the-fact summaries of important conversations, and theoretical memos to myself, all in the order in which they had occurred in the field. I kicked myself for not organizing and summarizing my fieldnotes at regular intervals while in Japan. Not only did I have to sift through and analyze mounds of data, but since my graduate funding would run out at the end of the year, I had to have the dissertation written in nine months. I wish I could say it went smoothly. While I was able to defend successfully, I would have to characterize the four years from dissertation proposal to finished thesis as a progressive lowering of my sights from National Book Award to a fervent hope that no one would read my dissertation.

The dissertation defense exposed several weaknesses in my data, especially a failure to take into account the "learning curve" and how the program was the result of evolving, as well as original, intentions. Failing to find a teaching job that year, I landed in a postdoctoral fellowship at the Program on U.S.-Japan Relations at Harvard. Once again, serendipity intervened: the Japanese consulate in Boston asked me to serve on the JET selection committee. Not only did this provide an "insider's view" of the selection process, it also allowed me to meet key officials in the Ministry of Foreign Affairs, whom I was able to interview later. The year also provided an opportunity to focus on the "big issues" in conversations with people whose work I had read but never dreamed I could meet: Ronald Dore, Merry White, Carol Gluck, William Cummings. This in itself was inspiration enough to keep the project alive and a book in sight.

Over the next eight years I was able to return to Japan four times (1993, 1995, 1996, 1999) for intensive follow-up interviews at all levels. The first three trips lasted three to four weeks each. Even by 1993, many of the people I knew had rotated to new positions. At first, this worried me, but in fact, tracking down those who had left the JET Program proved to be one of the most fruitful strategies I employed in the entire study. For example, I tracked down a former secretary-general and several program coordinators who were at CLAIR during the early years of the program. Not only did I interview Wada in his new job as a university professor, I even caught up with him during a summer trip to Bucknell University, leaving him shaking his head at my strange persistence in trying to understand the Ministry of Education's role in the JET Program. At the prefectural and school levels I was able to return for several long nights of socializing with Sato and Tanabe, Hayano, and other teachers. Altogether, these interviews were among the fullest and frankest I conducted.

The return trips also allowed me to track down several new people to interview, including four key bureaucrats and educators who were involved in the original negotiations about JET prior to the "Ron-Yasu" (Reagan-Nakasone) summit in 1986; an openly gay program coordinator who had a unique perspective on CLAIR; officials in the German, American, and Canadian embassies in Tokyo; and a former ALT and AJET chair, Robert Juppe, who had been hired as an ALT advisor in the Ministry of Education. Juppe met with me numerous times, and his long-term association with the program afforded me a different view of the behind-the-scenes operations in the Ministry of Education and indeed of the entire program. On each trip I also made an "official" visit to CLAIR and met with senior Japanese staff and program coordinators, most of whom were very generous with their time and insights. The negative media reports about JET had pretty much disappeared by this time, and I sensed a new openness about the program and a feeling that it had come of age.

In retrospect, the long-term time horizon of the project had many advantages. It afforded me an opportunity, first of all, to move back and forth between data and theory and thus see more clearly those dimensions of Japanese approaches that were contested and those that were taken for granted. It also allowed me to achieve a balance between breadth and depth in capturing a complex social policy. I was able to benefit from critical feedback from many people who read shorter articles I wrote or papers I delivered about the JET Program. Nevertheless, by the end of the decade I have to admit I was somewhat "jet lagged" by the tens of thousands of miles of travel by plane, train, taxi, and bus. The strengths of the slow but steady "hedgehog approach" notwithstanding, I was ready to move on to something new.

Notes

I would like to express my deepest appreciation to the students, teachers, administrators, and participants in the JET Program, whose assistance made this research project possible. For monetary support and sponsorship, I thank the Fulbright Program of the Japan-U.S. Education Commission; the School of Education at Kyoto University; the Japan Fund of the Institute of International Studies at Stanford University; the Spencer Foundation of the Woodrow Wilson National Fellowship Foundation; the Program on U.S.-Japan Relations and the Pacific Basin Research Center at Harvard University; The College of Wooster's Henry Luce III Fund for Distinguished Scholarship; the Great Lakes College Association's Japan Fund; and the Northeast Asia Council of the Association for Asian Studies.

1. I have used pseudonyms for all persons identified by only first or last name.

2. This stance was confirmed later by a Japanese professor, now at Tokyo University, who had tried to gain access to CLAIR. She was flatly denied.

3. My approach draws heavily on Thomas Rohlen's framework for analyzing postwar educational politics. Rohlen views each administrative level as a distinct sociocultural subsystem with its own set of priorities and its own manner of participating in a top-down intervention (Rohlen 1984). For a related account of the complexities of defining the field of study, see William W. Kelly's article on Japanese baseball (Kelly 1999).

Related Readings

McConnell, David L. 1996. "Education for Global Integration in Japan: A Case Study of the JET Program." *Human Organization* 55(4):446–457.
———. 1999. "Coping with Diversity: The 'Achilles Heel' of Japanese Education?" In Gerald LeTendre, ed., *Competitor or Ally? Japan's Role in American Educational Debates.* New York: Falmer Press, 47–64.

————. 2000. *Importing Diversity: Inside Japan's JET Program.* Berkeley: University of California Press.

————. 2002. "It's Glacial: Incrementalism and Japan's Reform of Foreign Language Education." In Gary DeCoker, ed., *National Standards and School Reform in Japan and the United States.* New York: Teachers College Press, 123–140.

McConnell, David L., and Jackson P. Bailey. 1999. "Power in Ambiguity: The Shido Shuji and Japanese Educational Innovation." In Susan O. Long, ed., *Lives in Motion: Composing Circles of Self and Community in Japan.* Ithaca, N.Y.: Cornell East Asia Series, 63–88.

David T. Johnson building research relationships with prosecutors.

DAVID T. JOHNSON

Getting in and Getting along in the Prosecutors Office

From 1992 to 1995, I spent a thousand days in Japan doing research about the prosecution of crime. This chapter is organized around three challenges I faced while conducting that study: getting in to the research site, getting along with my research subjects, and getting close enough to prosecutors to explain how they shape the Japanese way of justice (D. Johnson 2002).

Getting In

I arrived in Kobe on August 15, 1992, intending to study Japanese prosecutors *(kenji)* ethnographically, something no one had done before. It took five months before I actually began.

This protracted preliminary period started when a professor at Kobe University wrote a letter to the chief *(kenjisei)* of the Kobe District Prosecutors Office (KPO), introducing me and my research goals, asking for permission to visit the office, and stating that he would telephone in the near future to follow up on our request. The letter suggested that the KPO treat me as it did the legal apprentices *(shihō shūshūsei)* who rotated in and out of the office at four-month intervals.[1]

The chief agreed to consider this proposal and instructed me to call on Mr. Ono (a pseudonym), the "instructing prosecutor" *(shidō gakari kenji)* in charge of the legal apprentices. I telephoned Ono to arrange the date, and on October 2, 1992, made the first of some two hundred visits to the KPO. Ono was then in his mid-thirties, a ten-year veteran, and one of the procuracy's rising stars. He became my primary handler throughout the Kobe phase of research.

During our first meeting, Ono and I talked for about two hours, moving from self-introductions, favorite foods, preferred beverages, and sports interests, to family background, educational history, and marital status, to (finally) research goals and needs. In response to this interrogation, I told Ono the same story I provided all prosecutors in the months that followed: I am an American graduate student interested in Japanese law and society, and I want to understand the role prosecutors play in both. I also explained why I wanted to do participant observation and open-ended interviews in the KPO, justifying my request by noting that Japanese police had been the subject of numerous field studies but that prosecutors had received barely any academic attention. Ono said little in response to these requests. Instead, at the conclusion of this visit, he gave me a few brochures about the office, instructed me to call him in two weeks, and saw me to the door.

My follow-up call also failed to generate a clear reply to the request for access. It did, however, produce a second appointment, one month after the first. On November 2, Ono related two notable developments. First, although the Kobe executives were considering my request, it would probably "take a while" before they decided either way. This was unsurprising, for I knew that in a bureaucracy like the procuracy, no single prosecutor could make this decision on his own. It seemed significant, however, that the KPO had forwarded the research request, together with my mentor's letter of introduction, to executives in the Ministry of Justice for higher-level "consultation and approval" *(kessai).* At the time, I knew two truths about the ministry: prosecutors run it, and they are wary of outside scrutiny. I also knew that the key to access for Walter Ames, who studied Japanese police in the 1970s, had been "official permission . . . from the supreme authority—the National Police Agency" (Ames 1981, xi). Ono's second point was more discouraging. While agreeing that prosecutors are important but understudied, Ono said that conducting research inside the office would be "difficult" because prosecutors are obligated to protect the privacy of suspects, victims, and witnesses. He asked me to understand their position and saw me to the door with the same request he had made on my first visit a month earlier: to telephone again in two weeks. I parted with a plea to accept my research request. The incessant tick-tock of my Fulbright fellowship clock was growing louder by the day.

On Ono's invitation, I returned to the KPO three weeks later. There was little to report. Ono had urged the Kobe chief to answer quickly, but neither he nor the Ministry of Justice had yet responded. He again warned that I could be denied access altogether, told me to wait patiently, and promised to phone when he heard from his superiors.

I did not wait for his call. Instead, I phoned Ono several times in subsequent weeks to ask for updates. Eventually—three months after my mentor's original inquiry—Ono asked me to come to the office again, together with my mentor, so that we could meet the chief. We did, whereupon the chief granted access, albeit without explaining why it took months to make a decision that took minutes in a California prosecutors office (see below). My request to begin research immediately, in the middle of December, met with an authoritative suggestion that mid-January would be better because the office is busy at the end of a year and slow at the beginning of one.

Gaining access to prosecutors was the most critical factor in the success of my research. I was given that access on four conditions. First, I needed to keep secret the names of all persons encountered in the office, unless I gained permission to do otherwise. Second, I promised to submit one copy of my completed dissertation to the head of the General Affairs Bureau of the KPO. Prosecutors insisted on this condition in order to "avoid making errors about matters of fact" before wider publication, but agreed that they had no right to edit or censor my work. Third, I was not to interfere with daily life in the office. Most significant, I was permitted to move freely in the offices where Ono and the legal apprentices worked, but could contact other prosecutors in the KPO only through Ono. In the beginning, this gave him control over the people I could contact and the information I could collect. As it turned out, however, having my own "handler" had a thick silver lining, for in addition to his official obligation to control my activities, Ono gradually acquired a personal obligation to help advance my research. Though I never gained freedom to roam the halls and offices at will, I did acquire substantial autonomy, a development Ono encouraged because it saved him the trouble of serving as my go-between.

My difficulty getting in the Kobe office can be illustrated by contrasting it with an analogous experience in California. In July 1993 I returned to Berkeley to do comparative research among prosecutors in Alameda County. Getting in was almost effortless. A Berkeley professor called the local district attorney to explain my research proposal. Two days later we visited the deputy chief. Unlike Mr. Ono, he showed little interest in me or my research. By the conclusion of our thirty-minute chat I had been granted complete access to all people and practices in the office, including sensitive backstage activities such as plea bargaining. In the weeks that followed I learned that these American prosecutors were far more accessible (and candid) than their Kobe counterparts.

Ono gave two reasons to explain why the KPO let me in at all. First, the Kobe chief occupied a post that was off the elite path for prosecutors, and given his age and standing in his cohort, he stood little chance of boarding the elite train that circles, for the most part, the Ministry of Justice and the Supreme Public Prosecutors Office. Thus, Ono surmised, the chief probably believed that my research could do his career little harm. Second, Kobe was the chief's own "kingdom," and in matters like this (though certainly not in everything) he had considerable autonomy. At the same time, Ono said, if executive prosecutors had opposed my research, the Kobe chief would have had no choice but to comply with their directive. Thus, elite prosecutors could veto my proposal but could not force Kobe to accept it. In the end, the executives who reviewed my request neither approved nor disapproved it, thereby absolving themselves of formal responsibility for any unforeseen, deleterious consequences. As in the rest of Japan's elite bureaucracy, so in the procuracy: officials are evaluated through *shittenshugi* (the demerit system). Excellent performance is not so much rewarded as mistakes are punished, and the people who rise to the top are those with the most unblemished records (Miyamoto 1994). According to Ono, the consultations between KPO and the Ministry of Justice resembled a game of hot potato, with each side doing its best to ensure that the other would be seen holding the tuber of responsibility if I arrived at unacceptably critical conclusions.

Getting Along

Although getting in the Kobe office was troublesome and time-consuming, getting along with prosecutors—and gaining their trust and candor—were far more formidable tasks. To be sure, Ono's office was a prime place in which to observe a prosecutor at work. His room had three desks and a table. The prosecutor sat at the largest desk, facing the door with his back to a wall-length window. At a table directly in front of him sat suspects, guards, witnesses, and legal apprentices, depending on the occasion, and to his right was an administrative assistant who, among other duties, took dictation from the prosecutor during interrogations of the accused. I occupied a vacant desk to the prosecutor's left, from where I could hear conversations, watch interactions, and engage participants in conversation. However, getting along required more than having a place in the prosecutors' space. I also had to confront four practical issues faced by most field researchers: stance and style, factions and closed doors, language difficulties, and the researcher as subject of influence.

Stance and Style

The first issue was what "stance" to adopt toward prosecutors (Lofland and Lofland 1984). Field researchers speak with two voices on this subject, one advocating trust and the other suggesting suspicion. The ubiquitous Japanese distinction between *tatemae* and *honne* seemed to recommend a suspicious stance. *Tatemae* is the "official story," a statement that spells out the way things should be while veiling the fact that reality is otherwise. *Honne* designates the underlying truth—the real intention, fact, or essence. Officials in Japan often distinguish between the two when explaining and justifying their own behavior or analyzing the explanations of others. The ability to juggle this pair without conflict is "considered the mark of a true adult," and bureaucrats who inappropriately reveal *honne*—especially to outsiders— can be harshly criticized by their colleagues (Miyamoto 1994, 176). Many Japanese—defense attorneys, judges, journalists, defendants, ex-convicts, academics, and even some prosecutors—urged me to be suspicious of official accounts because prosecutors routinely manage appearances in ways that rationalize their interests and reflect well on themselves and their office.

In the initial stages of research I knew so little of the prosecutor *honne* that I had little choice but to adopt a mostly trusting stance. It was difficult to disbelieve an official account without evidence to contradict it, and for the first few months I had little disconfirming data. More importantly, even mild distrust seemed likely to make already wary prosecutors all the more guarded. So instead of suspicion I listened with faith that whatever I heard would instruct, either about the way things are or about the way prosecutors want me to believe they are. Over time I became able to test what I heard with what I learned through direct observations. As a result, the longer I stayed in the office the more I shifted to a stance of suspicion. By the six-month mark I came to recognize in my fieldnotes the same "debunking motif" that has been attributed to sociology's "built in procedure of looking for levels of reality other than those given in official interpretations" (Berger 1963, 38). The evidence I gathered does not discredit all official versions of reality, but it does reveal several claims to be exaggerated or false (D. Johnson 2002).

In addition to a stance, I also had to develop a style—a way of presenting myself so as to keep the flow of information coming (Lofland and Lofland 1984). I selected a straightforward style that changed little over time. First, since threatening prosecutors' beliefs, accounts, or self-confidence seemed likely to generate less rather than more disclosure, in most field situations I judged and argued as little as possible. Being nonthreatening extended also to dress. I donned the same suit-and-tie uniform worn by all male prosecutors. Second, in conversation I was as direct as I could be without sounding rude or coarse. It is well known that in communicating with each other, most Japanese favor the indirect and implicit over the direct and explicit. Though the conventions of Japanese forced me to be more oblique than I ordinarily am in English, I spoke as directly and explicitly as possible, a strategy that made a few prosecutors noticeably uncomfortable but that seemed to facilitate candor better than a more thoroughly "Japanese" style. Finally, when I was with prosecutors and we encountered outsiders, whether lawyers, judges, or police, I tried to signal that my first loyalty was to prosecutors by (among other things) refusing to betray backstage information. This style, premised as it was on "the defensive measures" of loyalty, discipline, and circumspection, provided protection against the common tendency for insiders such as prosecutors to be suspicions of outsiders like myself (Goffman 1963, 212).

Factions and Closed Doors

Getting along in the prosecutors office required managing two threats to access: factions and closed doors.

All organizations have discord, dissension, and other cleavages of conflict, but in Japan such fault lines can be especially difficult to see (Pharr 1990). The procuracy's *tatemae* asserts that the organization, from the prosecutor general at the top to the lowest clerk in the pecking order, is a unified, harmonious whole, and the first point stressed in many scholarly accounts of the procuracy is the "principle of prosecutorial unity." Although the organization does have more solidarity than the American offices I studied, it did not take long to realize that the *tatemae* disguises considerable discord.

Friction between Japanese prosecutors arises out of personality clashes, disparate educational backgrounds, case and job assignments, status and reputation inequalities, and so on. Some of the deepest resentments occur when a trial prosecutor *(kōhan kenji)* feels that an investigating prosecutor *(sōsa kenji)* has charged a case that could end in acquittal. This possibility compels the trial prosecutor to invest substantial effort sustaining the case at trial and, if the defendant is ultimately acquitted, still more effort afterward explaining to office managers (in exhaustive and exhausting detail) what went wrong. When I knew both parties to such conflicts it was easy to avoid causing offense, but when I did not know one side or, more troublesome still, who was allied with whom, it was difficult to discern what to say to whom. The world of Japanese prosecutors is small, and news travels rapidly through its dense networks. In the procuracy it does seem that everyone knows someone who knows the unknown other (Kubo 1989). Although I tried to be circumspect, I did not always navigate the factional cleavages successfully. In some instances the failures prevented me from acquiring valuable information.

Getting along in the prosecutors office did not mean getting access to everything or everyone I wanted. Some doors stayed stubbornly closed. This has not been the case for some other students of Japanese criminal justice. In his seminal study of Japanese police, for example, David Bayley states that "no attempt was ever made to deny me access to a location, an officer, or an operation." The police, he recounts, "were as accessible as I could ask" (Bayley 1991, xii). Japanese prosecutors were far less forthcoming. Persistent petitions were repeatedly refused: to read reports written by and for prosecutors; to observe a sample of prosecutors conduct interrogation; to witness case consultations between frontline prosecutors and their managers on more than an occasional basis; to attend office meetings; to read case records; to administer my questionnaire at other offices; and so on. Prosecutors were emphatically not as accessible as I could ask. When closed doors opened at all, they usually did not because prosecutors could be persuaded to cooperate but rather because I mobilized allies elsewhere in the office or sought the help of outsiders (judges, defense attorneys, journalists, and ex-prosecutors) who either possessed the information I wanted or could provide access to it.

Language Difficulties

To get along with prosecutors I had to get along in Japanese. I was constantly reminded that I was the only non-Japanese, and thus the only nonnative speaker, in the office (except for the occasional foreign suspect or witness). Some prosecutors insisted on speaking to me in impoverished English, even though we communicated much better in Japanese. English conversations could be a welcome relief from the fatigue I felt working hours on end in a second language. More often, however, they were an irritating obstacle to inquiry. Other prosecutors addressed me with the same sophistication that is used to communicate with a clever six-year-old child. Still others refused to examine (much less abandon) their conviction that a foreigner cannot possibly appreciate sushi or sumo, much less the subtleties of their professional lives. One result was that in many encounters I heard little more than prosecutor platitudes.

At the same time, language was one of my biggest challenges getting along in the office. Most prosecutors engage in little observable action (unlike the police, who walk or drive a beat and respond to calls for service). For the most part, prosecutors traffic in words. Reading, talking, and writing constitute the core of their occupation. It is primarily through language that they interact with police, suspects, witnesses, judges, lawyers, the public, the media, and other prosecutors. Understanding prosecution meant, first and foremost, comprehending prosecutors' language.

I understood that language imperfectly. When I began fieldwork in the KPO I had lived in Japan twice previously for a total of two years and had studied Japanese at an American university for an additional three. By some definitions I was fluent ("able to speak and understand smoothly and readily"). Nevertheless, getting along in Japanese was often a struggle, for many mundane reasons. Legal jargon was prolific and dense, expressions were perplexingly ambiguous, handwritten manuscripts were illegible, and the unfamiliar Kansai dialect was colorful but confusing.

These language difficulties had at least three effects on my research. First, and most important, they obstructed an accurate understanding of Japanese criminal justice. I tried to minimize such inaccuracies by cross-checking accounts with people who could test the veracity of my observations, but errors of fact rooted in problems of language no doubt remain. Second, since I cannot process Japanese as efficiently as English, this project took more time than would have similar research in the United States or other English-speaking countries. Scholars who intend to do field research in Japan should anticipate, as best they can, the time costs induced by linguistic obstacles. I went to Japan expecting to stay eighteen months but ended up staying about twice that long. Fortunately, since my learning curve was geometric, not linear, the extra time in the field yielded more than double dividends—in relationships and information. Finally, I had to be emotionally vigilant in order to keep from translating the accurate perception that my language ability was sometimes inadequate into what could have been the immobilizing belief that I was an incompetent researcher. Insecurity-induced depression has stalled many an ethnographic account.

The Researcher as Subject

In contrast to Charles Bosk (1979, 194), who found that the American surgeons he studied were "as a rule remarkably uncurious" about his research, many Japanese prosecutors cared passionately what I thought about them. Indeed, several cared so much that they made crude efforts to manage my impressions and influence what I wrote. Once, when I was eating dinner with two elite prosecutors and their former colleague (now a private attorney), the latter declared that if I ever wrote about prosecutor misconduct he would "not be my friend anymore." Japanese prosecutors (and police) are generally more reluctant than their American counterparts to admit mistakes or discuss sensitive issues (Bayley 1991, 73). Concerning controversial issues (such as the criminal justice system's extreme reliance on confessions), most prosecutors are closemouthed and keenly suspicious of inquiries. In the early stages of field research I stayed away from topics that prosecutors seemed uncomfortable addressing. Over time, however, I learned how to pursue delicate issues and how to defend the integrity of my research project against attempts to distort my descriptions and interpretations. Field researchers not only have subjects, they are subjects. As a result, getting along may mean managing relations with meddlesome people.

Getting Close

Getting close to prosecutors required earning their trust. Gaining that trust was often difficult, occasionally impossible, and always time-consuming. Introductions helped not just to gain initial access, but also to navigate inside the office thereafter. I received good introductions—something more than "this is Johnson-san and he is studying us"—only after establishing good relationships with the introducers. Introductions were a necessary condition for developing a more extensive network of relationships, but they were not at all sufficient. Getting close to prosecutors meant forging intensive relationships, one prosecutor at a time. Playing roles—in the office and at the bar—helped facilitate the forging.

Roles and Relationships

In my first few months in the KPO, Mr. Ono regarded me as he might a ghost, with "deep fear and suspicion in the guise of absolute indifference" (Hamabata 1990, 6). I did not escape ghosthood by suddenly crossing "some moral or metaphysical shadow line," as other field researchers have described (Geertz 1977, 422). Instead, I moved from ghosthood to personhood gradually, as the cumulative result of performing roles I assumed and was assigned. Through these roles I acquired a respectable identity and the rights, duties, and trust that afforded proximity to prosecutors.

My first role, and the one I stressed in self-introductions, was as a student studying prosecution in Japan. This role implied several duties: to be curious and interested without being discourteous or insubordinate; to be diligent; to trust that prosecutors know best; and (an especially salient duty in Japan) to avoid embarrassing my teachers. The student role also conferred privileges such as the right to admit ignorance and ask questions. In turn, these privileges implied a prosecutor duty to teach, a highly respected role in Japan and one many prosecutors seemed to relish.

Another role, as an American in Japan trying to make sense of things Japanese, overlapped with my role as student but provided additional license to ask questions about matters so taken for granted that few Japanese, even designated learners like the legal apprentices, felt comfortable inquiring about them. Jonathan Rauch has observed that Japanese tell themselves two "national lies": the "we Japanese are all the same" myth of homogeneity, and the "we Japanese are completely different than you foreigners" myth of uniqueness (Rauch 1992, 42). Many prosecutors subscribe to the latter, believing that their system of criminal justice stands in such deep contrast to the West that it can only be understood by people born Japanese. Convinced that their beliefs and practices must seem mysterious to outsiders, prosecutors accepted questions from me that, coming from a Japanese, they may have resisted or resented. My status as an outsider thus afforded special opportunities to ask and be taught.

This role as an American in Japan helped me manage relationships with prosecutors in another way as well. Through trial and error—by "blundering across boundaries" (Hamabata 1990, 6)—I learned that in some circumstances it pays to use English in tight spots. As described above, although few prosecutors are fluent in English, most know many English words. Their acquaintance with my language made it acceptable to resort to English when operating in Japanese proved especially difficult. Using English in tight spots reminded some reticent prosecutors that they are jointly responsible for helping construct conversation. At the same time, English conferred tacit permission to speak more directly than the conventions of Japanese allow. When discussing sensitive issues such as fairness, blame, and responsibility, this was a valuable privilege.

Thus, my principal role permutation was as an American student in Japan, but I had many opportunities to perform the complementary role of teacher, both formally and informally. Informally, my inquiries about Japanese justice often elicited parallel inquiries about the United States. Since the media in Japan devote considerable coverage to the United States and a disproportionate amount of that to crime and related problems, I was frequently asked to explain or defend some aspect of American criminal justice (juries and guns seemed two favorite topics). Prosecutors' questions permitted me to demonstrate that however little I knew about Japan, I understood American criminal justice, at worst, better than they did. That was a good way to repay some of the many debts I incurred while in the field. More important, prosecutors' questions promoted dialogue that deepened my understanding of the ways they think and act.

On several occasions I played a more formal teacher role by lecturing about comparative criminal justice. My first lecture occurred four months after getting in the office. I should have started earlier. Preparing formal talks made me articulate what prosecutors consider relevant and interesting, even if only in a provisional way, and the questions they asked during and after the lectures often provided additional clues about practices they deem different or significant.

Like many field researchers, I was eager to repay my debts and help my subjects (Lofland and Lofland 1984). During my first few weeks in the KPO, when I was more of a guest than a ghost, my hosts refused to permit me to provide even the most mundane forms of assistance—not even clearing books and papers off my own desk. Of course, since this special "guest treatment" could not have lasted the entire fourteen months I was in Kobe, before long I was allowed to answer the phone, take messages, relay requests to the legal apprentices, make photocopies, and perform other small services for

Ono and others. Once in a while I was asked to provide more substantial assistance, by interpreting during the interrogation of foreign suspects. I always agreed, partly to discharge my debt, but also because interpreting was one of only a few ways to gain entry to the otherwise inaccessible world of criminal interrogation. I tried to refuse compensation, explaining that I was only repaying the KPO for services rendered to me, and noting that Fulbright administrators had advised that accepting remuneration could create the impression that the researcher has been bribed. These explanations succeeded only in part. Prosecutors stopped trying to compensate me with cash the office had budgeted for this purpose, but they did insist that I accept books or book certificates instead. It thus proved impossible to help them without being helped in return. I often felt overindebted during my time in Kobe, and I sometimes wonder, even today, how that feeling may have shaped my interpretations.

Prosecutors offered me the complementary roles of sounding board and referee, thereby conferring duties to listen to their frustrations and to adjudicate disagreements about matters as mundane as whether the American wrestler Akebono would make a good sumo grand champion, or as weighty as what punishment a sex offender deserves. The more serious the interrogatory, the more I resisted the referee role. Being asked to umpire confused me. On the one hand, I was pleased that prosecutors trusted me enough to solicit my opinion, and since self-disclosure tends to breed self-disclosure, I wanted to respond in ways that would encourage candor. On the other hand, I did not want to influence case dispositions, and I feared offending or irritating those prosecutors who might dislike my reply. Despite my efforts to avoid this role, requests to referee continued. Sometimes I sought escape from the role through the large stock of ambiguous Japanese phrases that are used on awkward occasions. More often I just improvised.

In addition to fielding their criticisms and complaints, sometimes I turned critic myself, asking prosecutors the difficult questions they seldom ask each other. Of course, since criticism is more often expressed obliquely in Japan, I tried harder to assess the costs and benefits of disapprobation than I do when in America. These utilitarian calculations usually counseled silence, but in some cases planting a critical comment or question seemed the wiser course of action. Critical inquiries often yielded fruit by inviting replies that revealed more of an issue's complexity, and by prompting prosecutors to elaborate the critique. Still, Japanese prosecutors are, on the whole, an extraordinarily sensitive lot, and a few times I spoke when I should not have.

When my comments stimulated a defensive response I sometimes retreated to the less provocative role of listener-learner and, when the opportunity arose, recorded in my fieldnotes the emotions and reasons my inquiry had revealed. I tried to sustain disagreements only when I believed that the relationship could endure vigorous debate. Unfortunately, on one such occasion (a disagreement over whether Japan has plea bargaining—it does) I misjudged so badly that the offended prosecutor shunned me forever after.

Finally, some prosecutors acquired an intense interest in my research and began to consider me their emissary and advisee as well. After a few months in the field I knew a lot about how the procuracy works, knowledge that seemed to impress and concern my hosts. Many prosecutors were glad for the attention and grateful someone recognized their importance. Others knew I would publish the research and, anxious for good reports rather than bad, sought to shape my interpretations, as Japanese prison officials have done in an analogous context (Gerber and Weeks 1992). A few prosecutors did not even attempt to disguise their efforts to provide only information that flattered themselves and their organization. Most, however, were more artful, subtly directing my attention toward agreeable facts and away from disquieting ones. Since efforts to shape my views instructed me about what prosecutors consider sensitive and significant, I usually did not object. As the research progressed, however, and I gained confidence in my interpretations, I became increasingly unwilling to tolerate attempts to alter my conclusions, and sometimes told them so.

Liquor and Loquacity

I became friends with several prosecutors in Japan. Friendships there are, in many respects, like friendships in the United States, conferring similar rights, imposing analogous duties, and manifesting many of the same forms, sentiments, and intensities. To a much greater extent than my American friends, however, prosecutors in Japan expected and desired to drink together. This fact will not surprise readers familiar with after-hours Japan, but it is hard to exaggerate its importance as a means of getting close to research subjects.

In his classic ethnography of a Japanese bank, Thomas Rohlen (1974, 256) credits drinking as the "single most important means to friendship" and describes "a clear relationship between the helpfulness of people and the previous establishment of a personal relationship, usually through drinking." Similarly, in his account of life in the Japanese bureaucracy, Miyamoto Masao (1994, 61, 184) describes the transformative powers of alcohol. While drinking, Miyamoto observes, "nothing you say is held against you." As a result, some Japanese drink in order to acquire the liberty to say things they otherwise cannot. In Japan as much as anywhere, alcohol dissolves the ubiquitous bounds of propriety and thereby frees the drinker to "speak his mind."

I discovered the importance of alcohol to Japanese prosecutors early in my research. Indeed, on my second visit to Ono's office I had a stomachache, so I asked for water instead of the offered green tea. This prompted Ono to ask if I am a Mormon. He went on to explain that it is customary to drink beer and spirits in the office after the day's work is done, and eventually inquired if I drink liquor or object to being around people who do. I drink a little, I said, and I do not object to those who imbibe more vigorously. This reply was met with further inquiries—queries I would grow all too accustomed to hearing—about the reasons for my moderate consumption.

For the first few months in the KPO I refused most invitations to drink, thus foregoing valuable opportunities to hear guarded, circumspect prosecutors wax loquacious about their jobs and lives. Before long, however, I was drinking with my hosts regularly, having learned that wet conversations were far more revealing than dry ones. The following two examples (which could be multiplied considerably) illustrate the links between liquor and loquacity in Japan's procuracy.

At UNAFEI[2]—a government institute where I worked for fifteen months after leaving Kobe—I became acquainted with a prosecutor whom I shall call Mr. Suzuki. Nearly forty, Suzuki took pride in his ability to extract confessions from recalcitrant, unrepentant suspects. Like many of his colleagues, Suzuki was staunchly loyal to "his group," whether country, procuracy, team, or gender (Miller and Kanazawa 2000). No matter the subject—the Pacific War, prosecutor misconduct, the Tokyo Giants, or gender relations—Suzuki took a consistently conservative position, at least when he was dry. When he was drinking—and the important fact seemed to be not how much he drank but simply that he was drinking—Suzuki changed markedly.

One day Suzuki and I had an awkward conversation about how much control managing prosecutors exercise over their subordinates. I suggested that because managers decide job and case assignments, because most charge and sentence decisions must be approved by two or more supervising prosecutors, and because deference to authority is rewarded while defiance is punished, managers exercise considerable control over frontline prosecutors. Suzuki disagreed, citing the official *tatemae* that each frontline prosecutor is an "independent agency," free of hierarchical controls. That evening, however, when Suzuki and I attended one of UNAFEI's many parties, he told a very different story. Shortly after the bottles were uncorked, Suzuki charged into my conversational circle, glass in hand, and declared his wish to work in America because then he would be free from the "petty" controls he encounters in Japan's procuracy. Though I cannot be certain Suzuki's comment was *honne* (the next day he would neither confirm nor deny it), his pronouncement did reveal a layer of prosecutor reality I would not have seen but for the facilitative effects of fermented rice.

Alcohol promoted similar candor in the second example, which also occurred during my days at UNAFEI. In the spring of 1995, the staff of the institute took a "group trip" *(shūdan ryokō)* to a hotel in a neighboring prefecture famous for its hot springs. We left Tokyo's Shinjuku station on a chartered train at 11:00 A.M. Before we had even departed the station, several UNAFEI veterans broke out beer, and the liquor did not stop flowing until some sixteen hours later. That evening, after a catered dinner and the main party had ended, I went with several colleagues to the director's room for "round two" *(nijikai),* the informal second party that frequently follows the first. We sat on the tatami floor in a large parabola and took turns pouring each other drinks, telling stories and jokes, and otherwise making merry.

The director of UNAFEI (an experienced prosecutor) was known as much for his fondness for alcohol as for his informal style, fun-loving manner, and love for the institute he led. When he drank, however, the director occasionally violated norms about drinking behavior. On several previous occasions his subordinates had privately discussed what they could do to prevent him from (as they put it) "recidivating" and thereby damaging the reputation of the institute he administered. At the after-party, three UNAFEI instructors (one a prosecutor), emboldened by several liters of liquor, openly and directly rebuked the director for his drinking transgressions, warned him of the likely consequences such behavior would have for his own career and for UNAFEI, and urged him to adopt a lower profile at future UNAFEI events, especially when liquor was served. To my astonishment, the director listened quietly, even contritely, to these admonitions. Subsequently, he even changed his drinking behavior in the suggested direction (at least while on the UNAFEI campus).

Japanese prosecutors work in a rigidly hierarchical office where, as my first example shows, superiors wield wide control over their subordinates. The second story suggests that in the procuracy as in much of social life, conventions depend on context. I asked the man who rebuked the director if he had risked damage to his career by acting with such impudence. Different rules apply in different situations, he explained, and one key variable is whether the occasion is wet.

But Not Too Close

Relationships were my main tool for gathering data, and drinking was one essential way of deepening connections of various kinds. By playing roles in these relationships—as student, foreigner, teacher, helper, sounding board, umpire, critic, and friend—I gained intimate access to the work lives of my research subjects. Others can too. But be careful. "Getting close" can devolve into a "tyranny of access" that interferes with objective observation and analysis. In particular, field researchers must avoid the distorting influences of overrapport, overindebtedness, overgeneralization, and observer effects (Bosk 1979, 204). They must, in other words, get close but not too close.

I tried to get close enough to prosecutors to gain their trust and, thereby, reliable, revealing data about their work lives, yet not so close as to allow the gift of access to undermine objectivity. On the whole, getting close—obtaining access, turning entree into relationships, building rapport, developing trust, and acquiring information—was a much bigger problem than getting too close. Indeed, getting close was my methodological migraine—an intense headache recurring so regularly that even when I did not feel it I suffered from the knowledge that it would soon return.

There are many respects in which my experience getting in and getting along in the prosecutors office can serve as a good "negative role model" *(hanmen kyōshi)* for researchers contemplating similar forays into the field. I made many mistakes, and learned from some of them. The perspicacious researcher will have to do likewise. Nevertheless, I offer the following imperatives in order to sum up and simplify three ways in which my research experience may instruct others. If you do as I say and not just as I did, you will do better.

First, getting in takes time. Plan in advance and, if possible, gain access before you go. Failure to do so costs time, money, information, and insight.

Second, getting along means mastering Japanese. For foreigners doing fieldwork in Japan, language may be the most important subject of study.

Third, getting close requires trying on and trying out unfamiliar roles. Be flexible; rigidity inhibits research.

I hope my research stimulates others to conduct studies aimed at replicating, refuting, and refining what I have discovered, or prompts investigations that extend our understanding of the Japanese way of justice beyond its present bounds. If it has that effect, I wish my successors well getting in, getting along, and getting close at their research sites. May they possess patience and perseverance. They will need both.

Notes

For guidance and support of various kinds, the author thanks Malcolm Feeley, Setsuo Miyazawa, Franklin Zimring, the Japan-U.S. Educational Commission, the Earl Warren Legal Institute, and the Sho Sato U.S.-Japan Legal Studies Program.

1. Bar exam passers underwent two years of training under the supervision of the Supreme Court's Legal Training Institute. In 1992, only about six hundred people passed the bar, about 2 percent of all who tried. These legal apprentices then did six months of class work at the institute in Tokyo, followed by four months of training at each of four other sites: a private law office, a civil court, a criminal court, and a prosecutors office. The last two months of the apprenticeship were spent preparing for the final examination at the institute. In 1993, approximately thirty apprentices began their sixteen months of training in Kobe. They rotated through the KPO in three groups of ten, each group spending four months under the supervision of the "instructing prosecutor."

2. UNAFEI—the United Nations Asia and Far East Institute for the Prevention of Crime and the Treatment of Offenders—was established in Tokyo in 1961 by agreement between the United Nations and the government of Japan. Its main purposes are to train people—Japanese and foreign—in criminal justice administration and to conduct research about crime prevention and the treatment of offenders. Like the rest of the Ministry of Justice to which it belongs, UNAFEI is run by prosecutors. I moved to Tokyo in March 1994 in order to continue my study while working at UNAFEI as a researcher and editor. I stayed for fifteen months.

Related Readings

Johnson, David T. 1998. "The Organization of Prosecution and the Possibility of Order." *Law and Society Review* 32:247–308.
———. 1999. "Kumo no su ni shōchō sareru Nihonhō no tokushoku."
Jurisuto January 1–15, no. 1148, 85–89.
———. 2002. *The Japanese Way of Justice: Prosecuting Crime in Japan*. New York: Oxford University Press.

Sheila A. Smith
on the stern of an
MSDF destroyer
during antisubmarine
warfare exercises
in Tokyo Bay.

SHEILA A. SMITH

In Search of the Japanese State

My first research trip to Japan was in 1989, when I set out to do my Ph.D. dissertation. Japan was not unfamiliar, but the task of doing research was. I had studied the Japanese language at Sophia University and had lived in Tokyo for more than a year as an undergraduate. I was excited to return, but that excitement was tempered by the unknowns ahead. I was setting out to research Japan's national security policy, a policy cloaked in secrecy in almost any state. But in Japan, this was an issue that also inevitably conjured up images of a past Japan, a Japan very different from the bright postwar image of the world's only "economic superpower." It seemed then that I was venturing into mysterious and unexplored territory, and while I had some basic ideas of where to start, the journey was to be much longer than I imagined.

Although I did not know it then, I was about to witness a series of changes that would transform Japan's security policy debates. The Cold War was about to end, and in the years that followed, the relationship between Japan's long-time ruling party, the Liberal Democratic Party, and the bureaucrats who had crafted Japan's security policy was also about to be transformed. The puzzle that needed explanation at the end of the 1980s was Japan's resistance to change. I was looking to understand the well-advertised "taboos" and wanted to find out more about the one institution that seemed strangely missing from policy deliberations—Japan's military. Within several years, however, many of the taboos were being broken, and Japan's military had come out from the shadows and on to the front burner of Japan's foreign policy debates.

When I began my research, there was relatively little discussion of Japan in the academic literature on international security. In fact, like many fields, much of the theoretical work had been focused on European experience, and with some notable exceptions, there was little empirical work done on how Asian states (and their societies) were affected by the Cold War. Japan was absent, too, from the key policy debates of the Cold War. It was not a nuclear power, and there was little evidence that Japan's security specialists were as worried about the strategic dilemmas of alliance with the United States as their counterparts in Europe. Moreover, Japan's distinction as a state that had renounced war seemed to sit awkwardly with theories about the global nuclear balance, or even about the politics of grand strategic alliances.

As I set off to explore the Japanese state and its strategic impulses, it was this contradictory set of images that troubled me. I wanted to know how Japan organized its military given the postwar constitutional proscription on the use of force by the state. How did a government that was not allowed to use force to "settle international disputes" go about designing, equipping, and deploying a military? What was the purpose of such a military, and how did it factor into Japan's broader foreign policy goals? I assumed that Japan, like every other state, must have a process for developing strategy and articulating a national interest. I also assumed that Japan's military would be a constitutive element of this process. I thought that I only had to interview security-policy decision makers (including the elusive Japanese military) and observe the interplay between jousting policy advocates and I would be able to come up with the factors that determined the Japanese state's security goals.

So with questions and notebook in hand, I took aim at the institutions responsible for security policy formation. Gaining access to the Japanese Defense Agency and Ministry of Foreign Affairs and Japan's political and military leadership took much time and patience. Ultimately, I was very fortunate, but there were indications in many of my interviews that I needed to reconsider the way I had envisioned the roles of some crucial actors. I also had to contend with the persistent claim that two factors I had not fully appreciated were key to Japan's security choices. The first was the amazing consensus—shared by ruling and opposition political parties, as well as by local base protestors and Ministry of Foreign Affairs diplomats—on the determinant role of the United States in shaping Japan's policies. The second was the predominant view within Tokyo—again shared by such competing interests as the bureaucrats in Kasumigaseki, the civilian and uniformed members of the Japanese Defense Agency, and the politicians in Nagata-chō—that the Japanese public was an equally powerful influence over the policy-making process. Given the penchant of U.S. policymakers for claiming their influence over process, I was struck by how quickly and emphatically Japan's policymakers bemoaned their inability to influence the public or make changes in Japan's policies.

Over time, I managed to navigate this maze of interests and perspectives within the security policy-making community in Japan. I had considerable assistance and guidance from Japanese advisors and fellow researchers, but it took some time before I could see the larger linkage between what I was experiencing and the meaning these experiences had for my own project. My initial assumptions and choices as to where to start had to be refined and ultimately reevaluated once I had some distance from Japan. As it turned out, I had arrived in Japan on the eve of significant changes in the policy-making process. I went to Tokyo with a rather evolutionary vision—and therefore continuity-driven notion—of how Japanese security choices had developed. I had to reformulate my questions many times over. The world was changing, Japan was changing, and this research topic had to take into account much more than I initially had bargained for. But there were some very significant signposts along the way, and while I could not understand their meaning in the early stages of the project, I knew that they were pointing me in new and different directions.

Refining Early Choices and Gaining New Perspectives

Preparing to do research in Japan involves a number of initial choices. These early choices will require some thought, as they shape the initial phase of research. One of the most important is where to affiliate. An institutional affiliation is crucial for most researchers who intend to spend time in Japan. This will be the initial referent point for Japanese scholars, policymakers, and/or individuals whom the researcher will work with. More than simply giving you a professional identity to put on a business card *(meishi),* institutional affiliation also contributes to the credibility of the research itself and can help open doors to the policy community.

Academic affiliation is perhaps the most neutral of all options. For most graduate students, the initial choice of affiliation will be made in consultation with academic advisors who have had research experience in Japan. For those without direct access to a Japan specialist at their home institution, there are other avenues of soliciting advice from those who have had research experience in Japan. For example, the Social Science Japan Forum (SSJ-Forum), a list-serve organized and managed by the Institute for Social Science at the University of Tokyo, provides access to a broad array of Japan specialists in the social sciences, as does H-ASIA, a list-serve managed by the University of Michigan. In addition, many of the grant-giving agencies that offer fellowships for research in Japan also provide assistance in identifying an appropriate institution for formal affiliation. If at all possible, a brief preresearch trip to Japan can help identify the main institutes or individuals conducting research on similar subjects. In my case, a predissertation summer grant gave me the opportunity to meet with a number of Japan's scholars and policy analysts in international relations and security policy and to survey the terrain of research prior to writing my grant proposal. Once I had a dissertation grant my advisor at Columbia arranged for me to affiliate with a well-known scholar of Japanese security and international relations at the University of Tokyo. This university affiliation was very helpful in establishing my status as an academic researcher.

But affiliation with government-related think tanks was crucial to gaining access to policy debates on security issues. I was fortunate early on and was invited to become a research fellow at the Research Institute on Peace and Security, the only institute at that time focused solely on security issues. In return for assisting in the editing of the English-language annual periodical *Asian Security,* I had the opportunity to join in conferences and to meet many of the individual scholars from various Japanese universities who specialized in security-related research. Later in my stay, I was invited to join the Japan Institute for International Affairs. Both of these institutes were linked to Japanese bureaucracies, respectively the Defense Agency and the Ministry of Foreign Affairs. They brought together key Japanese specialists for seminars, conferences, and research projects, and I was able to gain considerable insight into the concerns of Japan's policy-making establishment.

Unwittingly, I found myself sitting on the walls of the Japanese state—peeking into bureaucratic wrangles and intra-agency squabbles. I was in the thick of things—watching as Japanese policymakers sought to contend with the implications of the end of the Cold War for Japan and to respond to (or "contribute to") the Gulf War—and it was a great spot from which to observe the policy-making process. However, I realized that my research could not fully represent the details and circumstances of decisions made. I had expected contentious public debates over the specifics of policy choices. But even getting basic information about Japan's military and the rationale behind policy decisions was a difficult task. The information I was privy to—as a member of research seminars or as a speech writer for policymakers or as a friend of decision makers—could never be substantiated formally, nor could the post-hoc stories of decision-making events be sufficient evidence from which to make inferences about the broader questions of what drives Japan's security policy-making choices. I was close enough to see some interesting behind-the-scenes wrangling, but ironically, I was too close to gain perspective on the relative importance of any particular wrangle.

A second set of initial choices that I needed to refine, and ultimately amend, as my research progressed was the basic assumptions that I carried to Japan. I arrived in Japan with the rather unquestioned (and in hindsight, naive) notion that I could easily find "where the buck stopped." I assumed, too, that I would be able to recognize the process by which Japan's security policy decisions were made. In part, I had counted on hearing firsthand from those involved in the process. I assumed bureaucratic politics were at work—and that I could identify individual and institutional interests. There were interests in conflict, but they seemed to be different kinds of interests than I had originally imagined. Almost all policymakers felt embattled, and apologetic, about Japan's lack of a clear security policy. With the exception of a few, there seemed little reference to operational needs or to strategic assessment. Military officers seemed reticent to discuss much of their work. Again, this raised a whole host of new questions for my research. What explained the reticence of policymakers to claim credit for policy changes? Why was the Self Defense Force (SDF) absent from debates over their professional goals and interests?[1] Why did senior political leaders in positions of responsibility feel discomfort when I asked them to expand upon the arguments they had made in Diet deliberations?

As time went on, several refrains became clear. First, I realized that I needed to abandon some of my attachment to the mental map I had unwittingly created of how I thought policy should be made. I assumed that public policy was the domain of the state bureaucracies and that the choices outlined by these bureaucracies would be subjected to scrutiny and review in the national legislature. I was only partially right about the first part, but the second assumption needed to be revisited. For much of the time I studied Japan's security policy, the bureaucrats in the Defense Agency and in the Ministry of Foreign Affairs were the chief architects of Japan's policies. But the political relationship between bureaucrats and the politicians that advocated these policies in the legislature was very different than I originally imagined. What happened in the Diet was less of a debate over the pros and cons of policy directions than it was an arena for defining, and redefining, the parameters of appropriate government action. In other words, it was a place for interpreting the intent or spirit of Japan's postwar Constitution, and more often than not the question and answers seemed more like a theological discussion than a debate over the merits or demerits of any given policy choice. The tone and tenor of policy deliberations, as well as my slow realization that they were taking place in different places than I had imagined, was the first sign that I needed to sit back and reconsider my project. Two other signposts were about to indicate a new direction for my work. The first was my growing awareness that there seemed to be a separate idiom for security policy discussions—a vocabulary and a phrasing of policies that called for greater attention. The second, and somewhat related, signal that I needed a different vantage point was the silences that seemed to crop up often when I sought to explore the relationship between policy-making within the state and its reception among Japan's public.

Listening to Language and the Signals It Sends

One of the least-discussed aspects of research is the dilemmas encountered when using a second language and in the judgments we make with regard to translating meanings, particularly in policy areas that are highly contested. For some, particularly those whose research depends heavily on quantitative data, fluency in Japanese may not be needed. Basic conversation skills may be enough to get access to the information required. For most of us with academic training, advanced reading and comprehension skills are a prerequisite to doing research in Japan. Working in a nonnative language carries with it the added burden of checking and double-checking that we have interpreted meaning correctly.

This process of interpretation has several facets. The most obvious is the mastery of the specialized terms used in our area of specialization. I had spent many years, both in Tokyo and in New York, honing my Japanese-language skills, and as I prepared for my dissertation research, I acquired the requisite vocabulary for "things military"—the names of weapons, the organization of military forces (battalions, squadrons, and flotillas, for example), the legalistic language of the U.S.-Japan security treaty, and so on. I had to memorize a vast vocabulary of weaponry and organizational concepts. I also had to sort through the bureaucratic jargon of government-speak. And then when I tackled Diet debates, I found a whole new set of terms that had no recognizable English equivalent, such as the distinction between "individual self-defense" *(kobetsuteki jieiken)* and "collective self-defense" *(shūdanteki jieiken)*. I had masses of note cards with military-related terms that attracted some curious looks when I was studying in coffee shops and on trains! But I needed this vocabulary for interviews, for reading the policy debates in public media, and for discussing the issues with other researchers.

There is another important way in which the language of my policy issue affected my research. As I became more comfortable with the terms used to discuss security policy, I realized that there were questions that I could not ask. I found, too, that there were words that carried connotations I had not understood. And, there was a lack of vocabulary for some of the issues I began to pay attention to. Translating and interpreting the nuances of policy terminology was a challenge, but struggling to do this provided me with significant clues to the dynamics of the policy-making process that were very valuable.

Several aspects of the language used to discuss Japan's defense struck me over time. First, the Japanese security world seemed to have developed its own ways of talking about security and defense. In a sense, a new language had to be created in the postwar period for discussing security policy issues, and many of these new words or phrases embodied a new interpretation of the purpose of Japan's military.

Today, weapons systems in Japan are named according to their operational functions, rather than referring to weapons in terms of their (lethal) capabilities, as is more common in military circles around the globe.[2] For example, Japan calls its naval vessels "self-defense ships" *(jieikan),* and its large naval warships are referred to as "escort ships" *(goeikan)* rather than as "destroyers." Military doctrine is now referred to as "exclusively defensive doctrine" *(senshu bōeiron),* defined not by the potential adversaries' capabilities but by the need to articulate Japan's limited military ambitions. In terms of security or military planning, the government avoids the term "war" *(sensō)* or "war capability" *(senryoku)* and uses a softer language to discuss the activities of the SDF, such as "U.S.-Japan defense cooperation" *(Nichibei bōei kyōryoku)* or "defense capability" *(bōeiryoku).*

Rather than endorse contingency planning exercises that involve assumptions about how Japan might find itself engaged in a war, the government has insisted in the Diet for much of the Cold War that the SDF is only allowed to conduct "studies" rather than to actually plan for war. The legal framework for contingency planning remains today a contested area of national policy. In the 1980s, the Defense Agency began to consider what kind of legal changes would be necessary to enhance its ability for "emergency planning" *(yūji kenkyū).* Much of this was driven by the difficulties the Defense Agency faced in its effort to expand military cooperation with U.S. forces. Yet it was not until a decade later, in the wake of the Cold War, that the Defense Agency had the political support needed to introduce this legislation to the Diet. In 2002, the Japanese government finally put forward the Defense Agency's draft legislation that will create the legal basis for extending government (and the Defense Agency's) authority in times of crisis or war, but it took the events of September 11, 2001, and the heightened concern about the prospects of attacks on Japan to create a political climate that would be receptive to this legislation.

Recognizing and interpreting the vocabulary of security and defense was my first task. But later, once I was more comfortable with this vocabulary for speaking about Japan's security policy, I realized that I also was having trouble even asking the questions I wanted to ask. What prompts a distinction to be made between defensive and offensive weapons? When most military weaponry can be used for offensive as well as defensive purposes, what makes Japanese policymakers think that they can label weapons by their intended purposes rather than their potential military effects?[3] Who are they trying to convince—neighboring countries who watch the military buildup and worry about a future Japan that will use these weapons offensively, or a domestic public that questions their government's intentions? Coming to recognize these questions was troubling, particularly after I had worked so hard to learn this new way of talking about "things military." I began to consider the possibility that the terms of Japan's defense debate were just that— a means of making things military palatable to a public that was less than receptive to the notion that Japan even has a military. Was this a conspiracy to hide policy from the public? Or a tactical approach by bureaucrats trying to avoid criticism in the Japanese Diet? Or did Japan's new vocabulary of defense represent a broader transformation in Japanese thinking about the purpose and utility of military force?

The power of the language and the associations it held for most Japanese was brought home to me when I wrote an article for a Japanese journal. At that time I was interested in the changing operational role of the SDF in the U.S.-Japan alliance. I wrote the draft in English, and one of my Japanese colleagues offered to translate it for me. I had spent much of my research effort trying to clarify the role of the Japanese military in the implementation of the U.S.-Japan alliance and made a point of making explicit references to the operational or military aspects of the relationship in the essay. But when I received the draft in Japanese, even I was shocked. The Chinese characters for "military" *(gun)* or "military personnel" *(gunjin)* leapt off the page. My Japanese colleague, knowing my conviction to clarify the operational aspects of the U.S.-Japan alliance, had been faithful to my English-language draft. But when we showed the draft to our professor, he immediately took out a red pen and rendered it vague and confusing—with all of the softening terms I had tried to avoid by explaining what the two militaries were actually doing. The initial draft was written—or so I thought—with the clarity that direct and plain English would provide. It was also clear about the military operations.

Even I had to admit that the image on the paper was that of prewar Japan, not of postwar Japan. My professor pointed out that if I did not refer to these policies as the Japanese policy community did, it would be identified as a critique of the sort launched by the left in Japan. The language I chose after much soul-searching was the language of the Japanese policy debate (S. A. Smith 1990).

I felt that the analytical clarity of the article would be lost, but I also realized that the translation of this most contentious area of Japanese public policy into a palatable vocabulary was part of the process by which Japan's postwar defense and security policies had been legitimized. The translation exercise was a valuable revelation into just how imbued with political position the language of public policy is. What I thought of as the "truth"—that is, what the U.S. and Japanese governments were actually doing—was obscured by a vocabulary that ostensibly pacified those aspects that the public (or government critics) would find objectionable. The other side of that revelation was that in the American public policy debate, it is perfectly legitimate for militaries to plan for contingencies that involve crisis and war. That is their job, and it is expected of them. In Japan, however, that sort of planning was not acceptable to many and was anathema to some (S. A. Smith 1999). The use of terms that sought to embody the reformed purpose of Japan's military was part of gaining public acceptance to the policies being generated by the government. But it also obscured what militaries do—prepare to use force.

The way in which Japan's security policy was discussed not only reflected this postwar project of redefining the purpose of a national military, but it also reflected a new prescription for how this military was to be treated within the state. The notion of establishing firm civilian control was established during the U.S. Occupation, and in the early years of the Defense Agency's existence in the 1950s, the civilian bureaucrats defended this rather harshly. Japan's postwar military officers were clearly not in the position to make policy recommendations, and they were routinely subjected to demonstrations of the new power of civilians. This was dubbed the system of *sebiro kontorōru,* or control by those in business suits. When I first encountered this reference, I found it an amusing twist of linguistic humor and promptly inserted it in my chapter. But the more I thought about it, the more I realized that this was not just a play on words. It was indeed a quite accurate description of the way in which civilian control had been interpreted in early postwar Japan. The visual image of suits outnumbering uniforms in the Defense Agency stayed with me, time and again, as I left the Roppongi compound. Interviews—unless I specifically asked for them to be with members of the SDF—were with suits, and rather senior suits at that. When I talked about civilian control and repeated the pun on suit control, I received fewer smiles than I had anticipated. In contrast, in interviews uniformed officers of the early postwar years would jokingly recall the ways in which civilians in the Defense Agency would demonstrate their new position within the decision-making hierarchy, such as talking to SDF officers as they sat with their feet up on their desks.

It was not until I had made several visits to interview policymakers in the Pentagon several years later that I managed to put both the visuals and the pun in clearer perspective. The U.S. system of policy-making, for better or for worse, includes many uniforms, and the offices of the Deputy Assistant Secretary for International Affairs, for example, are populated mostly by uniforms, even though the deputy assistant secretary is a civilian. But there is no formal resistance to the notion that uniforms can work under suits, nor is there a question of who makes the decisions in that office. The confidence in the system of civilian control in the United States, however, does not come from this relationship between civilian and uniformed bureaucrats. Rather, it comes from the knowledge that Congress is the elected decision-making body that will ensure that civilians make the decisions. In the Japanese system, however, the bureaucrats—civilian and uniformed—feared criticism from Japanese politicians who were intent on ensuring that Japan's military had no place of authority within the state. In the 1960s, Socialist Party Diet members were relentless critics of the government's policy and the activities of Japan's SDF. Given the hostility of the broader political environment to the role of the military in security planning, civilian control came to be interpreted as the task of the bureaucrats, the "suits," within the Defense Agency. In the face of widespread public hostility to the military institution, many Japanese SDF officers refused to wear their uniforms outside of the Roppongi complex for fear of personal attack or ridicule. Popular sentiment and sharp political criticism had made suits out of those who were in fact military personnel, in effect erasing their presence from the public consciousness.

There was a new way of talking about Japan's military, and its relationship to civilian authority, that reflected the need to demonstrate vigilance about its purpose. The repeated call in media editorials for putting "brakes" on the state suggested a military that was champing at the bit. But there was almost complete silence from that quarter. The silence of an actor that I thought would be at the forefront of policy deliberations gave me pause. Moreover, the antipathy toward Japan's postwar military that permeated discussions in policy circles provided little opportunity to hear this institution voice its thoughts. The silence was deafening and perplexing. I turned my attention to finding out what Japan's military really thought, and it was suggested to me that they would be more comfortable answering my questions if I moved away from the "high politics" of Tokyo.

The Advantages of Leaving Tokyo

Going out to various regions of Japan to see how Japan's military and its U.S. counterparts lived with local communities was an eye-opening experience. I had become intrigued by the relationship between Japanese citizens and their new, postwar military. Moreover, I already had an inkling of the complications of the U.S. military presence in Japan. I had been told repeatedly of the Japanese public's "pacifism" *(heiwa-shugi)* and its "allergy" *(arerugii)* to security issues, and to be honest, I had not questioned these assertions much. So, I temporarily set aside my search for the Japanese state and went instead to look for "pacifism" in action. The impact of these two militaries on Japanese society, it seemed to me, could best be gauged by visiting them where they lived, in peripheral regions far from the central government of Tokyo. I left the policymakers and their critics in Tokyo and ventured forth—north to Hokkaido and south to Kyushu and Okinawa—to see what the Japanese "public" thought of these two very different military forces.

Close to Tokyo and the front line of conservative-progressive confrontation over the postwar military, the SDF easily antagonized the media and, by extension, "the public." I had been taken on a sort of field trip to Yokosuka to watch the Maritime Self Defense Force (MSDF) demonstrate its antisubmarine warfare capabilities, only to witness the highly publicized capsizing of a Japanese fishing vessel by an MSDF submarine that was part of our flotilla. The media reaction was immediate and unforgiving, despite the crowded circumstances of Tokyo Bay and the question of whether or not the fishing vessel received the warning that it was in the wrong place at the wrong time. Condemnation of the MSDF officer in command of the submarine was harsh, and the public criticism quickly expanded to the entire Japanese military and to the Japanese state.

I anticipated, therefore, that local reactions to SDF bases, where aircraft were noisy and incidents were likely to be more frequent, would also be harsh. I was surprised to find that local sentiments were less critical and that SDF members I met were more willing to talk about their pride in their profession and their personal reasons for joining what had to be one of the most underrated professions in postwar Japan. I was warmly welcomed by the ground, air, and maritime SDF at Chitose, Sapporo, Misawa, Etajima, Kure, and Sasebo. In Hokkaido I was guided through the inventory of Japan's most modern army unit, the 7th Division, and much to my amusement, I was provided with a blanket on the tarmac so I could change from my heels into a pair of army boots and a flak jacket for my ride in Japan's most modern tank. I was photographed in the cockpit of an F-15J and on the top of one of Japan's diesel subs. I simulated piloting a Japanese destroyer through the straits of Shimonoseki, and I was given time to read the letters of kamikaze pilots collected in the archives *(shiryōkan)* of Japan's Maritime Academy in Etajima. I was told in Misawa of the troubles encountered by the Japanese Air Self Defense Force (ASDF) in getting the United States to fix the "black boxes" for the F-15s, and I was told (despite the official stance of the ASDF) that pilots would have preferred to fly an American F-18 than to build the FSX. Despite all the fancy hardware up north—close to the so-called "Soviet threat"—I was struck by the fact that some of these brand new aircraft were sitting without hardened shelters and that the tanks and other weapons systems had less than a thirty-day supply of ammunition. I wondered why mountainous Hokkaido needed such fancy tanks, but I had to laugh when one of the Ground Self Defense Force (GSDF) officers said that they actually spent more time preparing for the annual Sapporo Ice Festival than they did for a Soviet invasion.

I wanted to hear what Japan's military officers had to say about their country's security policies. I hoped that they would make sense out of the confusing debate over how to organize for an "exclusive defense" mission. I thought that with the SDF, I would not need to worry about language. The SDF was a military. It was equipped with as much of the latest high-tech weaponry the Japanese government could afford to give it, and it was an ally of one of the Cold War superpowers. In one of my many visits to the Defense Agency, I had been given a comic book (and a set of plastic dolls) that introduced me to "Pickles-kun" and "Parsley-chan."[4] These were the new faces of Japan's military—bright, cheerful, and disarmingly cute characters who rescued people from disasters and exuded "peace." Despite these and other public relations efforts to make the face of the SDF friendly and nonthreatening to the Japanese public, this was a military that looked powerful to most of Japan's neighbors, especially since it was backed by the presence of U.S. military forces on Japanese soil. The U.S. and Japanese militaries had increased their joint "studies" and exercises for more than a decade, and operational planning between the two militaries I assumed was proceeding rapidly.

But it was the impending Gulf War that focused attention on the role of Japan's navy, in particular. I visited Sasebo in late 1990, just as the debate over whether or not to send MSDF minesweepers to the Persian Gulf had instigated a national outcry of protest. I expected this topic to be off the table but found that after the official briefings were over, the MSDF officers I spent time with were frank and open about what they thought Japan should do in the Gulf War. Almost without exception these ship commanders and officers were ready to go and thought that Japan's navy should play a greater role in multilateral efforts in the Gulf. There was a sense of frustration with the hesitancy of Tokyo, and one officer remarked wryly that only in Tokyo was

Japan's navy not called a navy. And yet there was wide recognition that the Japanese public was not ready for its military to be seen flying the Japanese flag overseas. As this option was being discussed within the SDF, it was made clear that only those SDF who volunteered would be assigned to this mission.

My trip away from the center of policy power gave me a glimpse of Japan's military at work. While I had expected to see the attitudes of Roppongi reflected more strongly on bases around the country, I found the opposite. Engaged in the day-to-day operations assigned to them, Japan's military was more confident, professional, and at ease with itself and with the society it worked for. Moreover, in these communities, at least, there was little overt strife. For the most part it was not uncommon to see uniforms off base and on the streets. In Misawa and Sasebo, Japan's military was dwarfed by that of the United States. Housing for U.S. forces was luxurious in contrast to the apartments for SDF personnel and their families. And yet there was a rather quiet acceptance of this foreign military presence in these cities. More than once I was told jokingly by local officials that the U.S. military was only there temporarily! American base commanders also echoed this sentiment, as they told me all about the upgrades in infrastructure that the Japanese government made under its *"omoiyari yosan"* (loosely translated by policymakers as the "generosity" or "sympathy" budget) for U.S. forces in Japan. U.S. military officers were convinced that the long-term intention of the Japanese state was to improve base facilities for the day when Japan's own military would take them over.

But the situation I found in Okinawa was much different. And by the mid-1990s the pressures between local communities, U.S. forces, and local political leaders became the focal point of national attention. Okinawa's postwar history, its distance from metropolitan Japan, and the concentration of U.S. forces there all contributed to a much more contentious relationship between the prefecture and Tokyo, and the rape of a twelve-year-old schoolgirl in 1995 brought to light the backroom deals and the policy silences that had characterized Japan's (and Washington's) handling of the U.S. bases.

Had I not gone to local cities, towns, and villages in Okinawa, I would have again accepted the terms of the national debate. Moreover, I would have continued to view the Okinawa bases as being peripheral to the strategic goals of the U.S.-Japan alliance, and I would have thought that the issue was simply one of conservative-progressive difference over Japan's alliance. But in fact, base policy incorporates a whole host of policies, and had I not had the chance to investigate the way in which bases are managed, I would not have appreciated the terms of the bargain between local citizens, their local governments, and the national government. Moreover, I would have misinterpreted the impact of Governor Ōta's challenge to Tokyo. The protest by Okinawan citizens and their governor was perhaps the most startling challenge to national authority in recent years in Japan (S. A. Smith 2000). Whereas many participants in Japan's security debate in Tokyo saw the claims of Okinawa's governor as a throwback to the "old" political rhetoric of the 1960s struggle against Anpo (U.S.-Japan Security Treaty) or the 1970s Okinawa reversion movement, a new political idiom emerged from Governor Ōta's challenge to the primacy of national interest *(kokueki)* over local interests of Okinawan residents *(Okinawa kenmin no kōeki)*. Indeed, the overlay of antialliance rhetoric echoed themes of an earlier era of protest in Japan. But alongside this familiar set of complaints against the presence of U.S. military forces emerged a new coalition to protest Tokyo's handling of the bases in Okinawa, one that includes issues of women's rights, environmental protection, citizen access to the national policy-making process, and the accountability of Japan's government.

The policy solution identified, however, was one that has been a consistent part of the compact between the national government and the local communities that hosted military forces in Japan. Economic subsidies were the means of assuring local cooperation with national priorities. The dependence of poorer regions in Japan on the influx of funding from the center made the acceptance of U.S. forces—even in Okinawa—more palatable. Local politicians, conservative and progressive alike, had long traded local acquiescence to a foreign military presence for considerable economic benefits. Governor Ōta's challenge of the status quo on the U.S. bases in Okinawa, therefore, threatened not only national security policy, but also the stable supply of national funding to less advantaged local communities.

Leaving Tokyo and heading for Okinawa revealed most strikingly the social impact of a second national military force in Japan, that of the United States (S. A. Smith 2001). Far from the center of government, Okinawan citizens live with both of these militaries—Japan's and America's—in small and localized doses. This relationship—rather than an assumption of Japan's "pacifism"—became more central to understanding the nature of citizen opposition to Japan's security policy in the postwar period. Leaving Tokyo allowed me to explore the contours of the postwar Japanese state, but from a different vantage point than I had at the beginning of my research. The "island-wide protest" that erupted after the 1995 rape revealed how deeply

Japanese postwar politics has been influenced by the Cold War arrangement of combined U.S.-Japanese military power (S. A. Smith, forthcoming).

Studying the Policy-Making Process in Japan: Issues and Dilemmas

The study of public policy in Japan has long focused on the producers of policy, the bureaucrats, politicians, and opinion leaders in Tokyo who shape policy debate. The motivation for the study of public policy by U.S. and other scholars often is to identify key actors and decision makers so as to inform the way in which U.S. government and businesses negotiate their interests in Japan. But there is an increasing interest on the other side of the public policy debate—the impact of the consumers of Japan's public policy. How do Japanese citizens articulate their interests? Are those interests represented adequately in the policy-making process? Will the recalibration of the influence of Japan's bureaucrats and politicians make for a process of policy-making that is more responsive to citizens' interests, or not? These are the questions that are being prompted by the political changes within Japan over the past decade, and increasingly public policy research is encountered in a variety of institutions—some government sponsored, many others not—throughout Japan.

I had unquestionably made a number of assumptions that were being tried by my observations of the policy debate in Japan. The first was that public policy, and in this particular case security policy, was not public, at least not in the sense that we in the United States expect our policy-making to be. There was no Freedom of Information Act,[5] and until very recently the negotiations over the specifics of national policy did not take place in the national legislature. In effect, it appeared that much of the policy decisions made regarding Japan's defense and alliance policy were not subject to public scrutiny, despite policymakers' sensitivity to the well-known public "allergy" to military issues.

A second idea that I needed to rethink over time was how the public affects government policy. The policy community within Kasumigaseki had the advantage over the politicians in Nagata-chō who guided policy through the Diet. Even politicians who were noted for their expertise in the defense policy arena were less interested in the specifics of policy than they were in ensuring that the legislative reception of the government's policy was as minimally critical as possible. I was surprised to find that in Japan public policy choices were not shaped and negotiated within the legislative arena.

Or rather, the bureaucrats themselves provided the legislators with the text that they read to their colleagues in the Diet. Today, the relationship between the bureaucrats and politicians in Japan is changing, and Japan's politicians are publicly tested on their policy knowledge. This is true not only in the Diet, but also in the public media. Debates, TV talk shows, and party campaign platforms are more tailored to a public that expects policy debate.

When starting out, I spent much time trying to get my bearings and learning who was doing what, when, and where. I needed the picture to stand still, and in a sense, I started out with a rather static gaze on the policy-making process. I wanted to find out who made decisions, and why. But the more intriguing issue became what happened to this framework of policy-making as it was punctuated by change. The end of the Cold War revealed the limits of my original research question. Moreover, it opened my eyes to a more interesting phenomenon. I often joke that had I left Japan as planned, I would have been convinced that Japan would never have sent the SDF overseas. I would have agreed with the prevailing wisdom—without truly knowing why—that the dispatch of Japanese military forces abroad was unthinkable, or "taboo." I had come to believe in the rhetoric of continuity that characterized Japan's defense debate, but I had failed to reflect on what interests were being served by this interpretation. After new legislation was adopted in 1992, Japan sent the SDF overseas for numerous peacekeeping operations under the mandate of the United Nations. Legislation passed in 1999 allows the SDF to patrol international waters in case of a crisis in the "area surrounding Japan" *(Nihon no shūhen jitai)* and to assist logistically U.S. military efforts in Korea should a conflict arise. Immediately after September 11, 2001, additional legislation enabled Japan's SDF to deploy in the Indian Ocean and in South Asia in support of U.S. forces. Like many of the so-called taboos on Japanese security policy, the domestic constraints on Japanese foreign policy have been less than binding. The intriguing question for me was no longer trying to explain specific cases of decision making, but rather the shifting contours and dynamics of the process itself.

A word perhaps also needs to be said about how to do research on contentious public policy issues. As such, they present some challenges in terms of how the researcher copes with the normative dimensions of observing and interpreting political processes in Japan. Since Japan's security planning— and citizen complaints against U.S. bases—engage Japanese and U.S. policymakers, I found myself being sought out for comment on new policy initiatives. As an academic, my aim was to better understand the dynamics of change in policy-making. And yet there were many times when I found my own opinion and recommendations being solicited by journalists, bureaucrats, and politicians on both sides of the Pacific. This is perhaps a particular attribute of public policy research, particularly one, like defense policy and U.S. Marines in Okinawa, that engages U.S. government interests as much as it does Japanese. The position of the researcher, therefore, within or without the debate will influence the kinds of information that are available. It will also help identify the researcher with the agenda of the institution where s/he affiliates. There will be a trade-off between access to information and the credibility earned via the associations any researcher makes while in Japan. Nonetheless, I found that the latitude given to non-Japanese researchers is much greater than that given to those within Japan.

There has been tremendous change in the policy research environment on certain issues in Japan, particularly those related to international changes. The challenge of public policy research today in Japan is keeping an eye on the ways in which patterns of interest articulation are changing and on the factors that prompt new demands and new solutions to policy dilemmas. Individual academics or professional researchers within Japan are good sources of advice and insight on the way in which policy-making is done. So, too, are the social or political activists—those who are advocating change in the way in which policy is made. Learning to talk the policy issue talk, learning to hear the silences in policy discussions, and discovering more than one vantage point from which to view the policy debate all take time, but these kinds of signposts also offer clues to new directions at a time when the policy terrain is fluid.

Notes

I am grateful for support from the following institutions that has made my research possible: the MacArthur Foundation, the Japan Foundation, the Japan Society for the Promotion of Science, the University of Tokyo, the University of the Ryukyus, and the International Research Center for Japanese Studies. Particular thanks go to the many scholars, policy analysts, government officials, uniformed personnel, and Japanese citizens from all walks of life who have so graciously shared with me their personal and professional views on security issues.

1. The Self Defense Force (SDF), or Jieitai, includes three branches: the Ground Self Defense Force (GDSF), or Rikujo Jieitai; the Maritime Self Defense

Force (MSDF), or Kaijo Jieitai; and the Air Self Defense Force (ASDF), or Kōkō Jieitai. When speaking of Japan's present-day defense forces as a whole, the term "Self Defense Force" or "Jieitai" is used.

2. Comparable ships in the U.S. Navy are referred to proudly as destroyers, and Pentagon web sites emphasize ships' *battle* capabilities. In contrast, the Defense Agency on its web site and in its annual White Paper focuses attention on how many ships it has (or wants) and what exercises particular ships have participated in.

After September 11, 2001, particular attention has been given to the logistical supply ships sent to the Indian Ocean in support of the U.S. war in Afghanistan. While the United States wanted Japan to send its most modern (and in terms of battle capability, its most lethal) ship, the new Aegis-equipped destroyer, Prime Minister Koizumi declined, arguing that it would violate Japan's interpretation of its constitution.

3. For example, in 1988, when the Defense Agency and the MSDF were contemplating the purchase of a British Harrier VTOL (vertical take-off and landing) aircraft carrier, the result of the deliberations was to postpone purchase. But in the following year, the Defense Agency stated that Japan could not purchase "offensive aircraft carriers." By their very nature, aircraft carriers are designed to project force, and thus the idea that these ships may also be construed as "defensive" at some point in time reveals the lengths that Defense Agency officials have gone to try to find a way to label weapons in ways that neutralizes their function as instruments of war. Japan's intent may be to use military weapons for defensive purposes, but this does not diminish the capability of the weapons themselves.

4. The Defense Agency has had an active public relations effort over the postwar period. Some of the more recent efforts to change public attitudes toward the SDF have been in response to dwindling recruitment numbers. These efforts have been directed more toward younger Japanese. For example, when the movie *Top Gun* made such a splash in the United States, the Defense Agency cooperated with Japanese filmmakers in making a similar action drama (titled *Top Guy*) that featured Japan's ASDF pilots. The cartoon characters Pickles and Parsley have been made for children. You can get stickers, dolls, and comic books all depicting the Japanese SDF as contributing to public safety.

5. The information disclosure law *(Gyōsei kikan no hoyū suru jōho no kōkai ni kansuru hō)* came into effect in 2001, with significant restrictions on the kinds of information relating to national security that Japanese citizens can request of their government.

Related Readings

Smith, Sheila A. 1990. *"Henyō suru nichibei anpo."* Kokusai Mondai 369:15–28.
———. 1997. "The Wider Implications of the Bilateral Alliance." *Japan Quarterly* 44(4) (October–December): 4–11.

——. 1998. "Representing the Citizens of Okinawa." *Social Science Japan* (special issue on Okinawa) 14:8–10.

——. 1999. "The Evolution of Military Cooperation in the U.S.-Japan Alliance." In Michael J. Green and Patrick Cronin, eds., *The US-Japan Alliance: Past, Present and Future*. New York: Council on Foreign Relations, 69–93. (Japanese version, 1999. *"Nichibei dōmei ni okeru boeikyōryoku no shinten."* In *Nichibei dōmei—Beikoku no senryaku.* Tokyo: Keiso Shobō, 20–41.)

——. 2000. "Challenging National Authority: Okinawa Prefecture and the U.S. Military Bases." In Sheila A. Smith, ed., *Local Voices, National Issues: The Impact of Local Initiative in Japanese Policymaking.* Ann Arbor: Center for Japanese Studies, University of Michigan, 75–114.

——. 2001. "A Place Apart: Okinawa in Japan's Postwar Peace." In Akira Iriye and Robert Wampler, eds., *Partnership: The United States and Japan, 1951–2001.* Tokyo: Kōdansha International, 179–200. (Japanese version, 2001. *"Hedaterareta basho—Okinawa to sengo Nihon no Heiwa."* In Iriye Akira and Robert Wampler, eds., *Nichibei sengo kankeishi.* Tokyo: Kōdansha International, 212–232.) (Trans. eds. Hosoya Chihiro and Aruga Tadashi.)

Ellis S. Krauss
studying media
and society.

ELLIS S. KRAUSS

Doing Media Research in Japan

The mass media are ubiquitous in Japan and are an important institution connecting state and society. In the Japan field there are arguably fewer studies of the mass media, however, than almost any other significant type of social actor. The mass media present the researcher with a bewildering and complex variety of methodological issues and problems, many common to studying any Japanese organization, but some unique to this particular variety. The neat, textbook formulas for conducting research, from conception and access through data gathering, analysis, and write-up, are often irrelevant in the actual field situation.

The path of my own fifteen years of research on NHK, Japan's mammoth public broadcaster and the second largest (after the BBC) broadcaster in the democratic world, and on NHK's relationship to and consequences for politics in Japan illustrates this well (Krauss 1996, 1998, 2000). Research trajectories and practices are often not mechanical, preplanned, logical processes but the result of cumulative, ad hoc, and evolutionary ones. These processes, and thus the research outcome they produce, may in unexpected ways involve combining fortuitous serendipity with foresight, wedding makeshift responses to design, and creatively incorporating altered conceptions and unforeseen developments into original research plans.

Interest: Why Did the Trains Run in Prime Time?

One's conception of a research project rarely results from contemplating the "state of the field," then deciding on a project solely because it promises to discover new paradigms. The actual origins of a research project are often more complicated and interesting than this stereotypical fantasy of academic creativity would suggest. In my case, it was the result first of curiosity stimulated by a visiting friend's unexpected reaction to a Japanese experience, and eight years later being presented with a spontaneous but undeniable opportunity.

In 1975, a colleague and his wife, David and Rena Ziegler, visited us in Japan. I was proud of aspects of my adopted foreign land, and among these was NHK. Back home we had sometimes bemoaned American network news' dependence on dramatic visuals, hosted by "star" anchors. In Japan, I pointed out the solid, factually based reporting that concentrated on policy-making, presented by staid newsreaders and obviously working journalists. I was sure he would find my NHK news as superior to U.S. evening news programs as the elite Japanese newspapers were to American tabloids.

To my surprise, instead he found it uninteresting, unpolished, and staid and was scornful that its news had so many segments about, and visuals of, trains and train stations. Although surprised at his reaction, I began to watch the news with this new and different perspective, and eventually I had to agree. From that moment, my future interest in NHK was at some level an attempt to answer the questions—why was NHK's news so different from American news in style, content, and presentation, and why did they have so many segments about trains?

Once back home, my newfound interest in media led me to introduce a new course on "Political Communication," encompassing subjects such as media's role in election campaigns, television news' coverage of politics, and polling and its political uses, but only concerning American media and politics. In Japan in 1983 for research on political opposition in that country, my interest in media on the other side of the Pacific was further stimulated by conversations with Glen Fukushima, a fellow Fulbrighter that year. We both perceived especially print media coverage of the United States to focus so much on militarism, violent crime, and bizarre occurrences that it gives a very biased and one-sided picture of our more complicated society. Media was thus still very much on my mind during the last few months of this stay in Japan.

Initial Access: There Is No Such Thing as a Free Lunch

My intended research on political opposition in Japan, however, was not going well. Compared to when I had interviewed Diet members five years previously, this time they seemed more adept at giving evasive or merely formal responses. I sensed that Diet members in the intervening time had become quite conscious that what they said to foreigners was not always without an impact that reverberated back to Japan. I had worked hard, but felt like I had broken little new ground on the subject and was coming to the end of my valuable time in Japan with little to show for it in terms of my original research goals. Frustrated, I began thinking of perhaps doing some preliminary research on something to do with media to partially redeem the time on my grant.

I had discussed my interest in NHK and television news with one of my then-wife's and my oldest friends in Japan, a woman who was the granddaughter of a famous Meiji-era (1868–1912) government leader and the daughter of a man who had been head of a major wire service in Japan after the war. One day in June 1983 during a phone conversation she mentioned that her father had once been involved in some committee that had studied NHK and that she had remembered someone he had known from that time who was now one of its *riji* (managing director). Perhaps I would like to have lunch with him and tell him of my interest in studying NHK?

I went to the lunch hoping only that this initial contact might allow me to perhaps gain access to the NHK newsroom during some future visit to Japan so that I might see how the news was gathered and edited. I think I had vaguely in mind writing an article similar to the classic book *News from Nowhere* (Epstein 1973), in which analyzing the news process would elucidate why the news product turned out as it did. I was aware that to do this would require a good contact to get into the newsroom on a consistent basis.

Among the first problems a researcher may face is the difficulty of gaining access to what often can be a relatively closed organization. Journalists often like to justify their craft as a "watchdog" of government, constantly arguing for full access to information; yet when they find themselves the subject of someone else's scrutiny, they can dislike and attempt to avoid the experience as much as anyone else. Even among those in Japan who specialize in following the media, NHK's reputation for openness is low; as one has written, "[A]mong free journalists, NHK is getting a reputation as more difficult to gather information in than even the government agencies that we might expect to be called the symbol of bureaucratism" (Tokunaga 1981, 100).

As it turned out, my lunch appointment wound up making access problems the least of the research and methodological problems I faced during the unexpectedly long period in which I would conduct research on NHK. Instead, I confronted many other issues and dilemmas, including some brought on by the very ease in which I gained entrée to the institution.

The *riji* turned out to be a fine man who was most sympathetic when I explained my interest in someday studying NHK's News Center. He suggested we go back to his office, and once there, he called and told someone in the News Center to come up.

A few minutes later a relatively tall man with angular features respectfully entered. This was my introduction to one of the three associate directors of the News Center, a person who would play a key role in my research. After a few moments, the *riji* invited us to take a tour of the News Center. So, accompanied by the *riji,* my friend and I received a personal guided tour and introduction to the News Center from one of its highest executives. I could not completely enjoy it, however. I kept wondering throughout the tour whether my Japanese had been misunderstood and whether they had thought all I wanted was a tour that day, instead of consistent access at some future time to do research. I needn't have worried. At the end of the tour the *riji* turned to the associate director and told him that I was to have unlimited access to the News Center, that he should take care of me, and that he should make sure I learned as much as I could about the news process during the next couple of months I had remaining in Japan.

This development, of course, was far beyond anything I had hoped for. Access that many researchers might expend a great deal of time, effort, and connections to arrange had come to me suddenly, unexpectedly, and easily. Despite the complete lack of prior preparation or thought I had given to what my research goals or design would be, I ceased to focus on the research that originally brought me to Japan and for the next two months until my departure spent an average of three days per week at the News Center, learning as much as I could about how the news was put together.

Gaining such immediate and complete access in this fashion proved to have great benefits. I was able to observe the news process as it was taking place, as often as I liked. If I didn't understand or missed something on one day, or discovered a dimension I had not recognized previously, I could come back again to pursue or check on my observations. The ability to observe the complicated process as often as I needed was invaluable.

An additional aid was the associate director, who took seriously his injunction to "take care" of me. He not only introduced me to producers in the News Center, who were asked to provide me with information or introductions when he was busy, but on at least one occasion he gave me "homework." I was told toward the end of my stay to bring in a written comparison of the news process for both the 7:00 P.M. news and for "News Center 9:00 P.M.," a more American-style program called a "news show" with a *kyasutā* ("caster," a newscaster or news anchor in American terms) rather than an *anaunsā* ("announcer" or news reader as on the 7:00 P.M. major news program). He checked over my descriptions of the process and my evaluation of how the two programs differed, corrected minor errors, made a few additions, and confirmed my impressions. I had as my own personal "tutor" one of the most influential and knowledgeable veterans of the News Center who understood the journalistic issues involved in the way the structure and process worked and affected the product.

Whatever the type of organization, entrée through top-down-sanctioned access always entails some costs, however, as well as tremendous advantages. The most important is the trade-off of not learning about the organization from the bottom up. The *riji*'s blessing and the associate director's mentoring meant that I would have great access, but it always would be managed access: when I wanted to observe something or interview someone, it would be arranged by the associate director or one of the producers to whom he had introduced me and with whom I developed a personal rapport and a mentor-student relationship. Undoubtedly, when the others in the News Center asked who the *gaijin* (foreigner) was and what he wanted, they were told of my being there thanks to the *riji* and associate director's blessing. In so doing, I strongly suspect certain topics of discussion, and certain individuals as sources, were inadvertently or intentionally put "off-limits."

For example, through the associate director and my producer friend I came to understand that the newsroom was undergoing a major transition in an attempt to make NHK's news more visually oriented and less like the newspaper news on which NHK's was originally modeled, and this included raising the status and decision power of visual editors. Both these persons were important players in trying to bring about this change. They told me honestly about the fact that not everyone in the News Center—most especially the reporters who had dominated the previous way of doing things and who now had to cede some involvement to the nonjournalist editors—was happy with this change.

But any attempt to explore this topic with others, or to gauge the depth of the resistance, was difficult since those to whom I was introduced by my mentors were, I sensed, those who also supported the change or at least were not too opposed to it. Nor could I explore easily the issue of whether there were personal factions in the News Center and within the executive ranks of NHK for the same reason. And were—as I intuitively felt rather than knew— the issues of personal factions and differing conceptions of the news related?

I would have to learn more about this later through secondary sources, including a candid, professional autobiography critical of NHK's relationship to the ruling party by a controversial and short-lived president of NHK who had been the most influential of News Center executives, as well as through an interview arranged by someone other than my News Center mentors. Had I entered NHK through contacts with ordinary reporters first, I might have learned more earlier about the personal and professional factions and relationships that are often so crucial in a Japanese organization; but then I also might not have gotten the overall picture of the news process I did by having a veteran executive as mentor, nor very possibly had the ease of access to many others in the News Center. Whichever door to an organization you enter by—one at the top, in the middle, or at the bottom— comes with its own particular corridors that enable you to see some things better than others. All you can do is be aware of this and try to compensate in some way for what you may have missed by not coming in from a different entryway.

Interviews and Candid Views

In spending time at the News Center, I wanted not only to observe the organizational process, but also to conduct interviews with journalists to discover their definitions of news, their criteria for news selection, and their evaluation of the news-gathering and editing process. My status as a constant visitor and the journalists' schedules made this complicated. Usually one calls up and makes an appointment to do an interview, goes to the office of the respondent, and has a set amount of time to ask questions. At NHK, my potential respondents were all around me. My methods of approach were far more informal than the usual interviewing techniques.

Generally, when I visited I would go to my producer friend and tell him I was there that day. Sometimes he would ask what I wanted to know and then just take me to show me the process, essentially giving me a running interview. Often during that time we would meet other journalists sitting around —the journalistic enterprise at NHK as I discovered is one of great peaks and valleys, periods of frenetic activity and other periods when reporters would just be sitting reading the newspaper. If they were not busy I would ask them some questions or ask if I could interview them at a specified later time that day or on my next visit. Or, we would exchange *meishi* (name cards) and I would call them and arrange a future appointment. Sometimes I told my producer friend or the associate director that I would like to interview a given person. They would pick up the phone and call and arrange the interview, sometimes for a few minutes later. Not only was the interview scheduling informal, but often the interview locales were fairly informal as well. Some took place at their desks, other times at restaurants or coffee shops (there are cafeterias and coffee shops in the large NHK building).

One of the most important issues a foreign researcher faces in doing interviews is whether to tape record the interview. Ideally, if your language is so good that you have total confidence you will understand almost verbatim everything being said, and you have the ability to take notes rapidly, it would be better not to tape record to encourage more natural and open responses. The same would be true if you did not think you would need verbatim quotations, but only wanted the information for background purposes. I do not have such confidence in my language ability and have found it difficult to simultaneously concentrate on what is being discussed, anticipate my next question, and take notes. And, I often want verbatim quotes. For all these reasons, over the years I have often used one of two methods to record my respondents' information: tape recording or being accompanied by a Japanese research assistant to take notes as I conducted the interview.

There are major trade-offs to any of the methods used. Using no tape recorder or note taker means you will miss information and will not get direct quotes. Using either a tape reorder or a Japanese research assistant means you will get more complete information, but you run the great risk that your respondent will be less candid on important items.

I generally have found that the risk of lower candor is minimized by tape recording and maximized by the research assistant. I can only speculate on the reasons for this. While some respondents seem ill at ease at first with the tape recorder and are quite conscious of it, after a few minutes they forget it is there. When I ask them at the onset of the interview for permission to tape record I also reduce stress about candor by explaining that I do so to ensure I understood them correctly later on, and by assuring them that the information they give me is "not for attribution"—that I would not identify their words with their name, only by some vague and general reference to their position. Most tell me that they don't mind their name being used, but I usually tell them I will not use their names in final publication in any case to encourage candor.

If you are accompanied by a Japanese research assistant, however, it is more difficult for the person you are interviewing to forget that his or her words are being recorded in some fashion. It is more difficult to forget the presence of a live person sitting across from you scribbling away than a small, black object sitting on the table between you. Also, I think the presence of a Japanese national in the room sends up an unconscious "warning flag" to some Japanese elites that the information they give runs the risk of getting back to people in Japan: for some it is easier to subconsciously assume that talking to a *gaijin* is somehow "outside the system." Then there is the added complexity of scheduling appointments with a respondent when a third person's schedule is involved—tape recorders require only battery checks and can accompany you at your and your respondent's convenience.

I have sometimes wished a research assistant's notes had been more complete on a particular point. I have almost never been sorry that I used a tape recorder to record interviews. Sometimes, of course, I have had a respondent who was so conscious of the recorder that he or she obviously was being very cautious about what they said; but I have often found that the ability to go back sometimes months or years later to the verbatim interview to get information and check meanings is invaluable.

The most important drawback to recording is not its effect on the respondent—it is the enormous amount of work required to pick out what is useful or to have the interviews transcribed, and finally, to go through, select, and translate what I can use. If one does record, it saves a great deal of time later to spend time during the interview making brief notes on the subjects covered, their order, and noting potentially useful subjects discussed.

In any case I did not find any problem using a tape recorder with NHK journalists. If there was a little stiffness in responses, it can be attributed to the fact that journalists themselves are not used to being interviewed. Some seemed to feel a bit uncomfortable being on the other side of the interview relationship. Reporters, too, are quite aware of the consequences of misspeaking during an interview. After all, when a journalist does an interview it appears in the newspaper or on television almost immediately.

More informal and spontaneous interviews, or those held at restaurants or other natural settings, often elicited more candid responses from reporters. Offering to take respondents out for lunch, coffee, or a drink is often a good strategy, as long as it is a quiet locale. Just getting people out of their workplace environment reduces the fear that colleagues will overhear their opinions and thus encourages more relaxation and candor.

There was one kind of interview that only the opportunity to integrate myself into the News Center afforded—what one might call the "instant feedback" interview. I was quite interested in learning why journalists made certain news judgments. One of the best ways to find that out was to interview them immediately following decisions they made. Thus one day I arranged to talk to the main producer of the evening news right after he had made the final decisions as to which segments were going to be on the program that night and in what order. I then could question him about his thinking and the norms he followed in making those decisions. Another time I sat in on an editorial meeting of another news program and right afterward discussed with the program's *kyasutā* the arguments he had in the meeting and his view of the dynamics of the meeting. These "immediate postdecision" interviews were most illuminating and at once captured the thinking behind decisions.

Such techniques ultimately answered my friend's question about why there were so many trains on NHK news. It turns out that among the most important norms for judging the newsworthiness of events are whether it had a direct impact on the citizen and their family, involved taxpayer money, and was of nationwide significance. Developments affecting the role the extensive rail system played in Japanese daily life tended to meet these criteria.

Content Analysis, or "Morgues," Money, Monotony, and Methods

As any graduate student who has taken the most basic research design course knows, you should always choose your dependent variable first; yet here by virtue of the serendipitous way in which the opportunity to observe the news process had occurred, I had jumped into a project with great prospects for gathering data about my independent variable. I still didn't know, however, exactly what the news product was that this process was going to explain, or whether NHK's news product was unique or universal among broadcasters, both public and commercial. I intuitively knew it was different, but I had no firm evidence, nor was I sure it was different when it came to coverage of politics and government, my main interest as a political scientist. I needed systematic data, meaning I had to obtain news broadcasts of NHK's, and other networks' and countries' news programs, and then conduct a systematic content analysis of them. It sounded fairly simple; it became a nightmare of unexpected obstacles, gaps, and difficulties.

Conducting research on newspaper news product in Japan is relatively easy. One goes to a major research library and finds either their actual newspaper copies or, more frequently when one is dealing with issues from the past, the nicely indexed *shukusatsuban* (small-format, archival reprint editions) of one of the major national newspapers, such as the *Asahi Shinbun,* the *Mainichi Shinbun,* the *Yomiuri Shinbun,* or the *Nihon Keizai Shinbun (Nikkei).* Issues of content analysis format, categories, and reliability will have to be faced, but the basic data are readily accessible.

This is not generally the case with television news, in Japan or elsewhere, despite the great touting by the broadcasters of their role as visual "eyewitnesses to history" and the fact that television has been the major news source for the greatest number of people in all the industrialized democracies for over thirty years. In all countries, it is appalling the extent to which television news has been irresponsible about the most basic preservation and cataloging of their news broadcasts and has failed to treat them as important historical documents or to make them readily available to scholars.

In the United States, news broadcasts during the first two decades of television news were not even kept by the networks. It was only when the Television News Archives (tvnews.vanderbilt.edu) at Vanderbilt University began systematically collecting, indexing, and making them available to scholars that the American networks became interested in the subject—and then it was to sue Vanderbilt for their trouble. When that legal issue was worked out, the networks first began keeping their own record of their broadcasts, and the Vanderbilt Television News Archives also was able to become an invaluable resource to scholars in media studies, history, and the social sciences. Unfortunately, as I discovered, few other countries had its equivalent.

My first lesson in this was in the mid- to late 1980s, when I asked my producer friend if there was some way I could get several weeks of news broadcasts to analyze. He took me down to the Documents Division of NHK where he thought there were videotapes of NHK visual footage that could be accessed by a computerized indexing system. I was thrilled and thought it would be relatively easy to get the material I needed. It wasn't. It turns out that NHK's "morgue," to use the old newspaper term for its information archive, was in a somewhat different form than I expected. One typed in a name, and the computerized index would quickly find all references to it classified by subject; the problem was that the file footage was the raw footage the film crews had gathered. There did not seem to be any record or way to retrieve an entire edited, transmitted program by particular dates. This type of archive was functional for working journalists who needed file footage to put together current and future stories, the visual equivalent of a clipping file, but this was scant consolation to a scholar who needed records of particular whole programs.

Perhaps this has changed today, but I have some indications it may not have. In 1995, when I began doing research on TV Asahi's "News Station" for a comparison of NHK with a commercial network's news, I asked a TV Asahi producer if he could provide me with two or more weeks of the program for analysis. I had a period of NHK tapes and requested the corresponding period for Asahi. A week or so later the producer did send me a tape for one of the weeks I had requested, accompanied by an apologetic note explaining that retrieval of such past material was so time-consuming that they could send me only what I had in hand. I don't know what the problem is, but apparently it may still be difficult in Japan to easily retrieve or obtain the broadcasts of whole news programs from the broadcasters themselves.

I later discovered it was not much easier—but for other reasons—to obtain tapes of broadcasts in other countries for comparison to NHK. In the case of England, the BBC did have an archive of its broadcast programs and was perfectly happy to provide them for those not using them for commercial purposes. I wrote and asked the cost for three weeks of taped weekday broadcasts of the main news and received a letter providing the figure. It was not a cheap amount, but I thought perhaps it was manageable. When I wrote to ask them how I could provide the named payment, the response was a polite but firm admonition that I must have misunderstood—that amount was for *each* twenty-some-odd-minute newscast! I don't recall the exact amount, but this made the prospective cost fifteen times the original figure that I had thought barely affordable! Obviously, the BBC was not set up to provide their newscasts to scholars working on pure academic research on a small or nonexistent budget.

I was therefore left to my own ad hoc devices. My first set of NHK news programs was taped for me by a neighborhood photo shop. Later, through the years, friends, friends of friends, and relatives of students who were working as teaching assistants in Japan and in other countries taped sets of programs at my request. For France, no one, not even scholars of that country, seemed to know where to obtain such tapes. I finally learned that there were international broadcasts of France's public television via satellite. For the United States, Professor Doris Graber, a noted American media scholar at the University of Illinois at Chicago, kindly gave me the raw data from a content analysis that she had conducted, and I was able to recategorize that data for comparison to NHK's. For Germany and Italy, too, I retabulated data from other scholars' papers to make them correspond as closely as possible to my categories for Japan. In Sweden, a good friend's wife was a media scholar working on a project involving the analysis of Swedish television newscasts using a descriptive written log of news items, so I was able to use her data for simple rather than full categorization as in the other countries.

The lack of systematic archives of TV news programs in industrialized countries that would make such tapes available at reasonable cost to researchers made using these informal personal methods necessary, and the acquisition and analysis inconvenient and difficult. It also meant that rather than having the exact same days of coverage for each country's news programs, I had different weeks of different years. As my focus was on domestic coverage in each country and not on international coverage of the same events, this was not crucial. Nevertheless, my experience leads me to the following advice for anyone working on media research and who wishes to do content analysis:

1. Do not assume that the raw programs are readily available for analysis.
2. Plan a budget for the considerable expense of buying tapes in those countries that have archives and make them available.
3. Decide early what time period you want to analyze for each country and have a reliable source lined up far in advance.
4. Have collaborator(s) abroad if you are doing comparative research, and be prepared to coordinate with them to obtain consistent time periods across countries.
5. Be aware that there are copyright issues involved if you tape programs

yourself or have others tape them, and don't assume that the rules are necessarily friendly to academic researchers. Commercial and private interests tend to take precedence over the public good and historical veracity in the modern world, and few practitioners care much about the record of social life for the ages.

Incidentally, I found exactly the same problem later in getting photographs for my book. The public relations offices of both NHK and TV Asahi were happy to oblige, but unfortunately not to the extent I had hoped. TV Asahi gave me exactly two photos, and only after confirming that I was not working for an American news agency or going to use them commercially. NHK obligingly provided more, but they had only very old photos from the 1950s and 1960s and a few recent shots from the current News Center, but none of the News Center ten years ago or of past presidents of NHK beyond the last two. We social scientists tend to underestimate how much the people we study are concerned with carrying out their jobs in the present and place little value on materials for their historical or academic utility.

Another, more complicated, issue for content analysis was how to analyze the content of the NHK programs I was able to obtain. A larger proportion of major research on television news had been done in the United States (e.g., of the role of television in electoral campaigns) and Britain (e.g., studies of how labor is treated in the news). The research questions, and thus the categorizations, used in those analyses were often quite different than mine about which specific, important political actors were portrayed and how. I was struck also by how many analyses of television news surprisingly focused solely on the content of the narrative, but not on the visual dimensions of the news presentation. Because television is a visual medium and presumably at least some of the effect of television news on the viewer comes through its visuals and not just its narrative, I thought this a major limitation of many previous studies.

I thus realized I would not be able to simply adopt content analysis schedules and categorizations created by other researchers, but would have to design my own format that focused explicitly on political dimensions of the news and included detailed attention to visual styles.

Because my research extended over several years, however, and eventually included other networks and other countries' news programs as well, I learned an important lesson: make sure you plan everything you want to include in your analysis before you start. After analyzing the news during certain years, I discovered that there were some new dimensions of the analysis I would like to include—for example, not just who was covered and whether the journalist or announcer had stated their opinion about the event, but also some overall rating of whether that coverage was neutral, positive, or negative. This was difficult if not impossible to do without going back and reanalyzing and recoding all the programs that had been done previously—a very time-consuming task. So make very sure you have thought of everything you might possibly want to include before you analyze the first program.

Employing research assistants to do the coding of the content analysis data has its trade-offs. This task has to be one of the most tedious, time-consuming, and mind-numbing methodologies ever conceived. It thus is perfect work to hire others to do. But this creates other major problems. Students or whomever you hire must be trained well and long in exactly how to categorize material as you would have categorized it. This not only takes a great deal of your own time to conduct training sessions as well as to resolve questions that students have, but it requires constant checking of the results. Also, if the research is going to take place over years, as mine did, and involve data from several countries, then the problem is multiplied because students by their very nature (at least the best ones) tend to graduate and move on to more interesting and lucrative pursuits than content analysis. This means you have to train a new cohort all over again.

In the case of content analysis of Japanese materials, other issues come to the fore as well. Understanding meaning is crucial, of course, and the temptation is to use as your coders Japanese nationals who would have no trouble understanding the program content. Then, however, you have to be especially careful that your instructions, the meaning of your coding categories, and the methodology are understood. If you use Americans, even those fairly fluent in Japanese, you have the opposite problem: being careful they really understand the content. I also discovered that, because of the specialized vocabulary and need to understand context and history of a particular kind of segment, one should not assume that either a Japanese or American student fairly fluent in Japanese really understands everything in a news broadcast.

I have occasionally used students, especially graduate students, to do the content analysis. In most, but not all, of the cases I either found it took an enormous amount of my time to train and supervise them sufficiently or that I had to go back and redo several parts because I had not spent enough time training them. I was also concerned that if over time too many different students did too much of the various analyses, then consistency might become a problem. For all these reasons, I often either redid the analysis that students had done or wound up doing it myself. I know of projects where funding was sufficient that enough students were hired at one time, enough time spent on training them sufficiently, and enough supervision maintained that the results were fine. It is not impossible, but if you don't have the funding, the time to train and supervise adequately, or enough students to complete the project within the academic life span of these students, then doing much of it yourself is the only effective (default) option. Either way, it will take a great deal of your own time and effort.

Why Better Books (and Elephants) Have Longer Gestation Periods

My research on NHK took over fifteen years to turn into a book manuscript, an inordinately long time especially for someone who has always prided himself on completing projects by a deadline, even a self-imposed one. There are reasons (not excuses) for this, including two cross-continental moves to new positions, a divorce, and taking on several more lucrative projects to help pay my contribution to my daughter's tuition, all of which helped to delay completion. There is also the "moving target" problem in studying contemporary affairs: once delayed, events progress, and then one has to return to do field research to follow up on recent events. Closure becomes very difficult.

Whatever the old stereotype of the scholar working on their "magnum opus" for years, it isn't true today. The academic profession has become merciless about such long gestation periods and their consequences. Considering that during the course of those fifteen years I had produced three coedited books and over thirty articles in major professional journals and edited volumes, I wasn't exactly idle, but nonetheless I got the impression that not getting the book out sooner hurt my reputation among colleagues. Further, the longer a volume takes to research, the longer it tends to get. Yet editors today are ruthless about insisting a manuscript be under a certain size for financial and marketing reasons.

I also discovered some of the cross-pressures and contradictions in our profession. For example, in the course of one's career it is easy to be induced and seduced into editing volumes for the collective good of the field. Nonetheless, fields do not count all publications equally. Scholars in Asian studies tend to measure productivity quite subjectively, with the single-authored volume having a professional "payoff" beyond that of other publications.[1] In retrospect, I wish I had devoted more time and effort to my own volume and less to the several edited books I produced. As an editor, especially if one is contributing more than one article to the volume, one invests almost as much as it takes to complete a single-authored book. New entrants to the field, beware: you have nothing to lose but your reputations. I suggest resisting those collegial pressures to edit a volume and concentrate instead on your own book.

Despite some of the problems and delays I encountered, I am convinced that my book is a better and will be a more significant publication because it was done over an extended period of time. Had I completed a book manuscript just a couple of years after my initial field research, I would have implemented my original project on how the television news organization and process produced a particular type of television news, perhaps including a comparison of two of the major news programs NHK broadcast.

As time went on, I began to wonder about the broader question of why news organization and process are structured as they are and how those structures came about. I began to delve more into questions of the historical development of NHK and how NHK as an organization related to political authority.

I also benefited from the feedback I received from papers presented at professional meetings that made me think more about the potential political consequences of the product the news organizations produce.

In short, the delays in completing my research led me to reflect on far broader and more significant questions of origin and consequences. Developments in the field of political science emphasizing state-society relations also fed into and encouraged me in these new approaches. And, the most significant change in the area of television news in the postwar period—the growing popularity of Kume Hiroshi's "News Station" program on the commercial TV Asahi network, which undermined the television news dominance of NHK and presented a new style of television news in Japan—took place only since the late 1980s. Because I thus could incorporate these trends in my book, it is a far more interesting and deeper analysis as a result of the time it took to complete.

In many ways I was fortunate. I had tenure and was a full professor. I could afford the "luxury" of not rushing my initial ideas for this project into book form. The pressures for tenure continue to increase. It is no longer rare for assistant professors to need two published books or their article equivalents to be promoted, even at far less than elite institutions. The quality of some of the resulting books sometimes suffers, producing a volume that twenty years ago would have been only a journal article.

Let there be no mistake: I am not advising anyone to take as long as I did to complete my book. Certainly, however, there is something between churning out a book every three years to satisfy external pressures for quantifiable research standards and taking fifteen years to finish one because it always had to be deferred to other, more immediate, professional and personal demands. May we all find a happy medium!

Notes

With thanks for funding at various points from: Fulbright Fellowship; Joint Committee on Japanese Studies, SSRC-ACLS; Woodrow Wilson International Center for Scholars; Japan Iron and Steel Federation Funds, Central Research Fund, and Japan Program, University of Pittsburgh; Swedish-America Foundation. With thanks to friends Kazuko and Tetsuo Hisamori, and to the executives and journalists at NHK, who made the fieldwork possible, to many colleagues in the Japan field for their helpful feedback, to my many research assistants, and to my wife, Martha A. Leche, for her unstinting support.

1. Of course, in many disciplines in the social sciences, refereed journal articles may have more "payoff" than a single-authored book. This is one of the main cross-pressures social scientists in Asian studies must live with today: the need to meet several varying standards of professional judgment.

Related Readings

Information on my current research and recent publications can be found on my web site: www-irps.ucsd.edu/irps/expersheet/sh-krauss.html.

Budner, Stanley, and Ellis S. Krauss. 1995. "Balance and Objectivity in Newspaper Coverage of U.S.-Japan Frictions." *Asian Survey* 34(4):336–356.

Krauss, Ellis S. 1995. "Varieties of Television News: Explaining Japanese and American Coverage of the Other." *Studies of Broadcasting* 31:47–67.

———. 1996. "Portraying the State in Japan: NHK Television News and Politics." In Susan J. Pharr and Ellis S. Krauss, eds., *Media and Politics in Japan.* Honolulu: University of Hawai'i Press, 89–129.

———. 1998. "Changing Television News and Politics in Japan." *Journal of Asian Studies* 57(3):663–692.

———. 2000. *Broadcasting Politics in Japan: NHK and Television News.* Ithaca, N.Y.: Cornell University Press.

Mary C. Brinton consulting with a research assistant.

MARY C. BRINTON

Fact-Rich, Data-Poor: Japan as Sociologists' Heaven and Hell

Social scientists do not always make good predictions. The scholars who supervised my dissertation research later told me that they had been sure my research plan would fail. Fortunately, they were wrong. But unfortunately, their prediction was based on sound reasoning: they were cognizant of a major impediment facing social scientists attempting to do the type of research in Japan that I had proposed. That impediment is the virtual unavailability in Japan of individual-level data—"raw" data, as social scientists often call it—with which to carry out statistical analyses. This problem has hampered American research on Japan in a number of substantive and theoretical areas in sociology, political science, and economics. In the case of my own discipline, sociology, it has hindered the training of graduate students who are interested in joining the ranks of the handful of academic researchers who claim dual loyalty to Japanese studies and to sociology as a discipline.[1] In the extreme, the unavailability of data so discourages Ph.D. students that they make the unfortunately pragmatic choice of abandoning the study of Japan altogether in favor of a research site (often the United States) where high-quality, individual-level data are accessible. This seems a rash choice indeed, but it is a survival strategy in those fields in sociology that more or less require practitioners to carry out empirical research with large survey data sets.

The situation is even worse in labor economics. The Japanese government produces and releases some of the best GNP, corporate financial, and input-output data in the world. But microlevel labor data are available only to a handful of Japanese researchers and very rarely to any foreign researchers.

This chapter outlines the set of problems facing social scientists and would-be social scientists of Japan who need quantitative data for their research and suggests some strategies for overcoming these problems. I also discuss recent promising developments in the Japanese social science research community that will make some types of quantitative data more accessible to all researchers. While I speak from the vantage point of a sociologist, the issues and solutions I discuss are relevant to all researchers, academic and nonacademic alike, who find themselves in the position of needing individual-level data on which to carry out analyses. My purpose is not to try to convince readers that the best social scientific studies of Japan are necessarily quantitative in nature. Rather, I seek to deal with the "data problem" in areas that more or less require quantitative data. These include fields such as social inequality, labor markets, gender stratification, education, demographic processes, and political and social attitudes.

Who Needs Data?

Individual-level data refer to objective and subjective information on individuals that is typically gathered through interviews or written surveys, often of large samples of individuals representative of particular populations (e.g., national samples of Japanese men and women, regional samples of the voting population, etc.). I use "objective" and "subjective" in the typical senses of those words, with "objective" referring to characteristics of the individual such as sex, education, birthplace, father's education, income, and so on, and "subjective" referring to an individual's opinions and attitudes, self-perceived social class, and so forth.

Individual-level data are important for the analysis of any number of social science problems where one is trying to tease out causal processes. Suppose one is interested in the wage gap between working men and women in Japan and the causes behind that gap. Japan has consistently had the dubious distinction of having one of the largest male-female wage gaps of any highly industrialized country (Brinton 1993; Ogawa and Clark 1995). Within East Asia, it is outdone on this dimension only by South Korea. Gaining an understanding of this phenomenon and its intransigence is thus an important sociological endeavor.

When I went to Japan as an energetic Ph.D. candidate there were no data available to allow me to answer in a comprehensive manner the question of why the Japanese gender wage gap is so large, let alone answer the other questions about women in the labor market that I had proposed to study. I therefore decided to collect my own data by conducting a large-scale survey in several Japanese cities. That is the plan that made my committee members shudder. One might reasonably ask why published tables from census data or from surveys carried out by the Ministry of Labour would not suffice.[2] In fact, I was repeatedly asked this by a contact I had in the ministry. It was difficult for me to explain why published data—which she could easily obtain for me—would not suffice for my purposes. It helped when I asked her to imagine a table that included men's and women's levels of education, their major field in school, their years of work experience, age, occupation, the size of firm where they worked, the industry of the firm, their status as a full- or part-time employee versus a self-employed worker or a worker in a family enterprise, and their inclusion in a firm-internal labor market or not. These are some of the key variables required in order to tease out the possible sources of the male-female wage gap. As each dimension is successively added, one can assess how much of the wage gap it explains.

Of course there is no such published table, for there is no way of including all of this information in a two-dimensional or even three-dimensional table. This is a principal reason why researchers need the individual-level data from a survey rather than aggregate data. (Another reason, more easily resolved, is that occasionally the two- or three-way table one wants does not happen to be included in published statistics. I discuss ways of resolving this issue later in the chapter.) Individual-level data allow the researcher to use statistical techniques to essentially produce the type of table sketched out above that one cannot produce visually because there are too many dimensions involved. Multiple regression and other statistical techniques that are readily available in most statistical packages then permit one to assess how much of the wage gap is due to differences in men's and women's educational and work experiences, differences in the occupations in which they work, and so forth. These statistical tools take us a long way toward understanding important social phenomena such as male-female wage inequality.

There are of course many things that the analysis of individual-level quantitative data will *not* reveal. If all of the factors outlined above explain very little of the wage gap, the analysis does not point to what explains more. For instance, it does not reveal directly what the role of labor market discrimination is. But it does show how much variation in wages is explained by the variables included in the analysis. And this permits generalizability, a central goal of much social scientific research and of sociological research in particular. Being able to make statements of the type, "If Japanese working women had the same educational background as working men, X percent of the gender wage gap would be eliminated" or "If occupational sex segregation were eliminated in Japan, X percent of the gender wage gap would disappear" renders it possible to compare Japan with other countries for which such analysis has been done.

It is worthwhile to emphasize how important it is to be in a position to engage in such comparative work. First, it puts Japan scholars on equal footing with scholars who study the same issue in other countries and thus opens up a conversation between Japanese studies and studies of other parts of the world. Second, if one finds something different about the way the gender wage gap is produced in Japan versus other countries, this suggests ways that the Japanese case can inform theory building in the field of gender stratification (Brinton 1988, 1989, 2001). This is not a trivial accomplishment, since the field of area studies has come under attack for not contributing strong theoretical insights to social science disciplines (viz., the debates that raged around the dismantling of "traditional area studies" committees and programs at the Social Science Research Council in the mid-1990s).

In addition to making it possible to bring findings from Japan into a general theoretical discussion, the ability to parse out at least some of the principal causes of male-female wage inequality can provide important grist for social policy recommendations. If one can state that a specific portion of the wage gap is due to the fact that women in the labor force are less educated than men, it suggests that eradicating that portion of the wage gap will rest on drawing more highly educated women into the labor market. Or, if educational levels in the female population at large (not just the female workforce) are below males', one may advocate policy measures that equalize male and female education in the population. (A case in point where social science research has had this type of significant policy effect is in the area of women's education and child health. A large number of demographic studies in both industrialized and "developing" countries in the 1970s and 1980s showed that mothers' educational levels are highly predictive of child health. This created a strong incentive for governments in developing countries to promote female education [Mason 1989].)

This extended example of the type of data required to examine an important sociological problem is one among many that could be given. It illustrates not only how one can begin to disentangle various causes of a certain phenomenon with individual-level data, but how that capability itself enables Japan researchers to contribute to an existing field of inquiry (gender stratification) within the social sciences. So, why are individual-level data so hard to come by in Japan? Is this a case of "structural impediments" that block foreign researchers, or is it a more general problem for Japanese and foreign researchers alike? What strategies are available for dealing with situations where individual-level data for a large representative sample of individuals are inaccessible?

Where Are the Data?

The problems surrounding data inaccessibility in Japan cannot be fully explained by the concern for preserving the anonymity of survey respondents, the "selfishness" of Japanese researchers vis-à-vis foreign researchers, general East Asian social science traditions, or other facile reasons.[3] Japanese social scientists attempting to do empirical research on a large range of topics that require individual-level data (not only gender inequality but educational inequality, social class inequality, ethnic inequality, demographic topics such as marriage and fertility patterns, social and political attitudes, etc.) have been nearly as badly hampered as foreign researchers. The reasons relate to the two principal ways that researchers in any industrialized country typically acquire individual-level data—from the government, or from surveys conducted by other researchers and then released for public use.

In the United States, the Census Bureau and the Bureau of Labor Statistics make individual-level data based on representative samples of the U.S. population publicly available. Also, funding provided by the National Science Foundation (NSF) and other government agencies to social scientists carries the stipulation that the data collected will eventually be made available to the social science community at large for further analysis. Grant administration guidelines published by NSF state the following: "Investigators are expected to share with other researchers, at no more than incremental cost and within a reasonable time, the primary data, samples, physical collections and other supporting materials created or gathered in the course of work under NSF grants" (National Science Foundation 2002, 107). The Inter-University Consortium for Political and Social Research (ICPSR), established in 1962 at the University of Michigan, serves as a major repository of public-use survey data.[4] Data archives were also established in the 1960s in Germany, Britain, and the Netherlands, followed by nine other European countries in the ensuing years.[5]

The situation in Japan is significantly different. None of the major government ministries in Japan (including the Census Bureau, the Ministry of Education, and the Ministry of Health, Labour and Welfare, all of which carry out surveys extremely relevant to social-scientific concerns) routinely makes individual-level data publicly available, either to Japanese or foreign researchers. The exception is the case where Japanese social science researchers are involved in study groups on a specific topic organized by a government ministry and are granted access to a certain data set with the proviso that they will not share it with other researchers. In this case, these individual researchers may be permitted to publish papers in social science journals. But the stipulation that the data not be shared means that the pool of researchers who have access is very small, even within the Japanese social science community.

Furthermore, the amount of government funding available for individual Japanese researchers or groups of researchers to conduct surveys of their own has been extremely limited, and there is no provision that data from survey research conducted by researchers with the support of government funding need be released to nonrelated researchers or to the general public. The paucity of funding has meant that many fewer large-scale surveys have been carried out by social scientists at Japanese than U.S. universities. It also means that when Japanese social scientists do conduct survey research, it is often at considerable cost to themselves, with the necessary resources patched together through a combination of their own funds and the unpaid labor of their graduate students. These are hardly the circumstances that generate an eagerness to make one's data publicly available; so many of the costs have been borne by the individual researcher that there is a strong incentive to keep the data for oneself. The logic is similar in the case of major research projects undertaken by Japanese social scientists with the financial assistance of their universities. The university may offer support with the stipulation that the data not be shared with social scientists at other universities in Japan (let alone with social scientists in the United States or other countries). A large-scale demographic survey undertaken in the mid-1990s by social scientists at Nihon University comes to mind as a recent example.

In sum, the barriers to intellectual exchange and development in social science fields that require individual-level data from Japan have been formidable. This has had a strikingly negative impact on the volume of research and knowledge about Japanese social inequality, labor markets, education, and demographic processes in particular, all of which are major subfields in American sociology. What strategies are available to students and scholars of Japan committed to working in such areas? It is very tempting to decide to collect one's own data afresh. But making this initial decision and carrying it out successfully are quite different things. Data collection difficulties are magnified if one wants a sample of individuals that is representative of a certain population. I deal first with this case, which requires doing a large-scale survey. I then turn to the generally more advisable strategy of collecting data through a case study. Finally, I turn to strategies not of data collection but of gaining access to preexisting data sets.

Going It Alone: Large-Scale Surveys and Organizational Case Studies

In collecting quantitative data from a sample of individuals, the two things one must try to maximize are the representativeness of the sample and the response rate to the questionnaire survey. Both of these are critical in determining the publishability of one's results in major American social science journals and the acceptance of a book manuscript by a major university press, so they are well worth worrying about.

The Large-Scale Survey

Conducting a survey on one's own poses some tempting advantages. One can include all of the burning questions one has in mind. Moreover, one need not rely on permission from management (as in the case study of a firm), a school board or principal (as in the case study of a school), or other authority to reach individual respondents. On the other hand, without such an intermediary there is no guarantee that individuals will grant interviews or agree to fill out questionnaires, for it is entirely a matter of individual cooperation with the researcher. The attempt to survey a large representative sample of individuals was the route that I chose as a Ph.D. student and was the reason my committee cringed at the thought of sending me off to Japan on my own. A quick walk-through of what I did and the reasoning behind it will illuminate the beauties as well as the horrors of this strategy.

Since one of my central purposes was to understand the sources of the male-female wage gap, I decided that focusing on a single firm or business organization would not be an appropriate strategy. I wanted to ask questions of women who were not currently in the labor force as well as those who were, and I also wanted to have a range of workers in my sample—self-employed workers, unpaid workers in small family businesses, government employees, and full- and part-time employees in firms of different sizes. I also wanted to survey individuals in more than one area of Japan so that my scholarly audience would not accuse me of regional peculiarity in my results. To put it bluntly, I wanted my research subjects to approximate the type of nationally representative sample of men and women that the Japanese government uses in its surveys (those surveys for which I could not obtain individual data—the surveys that created the necessity for me to collect my own data in the first place!).

Inquiries in Japan led me to discover that each *shiyakusho* (municipal office) or, in the case of large cities, *kuyakusho* (ward office), has a comprehensive record of households in its administrative area that lists the name, sex, and birth date of each adult age twenty and over. This is the *senkyonin meibo,* or list of eligible voters. The government requires individuals to register a change of residence within thirty days of moving, so these records are continuously updated. I decided to sample men and women twenty-five to twenty-nine years of age and forty to forty-four years of age so that I would have individuals in my sample who had recently entered the labor market and were in the family formation stage as well as individuals who had potentially been in the workforce for twenty years or so and had gone through the stages of marriage and child rearing.

Obtaining a nationally representative sample would have involved sampling from a huge number of *shiyakusho* and *kuyakusho*. Thus I had to compromise. Given that I was mainly interested in the labor market fate of men and women living in urban areas, I chose three urban locations: Kodaira (a middle-class suburb west of Tokyo), Sapporo, and Toyohashi (a city close to Nagoya with a larger working-class population). This gave me an urban sample with regional as well as social class variation. All of the cities were chosen opportunistically; that is, I had at least one Japanese personal contact at each site. My contact and I sent a coauthored letter in Japanese to each *shi-*

yakusho (or, in the case of Sapporo, to several *kuyakusho*) requesting permission for me to visit and draw a sample of individuals in the sex and age groups specified above. The *senkyonin meibo* are open to public access, so theoretically my request could not be denied. Once granted permission, I spent several days at each office copying names and addresses of men and women in the demographic groups I had selected. Much of this tedious work was carried out with the assistance of undergraduate students of some of my contacts, to whom I paid a modest hourly wage.

I designed a fairly long (eleven-page) survey in Japanese that would generate the information (educational background, work experiences, parental background, spouse's educational background and work, number of children, etc.) I needed in order to carry out my desired statistical analyses. The survey had to be professionally printed, as this was in the mid-1980s, unfortunately just before Japanese word-processing became prevalent. The survey was then mailed to each person with a prestamped return envelope included. Follow-up postcards and phone calls encouraging return of the questionnaires had to be handled. A response rate had to be calculated. In Kodaira, where the initial response rate was particularly low, home visits were made to try to encourage people who had not sent in their questionnaires to do so.[6] Data had to be coded into computer-readable format, checked for consistency, and, many months later, analyzed. The extent of the undertaking was enormous. But the response rate to the questionnaire edged over the "acceptable" rate of 50 percent and, it turned out, rivaled the response rate that the Japanese government obtains on some of its (much more lavishly funded) mail surveys. The final sample of individuals numbered approximately twelve hundred men and women, a more than acceptable number on which to conduct the type of quantitative analyses I wanted to do on wage differences between men and women as well as promotional trajectories, on-the-job training, permanent or impermanent employment, and a host of other aspects of work. The results of the study appeared in a number of articles and in a book (Brinton 1989, 1991, 1993; Brinton, Ngo, and Shibuya 1991).

The moral? Large-scale data collection on the part of individual researchers is not *impossible* to carry out in Japan. But it is highly labor intensive in the best of circumstances (i.e., with plentiful funding) and extraordinarily so in less optimal circumstances. Mailing costs are high. Response rates are likely to be low. No sociology Ph.D. student in their right mind would attempt such an endeavor in the United States because it is not necessary when public-use data are available. To require Japanese or foreign researchers to engage in this type of work that is best carried out by survey research organizations or government agencies creates, as I have argued throughout this chapter, a disincentive to investigate issues for which such data are necessary and a disincentive to share data once they are collected. Also, it may very well be the case that the response rate I obtained from a mailed questionnaire in Japanese cities was higher than would be possible now, more than fifteen years later. Impressionistic evidence suggests that Japanese citizens are even more deluged with surveys now than was previously the case.

The Case Study

The major alternative to large representative surveys is the case study. Here, the researcher chooses an organization or community and uses this as the sampling frame, either surveying the entire membership or a representative sample. Using the example of the male-female wage gap, a logical strategy for dealing with the unavailability of data on a national sample of individuals might be to carry out a case study of a company, examining the extent of male-female wage disparity and the reasons behind it. Representativeness is a concern because of the importance of generalizability. Is the company representative of other companies, or is it a special case? This question should be addressed head-on when the researcher chooses the research site. For instance, one might target a specific industry such as banking, look at published data on the size and variety of banks, and determine which type of bank one is most interested in. From there, the researcher needs to use contacts to find a bank of that type to study.

Since permission to study a business organization may be difficult to obtain, it is more likely that the process of choosing a firm will not follow the logical sequence outlined above. The researcher may instead need to rely on contacts to gain access to a firm and then turn to published statistics to situate the firm in the relevant population of firms in order to assess its representativeness. There is no inherent problem with this. The central issue remains one of putting one's research site into context for the scholarly audience so that the audience will be able to interpret the findings knowing that this firm is representative of some larger population of firms. A successful recent example of an organizational case study where the researchers discuss the representativeness of the firm they studied is Spilerman and Ishida (1996). Ogasawara's study of Japanese office ladies (OL, ō-eeru) in a Tokyo bank, though primarily qualitative rather than quantitative in methodology, also required her to demonstrate to readers that the OL she studied could be considered representative of OL in other large Tokyo firms (1998, 2001). To do so, she also interviewed thirty OL from other firms and discussed their responses and experiences.

Unlike large-scale surveys, in case studies the response rates to questionnaires or individuals' acquiescence to be interviewed is typically not a major problem. Permission to distribute questionnaires or conduct interviews needs to be negotiated at the time the researcher is granted access to the company. The sensitivity of questions can be problematic in organizational case studies because of employees' possible fears that management will review the answers or the researchers' interview notes and identify "who said what." This is a separate set of issues regarding questionnaire construction and confidentiality assurances that this chapter will not specifically address.

General Lessons for Data Collection

When embarking on a data-collection project in Japan or elsewhere it obviously pays to first consider whom one knows and how they might be able to help. Social skills can be as important as intellectual skills in the initial stages of the project. Most researchers will follow the case study strategy rather than the large-scale survey strategy, so it is important to think about the myriad organizational affiliations that fellow Japanese professors, graduate students, or friends and acquaintances may be able to offer. For Ph.D. students, fellow Japanese graduate students can sometimes open doors. For instance, if one is interested in studying adolescent attitudes, a Japanese graduate student may be able to provide access to the high school from which he or she graduated. If the foreign researcher spends some time in the school, permission to carry out a survey of current students or former graduates may be granted by the principal. Establishment of a good relationship with that principal may clear the way for introductions to principals at other schools, if one wants to do a survey at multiple research sites.

A second critical point to remember is that information is always valuable to someone, as are research skills. Schools, firms, nongovernmental organizations (NGOs), social movement organizations, local governments, political parties, and many other groups and organizations rarely have the time, resources, or expertise to conduct surveys of the characteristics and attitudes of their own membership. An American researcher may be able to provide the time and expertise, and this can make all the difference in being able to gain access to lists of members or organizational affiliates. For example, an NGO that is attempting to help foreign migrants deal with employment, schooling, housing, and other issues may be extremely happy to have a foreign researcher distribute questionnaires in the local community to migrants and to Japanese residents, addressing attitudes of both groups on these issues. In such a case, the researcher can help NGO staff members formulate and word questions to be included in the survey and can typically add his or her own questions as well. The NGO may be able to provide assistance with the mechanics of data collection and coding, such as distributing questionnaires and coding responses under the researcher's direction. In short, offering services in kind to one another can be an excellent way of maximizing the complementary skills and advantages that a Japanese organization and an American researcher bring to a research issue. By offering help in survey questionnaire construction or expertise in sampling or data analysis methods, one may be able to persuade an organization to invest modestly in a research project that otherwise would not have been attempted. The payoff often can be substantial: important information for the organization and raw data for the researcher. (Of course, as with working through the management of a business firm, a cautionary note needs to be added that the nature of the organizational sponsorship may sometimes bias the responses one gets. This has to be thought through carefully in each case. For example, will respondents accurately report certain political attitudes if the survey is sponsored by the local government? How accurately will migrants who did not come to Japan on a work visa report their income to you or to the organization sponsoring a survey?)

Third, the researcher must be very clear about *what* he or she wants to know. In survey research perhaps more than in almost any other research enterprise, one can run into tremendous difficulties and expend useless effort in failing to *work backward from the research questions*. A useful way of thinking about it is that in survey research you cannot go back to the library if you did not ask what you needed to find out the first time around. If one goes to the trouble of devising an interview schedule or survey instrument, it is worth the time and energy to do it right. This typically means many drafts and several pretests with Japanese respondents in order to make sure questions and concepts are being interpreted in the way you intend, and in order to make sure that you have devised a coding scheme that adequately captures the essence of the answers.

Knowing what it is you want to know also generally maximizes the chances of gaining access to an organizational research site. Stating that you want to do a survey of workers or students is hardly a specific enough request for a business firm or school to pass judgment on. At the other extreme, stating that you want to study employees' perceptions of sex discrimination is not likely to get you in the door either. More appropriate but still sufficiently specific may be a request to study various dimensions of employees' satisfaction with their working life.

Strategies for Data Access: Personal Ties to Research Institutes and Scholars

The alternative to primary data collection is to access an existing data set. Given the lack of public-access laws or norms in Japan regarding individual-level data, the principal way of obtaining a data set is through personal ties. Any researcher of Japan recognizes that this is a long-term strategy involving the development of trust and the give-and-take of mutual exchange over a long period of time. Introductions to government research institutes by intermediaries can be very useful in the areas of research dealt with in this chapter. Long-standing ties with individuals or sets of individuals in the Ministry of Health, Labour and Welfare, the Japan Institute of Labour, and other government and semigovernmental agencies that engage in data collection can eventually make it possible for one to negotiate access to data sets that are otherwise not available to outside individuals, whether foreign or Japanese. But the emphasis here must of necessity be on the long-term nature of this research strategy; it is only feasible for scholars who already have a deep commitment to Japan and are "in it for the long run" no matter whether data are or are not available at the time that they would like.

A second strategy that is sometimes feasible is to inquire whether the organization holding data of interest can provide certain key unpublished cross-tabulations of variables. Sometimes the reason that published statistics are insufficient is simply because the tables most relevant to one's research question were not included in the research report. If one knows that data were indeed collected on key variables of interest, it may be possible to request that certain cross-tabulations be produced. This strategy has the advantage of being direct and avoiding the massive formal and informal red tape that usually accompanies the much more demanding request for the raw data themselves. In order to utilize this strategy one has to know exactly what one wants. But as discussed above, this is a requirement for any of the data collection efforts of the type discussed in this chapter.

A third strategy is to develop ties with Japanese researchers who have interests in similar substantive issues and to write grant proposals to submit for funding in Japan as well as in the United States for data collection. This does not obviate all of the disadvantages of primary data collection discussed above, but working in a research team on a data collection project can facilitate a division of labor that is more efficient and time- and labor-saving than striking out on one's own. If this strategy is followed, researchers need to remember that the NSF and other grant agencies of the U.S. government do require eventual release of the data to the public, so the willingness to do this must be shared by all of the principal researchers in the project.

An example of a highly successful team-executed survey in Japan is the Social Stratification and Mobility (SSM) Survey, first carried out in 1955 and subsequently repeated at ten-year intervals. Originally designed by Tominaga Ken'ichi of the University of Tokyo, the research team traditionally has included only Japanese sociologists, but in the 1995 round several foreign sociologists, including this author, were added. The tasks of survey design are divided up and assigned to different teams of researchers specializing in such areas as gender and work, family, education, work experience, and work attitudes. The data collection is funded principally through funds from the Ministry of Education, Culture, Sports, Science and Technology (MEXT). The main publications resulting from the SSM survey are a series of edited book-length volumes (in Japanese) covering major fields of inquiry in social stratification. Each volume contains six or seven papers, each written by a member of the SSM research team. Twenty-two topical volumes were published from the 1995 survey, covering areas such as the crossnational comparison of mobility, the structure of educational opportunity, structure and change in women's career patterns, and the regional structure of social classes in Japan (SSM Chōsa Kenkyūkai 1998).

Prior to the 1995 survey, only those researchers who were members of the survey team were permitted to use the individual-level data. New rules were created by the SSM executive committee for use of the 1995 data. As of this writing, current SSM committee members may use the 1995 data as well as data from all of the previous surveys. With written permission, their graduate students may also use the data. SSM committee members can also coauthor papers from the data with non-SSM members. But researchers who are neither graduate students of members nor coauthors of members are not permitted to use the data on their own. The new rules have thus considerably broadened the research community that has access to the data, but the rules do not yet permit public access. Full public access is under consideration by the SSM executive committee, and it is to be hoped that the arguments in favor of it will carry the day. If they do, social scientists of Japan will have a major data resource at their disposal that will greatly facilitate research in the areas of labor, social inequality, education, family, and social class issues.

Interpreting Quantitative Data

The importance of quantitative data for many areas of social scientific inquiry should not blind Japan specialists to the comparative advantages they have struggled to achieve. Talk may be cheap (though largely unquantifiable), and it can provide confirmation of results derived from analyses of quantitative data and provide grist for new hypotheses to test with such data. In other words, the ability to converse in Japanese remains a critical asset for quantitative researchers as well as their counterparts trained in ethnography or other methods of qualitative research.

Japanese-language competence is a capability worth using luxuriously, at every turn. Talking to everyone you can about the research questions that keep you awake at night may not seem like a scientifically valid exercise, but it helps you hear new ideas to test and it puts flesh on the bare bones of numbers. Moreover, just as one can capitalize on being an outsider by providing research skills to an organization eager to collect data, one can capitalize on being an outsider by asking questions about "how things work" that a Japanese researcher could never legitimately ask. Individual-level survey data will not completely reveal how a system of employment works or how schooling pedagogy is underlain by ideology, or shed much light on countless other issues having to do with how social systems and organizations are structured. Some of the other chapters in this book deal with strategies for getting at these institutional or system-level questions. But researchers hell-bent on collecting individual-level quantitative data do well not to neglect opportunities to gain an understanding through other, more qualitative methods of the broader social and cultural context in which to locate their quantitative research findings. This extends to researchers using published as well as "raw" quantitative data. Sociology journals are strewn with "comparative" articles that sometimes include Japan as a case only in the sense of having run regression or log-linear models on Japanese data. The quantitatively trained social scientist of Japan may *start* with such analyses but should not end with them.

A recent example from my own experience involves the interpretation of statistics collected from Japanese high schools about their recent graduates. Statistics published by the Ministry of Health, Labour and Welfare indicate extremely high rates of successful job placement for new high school graduates in Japan. In the course of conducting interviews in the mid-1990s at a number of Japanese high schools in Yokohama and Kawasaki, I asked teachers in the career planning and guidance office *(shinro shidōbu)* how they were able to achieve such high rates of job placement for their students. Several teachers pointed out to me that as the senior year wears on, students who are hard to place into jobs sometimes become discouraged in their job search and decide to go to *senmon gakkō* (vocational school) after graduation or to take an unstructured break from school and work rather than relying on school recommendations to help them secure a job. In such cases, some schools take these students out of the denominator when they calculate the rate of successful job search through the school. After all, the students took themselves out of the running. One need only think a moment to realize that if unsuccessful or discouraged students are subtracted from the denominator, the success rate will be very high indeed! This is an example of a case where the story behind the statistics is extremely important and can only be gotten through face-to-face conversation in Japanese with informed parties (Brinton 1998a, 1998b, 2000).

Recent Developments in the Japanese Social Science Community

I close with a recent, very encouraging development in the Japanese social scientific community: the creation in 1998 of a data archive (the Social Science Japan Data Archive, or SSJDA) at the Information Center for Social Research on Japan in the Institute for Social Science at the University of Tokyo. The SSM data are not yet available here, nor are individual-level data from surveys conducted by Japanese government agencies. Nevertheless, more than one dozen Japanese academic and corporate-sponsored research institutes and several teams of researchers had deposited over 256 data sets in the archive as of autumn 2002. This is a very significant first step in making individual-level data available to the social science community in Japan and abroad. As the archive grows, it will be important for anyone seeking

Japanese individual-level data on a social science topic to look in the archive before tackling other strategies.

SSJDA was established with financial support from MEXT. The SSJDA web page explains the urgency of the enterprise as follows:

> Social science overseas has been changing its focus from "macro analysis," which is based on cross tabulation, to "micro analysis," which uses micro data. Moreover, academic journals abroad require that the data which are used for the analysis be open to the public, because the principle of scientific work lies in its verifiability. For this reason, many scholars in Japan obtain data from abroad to conduct research. There is nothing wrong with conducting research with data obtained from foreign countries; however, Japanese researchers will have an easier time doing research on their own country if existing data are made available. In order to maintain and improve the level of scholarly work in our country, it is urgent to make existing data available for secondary use. (Social Science Japan Data Archive 2002)

This statement accurately captures the sentiments of this chapter and emphasizes an additional obstacle that Japanese and foreign researchers have faced in trying to publish papers in academic journals in the United States and most European countries: the guarantee that the data used by the author will be made available upon request by interested readers. Journals sponsored by the American Sociological Association explicitly require this of authors. Data not open to the public cannot be used in research published in these journals. The implications are sobering. Even if one cultivates "connections" over a long period of time in Japan and eventually is granted access to nonpublic-use data, papers based on these data will not be accepted for publication in many of the most reputable American sociological journals. This underlines the wisdom of the creation and expansion of a data archive in Japan such as SSJDA and the importance of the movement in social science circles in Japan and abroad to push for public access to individual-level data. It is neither necessary nor desirable for Japan to remain fact-rich and data-poor.

Notes

Support for the field research reported in this chapter was received from the Spencer Foundation, the Japan Foundation, the Social Science Research Council, and the Pacific Basin Research Center.

1. It is obviously impossible to determine the direct connection between problems of data availability and the small size of the Japan field in American sociology. But it is striking that only seven nonnative Japanese-language speakers produced *any* articles on Japan in the past two decades in either of the top two sociology journals in the United States. This is a very small number in a large discipline (the American Sociological Association has over six thousand members). Meanwhile, the pipeline of new talent entering Japanese studies in sociology is reflected by the number of people who have written dissertations on Japan. This constitutes about 3 percent of all sociology Ph.D.s awarded since 1980 in the United States and Canada (McSweeney 1999).

2. The Ministry of Labour and the Ministry of Health and Welfare were merged in a major government reorganization and became the Ministry of Health, Labour and Welfare on January 6, 2001.

3. Access to individual-level data in Taiwan, for instance, is relatively easy. Access is more problematic in South Korea, but a number of labor surveys are available at modest cost, and personal ties more often yield direct access to data than in Japan.

4. ICPSR was set up to facilitate the sharing of quantitative data in the social sciences. It is now the world's largest archive of computerized social science data. The consortium is a membership-based, not-for-profit organization that has approximately 350 members (colleges and universities) in the United States and fifteen other nations. With the rapid development of computer technology, major U.S. research universities either have the data sets that were previously accessible only through ICPSR or, if they do not have them on hand, can very easily access them for use by local researchers. The ICPSR data archive includes surveys on subjects ranging from urban poverty to political attitudes to education to health care, and some of the surveys are cross-national in scope.

5. The Council of European Social Sciences Data Archive (CESSDA) was established in 1976 to coordinate these archives. Non-European countries with data archives include Australia, New Zealand, Israel, and South Africa.

6. When making home visits I assured people, as I did on the interview form itself, that only the identification number of the questionnaire would be recorded rather than the name of the respondent, in order to preserve respondents' anonymity. Respondents generally accepted this assurance.

Related Readings

Brinton, Mary C. 1988. "The Social-Institutional Bases of Gender Stratification: Japan as an Illustrative Case." *American Journal of Sociology* 94(2):300–334.

———. 1989. "Gender Stratification in Contemporary Urban Japan." *American Sociological Review* 54(4):549–564.

———. 1993. *Women and the Economic Miracle: Gender and Work in Postwar Japan.* Berkeley: University of California Press.

———. 1998a. "Manufacturing Class: Urban Japanese High Schools at Work." *Hitotsubashi Journal of Social Studies* 30:49–60.

———. 2000. "Social Capital in the Japanese Youth Labor Market: Labor Market Policy, Schools, and Norms." *Policy Sciences* 33(4):289–306.

———. 2001. "Married Women's Labor in East Asian Economies." In Mary C. Brinton, ed., *Women's Working Lives in East Asia.* Stanford: Stanford University Press, 1–37.

Suzanne Culter with
coal miners in Yūbari.

SUZANNE CULTER

Beginning Trials and Tribulations:
Rural Community Study and Tokyo City Survey

I often wish I could say that I had an avid interest in Japan from the time I
was a small child and that I eagerly rushed into the first Japanese-language
class I could find in high school, but that isn't the case. I did have two Japanese pen pals in grade school, but Japan was as far out of my reach as the
moon. I was first introduced to the study of Japan while completing a Ph.D.
in sociology at the University of Hawai'i with a fellowship from the East-
West Center in Honolulu. The study of an Asian culture and language was a
requirement of the center. When I was fortunate enough to receive a Fulbright grant, I made my first trip to Japan in 1984 to undertake two years of
field research for my dissertation. I was forty years old, had never been outside of the United States, and had just begun studying the Japanese language
the year before. I continued an intensive ten-month program of Japanese-
language study after arriving in Tokyo before moving into the mountains of
Hokkaido to start the dissertation research project. I lived in the coal-mining
city of Yūbari and conducted an interview survey with over two hundred

households and forty city and company officials regarding the effects of community restructuring after the closures of the local coal mines. Nearly ten years later, I began another research project in and around Tokyo that involved interviewing officials at local government offices that had developed services for the new influx of foreign workers in Japan. Although a similar qualitative research methodology of structured interviews was used for both projects, there were significant differences in other contextual aspects that influenced whether the project was successfully completed as planned or completed with revisions.

Having conducted prior survey and interview research in the United States, I had gone into Japan with a research methodology "mind-set" that was geared to completing the tasks in an American setting. The dissertation research was my first awakening to the need for dramatic adjustments, but later projects brought even more unexpected lessons in the cultural differences and expectations regarding field research in Japan. In reviewing my research experiences over the past ten years, I feel there are several major areas that highlight the differences between conducting research in Japan as compared to a similar project in the United States and that also demonstrate the differences between the two projects I completed in Japan. These focal points often overlap and interact in any one situation and include: (1) language proficiency; (2) means of gaining access to the study population; (3) context of place, such as urban versus rural, or public versus private; and (4) context of person, such as the gender, age, and social status of the researcher and the participants. I can best point out how these issues were operating in the research settings I encountered by using examples from the two projects.

Language Proficiency

One's level of skill in using the Japanese language should be an important consideration in the planning stages of a research project. A number of different factors become involved in mastering a second language, and using that language in a research setting brings additional concerns. I found that I proceeded along a typical path for an adult learner of Japanese. I first began to develop listening comprehension then progressed to speaking and thinking in Japanese while trying to read and write the language as I studied. What I learned in the classroom, however, did not always carry over adequately into the field. I began studying the language at a later age, thus I progressed more slowly than an eighteen- or twenty-year-old. Being immersed in a rural city where no one spoke English soon increased my pace, but I was never as fluent as those who had begun their language training at an earlier age or who had lived in Japan while studying the language. Having less ability may initially slow down a project but should not prevent its completion. Which language skill is more necessary than another also depends on the project. Doing interviews, for example, requires more concentration on hearing and speaking than on reading or writing. Next, the location of the project may make a noticeable difference due to the variety of regional dialects in Japan. The dialect in Hokkaido is known to be similar to that of the standard dialect in Tokyo, whereas a project in a rural area of Tohoku or Kyushu would require more study in listening and speaking if one were to engage in interview research. An additional issue is that speech patterns of males and females, as well as those of various occupational groups, may differ to such a degree that extra preparation and attention is needed. When planning a research project for Japan, one must be aware that the vertical structure of Japanese society is reflected in the language through the many levels of formal and informal speech patterns and should therefore focus on those levels and patterns most likely to be encountered in the proposed project.

This latter point is one that I wish I had understood better when I bused into the mountains of Hokkaido. When I first entered Yūbari, I struggled daily to understand and to communicate my needs, whether to the city hall or to the local shopkeeper. What I had not anticipated was the amount of migration into Yūbari of miners and their families coming from other regions where mines had closed, such as Kyushu, or where work opportunities had dwindled, such as the coastal areas and farms of Tohoku. I not only had to comprehend the wide range of dialects, but also had to quickly learn the vocabulary of the coal-mining industry and the coal miner subculture. Few of the local people had ever met a foreigner, and no one was comfortable in trying to speak English. The younger residents who had finished high school or college had studied English but rarely had the opportunity to use it and declined the chance to try. The older workers, particularly the miners, tended to have less education and often had stopped going to school with the advent of World War II, when the teaching of English was suspended. I found that I could communicate with the younger, educated females but could barely understand the older miner or his wife who had come from the Tohoku seacoast.

If I were going to be able to carry out my survey, I saw that I would have to quickly gather a basic set of vocabulary commonly used in the city and to pay very close attention to male speech patterns. I soon learned that the majority of people I would be introduced to for interviews were going to be male city hall workers, business owners, and coal miners. My ears were far better attuned to the more expressive female speech of my teachers than the stiffer and abrupt male speech. The women opened their mouths in a more emotional and expressive speech, but the men barely moved their lips in immobile faces. I would find myself staring rudely at their mouths close-up in an attempt to decipher their words.

In order to conquer what I often felt to be an insurmountable language barrier, I decided on a multifaceted approach. I read newspaper and magazine articles on coal mine closures in Hokkaido and watched television documentaries on the effects of the coal industry restructuring on similar communities. But the crucial task was completing the first twenty interviews using a structured questionnaire and a tape recorder. If I did not understand a reply during the interview, I would ask it again using different words until we mutually understood the question and answer. I then spent many hours playing and replaying the tapes until I had an extensive list of local terms, place-names, and coal miner jargon, which I then defined with the help of dictionaries, friends, and neighbors. For each occupational group I interviewed, whether coal miners, shopkeepers, farmers, or government employees, I added key terms to the list. Each interview in the beginning took at least two hours, until I gained a better understanding of the vocabulary. This slow and laborious process was possible for the project in Yūbari because interviews were conducted in people's homes and outside of work hours and because people were keenly interested in meeting a foreigner. But more important, the people in Yūbari who were being affected by the mine closures wanted to share their stories and wanted someone to listen to what was happening to them. I found that the majority of people in this working community spoke a simple and direct level of Japanese, rarely using the more formal and distance-inducing polite levels when talking with me. Because they wanted so much to convey their thoughts about the changes going on and because I as eagerly wanted to understand, we worked in unison on communication, often imperfect and stumbling, but so gratifying and enlightening when we would finally grasp each other's meaning. Progressing through anger and tears, then laughter, became an expected part of this story-telling path.

When I went into Yūbari, I took with me a memory of a friend's conversation. Her mother was Japanese, and she had grown up living in both Japan and the United States. She told me that when she first began learning Japanese in her youth she wanted every word to be correct and her grammar to be perfect before she spoke. She would rehearse and translate repeatedly before speaking aloud. Consequently, she said, her speech was always slow and hesitant for fear of being wrong. She felt she was always seen as unfriendly or rejecting because of the "word shyness." Her brother, on the other hand, jumped in with both feet immediately and created his meaning as he went along. He would try out patterns and combine words until he made himself understood. He didn't worry about the correctness of his speech but about whether he could get what he wanted or connect with the other person. I decided I would have to try the brother's technique in Yūbari or I would leave the research field empty-handed. I had also been told when I entered Yūbari that I should conduct the interviews alone since the people were very suspicious of outsiders and government workers and would most likely talk more openly with a foreigner they knew would leave than with another Japanese. This advice coupled with the fact that no one in the community spoke enough English to serve as an interpreter meant that I had to find the best way to do the interviews myself. Thus I jumped in and often badly mangled the grammar as I did, but this method worked well for my research topic, the length of time I had, and the location.

When I later conducted research in Tokyo, I soon realized that using the same approach would not be appropriate for the project. English is more widely used in a metropolitan area like Tokyo, and I would be interviewing local government officials with higher education and thus more English-language capability. Ironically, the people I would be interviewing in Tokyo were more familiar with English language and with foreigners than Yūbari's residents, but I used an interpreter for each interview in the Tokyo project. The reason was not the vocabulary this time but the prevailing use by government employees of formal, polite language structure and the need to conserve time since the interviews were conducted at the workplace. I was dealing with very busy officials operating services for foreign workers who were not very interested in meeting one more foreigner, and who were responsible for providing me with sanctioned information and statistics, not personal stories. The majority of the participants were male officials intent upon completing an efficient delivery of requested information in the allotted time period, thus the use of an interpreter permitted a smoother completion of the process.

I found, overall, that the level of my language ability affected different people in different ways. Some would feel protective since my language would convey me as young and nonsophisticated. Others would sometimes talk around and over me thinking I could not understand. Those unwilling to adjust to the level of my ability simply dismissed me. I let the pretentious posturing slide on by, because I knew that those who wanted to communicate would find a way and would generally provide a far richer commentary. They would be patient, I would listen, and we both would learn.

Gaining Access

If I wanted to conduct a community survey in the United States, there are a number of different methods I could employ. I could first make contacts with neighborhood groups or organizations who would serve as an entry point, or I could mail letters of introduction and make telephone calls, or I could simply knock on doors and request permission to talk to the person. In Japan, I did not have this freedom to organize and conduct my own research agenda. A network of connections and introductions and the relevant authority's permission and advice were all necessary components of the research process.

A formal introduction was necessary not only for me to gain entry into Yūbari but also for each interview conducted. First, to officially conduct research in Japan, an appropriate research visa is required, which means sponsorship by an institution willing to supervise your work. Of course, one can enter Japan on a tourist visa and attempt a research endeavor. If you get into any trouble during the process, however, you may find yourself in very hot international waters. To introduce yourself formally as a researcher and to get access to official documents, statistics, or key people, a proper visa and sponsorship are important.

When I began the research project in Yūbari, I was a Fulbright grant recipient. In addition, I was also being sponsored by the Nihon University Population Institute in Tokyo. This institute had a working relationship with the East-West Center Population Institute where I was on a graduate fellowship. I had met a visiting staff member during his stay in Hawai'i. As a friend, he introduced me to his boss at Nihon University. When I decided to do my research in Hokkaido, this administrator introduced me to a colleague with academic connections to Hokkaido University, who made arrangements for a Hokkaido professor to introduce me to city government officials in Yūbari.

The Nihon University administrator completed the necessary paperwork, including a background history, curriculum vitae, and photograph. He also flew with me to Hokkaido, met with Yūbari officials, and stayed overnight in Yūbari to make sure that my entry was accepted and my living quarters appropriate. This interlocking set of connections and introductions were vital for gaining entry into the city and for my being allowed to conduct the research.

I was now allowed into the community, lodged in a Japanese inn, and placed under the supervision of the city's Department of Education, which promptly turned me over to the city library staff. The city hall, and particularly the library staff, had never before been responsible for setting up a research program for an American foreign scholar, and no one knew how to proceed. The library staff was both intrigued and exasperated. They wanted to know what I planned to do but didn't know how to get me started and were frustrated with having to take care of the strange *gaijin* (foreigner). The result was that I was assigned a desk placed against the back wall of the main library room. The desk was walled off with a folding screen from the rows of tables filling the room. I was instructed to come to the library every day and become acquainted with the written materials and statistics on Yūbari. I was told that the screen would protect me from the middle school and high school students who came to study there. Whether the screen was to protect me or to protect them was never quite clear, but the students could never be fooled by such simple tactics. Upon spying me in the library, they immediately pushed their tables up against the same back wall so that we were parallel and in full view of each other. Many tedious hours were gratefully interrupted by their giggling attempts to use English and whispered questions of "Who are you and what are you doing in Yūbari?"

As time went by, I began asking myself that same question, "What am I doing here?" And my echoing answer was "Not much." I would come to the library every day, but I was not being introduced to the communities nor allowed to set up interviews. When I asked about developing a schedule, I would be taken on tours of the region by a staff member. Months were passing, I had analyzed all of the relevant statistics, my questionnaire was ready, and my money was dwindling. I decided that I could wait no longer and went into the local shopping district intent upon interviewing shopkeepers I dealt with on a daily basis. When I explained my purpose, they smiled and agreed on a time to meet. I went and I waited. And I waited. They never arrived. After the first time, I assumed it was a misunderstanding, but after the third and fourth attempts, I knew that some other factor was operating. I was then kindly reminded by the library staff that they were in charge of my schedule. They told me to be patient. They said that the people were not used to foreigners and first had to become accustomed to seeing me around before they would be able to speak with me. In other words, I had not yet received their permission to conduct the interviews, and the people I had approached knew that. They all had notified the city hall when I attempted to proceed on my own. So I pulled out my patience and sat on it until six months had gone by and I was convinced that I would never be permitted to talk to anyone beyond the perfunctory greetings. I went to the library director and informed him that I was making arrangements to leave Yūbari and return to Tokyo since I had not been able to do the research and my money was running out. At that point, an older female city employee who had become interested in what I was doing turned to the director and sweetly remarked, "I'm sure the mayor will be upset when he finds out that the *sensei* (teacher) was not able to finish her project." Since it was the mayor who had formally agreed with Nihon University to my doing the research, the implications of my failure and the library staff's responsibility circled the room with lightning speed. By the next day, I was scheduled to enter the first community in Yūbari where I would begin interviews.

The library director was now willing to listen to how I wanted to proceed. First, he reviewed my questionnaire and determined which questions would be inappropriate and suggested how I might change them. I told him that I would like to have at least thirty households in each of the seven districts and gave him the number of coal miners, farmers, shopkeepers, and government employees per district. He, in turn, reminded me that for each person to be interviewed, I would have to have an introduction from a city hall employee. This process meant that the households selected would have to be known by the district city hall personnel since they were basically asking a favor of the household. Selecting a random sample was impossible under these circumstances. The best I would be able to do would be to obtain a selection across all seven districts and among all of the desired occupational categories.

When I arrived in the first community district a few days later, I soon realized that my test of endurance had just begun. It was the middle of the winter in Hokkaido with day after day of extremely cold weather and heavy snowfalls. The district the city had selected for my trial run was a remote coal-mining area that had been one of the first to collapse when its mines shut down. Shops were closed, the hospital was deserted and caved in, concrete housing units stood empty on vacant sites, and it was the coldest spot at the highest elevation in the city. I was taken to a Japanese inn where workers used to board but where now only the caretakers lived. I was led to a second-floor room far away from the innkeeper's quarters and was the only resident in the cold, empty building. As the innkeeper's wife pulled out the ancient, heavy futon covered with dust, I eyed the coal stove in the middle of the tatami floor and wondered if I would make it through the night. After she had sandwiched me between the heavy futon with only my face exposed to the frigid air, I was unable to move and watched warily as she put fire to the coal in the stove, scattering sparks on the old, broken tatami. I didn't know if I would die that night by freezing or burning, but I was sure the end was near.

The fire burned out in the night and water froze in my glass, but I woke up very much alive and well the next morning. I gathered my notebook and tape recorder and set out to climb through the snow to the homes selected for my interviews. By the end of that week, I knew how to keep the fire going in my coal stove, had grown accustomed to a layer of coal soot on my body and clothes, and had completed twenty interviews. I was satisfied that I could do it and that my method was working, and evidently so was the city hall. As I was packing to leave, I heard car horns outside. Three carloads of the library staff and district city hall employees climbed out with boxes of food and drinks. We were all ushered into one of the inn's former dining rooms, which had been heated and prepared without my knowing it. The library director made a speech congratulating me on my success, I returned the honor with my thanks for everyone's help, and we ate and drank our way through a fun-filled afternoon of mutual admiration and gratitude. Having passed my first major hurdle without causing serious offense or damage to anyone, I had no further difficulty in completing interviews in the remaining districts. At the conclusion of the study, I had completed a survey of 212 households and 40 city and company officials.

The Place Context

When I began the research project in Tokyo several years later, I encountered a very different set of dynamics that I feel could be attributed to such factors as a different mainland location, the urban environment, and, primarily, the project being supervised by a university research center and academic staff.

The original research plan for which I had received funding involved a study of small companies' hiring practices of foreign workers. A university professor who had conducted similar studies had agreed to supervise and assist in setting up and carrying out the research. Although this professor had been cooperative in person and in letters in discussing how the project would be conducted, there was no formal contract or arrangement, as is often the case between academic colleagues. Obtaining funding for the study took over a year to complete, and by the time I arrived in Tokyo ready to get started, government policies regarding the hiring of foreign workers had changed, causing many workers to return to their home countries. The once cooperative professor was now unwilling to be involved. Fortunately, a research center in the professor's university agreed to sponsor my study but did not have the necessary set of contacts to permit the original plan. A major revision of the research focus was necessary in order to continue. It was finally agreed that I would conduct a survey of a selected group of local government offices to examine the new policies and support programs that had been developed to assist the increasing number of foreigners living and working in their communities. We had agreed upon the topic and even came to an agreement on the selection of sites. But as the project unfolded, I came to find that we did not mutually agree upon the method.

I intended to use the procedure that had worked so well for me before. I would develop a set of interview questions as a guide, use a tape recorder, spend at least an hour for each session, and for this setting I would also enlist the assistance of an interpreter. The difficulties began when I had to go over the questions with the research center staff. Because a number of the staff spoke English, I started with a review of the English version. I then brought in a version that had been translated by a Japanese-language teacher. And that began a long, arduous debate that lasted for weeks. I had written a guide for verbal interviewing, and the translation had followed that format. However, the members of this academic unit were familiar only with the use of written questionnaires and the gathering of coded information for statistical analysis. Their intent was to create a standardized questionnaire that would be mailed to each site with a letter of introduction. The completed questionnaire would be returned to me, and I would miraculously have my data ready for coding and analysis. They attacked my presented set of questions, and my credibility as a researcher for writing such questions, with vigor and venom.

The more I tried to explain the purpose and method of the questions and interview format, the more reasons I heard as to why doing interviews would be impossible—it would take too much time, people would be at their workplaces, people would not talk openly with me, my questions were not useful, and so on. When I asked what the normal response rate was to a mailed questionnaire, without blinking they admitted that most would probably not return the questionnaire. Again I pointed out that the probability of a low rate of response was a good reason to do on-site interviews. We cajoled each other, we fought each other, we bribed each other, and at the point of giving up, a compromise was reached.

I had, as a last resort, asked for the help of a Japanese friend who was a member of the same unit but worked in a different branch. His English-language skills were perfect, and he had studied my discipline's research methods in the United States, so I knew he would grasp what I was trying to do. He contacted the center's director and explained what I had been trying to convey over a period of weeks, and the gap in understanding was finally bridged with concessions on both sides. We were able to agree upon a strategy for carrying out the project. I permitted the staff to rewrite the questions into a formal questionnaire format. A cover letter of explanation with a request for an interview was attached, and the packet was mailed to the selected official at each site. The director of the research unit had pulled in favors again by using his many contacts in order to get permission at the chosen sites. When the officials responded with a date and time for an interview, the information was entered into a master schedule. On the appointed day, an interpreter from the research unit and I would go to the local office. I would have with me my set of guiding interview questions, and the official would have his formal questionnaire with previously prepared and approved answers, along with a packet of information requested in the questionnaire such as regulations, statistics, and guidebooks in foreign languages. This method allowed the officials to follow the proper procedures in providing the information since they were acting as government representatives, and it also saved time for everyone. On the other hand, my interviews in person also permitted more nonofficial probing, as well as a tour of the locality and observation of the actual settings where foreigners were being offered services.

In some cases, the officials organized a group of workers, each person responsible for the items on the questionnaire that they knew best; thus the interview process became a focus group. Discussion in this kind of group setting can become quite lively or can be as dull as each person reading off an answer to a question. I found the difference in the responses to be tied to the personality and approach of the senior leaders. The livelier the leader, the more spontaneous the group. But the more excited debates also required a strong command of the language, since tape-recording twelve to twenty interacting voices is not very helpful. Even the interpreter can get lost in deciding which points to make sure you take note of. By the end of the four-month research period, I had completed eleven sites, and the procedure we had used worked smoothly in most of the locations. It is an appropriate method for collecting official regulations and statistical information. The personal contact allows for more descriptive information to be included.

In both the Yūbari and the Tokyo projects, the difficulties encountered in gaining access or in using specific methods seemed to be related to inexperience or misunderstanding. The more unclear the intent, the greater the distrust, and the tighter the controls implemented. Once the objectives and process were clarified and understood, the research was continued with little interruption, unless there was a change in the power structure of the sponsoring organization. If this kind of shift occurred, it was often necessary to repeat the trust-gaining cycles before the project could proceed. For example, in Yūbari the library director was transferred in the middle of the project, and the new director refused to continue the introductions to the communities. Another round of negotiations was necessary before the work could be restarted.

The Personal Context

As I have reviewed the two projects, differences between rural and urban locations and public versus private settings have been pointed out, but I have not yet addressed the issues included in the "personal context." Perhaps I have left this category until last because elements of the "personal" are harder to describe and will undoubtedly vary across so many different factors. If you have sufficient language skills and have gained access to the study population, then what other issues could possibly affect the research process? I would propose that for a study conducted in Japan, the researcher should keep in mind their physical appearance, gender, age, and any other relevant social status indicators.

One of the first personal factors I became aware of when I entered Yūbari was my physical appearance. I was a tall, heavyset, blue-eyed, white person surrounded by many smaller staring people. One little girl was so mesmerized that she ran her bike straight into a wall. I wanted to pick her up but was fearful of further terrorizing her. I had long legs that wouldn't bend into the proper kneeling position and were also too big and long to go under the low tables. When young people found they could see their reflections in my blue eyes, I had to cope with some very close encounters. And when I was acutely tired and stressed and just wanted to disappear into a crowd, my white hair riding a foot higher than the wave of black tresses made me easily identifiable wherever I went. The contrast was more remarkable in Yūbari, of course, than in Tokyo. In the metropolis I was just one of many foreigners, and as the years went by and more Japanese traveled abroad, my foreign body might still bring amusement to some, but not the curious stares. Over time, I had to learn to adjust my physical self to fit the Japanese environment and context and to tolerate the curiosity and periodic insensitivity. I came to see it as an exchange. They were studying me just as I was studying them.

Gender and age are also on the list of personal context. A female doing research in Japan can expect to encounter behavior and attitudes that a male does not and that she may not have to deal with in her own culture. A younger person may not be given the respect that an older researcher will receive. Again, however, whether gender and age are assets or impediments often depends on the situation. When the male directors on both of my projects refused to follow the methods I chose, I felt it predominately as a gender-related dismissal, because the compromise only occurred after the intervention of another male authority. On the other hand, as a middle-aged female, I found that people being interviewed in Yūbari talked openly with me, even crying throughout the interview, perhaps because of my matronly appearance and calm acceptance. My white hair and older appearance would often gain a higher status for me among the young but would be of no use in dealing with older academics or professionals, who expected because of my age that I should be more skilled and better informed.

Status holds an important place in the hierarchical structure of Japanese society and can directly influence research proceedings in formal and informal ways. Gender and age are related to ranking in the society, as are education and social class. As a student doing research in Yūbari, I was given a slightly elevated ranking because I was in graduate school, and that meant more cooperation in the fieldwork. However, when I interacted with academics or government officials, I was naturally dropped to a lower ranking. The supervising professor of a research project is also an important status symbol. I will never forget the day an American male researcher came into town with his well-known Japanese professor. In one hour, he received a complete stack of documents and statistics that had taken me three months to get. Even after I had become an assistant professor, my status would fluctuate depending upon the context and the contact. In the academic world of Tokyo, the importance was focused not on whether I was an assistant professor, but on my university, my publications, and my Japanese affiliation. Gaining the access, cooperation, and assistance needed to carry out a successful project in Japan often requires a delicate balancing and matching act that incorporates a wide variety of these status-related issues.

In planning a research project, it is always important to pick a topic you have a deep interest in. However, it is often just as important to match yourself with the context, particularly if you do not have a Japanese academic paving the way for your project. Of the several research projects that I have undertaken in Japan, the best match I created for myself was a project on children in institutional care. I worked with Japanese social workers, most often women, who had the same interest in child welfare. I interviewed directors of the children's facilities, people who were deeply committed to providing care and therefore saw the interview as a possible means of helping their situation through continued research. Most of the organizations were private, often church related, and not inhibited by political restrictions. Since I was a middle-aged female, my interest in the welfare of the children was seen as natural and did not create suspicion as to the motives for my research and use of my research findings. Thus the interviews were mutually conducted in an open, cooperative fashion. The entire process was the least stressful, most enjoyable project I have attempted, and I hope to continue with it in the future.

Conducting field research in Japan requires being aware of the many different aspects of the environment and culture being entered and the possible interactions between the setting and the self. A method that works in one location may not automatically transfer to another. Adjust the research method and your expectations to the specific territory and task. Strive for the best possible match, but if one attempt doesn't work, revise the plan and try another. In qualitative field research, do not be intimidated by the rhetoric of standardization and generalization. The richness of your research will come from being as creative as you can within the confines of the context.

Note

My research has been conducted with generous support from the East-West Center Population Institute; the Fulbright program; the Joint Committee on Japanese Studies of the Social Science Research Council and the American Council of Learned Societies; the University of Hawai'i Japan Studies Endowment; the Reischauer Institute of Japanese Studies, Harvard University; and the Social Science Research Council of Canada. In Japan, affiliations with the Nihon University Population Research Institute and the Institute for Comparative Studies of Culture at Tokyo Women's University, and the sponsorship and kindness of Kuroda Toshio, Kawarazaki Fukuchi, Kurihara Mitsuyoshi, and Yamada Noriko made fieldwork possible. My deepest thanks to these institutions and individuals and to the people of Yūbari.

Related Readings

Culter, Suzanne. 1992. "Coal Industry Decline in Japan: Community and Household Response." In Dan A. Chekki, ed., *Research in Community Sociology,* vol. 2. Greenwich, Conn.: JAI Press.

———. 1994. "Industry Restructuring and Family Migration Decisions: A Community Study in Japan." In Lee-Jay Cho and Moto Yada, eds., *Tradition and Change in the Asian Family.* Honolulu and Tokyo: East-West Center and University Research Center, Nihon University, 247–270.

———. 1997. "Reflections on Being a Foreigner Doing Research on Foreigners in Japan" (Part I). *Hikaku Bunka* 44(1):20–24.

———. 1998. "Reflections on Being a Foreigner Doing Research on Foreigners in Japan" (Part II). *Hikaku Bunka* 44(2):16–20.

———. 1999. *Managing Decline: Japan's Coal Industry Restructuring and Community Response.* Honolulu: University of Hawai'i Press.

John Creighton
Campbell singing
karaoke ("My Funny
Valentine") during
a night out with
bureaucrats.

JOHN CREIGHTON CAMPBELL

Research among the Bureaucrats:
Substance and Process

For some thirty years now I have been trying to study various issues of public policy in Japan. Although unfortunately policy studies are not very trendy
in the general field of political science at the moment, they have been popular among Japan specialists for a long time and are still seen as mainstream.
While some who do policy studies emphasize a structural approach (particularly in political economy) and others mostly employ a "unitary rational
actor" model (particularly to analyze foreign policy), people like me try to
relate aspects of political process (what bureaucracies, parties, or interest
groups actually do) to the substance of policy (what governments do, why
they implement one kind of policy—good or bad—rather than another).
Any of these approaches to public policy can be substantially enriched by
comparing Japan with other countries.

Policy research is often on rather contemporary subjects and must be carried out in and around the bureaucracy. Techniques like interviewing and
gathering government publications and other kinds of (often fragmentary)

documentary evidence are particularly important to policy researchers, though scholars in other fields not infrequently need them too. Some problems, such as finding a mentor and just plain getting started, are probably common to all kinds of field research in Japan but can have a bit of a policy nuance. Of course, for every project, one has to pick a topic, which is a good place to begin this account.

What Did I Work on—and Why?

My dissertation and first book was on budget making (Campbell 1977). That was by its nature almost entirely a process study, with policy substance treated only as a few tiny case studies and a brief discussion of fiscal policy. It was comparative mainly in the sense that it was patterned on a famous study of budget making in America by Aaron Wildavsky (1964). Doing a "replication" study was a good idea for my dissertation, especially since it turned out that Japanese budgeting was better described by Wildavsky's "incrementalist" model than was American budgeting.

My second book, many years later, was half about process (using a fairly elaborate model of "policy change" I developed myself) and half description and analysis of virtually all the *rōjin taisaku* (policies for the elderly) initiated from the mid-1950s until 1990 (Campbell 1992). Other than a discussion of how the development of the welfare state in Japan differed from other countries, it was not very comparative. Given that the research and writing used up fifteen years and 418 pages, actual comparative research would only have been possible at the expense of much of what I hoped to do about Japanese process and policy.

My third book, coauthored with Naoki Ikegami, was an attempt to figure out how the Japanese medical-care system works (Campbell and Ikegami 1998). Although little space was given to historical narrative, we described the biennial decision-making process for price setting in detail, and one of our basic arguments was the importance of maintaining "balance" among the powerful interests in this field. The book included many comparisons with the United States, even though European systems are more similar and would have been more logical to use, because we wanted the book to be understandable to American readers.

My current project looks to be half-and-half on process and policy. I am working on Kaigo Hoken, the new mandatory public, long-term-care insurance system that started on April 1, 2000 (Campbell 2000). The question of what to do about care for frail, elderly people is becoming a key policy issue in many industrialized nations, and I am trying to figure out whether and how the various policy choices made in Japan make sense, to some extent in comparison with Germany, Scandinavia, and Israel (I made brief research visits for that purpose). I also want to trace the rather convoluted process of decision making among bureaucrats, politicians, formal and informal interest groups, and local governments, all the way from the idea's early glimmerings around 1990 through, I hope, the early stages of implementation.

These four projects have several common elements. The advance preparation was always inadequate. Each really started with a stay of a year or so in Japan, financed by a fellowship, followed by shorter trips for updating and tying up various loose ends. For each of the first two projects I did well over one hundred interviews; for the second two, fifty each at least. For each project I brought back home a couple hundred pounds of materials, much of it actually purchased, a large portion of it never used for anything (but *which* portion is what one can't tell in advance). The writing was nearly all done in the United States and is just as hard to do now as it was at the start.

Two additional points need to be made about policy research as communication. First, in each of these projects (except the first) I got involved in serious discussions of policy substance in various ways, sometimes by organizing conferences. It is a good experience to have to deal with policy people and a general audience—neither with any interest in academic political science—on their own terms. Second, maybe partly due to the amount of substantive policy content, a lot of my work has been published in Japanese as well as (and occasionally instead of) English. That seems to be appreciated and, one way or another, to help subsequent research projects a lot.

Mentoring

The kind of research I do requires a lot of working knowledge not easily obtained on one's own, and besides, as we all know, Japan is a place where introductions count for a lot. Being able to rely on a Japanese expert who is knowledgeable and well-connected can make all the difference for a successful project. How to find one? Mainly a mentor has to pick you, and you cannot do much more than try to meet such people and act a bit respectful and attentive while still being yourself. My impression is that one's formal sponsor often does not play this role; meeting a mentor is usually more serendipitous.

Four people have helped me a lot in this way, and perhaps saying something about them gives a sense of how mentoring can work. For my first project on budgeting, my main mentor was Kojima Akira, who was then an expert on public administration, including fiscal matters, at the Legislative Reference Bureau, National Diet Library. Kojima was busy translating the same book on American budgeting I had taken as my model. The author, Aaron Wildavsky, had asked me to get in touch with Kojima to help him with the translation. Another mentor for that project was Ōuchi Yukio, a veteran NHK reporter and commentator who knew everybody in the world of economic policy; he went with me to many early interviews until he was confident I wouldn't embarrass him on my own (including my getting a haircut). I met him through a letter of introduction from Nathanial Thayer, a *senpai* of mine from Columbia University. (*Senpai*—the people who were ahead of you in school or in an organization—are very important in the contexts of Japanese introductions and bureaucratic favors.)

For my research on policy for the elderly in Japan, which began in 1975 and in a sense is still going on, my mentor is the man who for many years was the key mentor (or the less polite word is "boss") for the entire social welfare field in Japan, Miura Fumio. He was a department head at the Shakai Hoshō Kenkyūjo (Social Security Research Institute) connected with what is now the Ministry of Health, Labour and Welfare, and we first met when I went to interview him (introduced as I remember by Maeda Daisaku, who was at the Tokyo Metropolitan Institute of Gerontology and was my wife Ruth's mentor when she was working there). Later he became president of Japan Social Work University and is now retired but doing many jobs and still a source of good advice.

Then in my work on health care as well as long-term-care insurance I have had a very close relationship with Ikegami Naoki, who is a professor at the Keio Medical School, serves on lots of committees, and is well known in Japan and abroad as an expert on health policy. We were introduced by a mutual friend and fellow specialist on Japanese health care, William Steslicke —I remember calling Ikegami on the telephone to ask for an interview and trying to describe my project (which was not very coherent at that point) for fifteen minutes in Japanese before he interrupted to say I could talk in English if I preferred (actually he had grown up in England).

My mentors were three researchers—two of them then connected with the government—and one journalist; all four people who got around a lot. Kojima and Miura later arranged and supervised the translations of my resulting books, and Ikegami and I wrote one book (Campbell and Ikegami 1998) and edited two together. I presume that each of these men benefited in some way from their relationship with me, but clearly I got much more from them in knowledge, advice, and direct assistance, so they were all important mentors (even when, as with Ikegami, considerably younger than I am).

How to Get out of the House

The first problem I faced in my first research project was starting. Since at the time there was hardly any secondary literature on the politics of budget making, I knew I would need a lot of interviews. But I didn't know whom to interview, how to reach them, or what to ask them. For that matter I had no confidence that I could ask a question in a way my informant could understand, much less that I would understand the answer (even just to the extent of being confident that my next question wouldn't be the one he just answered). With little kids in the house and my wife teaching English, on any given day I had ample excuse to stay home, and for three or four months that's mostly what I did.

That was thirty years ago. Since then I have carried out three sizable research projects on Japanese public policy and decision making, plus several smaller ones, all of them based to some extent on interviews and other scary methods that go beyond visiting libraries or peering around on the Internet. I wish I could say I had conquered all these doubts and fears, but I still have all of them, and they still cause me to sit around the house (or International House, most often when I am in Tokyo) more than I should. Experience has given me some confidence I'll be able to get over it, however, and also a few contrivances to get me started and to produce something useful while gearing up to full-speed research.

I'll mention a couple. First, there is always something worth reading. For nearly all policy topics it is easy to find a lot of substantive literature written by specialists either for other specialists or for the general public. I usually buy dozens of such books and even read parts of them, but they are often tedious to get through. A better idea especially at early stages is newspapers: you can usually find *shukusatsuban* (small-format, archival editions) for the various dailies, and if you know a date for some event or decision you can find that story and then see how it is indexed. Looking at the index of each volume, it is quick work to find all the articles for a year or two. It is less quick to read them, of course, either at the library or on photocopies, but it is remarkable—even with not-so-good Japanese—how quickly you will be able to read the third or fourth article you encounter on the same subject, and before long you can read articles in your own subject almost as quickly as English (unbelievable but true).

Newspapers have the advantage of being written for the general reader. Between the main articles, the little "analysis" pieces that often accompany them, the op-ed pieces, the features on some topic that often appear as a serial (two to two hundred installments), and the editorials—the authoritative source for conventional wisdom, or wisdoms if you read, for example, both the *Asahi Shinbun* and the *Yomiuri Shinbun* on a controversial issue— you will learn a lot. Methodologically it is no small point that the papers are the main source of information on policy for almost everyone in and around the government.

The second contrivance is to go ahead and force yourself to do some interviews with people who are not, as individuals, critical to your research. Many policy topics have a local government dimension; there are lots of local governments, so if an official in city or prefecture A turns down your request or you do a lousy interview, you still have city or prefecture B–Z to try with no harm done. Academics, reporters, staff members for interest groups, and for that matter Diet members often fall into this category. If you can learn to live with rejection, and again so long as the person is not somebody you absolutely have to see, it is perfectly possible to get interviews with a cold call out of the blue.

Both these techniques will get you useful information at low risk, will be excellent preparation for the rest of the project (e.g., the newspapers will give you some good questions as well as knowledge and vocabulary), and will generate confidence and a sense of momentum. Even a horrible experience with an interview demonstrates that the world doesn't end whatever you do; remember it was an American president who threw up on a Japanese prime minister, and U.S.-Japan relations survived.

"Real" Interviewing

Let's say you have done that and are ready for some serious interviewing with "important" people. Important doesn't necessarily mean high ranking. If you need to learn about something from a particular junior official no older than yourself, you need to think as hard about getting access as for a bureau chief. That means, of course, getting some kind of introduction.

Introductions generally fall into one of two types: from someone who is connected to the person or from someone who is connected to you. In the former case, obviously it is easier to the extent that the introducer (or real "go-between" [nakōdo] in the extreme case) knows the subject personally, is in the same or a related organization, and is of higher status. Any one of the three is usually sufficient, and none are necessary. When one is interviewing at a pretty good clip, it is usually possible to keep going just by snowballing, getting further introductions from the people you are interviewing.

How do you do that? Your subject mentions a name (or more likely an organization, a bureaucratic section or something), or perhaps you muse out loud, "I wonder who knows about that . . ." and he suggests somebody. Then ask if the subject thinks you could talk to that person or to somebody in that office. Then ask if the subject can help. He might telephone then to arrange an appointment for you, he might write a little message on his business card (meishi) and leave it to you to call, or he might just tell you to mention his name.

A special case is doing interviews in local governments—and you should note that getting a bit closer to actual implementation is very valuable in public policy research. The most memorable month of my first year studying old-age policy was spent in Kochi, the prefecture of mountains and sea and of (that year) the highest proportion of old people in Japan. I had one contact from the Ministry of Health and Welfare with the prefectural office in charge of old-age policy, and they provided contacts down to their counterparts at the municipal level. My mentor also called someone at the local Social Welfare Council, and whether because of their relationship or the intrigue of squiring a foreign researcher around, he really put himself out.

Everyone in Kochi was more than accommodating, and snowballing contacts was easy. At the opposite extreme was Kyoto, where I did some research on long-term care twenty years later. Kyoto people are famous for being standoffish, and it was tough going to meet the right people in or out of local government or have them say much (with some big exceptions, of course). In my experience, most localities are much closer to Kochi than Kyoto in making foreign researchers welcome, and in fact, often enough when out in the boondocks somewhere (or even once in Hiroshima), I would just find the right counter in the municipal (or even prefectural) office building and ask to talk with the boss. It usually worked quite well.

Getting back to go-betweens, the second type of introduction, where the introducer is connected with you, is generally more efficient in that one person can get you lots of interviews. Whether or not you have been lucky enough to have found a mentor, it is more possible than one would guess to meet someone who is willing, on the one hand, to devote some time and energy to helping you out, and who is famous enough within your field of interest, on the other hand, that even the people he or she doesn't know will have heard of him or her.

Let's assume that one way or another you have gotten an interview with someone of medium-high status like a section chief *(kachō)* on a topic you know a fair amount about. What is important to keep in mind? Some pointers should be obvious: dress nicely though fairly conservatively, leave enough time to get there, have a few *meishi* on hand in case you get introduced to a bunch of people, be prepared to explain your project in a minute or so. Having a description typed out in Japanese (no more than a long paragraph or a set of bullets) is a good idea, but you should be prepared to give a short verbal introduction of your topic.

Be prepared for the worst: the subject might be obnoxious; dumb; the strong, silent type; or just arrived on the job and doesn't know anything yet; or you just don't hit it off. Unless you are awfully confident, you should have a pretty good list of questions to ask—write them down on a page in your notebook you can get to without fluttering a lot of pages (otherwise you will forget them). Some should be general enough that anybody can answer.

The most common roadblock in interviews is the subject who insists on explaining the most basic, obvious stuff at great length, as if you just got off the boat. If this is irritating to a graduate student, you can imagine how galling it is to someone who has recently published a book in Japanese on the same topic that your subject just told you he read. In my experience, there is no way to head this off. An interruption designed to show that you are really quite sophisticated will annoy him; he will just go on or, often enough, start again at the beginning. Wait it out and write it down (he may say something interesting, and anyway it keeps you awake and concentrating). You might be able to pick up on something he says to ask a question that will take him in a more productive direction, but usually there is nothing to do but wait.

The most important decision to make about interviews is whether to tape record them or not. I recorded nearly all the one hundred-plus interviews for my first project, a few in my second project, and all in a well-funded, small project I did on the government and the auto industry (where we had three interviewers and, more important, enough money to pay somebody to transcribe them). Now I do very rarely. Taping all the interviews in my first project was the right choice, for three reasons:

- My Japanese really was pretty poor and I would have missed a lot.
- The project was more about describing a process and how people did their jobs and thought about them than about facts, and having their own words verbatim was invaluable.
- I learned an awful lot of Japanese in transcribing, listening to parts of those tapes over and over again.

Why don't I do it now? Mainly, transcribing is horrible. Do three one-hour interviews in a day and face some nine hours of tedium. Also, my later projects were more about gathering information, which is easier to write down. I miss being able to use as many direct quotes, but when somebody says something memorable I make him stop while I write it down properly (the subject is always flattered).

When I taped, I always said I would like to do it because I found it too hard to talk in Japanese and take notes at the same time and (usually) that the interview would be anonymous. Only two or three times did anyone ask me not to tape, and I rarely had the feeling it affected what the subject said. On the other hand, it does make the interview seem a bit formal.

When not taping, if the material seems important, you have to be sure you understand it on the spot, and so often have to ask the subject to say it again or explain it more. That is actually a big advantage for the foreign researcher—one can act quite dumb (about facts and situations as well understanding words) and so go on asking questions that would be mortifying in one's own country.

Most interviews run forty-five minutes to an hour. If a subject lets you know he has had about enough, you can get away with one last, short question but no more. Even when the subject is really polite it is better to end a little early than a little late. You signal the end by saying *"Oisogashii toki ni . . ."* ([Pardon me for bothering you] at such a busy time). Occasionally I have asked if we could make another appointment, but more often, if I want a follow-up, I wait a week or so and then call.

After an interview, it always pays to go to a coffee shop or someplace and write down what you can remember, filling in your written notes or even noting the atmosphere if you taped. If not done within the hour most of it is gone forever. Adding in reactions, speculations, and other things to find out helps later, too. The two other things to do after an interview: be sure your notes are organized so that you can figure them out later, and send a thank-you note afterward. Oddly enough, an ordinary postcard is fine; it should be handwritten, but the message is conventional and 90 percent of it can be used again and again. (When my wife interviewed older people, she would take a picture and send that with a thank-you card; that would probably work well with bureaucrats, too, but I never could bring myself to try it.)

In general, it used to amaze me that people were willing to talk to me and tell me so much. Later, having been interviewed myself for one reason or another, I came to realize that most people rarely have a chance to talk about what they do or what they think to someone who actually seems interested. They enjoy it. Of course, it depends on who and what: most of my interviews have been with people who don't get a lot of attention (certainly from foreigners), and I am not asking about highly political or secret issues—unlike, for example, Richard Samuels (1994, preface), who was chagrined when informants covered up or even lied about defense issues.

How much can one rely on interviews? That's an unanswerable question —it depends on what you want to know. If you want to know how people think about things or usually act in certain situations, interviews are great. If you really need to get "the facts" about something, particularly a specific process, rely more on documents for the basic story and use interviews to fill in the gaps or to add more interpretation into the sequence of events. If you want to know "why" something happened, keep asking in different ways—it is a profoundly difficult question, and you will want to hear a bunch of answers.

Everybody makes mistakes when doing interviews. Usually they aren't fatal but are better avoided, and one can learn by doing. My usual sin, not an uncommon one, is talking too much. I find myself trying to impress the subject with how much I know, or I get caught up in something he says and start to discuss it (or worse, argue with him). In strict moderation neither is bad, but remember the old cliché—you don't hear much when your mouth is open.

Getting Written Information

It is an easy and certainly convenient assumption that anything written down is true, at least if it seems to be coming from an authoritative source. Doing research on a policy issue is a quick way to lose that assumption. In my first project on budgeting, I wanted to analyze how decisions were made by tracing a few programs through the process. I needed to know the money amounts for several programs at several stages over time. I knew that for numbers I would need some materials to cite, not just offhand examples from interviews, so I went out to get some documents.

It turned out I could get plenty. The bureaucratic sections in charge gave me some of their detailed materials on the specific programs (material like this is often published as well); I found I could get the actual tables that were used during the process of drawing up requests at the ministry level; a friend at the LDP obtained some of the tables used in the "political" markup of budget requests; and although I was not able to obtain internal Ministry of Finance (MOF) working papers, I did of course have the official budget publications that give the actual amounts as approved by the Diet (in that period the Diet was not amending the expenditure budget, so these represented the final MOF draft).

I thought I was in good shape until I started looking at the numbers. They were all different. In fact, I found I had a very hard time just identifying particular programs in each set of materials. There are actually various ways to classify what government does for budgetary purposes, and the most convenient classification at the moment seemed to have been adopted at each stage. Another complicating factor is that there is no equivalent in Japanese for our common word "program"—words like *jigyō* (activity), *seisaku* (policy), *kōmoku* (budget item), *purojekuto* (project), and indeed even *puroguramu* (program) overlap but have different nuances. And even when I was confident the same thing was in question, the numbers themselves were different.

What to do? Give up is one rational response, but this particular analysis was important to me, so I brought the documents back to some friendly officials and asked them. They, too, were somewhat perplexed, but one way or another I worked up a table that seemed consistent and—I hoped—"correct."

I later told this story to a more experienced scholar, and he rather patronizingly welcomed me to the real world. Time and time again, when one gets materials from different sources, even quite official publications, not even the numbers much less the softer facts and explanations will match up. In most cases, the differences are not so big as to invalidate the analytic point you are trying to make, and it is safe enough to pick whatever seems to be the best source and just allude to the discrepancy in a footnote.

However, the frequent occurrence of such problems indicates that when the data you are using are very important to you, or when they seem to have some internal inconsistencies, further exploration may be worth doing even if you are not confronted with different numbers from another source. (After all, that is probably because you didn't happen to find the other source.) One advantage of doing research in Japan is that nearly always the people who gathered and published the data are in Tokyo, and you can go ask them where the numbers came from.

I have done that four or five times and have always been glad I did. In one case, I discovered (somewhat to the embarrassment of the officials in charge) that the data collection methodology was so unreliable for what I was interested in (changes over time in the incidence of various illnesses among older people) that I gave it up, but more often I came away with a better understanding of what the numbers meant that helped my own analysis.

I should add that this problem is by no means peculiar to Japan. A former colleague at Michigan, Tom Anton, once got suspicious of the numbers that were always used to compare allocations of budget money to American regions (e.g., to show how the "Rust Belt" was losing out to the "Sunbelt"). When he looked into it, he found that the figures ultimately came from forms filled out by clerks at the county level with no checks for consistent definitions or even veracity. The resulting reports had been accepted for years by newspapers and politicians as well as academics, but they were worthless. Thus alerted, he was able to construct more accurate statistics by drawing on little-used official sources (Anton 1980).

One should never hesitate to go and ask at the source, particularly with regard to numerical data. If the data collection was carried out by a government agency, or with public funds, it is certainly the responsibility of those in charge to respond to legitimate scholarly inquiries. Actually, in my experience they are usually happy to explain shortcomings in the data because most often the cause is some bureaucratic or financial constraint that they feel more keenly than you do. Also, if you are going to be working in the same policy area for some time, it is good to get to know the people who do the actual work.

I am speaking here of cooperation in explaining published data. What if what you need is unpublished data? In some respects, that hurdle is higher in Japan than elsewhere, but there are some strategies that may help in getting what you want. Situations vary so much that a more detailed discussion is needed, starting from the hardest case.

Detailed Data

Data from governmental surveys that you need in a more disaggregated form. The issue that comes up most often is official census data, which are not available at anything like the minute level of aggregation as the U.S. census, but similar problems often arise with many data compilations on employment in workplaces, consumption by households, patients treated by hospitals, or votes at polling stations, among other examples.

Requests for such data are often met by the simple assertion that release outside the government is illegal, usually for privacy reasons (the possibility of identifying respondents). You might have reached a dead end, but in some cases a little polite pushing can get results, especially if you have a sympathetic acquaintance higher up in the organization. In my experience, one is unlikely to get machine-readable data this way, but sometimes you will be given permission to photocopy internal documents with more detailed tables.

Another possibility, particularly if you really need the data in electronic form, is to work with a researcher who is already connected with the agency that collected the data, such as a university professor or think-tank employee, ideally a member of the advisory committee for that survey. They often seem to have access to data sets for their own research, which can include working jointly with an unconnected researcher. Of course, this strategy depends on personal relationships.

Internal Government Documents Used in Policy Development

These include reports drawn up by junior officials; surveys of, for example, local government officials; and minutes of the meetings of advisory committees. The latter may be a wonderful source for someone trying to trace the evolution of policy, since the most interesting question can be how problems are formulated and what solutions are seen as valid possibilities. The usual course of policy development in Japan is a progression of discussions in various advisory committees, ranging from quite informal and temporary groups (known as *kondankai, kenkyūkai, purojekuto chiimu,* or many other names) up to the legally responsible *shingikai* under the agency in charge. Often a final report of the *shingikai* will become the official draft for legislation or a regulation.

Such internal documents are not regarded as all that secret unless they are about matters that are sensitive in terms of controversial policy or some big fight inside the government. However, the academic researcher certainly has no "right" to see them (at least until "freedom of information" principles are more widely implemented), so a genuine favor from somebody is needed. It may depend mainly on whether there is an extra copy around. Members of committees might be willing to part with their copies of the minutes, which sometimes can be a virtual transcript, in handwriting in the old days though happily now generally from a *wāpuro* (word processor).

How do you know what to ask for? Usually you don't—it just was mentioned in an interview. On big issues you might see citations in regular newspapers, but the best systematic guide is the trade press, the newsletters that track policy for insiders. They often list reports and give summaries of advisory committee meetings (as well as many other useful materials). Incidentally, it is hard to find these periodicals in any but quite specialized libraries, but the publisher will often let you read the collected back numbers and make photocopies. Ask some friendly official which are best, and maybe for an introduction.

Officially Published Materials

These go well beyond reports directly published by the government. Many important materials (especially specialized annual compilations of statistics and regulations) are compiled by a bureaucratic agency and published by a specialized commercial publisher or an affiliated organization *(gaikaku dantai)*. The fact that these often bring nice honoraria for the bureaucratic authors became a bit of a scandal in 1999. Other types of materials that may be useful include big policy pronouncements (often advisory commission reports, including the many famous MITI [the former Ministry of International Trade and Industry] "visions"), think-tank reports commissioned by an agency, and monthly or quarterly journals produced as ministry PR (e.g., *Fainansu*).

Most of these publications are perfectly open, and some are available in libraries, but they present problems because they are "gray" or ephemeral (i.e., sold only for a brief period and not routinely collected by libraries) and because they are too voluminous and expensive for the intellectual and financial capacity of most researchers. When in Japan, the easiest way to keep track is to visit the government publications bookstores in various cities (at least the one in Kasumigaseki is also a useful source of ordinary books and periodicals on policy matters in many fields). The bookstores nestled in the little basement shopping centers in every ministry can also be a good source.

In the United States, the Japan Documentation Center at the Library of Congress gathered lots of these publications plus many semi-internal documents and supplied copies of them to American researchers, through the 1990s. Although the program itself ended in 2000, its collection is still available. Otherwise, Harvard, Pittsburgh, and some other universities try to collect such materials related to public policy, and a good Japan librarian anywhere can be helpful.

Finally, the World Wide Web: my personal experience is limited, but with regard to the official ministerial sites I can say that for some topics lots and lots of documents are being made available, often in PDF format so the tables and so forth are quite readable, sometimes within a day or two of official release. The Ministry of Health, Labour and Welfare web site, for example, has become a fabulous source of information for my current topic of long-term-care insurance (because the subject has generated so much interest in Japan). On the other hand, as seems to be true of much of the Web, coverage is quite spotty. It is often the best place to look first, but rarely last.

Others

A few additional types of publications are worth a brief note since they can be so helpful in policy research. One is collections of memories of an agency's "old boy" officials, sometimes published in a small book and sometimes run as a series of short articles, or more often a group discussion *(zadankai)* in some magazine connected to the agency. Another is essentially journalism—magazine articles or paperback books often by moonlighting newspaper reporters or "commentators" *(hyōronka)*. More often than not their avowed theme is to tell the dirty truth, at last, about how the bureaucracy works. The best works of this genre tell detailed "inside stories" of policy-making—not totally reliable, of course, but probably more so than interviews on average.

Finally, when looking at the more serious and academic literature, you will probably not find much on your topic by political scientists (though it is certainly a boon if someone like Ohtake Hideo has happened to pick up on your policy problems). Mostly one relies on research by specialists on the subject matter—in my case, public finance, public administration, social welfare, social gerontology, health services administration, and health economics.

Keep in mind that each of these scholarly fields in Japan (as in the United States) has its own paradigms, traditions, and academic disputes, and it is hard to interpret (or even understand) what you are reading without a rudimentary grasp of its academic conventions.

A Few Avuncular Remarks

American social scientists who work on Japan have a tough time. On the one hand, their research has to live up to expectations at home, and in most fields those expectations are deeply embedded in American academic traditions. That problem is most worrisome at the dissertation stage and for people trying to write an article for a leading disciplinary journal, since they must satisfy their committee members or journal reviewers who will take current American paradigms pretty seriously. Book publishers worry less about defending the faith and are more willing to accept a work that is interesting on its own terms. At the more senior level it is up to each of us to decide how we want to relate to our own discipline and colleagues back home.

On the other hand, of course we all have to work in a foreign language and must learn a lot about a system quite different from the one we grew up with. Moreover, to the extent we are defining our questions and approaches on the basis of our American training, outside of the field of economics there probably will not be much academic literature in Japan to provide a base. For example, a political scientist interested in the impact of legislative committees on public policy in the United States can start by reading perhaps fifty books and five hundred articles of some merit close to that topic; for Japan, just a handful.

The public policy field has its own special difficulty—we have to learn an awful lot about a substantive policy area. How much time and energy that takes depends on how complicated the policy area is: I found social welfare policy in Japan not too hard to grasp, pension policy quite technical but narrow enough to study in a straightforward way, and health policy a morass. It took me months to get any idea of what was going on. Another dimension is the degree of similarity of the policy area, and the academic field that studies that policy area, to their equivalents in the United States (or perhaps Europe). Obviously it is easier to try to get a grip on policy issues by reading in English and talking to people at home and then apply that knowledge, as best one can, to what is going on in Japan and how people are writing about it.

To an optimist—and pessimists shouldn't go into this line of work—these problems can be seen as opportunities. If you take social science theory seriously, the opportunity to test homegrown approaches or hypotheses in a quite different environment can lead to some genuine theoretical insights that may even impress your non-Japan social science colleagues. Moreover, Japanese disciplinary colleagues will enjoy talking with you about fashionable American theories. When your topic has been little studied in Japan, you have the opportunity to grab a big, important chunk for yourself and establish a nice little reputation as a theorist.

And, to someone who is interested in public policy as both intellectual puzzle and important in the real world, there is a lot of satisfaction in trying to figure out how things work and maybe even how they can work better. In my experience, many policy experts and practitioners in Japan are surprisingly willing to exchange views on their own subject with an American who is able to talk intelligently, even if a bit amateurishly. One is even invited to do talks to specialized groups or write articles in newsletters, just as if one were a real expert. Many come to find these specialized policy worlds at least as gratifying a locale for serious work as one's own academic social science discipline, in both the United States and Japan.

A Final Hint from the Real World

Here is an e-mail from Margaret Gibbons, a fine political science student at Michigan, sent when she was doing pre-dissertation fieldwork on the politics of pollution-related litigation. It is used with her permission and is verbatim except to eliminate a couple of names.

> Hello,
> I finally got around to contacting the person you got me an introduction to. Unfortunately the prefectural assembly is in session from now until after I leave so I can't get an appointment.
> [My sponsor] contacted the company's attorney on my behalf. Again the attorney said that he would be happy to meet with me. Again I called his office and was again told by his secretary, after telling her that he had agreed to meet with me, that he was very busy but that she would pass on the message. Tomorrow is a national holiday, and this weekend I plan to visit the town again since the town assembly administrative office will now let me look at the *gikai* [assembly] records (since the mayoral election is over). So I can only hope that the attorney calls me before I sell my phone line next week.

Met the upper house rep that [my sponsor] called for me in Tokyo. It was a breathtakingly useless meeting. I can't decide if he was really ignorant or was feigning ignorance to avoid having to really talk to me. [An advocacy organization] gave me the name of a relatively helpful [ministry] person who had unfortunately been transferred. Did a five minute foot in the door phone interview with someone else in the dept. and they did give me a copy of an old *shingikai* [advisory committee] report that I requested.

I am sorry that I didn't act sooner on your letter of introduction. . . .

Maggie

This message is unusual only in being so succinct. All these problems happen all the time. The good news is that Maggie did get enough information to write a good report on this project, and it served as a building block for her current dissertation fieldwork. The key is determination to *ganbatte* (hang in there). And, at least in retrospect, she actually enjoyed the experience.

Note

My thanks to the mentors mentioned in my chapter; to the benefactors who allowed me to carry out the research I described (including the Ford and Japan Foundations, the Fulbright program, and the University of Michigan); and especially to my colleague and wife Ruth Campbell, who enriched all these fieldwork experiences.

Related Readings

Campbell, John Creighton. 1977. *Contemporary Japanese Budget Politics.* Berkeley: University of California Press. (Translated as *Yosan bundori: Nihongata yosan seiji no kenkyū.* Tokyo: Saimaru, 1984.)
———. 1992. *How Policies Change: The Japanese Government and the Aging Society.* Princeton, N.J.: Princeton University Press. (Translated as *Nihon seifu to kōreika shakai: Seisaku tenkan no riron to kenshō.* Tokyo: Chūō Hōki Shuppansha, 1995.)
———. 1999. "Administrative Reform as Policy Change and Policy Non-change." *Social Science Japan Journal* 2(2):157–176. (Reprinted 2001 in Friederike Bosse and Patrick Köllner, eds., *Reformen in Japan.* Hamburg: Mitteilungen des Instituts Für Aseinkunde, 111–135.)
———. 2000. "Changing Meanings of Frail Old People and the Japanese Welfare State." In Susan O. Long, ed., *Caring for the Elderly in Japan and the U.S.: Practices and Policies.* London: Routledge, 84–99.

Campbell, John Creighton, and Naoki Ikegami. 1998. *The Art of Balance in Health Policy: Maintaining Japan's Low-Cost, Egalitarian System.* New York: Cambridge University Press. (Translated as *Nihon no iryō: Seido to kōzō.* Tokyo: Chūō Kōron Shinsho, 1996.)

———. 2000. "Long-Term-Care Insurance Comes to Japan." *Health Affairs* 19(3):26–39.

David M. Arase
(back row, far right)
with his research
institute.

DAVID M. ARASE

Dealing with the Unexpected:
Field Research in Japanese Politics

When I think back on my dissertation research experience three themes emerge: adjusting to unexpected problems; taking advantage of the lucky break; and confronting the limitations of interview-based research. After finishing my qualifying examinations in the mid-1980s I began to consider possible dissertation topics in Japanese politics. At this point my adviser, Chalmers Johnson, suggested that I research an individual ministry that had not yet been analyzed by a Western academic. I was not averse to this idea. At that time a central debate in the study of Japanese politics—inspired in part by Chalmers Johnson's path-breaking book, *MITI and the Japanese Miracle* (C. Johnson 1982)—revolved around the question of how powerful and autonomous was the Japanese bureaucracy vis-à-vis elected politicians and societal interest groups. The kind of institutional study that Johnson suggested I do could not fail to address this debate. And this kind of research would be fairly easily done since the research domain (policy-making within the ministry) would be clearly delimited and the relevant information would be accessible through interviews and normal library research.

At the same time, however, there was the matter of my own personal interests that had been shaped by my Japan-related experiences prior to entering the Ph.D. program in political science at the University of California, Berkeley. I had a two-year experience teaching English in Japan after finishing college. This got me interested not only in Japan, but also in international affairs. I then went to the Johns Hopkins School of Advanced International Studies (SAIS) and completed a master's degree specializing in Japan and East Asia. While at SAIS I also worked part-time for Japanese newspaper bureaus and the United Nations Association gathering news and information on Capitol Hill. After finishing the master's degree program I spent a year studying Mandarin in Taiwan before going to Berkeley. Aside from an interest in Japanese domestic politics, these experiences left me with interests in international relations, U.S.-Japan relations, and Japanese foreign policy especially as it related to East Asia.

So the problem for me in choosing a dissertation topic involved finding something that matched both the central concerns of my field and my own broader interests. In running over the main themes of Japan's foreign policy at that time I rejected Japanese security policy as being too policy oriented and too distant from central concerns in the study of Japanese politics. What caught my eye, however, was the Japanese foreign aid program. It had grown quickly in the space of a decade to rival the size of the American aid program. Almost out of nowhere it had become the centerpiece of Japan's foreign policy rhetoric by the mid-1980s. And this aid had a distinctive profile because it was almost exclusively economic. The fact that there was no serious academic research into the causes of this much talked about policy phenomenon made the topic look promising. It addressed my interests in international relations, but what about its relevance to the study of Japan's domestic politics and policy-making?

The literature on Japan's foreign aid policy-making at that time was rather thin. The two major interpretations of Japan's foreign aid were not in agreement about who decided policy and what Japan's policy intentions actually were. One interpretation had it that policy was decided by four ministries interacting through routine and incremental bureaucratic policy-making procedures. Policy therefore had little overall strategic intent. The other interpretation claimed that the Ministry of Foreign Affairs really was in charge and that foreign aid was deployed strategically to support U.S. containment policy in East Asia. These views couldn't both be right, and they might both be wrong in certain ways. Perhaps I could make a contribution by revising these conflicting models of policy-making.

In addition, I was genuinely curious about how the Ministry of Finance, the Ministry of International Trade and Industry (MITI), and the Economic Planning Agency—all rivals on economic matters—and the Ministry of Foreign Affairs could jointly administer this program. It would be novel and interesting from an academic viewpoint to focus on policy-making *between* ministries, as opposed to policy-making *within* a single ministry. I was also taken by the Japanese government's moralistic portrayal of its aid as a peaceful and humanitarian contribution to international society. Wouldn't it be nice for a change to draw attention to this kind of foreign policy? And finally, the topic itself seemed fairly easy to research. Why wouldn't the Japanese government want to throw open the books to document its good deeds in foreign aid? Chalmers Johnson and my other advisers gave their blessing to this proposed research and were fully supportive.

Having settled on a topic—the causes and consequences of Japan ramping up its foreign aid program—I set about designing an approach to my field research. Because so much of what I had to do involved tracing actual policy decisions and assessing policy intentions, it was natural to assume my method would rely heavily on formal interviews of government officials. This was the method most often used by researchers studying contemporary Japanese policy-making. And in line with the received wisdom about bureaucratic decision making, I assumed their policies would be determined by technocratic factors and organizational self-interest and that decision making would be routinized and fairly straightforward. But I also had to understand how elected politicians and societal actors did or did not have access to decision making. So I painstakingly constructed an interview survey form in both English and Japanese that I would use in each and every encounter I had with an official who presumably would give me honest and straightforward answers. The form would help ensure that I would be gathering a consistent set of comparable data, and it would also help overcome the language barrier. At that time I had not yet done intensive Japanese-language study, and I doubted that I could handle an unstructured interview in Japanese. With what little actual knowledge I had of the topic at that time I tried to imagine what the key issues would be and worded the survey questions in ways that would minimize bias. I used multiple-choice questions where possible in order to generate quantifiable data.

In addition, given the need for access to government officials, it was important to have the proper introductions to the Japanese policy-making establishment in foreign aid. Luckily for me my advisers were able to give me crucial help. Through their introductions I was able to meet with key academics and bureaucrats in this field and ask for their help. More often than not help from these Japanese contacts was forthcoming. To this day I still feel gratitude toward these Japanese benefactors, along with some guilt that what I eventually wrote may not have sat well with many of them because it was at variance with the official government rhetoric explaining the origins and nature of Japanese aid.

After advancing to candidacy and gaining approval for my dissertation topic, I went to Tokyo for full-time Japanese-language training at the Inter-University Center. During this period I did not plan to conduct any formal research, but I did make some initial contacts that proved to be very useful. The most unsettling contact I had in this period was with a senior expert in a prestigious economic think tank. I chose this person to do a trial run of my interview method because I considered him knowledgeable but not central to aid policy-making, so if I made a total mess of things it would not have been with anyone on my "A-list" of contacts. When I met with this expert I explained my purpose and read off my list of naive questions for him to answer. About halfway through the list he cut me off and asked me what I thought I was looking for. I replied that it was clear to everyone that the Ministry of Foreign Affairs had gained the upper hand in making foreign aid policy and that I was trying to identify the officials and procedures that were making the key policy decisions. My naive list of questions and my presumptuous reply to his question must have been deeply irritating to him. He responded by saying that I had it all wrong and that the officials in the process were just the tip of an iceberg. He said there was an informal "aid mafia" in Tokyo numbering several hundred members who lived in various walks of life but were connected by deep involvement in aid policy and implementation issues. And I suppose he thought I was hopelessly in over my head because he then dismissed me by saying I would never find them!

I now laugh at this initial stab at field research, but at the time I was dumbfounded and wasn't sure what to make of his fit of pique with my questions and me. He was so impassioned that I had no doubt he was giving his truthful opinion, but was he actually right or wrong? It seemed unlikely that he could be right. All the academic and government literature attributed policy to government officials and government procedures, and there was no significant attention paid to "subgovernments" or "iron triangles"—the characteristic patterns of Japanese policy-making in which outcomes are determined in an insular fashion by the ministry with formal oversight authority over an issue, the regulated element of civil society, and elected representatives who play established intermediary roles between regulators and regulatees. Certainly, nothing was written about "mafias" in the Japanese bureaucracy. If he were merely eccentric and wrong, then nothing in my basic approach would have to be changed. But what if he was right?

As I mulled over this question in the succeeding weeks, which were still being devoted primarily to language training, I used a few more introductions provided by my advisers. Chalmers Johnson gave me the name of a very senior adviser to the chief aid loan agency in Japan. As a retired senior official from MITI, he was in effect the voice of MITI in this agency's governance. When I interviewed him I was still using the old questionnaire I had devised. In retrospect I think I must have seemed to him naive but earnest, as indeed I was. He was very supportive of my research interest perhaps because he felt the outside world should know more about the good work of his aid agency. In any event, this man did the equivalent of parting the Red Sea for me. He called in the agency's executive secretary and ordered him to arrange for me to have a desk for my personal use in the policy research division.

I was treated as a normal employee in the sense that I had an employee's pass and could come and go as I pleased, talk to people, and use all its facilities. In other respects I was very abnormal because I was a kind of *rōnin* (masterless samurai) with no set schedule. On the days I came in I spent most of my time in the agency library. (Incidentally, this arrangement is not very common in Japanese government agencies. Foreign researchers are normally placed in affiliated institutes that provide some access to agency information but that still keep researchers at some distance from actual operations and personnel.) When I was at my desk I was deferential and careful not to make my comings and goings disruptive to my division mates or to others in the organization. I also volunteered to help out with English copyediting and translation work in order to make myself useful and in some way pay back the favor they were granting me. Finally, not often, but on occasion I made time to socialize with office mates after hours in order to satisfy their natural curiosity about this outsider who was suddenly thrust among them. I gained a great deal of respect for the professionalism and dedication of these aid agency workers after I learned what they actually do. By and large they are idealistic and dedicated to improving development assistance. And through them I was able to see more clearly how the larger aid-policy decision making and implementation system actually operated.

By examining the organization, staffing, and functioning of this agency I began to understand what my first informant was talking about. The agency was nominally under the supervision of the Economic Planning Agency of Japan, but in fact things were not so straightforward. The president was always a retired Ministry of Finance bureaucrat, the directors were retired bureaucrats ("old boys," or OBs) from other key ministries, and at any given time one-third of my aid agency's permanent staff was out on one- or two-year temporary postings to other government entities and private sector enterprises, during which time they were replaced within the agency by staff mostly from the private sector. The actual organization and function of my aid agency suggested that Japanese aid policy was run by an informally networked community of government agencies and big businesses that was obscured by the neat hierarchical organization charts of aid policy-making found in official documents. Further research confirmed that this informal network was real, and that the old hands working within this network did indeed constitute an informal community hidden from normal view that determined the scope and direction of policy.

The other great breakthrough that I made courtesy of my adviser's introductions was an affiliation with a key Ministry of Foreign Affairs think tank. Good fortune smiled upon me because this think tank needed a native-speaking foreigner to help with a high-level, multilateral economic cooperation initiative. I was simply in the right place at the right time and became the institute's first-ever visiting foreign researcher. This institute also happened to be a focus of foreign aid policy research for the Ministry of Foreign Affairs. Later when I took up my research full-time I was allowed to sit in on meetings of aid-related *benkyōkai* and *kenkyūkai* (study groups). It was in one of these sessions that I realized my approach to field research would have to be rethought.

One evening the *kenkyūkai* invited an American academic who stressed the strategic basis of aid policy-making to speak about his research. After he described how Japanese aid was determined by the changing geostrategic situation in East Asia, some of the group members were smiling. The American asked why they seemed amused. There was an awkward silence, and finally one member said that his argument was interesting but not too persuasive. The American was perplexed and replied that a few years back he had interviewed many of the members present in the room and at that time they assured him this was actually the case. The response was that nevertheless, that was not the true situation back then or today. The American researcher paused to take this in and then stiffly said their understandings of their behavior as participants in the aid policy process may not be as objective as what an American social scientist could see as an outside observer. A *kenkyū-kai* member then joked that only an American political scientist would ever think to say that, and the tension melted into laughter.

Others might lightly dismiss this scene as a joke played on this visiting American, but I could not do so. In previous meetings of the *kenkyūkai*, Ministry of Foreign Affairs officials in charge of aid policy had come in with little to say about the geopolitical and strategic uses of aid. Instead they dwelled upon the balance of political and economic self-interest that informed their policy thinking. I could not cite or quote these remarks because the *kenkyūkai* discussions were private and confidential. More generally, I found that aid insiders in Japan would lay bare this kind of thinking only on a confidential basis, but would retreat to the diplomatic aid rationales thought to please an American audience if I asked them to go on the record in an official interview. Evidently, what the American had done in his field research was to make the rounds conducting on-the-record interviews and then treat the responses as valid depictions of reality.

For me this episode brought my methodological conundrum into clear focus. I risked mis-specifying the whole aid issue if I persisted in my original design of focusing on who and what was responsible in the bureaucracy for introducing the higher diplomatic profile of Japanese aid while ignoring the economic and informal side of aid policy that was coming ever more clearly into view. But if I wanted to get at the less documented economic and commercial side of aid policy, which in some ways undermined the official policy rhetoric, how could I get the policymakers to frankly acknowledge and describe this dimension on the record? If I persisted in my original intention of using on-the-record interviews and questionnaires, I risked having my subjects tell me only what they thought Americans and the Japanese Ministry of Foreign Affairs wanted to hear.

What made this problem particularly interesting was the outside-versus-inside distinction (in Japanese, "*soto* versus *uchi*") in the group-oriented culture of Japan. This distinction is also termed in Japanese "*omote* versus *ura*" (outward appearance versus seamy side), and in other circumstances it is called "*tatemae* versus *honne*" (rhetorical rationale versus bottom-line interest). Those inside a self-conscious Japanese group, whether the group is kin based, workplace based, movement based, or faction based, or even Japan as a nation, will tend to protect the *ura* or *honne* of group life by showing to outsiders only the *omote* or *tatemae* of the group. Insiders can be persuaded to talk confidentially about the *ura* or *honne* situation; indeed, they may eagerly volunteer their views on what is really going on inside their group to an outsider who becomes familiar to them. But they will hesitate to air the dirty linen on the record because this will embarrass and offend fellow insiders and can invite ostracism or even "ejection from the village" (*murahachibu*).

As an American of Japanese descent I sometimes wondered whether I had an advantage in gaining acceptance in Japanese groups. In a sense I was not a "real" foreigner (usually imagined by Japanese to be white), but neither could I ever be a "real" Japanese. My Japanese-language skills made it impossible for me to pass as a native, but in appearance only I might have passed a cursory inspection. Upon reflection I believe the access I gained did not come from being accepted as Japanese. Ironically, it came from being acknowledged as a foreigner who was seriously interested in how Japan worked. A Japanese academic could not gain entry to the range of groups I gained access to, nor could I have done so if I had tried to pose as an ordinary Japanese. The one good thing about the group orientation of Japanese culture for foreign researchers is that foreigners have the advantage of being easily welcomed as guests into Japanese groups. It was always on this basis that I entered a group, and I never tried to abandon my role as a guest. The advantage of being a foreigner with passable Japanese-language skills, cultural sensitivity, and a serious purpose (but not overly serious in manner) is that information-gathering opportunities can open to you at many levels of society. For the "real" foreigner (i.e., a white person) your obvious foreignness will make you more sought after as an acquaintance, and you will have greater opportunities for exploring Japan. Paradoxically, you will be more successful in taking advantage of learning opportunities when you remain in the role of a guest and do not expect to be treated as an ordinary Japanese.

In short, the in-group/out-group distinction creates certain problems and opportunities to foreign researchers. On the one hand, the carapace of *tatemae* can make issues appear to be simpler than they really are, and in turn this makes doing effective research design from a distance more difficult. It also means that in researching sensitive issues you cannot expect a quick round of formal interviews to return reliable results. Subjects will be reluctant to be frank if they are unfamiliar with a researcher who will report their answers to delicate questions. On the other hand, the willingness of many Japanese to court foreign acquaintances and to divulge the inside scoop off the record can be a boon to researchers. In this regard, knowing how to behave in group settings and cultivating subjects during informal lunchtime discussions or after-hours socializing is necessary to take advantage of the openings that become available. But even if you are able to learn what the *honne* is, the problem of documenting this kind of information remains.

As I turned to the commercial side of Japanese aid policy I came to realize the *tatemae* versus *honne* problem was particularly acute in my policy area. Overseas development assistance (ODA) can range from huge infrastructure projects such as hydroelectric dams and airports to small, village-level health and sanitation training programs. Japanese aid projects in the 1980s tended to be large, capital intensive, and closely aligned with the strategic plans of Japan's economic ministries and large-scale exporting industries. The first level of difficulty for me was that this pursuit of Japan's own economic self-interest was not part of the *tatemae* of Japanese aid policy even though it was plainly in view to those who looked at the actual pattern of project implementation. The second level of difficulty was that Japanese aid had all the embarrassing pork-barrel characteristics of Japan's domestic public works programs. Expensive projects such as dams, bridges, roads, and hospitals often were chosen according to commercial and political criteria rather than real developmental criteria, and their construction was contracted out to Japanese firms through secretive and uncompetitive bidding practices complete with fraud, bribery, and kickbacks. I should say that Japanese aid has improved due to reform efforts that began in the 1990s and continue today, but back then it was not an exaggeration to say the humanitarianism featured in Japan's aid *tatemae* and the economic and political *honne* were at odds.

In order to explore these new dimensions of the Japanese aid problem, I tore up my original research design. I widened my circle of acquaintances to include not just Japanese government officials but also individuals in private firms, business associations, citizen's groups, universities, and recipient country governments. I also visited aid projects and interviewed recipient government aid officials in Thailand, the Philippines, and Indonesia. All this sounds impressive, but it can be done quite simply. I used the personal and institutional networks available to me.

For example, after getting to know staff inside the aid agency and at the research institute, it was quite surprising to discover the range and diversity of personal contacts they maintained. If I wanted to meet a nongovernmental organization activist, or an academic expert, or a staff expert from the powerful Keidanren (Federation of Economic Organizations), eventually a friend, or a friend's friend, would come up with some contact information. If one then called with a polite and solicitous manner explaining who told you to call, what your own affiliations were, and why you needed to interview him or her, you had a good chance of success. It helps tremendously if you can demonstrate on the phone that you have done your homework and will spare that person vague and vapid questions.

I was able to use institutional networks by asking permission to visit the overseas representative offices of my aid agency in certain countries. I had decided that actual overseas project and program site visits were necessary for me to understand the entire aid project cycle. I was granted permission, and it was left to me to plan and coordinate visits to these offices and with their help to arrange site visits and interviews with recipient government officials. But I knew these overseas offices were very busy and chronically understaffed. I wondered whether the staff could take time off from their normal duties in order to help me very much. A friend suggested that I send additional references to these offices. I used a contact on the staff of a powerful Liberal Democratic Party (LDP) Diet member who agreed to send a fax on my behalf saying the Diet member would appreciate it if I could be assisted in my research. I am not sure how necessary this step was, but in any event, when I visited these countries the field offices had lined up full schedules of visits and interviews, even to remote projects such as the Asahan project, a hydroelectric dam and power lines, an aluminum smelter, and a port facility located in the mountainous middle of Sumatra. More surprisingly, I was escorted by a private car with driver on these forays.

Through the help of the field offices I was able to meet key Thai and Indonesian officials managing Japanese aid in a variety of staff and line positions, which helped greatly in understanding donor-recipient relations. I should mention that a Japanese field office staff member always accompanied me on my visits to recipient government officials. Understandably enough, my interview subjects were a little reluctant to get into the problems of Japanese

ODA, but on the whole they were forthcoming and willing to answer questions. The same could be said of the Japanese field staff, who could be surprisingly frank in discussing ODA policy as we toured around. On my own I lined up interviews with local academics and U.S. officials handling aid in these countries, and these contacts cast useful sidelights onto the issue of Japanese ODA.

From this wider range of sources I found a serious concern by aid professionals to fight for effective projects. But there was also a convincing pattern of evidence to support the thesis that economic and commercial agendas also explained a lot of the design and implementation of Japan's aid, at least at that time. For example, it was quite normal for a Japanese firm, often a general trading company, to hand a recipient government ready-made plans for projects that it wanted to build. The plans would be submitted to Tokyo for bureaucratic approval. There, LDP politicians aligned with the businesses as well as bureaucratic interests would push for pet projects. Once approved, a project would be costed out and the recipient government would be allowed to select a Japanese firm to manage the construction (invariably the one that originated the proposal). One result of this systematic pattern was that projects often failed to address the problems of poverty and development in recipient countries, and the system was vulnerable to corruption, fraud, and mismanagement.

At the conceptual level my problem became one of reconciling this result of my field research with what had already been said about Japan's aid. At the practical level I had to consider the fact that this picture of Japanese aid would not please those in official circles because it conflicted with Japan's aid *tatemae.* The challenge was to document this interpretation without relying on off-the-record comments by interview subjects who might (if asked) deny ever saying anything to me. Ironically, this led me to rely more upon archival and library research.

For example, informal conversations in Tokyo got me interested in visiting the Sumatra hydro-dam project mentioned above. Conversations during the actual site visit were frank but understood to be confidential. In this case and others like it I believed I could find a clear and convincing pattern of documentary evidence to support what had become clear from my informal interviews. In this regard, it became critical to use Japanese-language materials, especially government documents, government-commissioned reports by official and private think tanks, industry association reports and reference works, private firm publications, specialized journals and magazines, newspaper resources, popular media, and conventional books and monographs. This sounds daunting, but it is easy to search widely if one already knows the key search terms. In the case of the Sumatra hydro-dam project it was not difficult to find information from all the types of written materials just mentioned.

The Japanese are avid information gatherers and archivists, and this fact greatly helped me. For those who are interested in tracing institutional developments it may be useful to know that government agencies and large businesses often have their histories written, usually in commissioned works or by retired employees who take up the task as a hobby. They can be meticulously detailed and quite useful, but often they are not available in libraries or through book vendors. You should ask senior members of the organizations you are interested in about histories that may exist or the published (or unpublished) memoirs of its past leaders.

Another way to find documentary evidence is to use the major Japanese newspapers. Searchable full-text CD-ROMs such as *Asahi Shinbun*'s HI-ASK are now available at research libraries and are convenient to use. But it may be worth knowing that the major dailies maintain internal news-clipping files organized by story heading for the convenience of their reporters and editors. They clip not only their own stories, but also those of their competitors, including other kinds of publications such as weekly magazines and small local papers where relevant. Reviewing a case study through these clipping files can be a real time-saver if you can get access to them.

Another thing I found useful was the specialized libraries or archives *(shiryōshitsu)* that large organizations often maintain. I am not referring to the information libraries that government and private-sector organizations make freely available to the public, although these can be invaluable. Instead I am referring to the reference libraries in the working areas inside the organization that its officers and researchers regularly use. These collections normally have restricted access, but if you know enough to ask, you may be granted special permission to view the collection and take note of the kinds of reference materials stored there. Only here can one find conveniently arrayed the relevant "gray literature" of specialized reports and studies conducted by official, semiofficial, and private research organs. These commissioned reports are often confidential, but they can be quite useful in helping one to understand and document policy intentions without having to cite anonymous interviewees.

Through my own research I was able to show, using documentary evidence, that while interministerial politicking was a key part of the Japanese aid process, more ministries were involved than previously thought. Also, bureaucratic politics alone could not explain aid policy-making and implementation due to the heavy involvement of business firms at every stage of the policy process. And while Japanese aid to countries of strategic importance to the United States was forthcoming, economic interests heavily conditioned the modalities of such aid. I concluded that overall Japanese aid policy was not keyed to a geopolitical strategy, nor was it particularly effective in promoting development. My view was that in the end it was a messy process designed to serve a comprehensive security strategy set by the Japanese government. This stressed inclusion of strategic industries in policy-making and implementation, and it balanced three aims: Japan's continued rise in economic stature, the maintenance of its security relationship with the United States, and an enhanced political relationship with the developing world. I sensed this interpretation was unwelcome and cost me some friends when, after I presented my preliminary conclusions at a panel discussion in Tokyo, I was accused of dreaming up conspiracy theories by an official from my aid agency. When I returned to the agency to do some follow-up interviews and say a few hellos, I was sequestered in a meeting room by a staff member who asked me to submit any questions I had in writing. I am not the one to judge how successful my field research was. But I later heard something interesting from another researcher who was looking into Japanese aid policy. After my book (Arase 1995) came out, the aid agency assigned a worker full-time for a month to investigate how I actually conducted my research. I was flattered that someone there cared enough to try to find out!

Note

I would like to acknowledge the Japan Foundation for fellowship support of my dissertation research, as well as the Ministry of Foreign Affairs and the Overseas Economic Cooperation Fund (now renamed the Japan Bank for International Cooperation) for providing me access to information and contacts.

Related Readings

Arase, David M. 1994. "Public-Private Sector Interest Coordination in Japan's ODA." *Pacific Affairs* 67(2):171–199.
———. 1995. *Buying Power: The Political Economy of Japan's Foreign Aid.* Boulder, Colo.: Lynne Rienner.

Andrew Gordon
touring the NKK Keihin
Steelworks, ca. 1991.

ANDREW GORDON

Studying the Social History of Contemporary Japan

In this chapter I seek to pass on some of the lessons I have learned by trial and frequent error in the course of roughly twenty years of research in modern Japanese social history. I have studied various aspects of the history of labor-management relations and the politics of the labor movement in Japan over the past century and written three books as a result (Gordon 1985, 1991, 1998a). This is probably an excessive, even an obsessive, degree of attention for one person to devote to a relatively narrow set of topics, and I doubt I will ever write another book about labor in Japan. In this spirit of moving on, the remarks to follow focus less on doing labor history than on more general suggestions for historians of contemporary Japan in a variety of fields.

Access to Archives

For the historian, the library and the archive are the most common sites of what one might call our fieldwork. Seeking and making sense of documentary evidence is a core method of the discipline. Figuratively "excavating" material from archives is one of our defining research activities, comparable to the literal digging in dirt of the archaeologist or the participation in a local festival of the anthropologist (see Cohn 1980, 198–220, for a lovely essay comparing historical and anthropological fieldwork and methods). This is certainly the case in Japan, where the verb most often used to describe the gathering of documents by a historian is *hakkutsu,* literally "to excavate." The need for historians to search out and then tease meaning from documentary evidence of course transcends national boundaries, and the arts of excavation and interpretation have been the subject of considerable learned discussion (even granting that historians are among the least methodologically self-conscious group of scholars). But certain issues of access and discovery of archival material strike me as to some extent specific to Japan, if certainly not uniquely unique.

The first point to make is an apparent paradox. On the one hand, there may well be no other place in the world where organizations so assiduously—indeed obsessively—write their own histories. On the other hand, despite a plethora of organization histories, archives in Japan are in relatively poor repair, and access to them is difficult.

Virtually every major company and labor union in Japan, many other nonprofit organizations, and most units of government from town to prefecture to national ministries have produced in-house histories. These include both histories of the organization, such as a company or ministry, and studies of the area, whether a village, town, city, or prefecture. Many companies and unions revisit their history regularly; the steelmaker I have studied in most detail, Nippon Kōkan (NKK), located in the industrial city of Kawasaki between Yokohama and Tokyo, published its *Twenty Year History* in 1932 and has marked *every* subsequent decade through the *Eighty Year History* of 1992 with a new publication, including the thirty- and forty-year histories brought forth in the crises of war and postwar impoverishment. The plant-based and company-wide union federations have been almost equally prolific.

None of these publications are flimsy pamphlets. A typical NKK company history runs five hundred or more large pages, and NKK union histories range from three hundred to six hundred pages of text, tables, and photos. In general, the earliest of these works, especially those prepared before and just after World War II, are the least self-consciously laundered for posterity. Some early postwar union histories in particular include fascinating first-person narratives collected from key participants. Although frank and critical analysis of decision making and internal conflict is certainly rare in the company histories, especially, these works present much valuable basic information.

The histories prepared by local government offices differ in that they present not a history of the government itself but a wide range of information on social, economic, and political history of that area. Some of these projects have been undertaken at great expense for a decade or more, drawing on the expertise of established scholars and graduate students as well as government employees. When I visited the Yokohama offices of the Kanagawa Prefectural History Project at its peak in 1979, a full-time staff of at least a dozen government employees was assigned to the project, in addition to numerous teams of scholars and their students engaged as consultants. The output of such a project typically includes document *(shiryō)* volumes as well as volumes offering a narrative overview of the area's history from ancient times to the present *(tsūshi),* and specialized articles on particular topics *(kakuron).* These works are an essential point of departure for historians and students of the contemporary era of any field and for earlier history as well.

Turning to the other hand of this paradox, one finds a general lack of archive consciousness or expertise even in the organizations that go to great effort to compile and produce these histories. NKK, for example, is typical in not having created a permanent archival collection even though it sets a group of employees to work once a decade to prepare yet another company history. One does find exceptions, and the Japan Business History Association encourages companies to preserve records and commission outside scholars to prepare more analytic histories, but in the typical case a company will assign a veteran manager, well off the fast track and often about to retire, to oversee an in-house team in compiling its most recent history. After the book is published, the records gathered in the process are often boxed and stored until the next iteration, and sometimes they are thrown away. While the archival material thus often exists, it is not easy for an outside researcher, whether foreign or Japanese, to gain access to this material or to use it once located and made available.

While Japan certainly has a reputation as a fastidious and ordered place compared, for instance, to Italy, I was astonished (reflecting this prejudicial stereotype, no doubt) on a recent research visit to Italy to discover that a *regional* union in Milan had an archive comparable in size and sophistication to the collection of Japan's major public center for labor studies, the Japan

Institute of Labor, and far larger and better organized than that of any national, not to mention regional, union federation or employer association in Japan.

The paradox of obsessive organizational history writing combined with poor archiving confronts the researcher with opportunity as well as frustration. The key is to be inquisitive and persistent. If an organization of interest to you has a published history, even one of limited value, try to find out who prepared it and ask for the whereabouts of the materials upon which it was based. In the case of the Kanagawa Prefectural History Project, I found tantalizing documents such as a shipbuilding company's work rules and minutes of NKK's executive meetings in a published volume. These were not precisely what I was seeking, but I hoped that more relevant materials might have been collected but not published. The list of consulting professors to the project included a colleague of my adviser, who introduced me to the project staff, who were glad to offer access to the "extra" materials. It turned out that the project staff had collected about ten times more documents than they eventually published, and some of the other 90 percent were of great value to me.

The scarcity of archives coexists in Japan with the fact that organizations possess formidable esprit and commitment to precedent and institutional memory. This means that historically significant materials can be lodged in the desks and notebooks of current and retired members of the organization. In searching for such materials, the boundary between oral and archival research blurs, at least for the historian of the twentieth century. One practical lesson is that one should always ask oral history subjects whether they have any documents in their possession. This can yield great treasures. In 1979 as a graduate student doing dissertation research, I was asking a personnel manager at a shipyard about the history of wage systems. He pulled from a drawer a three-ring binder containing the company's wage regulations arranged in chronological order. The most recent set was from 1979. The oldest set was dated 1935, and it offered crucial evidence of prewar practices directly connected to the "present" of 1979.

A related practical observation is that important documents tend to become the personal possessions of retired members of organizations. Although one wonders if it reflects a culturally specific, individualistic notion of "intellectual property," this is surely not a happenstance limited to Japan. In any case, some of my best documentary finds came from the homes of former managers, bureaucrats, or union activists. Upon retiring they had taken home from their offices those items they felt had most significance. A high-ranking retired official of the Ministry of Health and Welfare took home a set of internal guidelines describing how the ministry was to implement the detailed provisions of a wartime "Order for the Management of Labor in Strategic Industries." He believed, quite correctly I decided, that as the government enforced this order, it imposed a rigid version of "seniority-based wages" on thousands of companies and significantly influenced wage practices nationwide for decades. In its value as virtual proof of the impact of the state on society, this document was in the "smoking pistol" class. Years later I was able to pass the document on to the historian Takemae Eiji, who included it in a published collection of sources on Japanese labor history (Takemae 1994, 253–257).

Other documentary treasures that turned up in the course of gathering oral histories included a set of one union leader's appointment calendars and a top-secret, in-house manual on union busting. The former ran from 1957 to 1962 and numbered some five thousand pages. It included notes on votes at union assemblies, points raised in discussions at union meetings and in visits to various locals, as well as bargaining sessions with management. The latter was a two hundred-page, handwritten account of one manager's in some measure illegal efforts to break the powerful grip of a small, left-wing union at a subsidiary of a major steelmaker, given to me with great pride and some trepidation by its author.

A final point concerning access to documentary sources concerns the critical importance of personal connections and introductions even to use ostensibly public collections such as those held at the libraries of national universities. If you are affiliated with a particular university or research facility and then venture forth to another institution for additional information, be sure to obtain a letter of introduction from your home institution in Japan as well as your home institution at home.

Even (or perhaps especially) inside the storied "Red Gate" of the University of Tokyo, I found such introductions necessary to use various branches of the university library. In 1984 I was a visiting scholar at the economics faculty of the University of Tokyo. This is a prestigious enough place when viewed from outside the campus, but the staff at the same university's law faculty did not find it particularly impressive. One day I naively walked the one hundred meters from the economics library to the law library, in search of records of some early twentieth-century trials of rioters charged with arson and political conspiracy. When I introduced myself as a visitor from economics, the reference librarian waved vaguely in the direction of the card catalog and suggested that if the library had any trial records, they'd be noted as such in the catalog. I came up empty-handed and continued searching elsewhere.

A month or so later one of the extremely competent librarians in the economics library asked if I would take on the job of running an English-language class for about ten library employees who met once a week over lunch for conversation practice. The class had been passed from one foreign researcher to another over the years, and the most recent teacher had just left Japan. By this point I was an assistant professor, and my first reaction was to feel that part-time English teaching was no longer appropriate to my elevated station in life. But the dollar was weak, the yen were real, and the requestor had been very helpful on many occasions. What I did not realize yet was that the students included library staffers from all across the university. Once I got to know them, all doors were open. I was assured all possible help tracking down materials from the main university library, the Meiji newspaper archive, the Institute for Social Science library, and even the law library.

Individual guidance in library use by a person familiar with the quirks of that collection is of particular importance in Japan. This reflects the relatively haphazard state of library cataloging. Librarians are important and under-appreciated members of the academic community everywhere, including Japan. The librarians I met in Japan were invariably competent and dedicated people. The University of Tokyo Law School case notwithstanding, they were almost always anxious to do whatever they could to help me find materials. But formal training in the field of library science is a relatively new phenomenon. Classifications by subject, in particular, are capricious and unsystematic, and of course searching by author is complicated by the unpredictable ways in which Japanese names can be pronounced. Electronic access to data has been relatively slow to emerge, although this situation has changed dramatically in the past few years. Even so, finding the treasures of many of the older collections in particular (and for a historian these are by definition the most valuable ones) depends on asking the right question of the one or two people who might know the answer. And of course in such a situation browsing in the stacks is always important, however unscientific and time-consuming it may be.

A related point worth mentioning briefly concerns the structure of universities in Japan. Students taking American practice as the norm—always a dangerous assumption—will be puzzled by what they find. Most universities are constituted along continental European lines in larger clusters than the typical American "department," for instance, in faculties of economics, of social science, of law, or of letters. In each of these, one will find scholars who do historical research and writing, both on Japan and other places. Few universities in Japan organize the study of history into a specific unit called a history department. My own primary mentors in Japan at Tokyo and Hōsei Universities were affiliated with the faculties of economics and social science, respectively, and they would not have identified themselves as "historians," although by my American reading this is exactly what they were. In sum, one must look for one's advisers and colleagues in a variety of institutional locations and not be misled by labels.

Doing Oral History

For historians of the contemporary era, which at this point in time is roughly the years since the 1930s, living human beings offer another rich source of historical evidence. Of course, memory is treacherous, and one must treat oral testimony with care. But the alternative to "unreliable" oral accounts is not reliable written ones. Documentary sources are no less problematic presentations of "what really happened," and they, too, require great care as one assesses and teases meaning from them. Here, rather than discuss generic problems of the use of oral evidence, I offer some remarks on procedures and methods for gathering this evidence in the first place. Some of these apply to oral history wherever it is practiced and some apply especially in Japan.

Common to everyplace, but worth mentioning on every occasion, is that preparation is everything. Barring a truly unavoidable circumstance (e.g., you finally connect with an interviewee the day before you are scheduled to leave the country), the oral interviews would come after extensive preliminary research with written records. One should never undertake an interview before gathering as much information as possible by other means about the person and the events or issues to be discussed. In addition, I usually tried to send in advance a brief list of the kinds of questions I was interested in asking, and this often led the interviewee to bring some relevant materials to our meeting. Also, whenever such information is available, it is a good idea to prepare two typed copies of a simple chronology of the interviewee's work career or life history. Each of you can refer to this as the session proceeds, and it helps jog a person's memory.

Follow-up is as crucial to successful oral history as the preparation and the interview itself. One should never be tempted by the false security of the tape recorder to postpone typing out interview notes. Listening to the tape and taking notes from it are extraordinarily time-consuming. Far better is to take good running notes during the interview and then type them into your computer (well backed up and with printed hard copy) later that day or the next at the latest. This, too, is time-consuming (in my experience, the note typing takes about as long as the interview, or longer), but if you put it off you will discover that your recall of the details of the interview deteriorates rapidly. If you have poor handwriting, as I do, your very ability to read the hurriedly scrawled notes will decline as the hours and days pass.

Finally, a good way to thank the interviewee and preserve a record of the occasion is to have a photograph taken of the two of you and send her or him one with a thank-you note. Keeping your relationship with the interviewee for the long run is a matter of research strategy as well as basic politeness. You should if at all possible leave time to schedule a follow-up session after having had the chance to digest the results of an interview and compare it to other oral accounts as well as documents. It may even be a year or several years later, when you are writing a book or an article, when you realize you should have asked something else. If you've kept in touch with New Year's cards as well as the photo, a sudden phone call or letter with a further query, even from overseas, would not be inappropriate.

The choice of whom to interview will largely be determined by the particulars of your interests and the happenstance of introductions and longevity, as well as your own careful sleuthing. Usually, when any appropriate person is willing and available to meet, you will have no hesitation about taking the opportunity. But if you are unfortunate to have limited time and fortunate to have many potential subjects, you will have to choose to meet some people rather than others. In such a happy case, I advise first seeking out the stories of the less rich and famous.

This preference is not simply a matter of populist sentimentality. I have interviewed former cabinet ministers and presidents of national union federations as well as "unknown" working men and women. Nearly without exception, the interviews with the latter were richer experiences. Men of power, wealth, and fame, one is not shocked to learn, tend to have well-rehearsed and guarded presentations. Even if retired, they are likely to remain involved in their former worlds and speak with an ear toward protecting or supporting a certain political interest for the present as well as for posterity. They are also likely to be busier and less willing to talk at length.

It would be naive to suggest that less well known people, in contrast, have no agendas. Every interviewee will offer a present-moment interpretation of experience and events that will in some sense be intended to justify as well as make sense of commitments both past and present. But I have found that such people are more flattered that you have shown interest (and come such a long way to meet them), more generous with their time, and more interested in listening and responding to the sense of the questions. Compared to more prominent interview subjects, their presentations were less practiced and less self-consciously packaged. I was often the first person ever to be asking the interviewee my questions in such a structured context. If the replies of a famous subject were comparable to polished essays, the answers in these cases were akin to the draft of the essay or even the scattered preliminary notes.

The above advice is generic to the enterprise of oral history. More Japan-specific are the following suggestions. First, never come to an interview empty-handed. Your gift, or *omiyage,* need not be grand. A token from your home is best, but if you've been in Japan for months your supply of such items will probably be exhausted. Flowers or fruits bought at the train station en route were certainly welcome by people, in my experience, despite protestations that "you needn't have." Of course, if you are meeting at someone's office or a distance from their home, make sure the gift is easy to carry.

Second, give some thought to the location. A meeting on the home turf of the interviewee, whether workplace, home, or a site in his or her neighborhood, is always preferable, not only in terms of etiquette, but also as a spur to the person's memory. In a visit to a private home, in particular, ask about photos and memorabilia. If at all possible, avoid coffee shops. Although your ten-dollar outlay for two cups of coffee buys you unlimited time to sit and talk, and the coffee shop has an aspect of safe, neutral territory, establishing a close tie to the interviewee is your goal. A "neutral" site is not necessarily best to achieve this. In addition, the coffee shop chairs in Japan are usually uncomfortable, the tables rarely suited to note taking, and the background noise distracting.

Finally, there is the matter of your status as a foreigner. It is a fact that defines the context of your discussion and makes it different from that of a Japanese researcher. You cannot change this, and you should not ignore it.

Foreigner status has some disadvantages. In research that touches on controversial, contemporary international issues, being an American, in particular, may lead your interviewees to be suspicious and reluctant to talk. Or it may elicit a presentation packaged for "external" consumption, as the interviewee sees this. And in all cases, as an outsider (and nonnative speaker of the language), you will certainly lack some basic "intuitive" experience and knowledge that might impede your ability to gather and understand information.

At the same time, outsiders can bring fresh perspectives that produce unexpected insights. In addition, there are two privileges or advantages of being a foreigner that, if not abused, can be of great value to your research. The first is the prestige factor for those who are Westerners in Japan, in particular those who are Americans, and more particularly those who are white males (Dorinne Kondo has written a sensitive account of the different constraints and opportunities facing a Japanese American woman in an anthropological project [Kondo 1990, 11–26].) The pejorative of "special foreigners' rights" *(gaijin tokken)* can be applied to the facts that despite recent U.S.-Japan trade wars and resurgent nationalism in Japan, not to mention the scars of World War II, such foreigners encounter a desire to please and an ease of access that others do not. In addition, one's ignorance and breaches of etiquette tend to be readily excused. Of course, on a deeper level such foreigners may face barriers that an ethnic Japanese (or even another Asian person?) can more easily transcend, but in the practical matter of making contacts and convincing people to talk to you, it scarcely seems wise (and in any case is hardly possible) to reject all benefits of being an outsider, even as one ought to make good-faith efforts to follow the protocols common within Japanese society.

Second, and more directly relevant to research in oral history, the foreigner comes to interviews as a nonpartisan in a way that Japanese scholars are unable to do. In studying the history of labor, as in many other subjects, one is entering a politically contested terrain where Japanese academics have a certain reputation, both as individuals and as a collective. In my own work, the lines of division not only set managers against workers, but also set union factions of the communist left, socialist left, and socialist right against each other (to somewhat crudely caricature the situation). One also found alliances between managers and the "cooperative" wing of the union movement against those unionists of more militant persuasion. A Japanese academic would invariably be associated with one side of this debate, either by his or her own writings or (as a grad student) by the adviser's reputation. As a foreigner, I was seen (falsely, one might add) as a relatively neutral figure. In some cases, I was also seen as a potential ally in telling the "proper" version of events to posterity. In other cases, the fact that I would be publishing my results in another language, in a faraway place, made me a safer person to talk to. My Japanese colleagues were astonished at how extraordinarily willing all sorts of people were to tell me their stories and at how relatively unafraid they were of how I might use them.

But finally, I learned only through trial and error that one should not take a neutral reputation to mean that one must avoid raising sensitive issues. In talking to managers and their cooperative union allies, one topic I wrongly thought a taboo was the sensitive matter of acts that walked on the wrong side of the law when companies and some unions tried to combat other unionists deemed obstructive and too far to the left. At first I erred in not asking about this issue, fearing it was too sensitive. But interviewees, both personnel managers and union leaders, who may have feared opening up to a Japanese scholar with a known political stance, did not hesitate to raise these matters. Indeed, they were delighted to boast of heroic acts in old battles in a just cause. To be sure, these managers and their union allies were not so much assuming I was neutral as they were deciding that as an American doing interviews in the last heady days of Japan's "bubble" economy and the immediate post–Cold War triumph of capitalism, I came to them as a friend of the enterprise-dominated society who would understand the justice of their cause. Indeed, Japanese labor historian colleagues on the left encouraged me to take advantage of these attitudes to talk to people who would not talk to them.

Fortunately, the assumption that all Americans were fervent Reaganites was not so profound as to hinder my efforts to reach those on the other side. As outsider, I did retain some image of neutrality. In addition, I was asking about battles long past. The pleasure of recalling those times, for unionists of all persuasions, was greater than the lingering bitterness of defeat (a bitterness that was sometimes quite powerful, still). Indeed, one interviewee would often offer to introduce me to another good source, including those on the opposite sides of a long-ago struggle.

The only exception was one veteran union activist who remained a long-time Japan Communist Party (JCP) member. When I contacted him, he simply refused speak to me after an initial phone call, although it had been preceded by an introduction from a union member who felt the two to be on good terms. This man explained on the phone that as someone from imperialist America, I would not possibly understand his story. But this experience seems to have reflected one man's personality as much as a commitment to letting the party tell its own story through official channels, because another veteran JCP unionist was quite willing to share his experiences in an interview.

Conclusion

In the end, the success of historical field research, whether digging in the archives or talking to living witnesses, depends on the historian's own creativity in making sense of the evidence and the research experience in a context of ongoing discussions among historians and their present-day audiences. This problem of how to combine analysis, theory, and research findings is a topic for another essay by another writer. I might conclude nonetheless with two comments. First, to give fullest meaning to one's research, it is crucial not to view Japan as merely a site for evidence gathering. One must also personally and intellectually engage the work of Japanese colleagues who are central figures in defining and elaborating the ongoing discussion about the meaning of the past. Certainly this is true for labor history, where one finds rich and varied, and mutually opposed, analytic traditions as well as rich repositories of data.

Second, as an outsider one has a particular opportunity in contributing to this discussion. Traditions of historical analysis in Japan are often not only opposed but quite separate. They sometimes proceed as if the work of others looking at similar problems with different assumptions did not exist. (Of course, one finds this state of affairs in the United States and elsewhere as well). As an outsider, one is freed from pledging allegiance to any one school and can talk to and learn from scholars who ignore each other. Ultimately it may be necessary to adopt one viewpoint over another, or risk producing work that lacks vigor or focus. But the freedom to cross boundaries in the process of research can be intellectually enriching. By all means, embrace it.

Note

I want to thank all those people who shared their time and memories of long-ago struggles so generously and eloquently.

Related Readings

Gordon, Andrew. 1996. "The Disappearance of the Japanese Working Class Movement." In Elizabeth J. Perry, ed., *Putting Class in Its Place: Worker Identities in East Asia.* Berkeley, Calif.: Institute of East Asian Studies, 11–52.

———. 1997. "Managing the Japanese Household: The New Life Movement in Postwar Japan." *Social Politics* (Summer):245–283.

———. 1998a. *Wages of Affluence.* Cambridge, Mass.: Harvard University Press.

OUTSIDERS IN INSIDERS' NETWORKS

Christine R. Yano (on the left) with the head of Umezawa Tomio's fan club behind his tour bus.

CHRISTINE R. YANO

Unraveling the Web of Song

Exploiting the Home Advantage

In June 1991 I prepared to conduct dissertation research in Tokyo to study *enka,* an old-fashioned popular-music genre whose reputation both as an expression of "the heart and soul of the Japanese" *(Nihonjin no kokoro)* and as "crying song" *(naki-bushi)* made it a likely candidate for sites and practices of Japanese identity and emotion. I was not a fan of *enka,* but I was lucky enough to be living in Hawai'i, where *enka* was popular with at least some Japanese Americans. Preparing for the field was a matter of seeking out all the opportunities and knowledgeable people who were right in my backyard. I had only two months. My pre-fieldwork fieldwork began.

At the very least, I had to familiarize myself with the music. My first stop was Hokama's Music, the only music store in Honolulu fully dedicated to Japanese music at the time, still run by Mrs. Hokama herself, a frail but steely woman in her nineties, and her daughters. Stepping into Hokama's was like stepping back in time: dust-covered plastic sleeves covered vinyl record albums; fading posters of past singers hung high on the walls; no Visa or

Mastercard signs adorned the cluttered desk—it was cash or check only. This was fieldwork in itself, ready for the tapping. Who were the most popular singers? Which were the most popular songs? When did record companies start using the word *enka* in their labeling? The staff could easily answer the first two questions and even helped dig around in answer to the third. I bought items as my pocketbook allowed: a highly recommended CD of greatest *enka* hits, a lyric book, and the most recent issue of *Enka Jānaru* (Enka journal), the main fan magazine of the genre. I was thus equipped with the primer texts of my pre-fieldwork education.

At the same time, I contacted the best-known teacher of Japanese popular song in Honolulu, Mr. Harry Urata. Mr. Urata came highly recommended as one who had grown up in Japan, returned to Hawai'i shortly before World War II (during which he was interned), and remained continually active in the local Japanese music scene. He had knowledge of Japanese songs and singers that went back to his youth in Japan in the 1920s and 1930s. He also had connections with the Japanese music business. Under his tutelage, I studied five songs, translating and singing each one.

Studying five songs in two months is considered quick, even hasty or rushed, in Japanese popular song instruction. More likely, a student learns one song at a time, dwelling on the one song for perhaps two to three months or longer before going on to another song. In my case, I explained to my teacher at the outset that my goal was to learn, at least superficially, as many songs as I could in the time I had available. (Furthermore, a repertoire of five songs is sufficient for many *karaoke* sessions, given that at most outings with five or six people, no one person sings more than three songs. A repertoire of five songs, then, can see one through a surprising number of *karaoke* outings, even with the same group of people.)

This preparation with Mr. Urata proved invaluable. Each song became a springboard for talk about *enka*. In discussing a song with him, I gained an understanding of some of the background of the lyrics, the popularity of particular singers, and a sense of the emotions in this genre. This kind of interaction structured around music lessons, but encompassing far more, became one of my most valuable templates for fieldwork in Japan. Moreover, knowing even this much about *enka,* and in particular knowing how to sing these five songs, elevated me from complete neophyte to one who could hold her own at *karaoke* sessions. This was an important prerequisite for much social interaction in Japan, and especially for my fieldwork on *enka*.

I quickly became his pupil of local renown. He arranged for an interview with a local Japanese-language newspaper shortly before I left for Japan. The interview and accompanying photo with Mr. Urata at my side made me (and my project, as well as my affiliation with him) known throughout that segment of the Japanese American community who reads Japanese. He also later sent a clipping of the article to a friend of his in the entertainment world, who became my first *kone* (connection) in Japan.

Every moment I spent preparing for the field gave me an important home advantage whose rewards I reaped many times over while in the field. My continuing web of connections, back and forth between Japan and Hawai'i, may have been unique to the proximity of my home base to the research site, as well as to the many Japanese and Japanese Americans living in Hawai'i. However, I feel it also reflects the changing nature of global flows of information, people, and goods in and out of Japan to points beyond. With sushi restaurants in Kansas and bonsai plants sold in Maine, the presence of Japan can be found in backyards scattered widely. Even in places far less proximate to Japan than Hawai'i, one can often find at least one or two Japanese to consult (including Japanese-language instructors at one's university) and practice interviewing. Moreover, researchers these days can also consult Japanese web sites for abundant information.

In fact, talking with Japanese about their thoughts and feelings may be far easier and more productive outside of Japan, where people may not be as bound by social conventions or more easily persuaded through distance to candor, than in their home country. One has to keep in mind, however, that Japanese living outside of Japan are often a self-selected bunch, not necessarily a representative sample. Nevertheless, I found oftentimes greater access to research opportunities, singers (some with vacation homes in Hawai'i), and Japanese fans (some traveling as part of fan-club tours) in Hawai'i than in Japan. Exploiting the home advantage, then, is, like fieldwork itself, a matter of ingenuity, persistence, and initiative.

Fieldwork with Family

I arrived in Tokyo well prepared for research, less prepared for everyday living. I was far from the model footloose fieldworker. With me were two children under the age of five, a husband seeking work, and ten bulging suitcases and boxes. August was sticky, the freeways and urbanscapes of Tokyo uncomfortably crowded, and I could only wonder at my audacity in pulling a family of four from the comforts of the life they knew to this challenge of living in a foreign country. My research site—the dense, urban complex of Tokyo—was everywhere I looked and therefore nowhere. I felt overwhelmed and intimidated.

Because I was enrolled to study for the first year at the Inter-University Center for Japanese Language Studies (IUC) in Yokohama, I felt no compulsion to rush into field research immediately. Instead I put on the apron of mother and got involved in the process of setting up house, as well as settling my children into their new school. There was no shortage of things to do: we had an apartment to furnish, neighborhood police to check in with, and health insurance to register at the ward office. We also had to ensure that the children enjoyed this new home, so we took time out from settling in to seek out all the parks and playgrounds near and distant. I became, for all intents and purposes, an urban Japanese housewife.

I mention these unacademic aspects of my field experience as self-indulgence with a rationale: fieldwork is not only about research, but also about the needs, stresses, and pleasures of day-to-day life in a foreign country. This holds all the truer when one enters the field with other human beings and particularly with children. My research agenda was only one of several components to be juggled amid the daily needs of four people. Nevertheless, this was no family vacation. The purpose of being in this distant place was to conduct research; therefore, getting that research done was an important, highly prioritized component. It was a critical ball to juggle. Field diaries such as Mead's (1977) and (notoriously) Malinowski's (1967) fill hundreds of pages with the minutiae of daily life. These form the background hum to research and inevitably color what we produce. Fieldwork is in large part about life in the field, with all its starts and stops, great moments and long lulls. There is another aspect of minutiae that is a quintessential part of fieldwork. Our research takes place in an unpredictable, unstable laboratory of human beings going about their lives with little care for or understanding of the work we do. It does not proceed apace as a story that unfolds evenly, but instead stumbles forward in a headlong rush, only to get mired in small details.

Conducting fieldwork in Japan with family in tow had its own rewards emotionally, intellectually, and in terms of research. Some of the lessons that appear in my lectures, writings, and thoughts on Japan I derived from experiences as a field researcher with a family. Other rewards are far less academic. For one, it brought us together as a family unit, particularly the children, who had spent their young lives drawing battle lines on opposing sides of sibling wars. Now in this foreign country, they became each other's best friend.

Second, children indeed *are* gods in Japan. This holds particular relevance for foreign (that is, Caucasian or part-Caucasian, as mine are) children. Everywhere we went we became recipients of smiles and attention. We became photo-ops for Japanese strangers intent upon recording the moment of their proximity to an American child. I'm not sure that my children always welcomed the spotlight, but they came to believe that Japan was a place filled with warm indulgence on their behalf. The sun shone on them in this foreign land. And I became firsthand witness to these particular giddy interactions that shape some of my thoughts on Japan and its relations with foreign others.

Third, the presence of family in Japan defined my status as wife and mother. The picture of me became clearer to those Japanese I met, including those whom I studied. If my interviewees showed any interest, I brought out photos of my children. Steering the conversation toward children framed me as immediately human and trustworthy in their eyes, rather than suspect or liminal. How could I be both monstrous and maternal? The photos led quite naturally to asking about their children and families. This shifted the conversation toward them as people with lives well apart from the entertainment profession. Children became our common ground of humanity.

Finally, being part of a family made me a far more socially embedded member of a community than I would have been otherwise, with lessons on life in Japan from which I draw daily as I teach now several years later. Like many mothers in Japan, I made friends through my children with other mothers. Although these women had nothing to do with the entertainment world I was there to study, I found their presence and our interactions invaluable. They became a reality check for bookish, sometimes high-minded ideas. They included a woman I found out was actually Korean, who spoke with me at length of the discrimination she had grown up with in Japan, as well as her love of *enka*.

I taught English to some of the mothers. There, sitting around my dining table on Tuesday and Thursday mornings after dropping the children off at school, I led women into discussions of their husbands, children, and hopes with the kind of frankness that foreign-language conversation classes sometimes allow. The chorus of complaints rose in halting English, as I heard of fathers who were strangers to their children, children who were strangers to their fathers, and mothers whose interrupted careers had little hope of resumption. Most of all, I heard mothers whose knowledge of and over-whelming concern for their children surpassed any mother I had previously met. All these lives and concerns continue to reappear in my lectures and thoughts on Japan.

Edging into the Field

Even before I had conducted a single interview, I was busy in the privacy of my home edging into the field while pursuing language study. I continued to follow up on the preliminary fieldwork that began in Hawai'i. There was much I could do at a distance from the actual people of my study. I sub-scribed to the primary fan magazine, *Enka Jānaru,* to familiarize myself bet-ter with this particular world of song. I watched, listened to, and recorded every *enka* program on television. Buying *TV Gaido* (TV guide) weekly, I looked for their listing of music shows, which was subdivided by genre. Each week there were typically three or four. By the end of fieldwork, I accumulated over two hundred videotaped hours of these shows, which have become some of my main primary documents. I began to list the per-formers who appeared on these shows, and in particular on one show, *Enka no Hanamichi* (The flower-way of enka), the flag bearer of the genre.[1] I kept index cards of the performers, the songs they sang, and the televised appear-ances. This helped me get a sense of the key players and songs. Eventually I used this information to derive the corpus material that I analyzed as text, music, and performance. I consulted the weekly Tokyo entertainment guide, *Pia,* for *enka* concerts. I could not afford to go to most, since each cost on average five thousand yen, but I duly noted the following kinds of features: day of week, time of day, cost of ticket, performance venue.[2] These aspects increased my understanding of the relative place and marketing of *enka* within the music scene in Japan.

At the urging of my music teacher in Hawai'i, I decided to make use of his *kone* with executives at a major television station, TV Tokyo. This became one entry point to the music business in Japan. Through this *kone,* my teach-er's contact arranged for me to have dinner with "Mr. *Enka.*" As luck would have it, TV Tokyo was the commercial station that specializes in *enka,* and the man seated next to me at the tiny, exclusive restaurant specializing in *kaiseki ryōri* (elegant Kyoto-style cuisine) was the executive director of *enka* programming. For one heady night I was treated as a guest of "Mr. *Enka,*" who regaled me with tales of the business and then sent me on my way in a paid taxi all the way from Tokyo to my apartment in Yokohama (the bill was over ten thousand yen). "Mr. *Enka*," however, was a busy man, and our contact did not extend much beyond this meeting.

Halfway through my course of language study at IUC, I felt ready to embark on "real" fieldwork—that is, meeting and talking to people. My night with "Mr. *Enka*" was a one-shot deal, with only promises for future help. Besides, I did not feel ready yet to knock on doors at the top. The question was: how to tackle such an intimidating subject as a commercial pop-music genre? One of the most useful purchases I made at this early stage of fieldwork was the *Oricon Yearbook,* an annual two-volume compendium, directory, and watchdog of the music industry. Armed with the *Oricon Yearbook,* I was able to easily secure the names and contact information of all record companies, singers, and official fan clubs. Here was my guide to the field. I decided to start at what I thought would be the low end—the fans. I contacted and made appointments to interview people at several different fan clubs, created my list of questions, and set forth. (Another useful but expensive purchase I made early on was a fax-phone. Finding an address is notoriously difficult in Japan, even with a general Tokyo map and the best-laid verbal directions. Most people and companies, however, were willing to fax me a map and written directions of their own.)

To my surprise, what I found at each fan club was not fan-led groups, but rather company-led organizations of fans. In contacting fan clubs, I was actually contacting the publicity arm of record and production companies. The person in charge of each club was a paid company employee whose own aesthetic preference might as easily run to other singers as to this one. One young woman I spoke with confided that she herself was not a fan, but this did not prevent her from carrying out her duties—selling autographed goods, arranging for special tickets for fans at upcoming concerts, and answering phone calls from fans concerned about the release of the singer's newest single. Employees were fan club supporters for hire who could never let on to the general public that they were anything but fans themselves. This realization provided an important lesson for me as a student and fieldworker of popular culture: never underestimate the far-reaching power of the company. The structure of culture industries in Japan extends its hand into areas a researcher may not have suspected.

My reception at these fan clubs varied widely. At one singer's fan club I was politely ushered in and then out in record time, during which I received brief, curt answers to my questions. At the end of fifteen minutes, the woman with whom I had been speaking rose purposefully, looked at her watch, and turned to go about her business. At another singer's fan club I was greeted warmly as a potential fan, shown around the offices, and given fan club literature without asking. At yet another singer's fan club I spoke by chance with a new employee because the head of the club was out of the office. This turned out to be a wonderful opportunity, because the new employee spoke with a candor not found in veterans of this business. She gigglingly disclosed stories of elderly fans calling early the morning after a televised appearance of the star. "Is he alright? He doesn't look well. Make sure that he eats enough," they would say. She revealed fans' intense displeasure at the recent issue of the club newsletter that was folded in such a way for mailing as to cut the star's face in half. It is stories such as these that brought the fan-star relationship into clearer perspective, and they came more readily from the mouth of a junior employee, not yet socialized into the protective ways of the company-run club, than a senior head. She, a newcomer to this profession, gave responses that were more open, less guarded, and a welcome source of insight, precisely because of her low status and relative freshness. I learned through her that it is often more productive to look lower in the hierarchy to understand the workings of an industry or organization.

Negotiating the Terrain of Fandom

In an attempt to create a socially acceptable identity for myself, I joined fan clubs. Careful not to overstep boundaries of allegiance, I joined the fan clubs of one top male and one top female singer, neither of whom would compete directly with each other. I chose the clubs to join solely on the basis of the reception I was given at these initial contacts. Through membership I received monthly newsletters that provided rich primary materials, including fan letters, announcements of the infrequent meetings, which turned out to be infomercials with the singer's manager and other record company employees, the opportunity to purchase advance-sales tickets for concerts, and an invitation to purchase tickets to attend the yearly dinner show with the singer. Membership did not mean regular meetings of fans talking with one another. It did mean that I was put into proximity with fans in formal settings. This does not necessarily translate into interaction. As most field researchers in Japan know, one does not readily speak with strangers. I felt that I needed more contact.

Taking vows of participant observation, I waited for the next concert. As the singer started up the song with which he typically ends a performance, I sensed movement. First one figure, then another, then another was moving hurriedly toward the stage. I was sitting two-thirds of the way in the back of the auditorium. It took me a split second to decide to join them. Quickly stuffing all my belongings under my seat, I rose and made my way to the aisle. Walking down the aisle, I found myself moving too slowly for the women behind me, who had broken into a matronly trot. I quickened my pace to match theirs. This was a race to rush the stage. I was a head taller than most of the women and ten or more years younger, yet I found myself being gently but insistently shoved aside. Surprised, I stood my ground. By the time we had reached as close to the stage as we could get, I felt pressed in on all sides by shoulders, stomachs, buttocks, palms of hands. I looked back and peered into the earnest faces of these housewives who looked well past me to the object of their affection on stage. "Mori-san!" they shouted and waved. He turned toward them. With the bright lights of the stage in his eyes, he could not have seen any of his fans except those in the very front, yet I'm sure each one thought he was looking at them. He smiled and waved—a small gesture, but one that would live on in subsequent letters to the fan club and their publication in the club's monthly newsletter. "I smiled at him and he smiled at me. I waved to him, and he waved back!" the letters would gush. I had read the letters before, but in this instant I found myself a part of the incident that triggered them. I could feel their excitement at being "with" him, with each other, and with the moment. And I wasn't even a fan. Jumping into the very motions of fandom proved invaluable in learning some of the more public yet intimate practices of consumption. Although it did not necessarily solve my interaction problem, it gave me firsthand experience in the physical and emotional seductions of fandom.

In the end, I gained opportunities for interaction only after attending enough events so that a few fans began to recognize me from one concert to the next. Progressively, a smile, a nod, a greeting, became the first steps toward a conversation. The conversation opener inevitably focused on the star singer's performance—"That was wonderful, wasn't it!"—proceeded to successive revelations of intimacy—"Would you like to see my photos of me with Mori from last year's fan-club dinner and the year before? I keep them with me all the time in my wallet"—and ended with "See you next year!" These fleeting connections were conducted over the rumble of the train, in the span of time before our respective stops. These represent the challenges of fieldwork conducted amid a community whose face-to-face contact is restricted to special occasions. Conversations become talk on the run, but talk conducted with the intensity of a devotee.

Learning the Dance of a Closed-Door World

One aspect that made my fieldwork different from the classic anthropological tradition was its multi-sitedness (Marcus 1998). I was studying simultaneously a group of fans, a major commercial industry, and an aesthetic expression. Part of the multi-sitedness was by design, but part of it was by default. Rather than focusing on one aspect of *enka*, I chose to paint the broader picture with swaths bridging the relationship between product, producers, and consumers. I would have loved to study a single company or follow the training of one singer. Although I tried, this was not to be. I came armed with introductions to media executives and academics. But even these could not get me in the door held no more widely open than the rules of politeness required. Record and production companies would not take me on because they could foresee no profit for themselves from the endeavor. I was a poor investment.

I learned well the many ways in which one may be refused in Japan without ever hearing the word "no." One of the most effective ways is through extended silence, not face-to-face, but at a distance. For example, I had an interview at Nippon Columbia, the largest and one of the oldest record companies in Japan. My interview was with an *enka* record producer in Columbia's lobby-lounge where vending machines sell coffee and cigarettes. The interview was going well as we sipped coffee from Styrofoam cups, so long as I asked questions that could be easily answered on the spot. How many newcomers does Columbia take on every year? How often are auditions held? How long is a singer trained before her debut? However, the interview took an uncomfortable turn when I asked if I could possibly shadow one of Columbia's singers in training. At that point, I saw the shift in his bodily posture, cocking his head to the side, averting his eyes, tensing his jaw ever so slightly. I heard the well-known drawing in of air between loosely clenched teeth that signals hesitation and ultimately unspoken refusal. He said that he would check and see. In the next moment, he seemed to recover his composure and suggested that we go upstairs to the company offices.

The moment of hesitation was a blip in the smooth proceedings, but it was significant enough to suggest a change in direction. Once in the upstairs offices, he smiled broadly as he loaded me with CD demos of *enka* and sent me on my way. Elated, I thought I had secured a research site and subject. I waited one, then two months for his call. Silence. A Japanese friend I consulted urged me to call him back. When I finally mustered the courage and made the call, I heard the same intake of air, but briefer this time and softer. His reply took a firmer stance: "*Chotto* . . ." (Well, it's a little . . .) At that point I knew there was no hope.

I took up my cue immediately, acquiescing, apologizing: "Oh, that's fine. It's no problem. I was just wondering . . ." .

He quickly countered: "Well, there's an audition coming up at Columbia. Would you like to attend?" I jumped at the chance.

This dance, then, between refusal on one front while proffering a (consolation) gift on another front became the modus operandi of dealings in the field. I came to expect it. Requests may be refused and promises unfilled. However, what takes their place is a countering of offers, extended on company terms. As a fieldworker, I fed on these first as crumbs or leftovers from my requests with a mixture of disappointment and elation. Ultimately, however, I realized that they were lessons in themselves. I learned the elements within a record company that are set aside structurally as hospitality items— sample CDs, seats at an audition, tickets to a concert—which may repay a small debt or curry favor. The potential benefits they accrue far outweigh their small cost in money or time. Stacks of CDs lie waiting on shelves ready to line pockets with small deposits of social and economic lubricant. I also learned the ways of a business world whose own interests in profit and promotion are always paramount.

Singing One's Way into the Field

Multi-sited fieldwork became a matter of necessity for the single site that I was not able to secure. It meant, however, that I sought more widely than I would have imagined. One of the sites of research became singing lessons and ultimately *karaoke*. Here was extended, costly participant observation. I found my first teacher through a newspaper advertisement. "*Karaoke* lessons. Shibuya." I had no idea what kind of music would be taught, but I decided to give it a try. This singing school included a wide variety of genres, but its young head teacher turned out to be the son of an *enka* composer, just beginning to compose *enka* songs himself through his father's influence and connections. I paid for lessons and began my weekly commute to Shibuya, but the main advantage I gained was the opportunity to talk with the composer/teacher about the *enka* world. Eventually I got to attend a recording session with a singer whose debut song was written by my teacher and became an honored guest of the composer at her debut party.

The debut party proved a rich source of information and insight as to one slice of the *enka* world. The singer was a sixteen-year-old from the northern suburbs of Tokyo whose mother ran a *sunakku* (a bar) and, apparently, took charge of the family. I rode the train to the debut party with my teacher, talking with him along the way about this singer, the song he had written for her debut, and this process of debuting. When we arrived at our destination, I bought a bouquet of flowers on whim to give to the debuting singer. At five thousand yen for a simple bouquet, this was no small outlay for my pocketbook, but I was soon to realize it was little compared to what others brought and what I eventually received.

The party was held at a commercial establishment more typically used for weddings than debut parties. At the entrance to the party, young women seated at the reception desk duly took my bouquet, wrote my name in their guest book, and indicated my table number. Other people arrived with envelopes of money. Three walls of the room were lined with flowers. My bouquet looked like a poor cousin to these twenty-eight elaborate floral arrangements. Each was mounted on a pedestal and bedecked with a sign indicating the giver: the composer, the lyricist, the record company, other record companies, family members, Saitama Prefecture Popular Song Association, an already-established *kōenkai* (a support group or fan club). (A Japanese friend later estimated that each of these floral displays cost well over ten thousand yen.) I started recording the names but decided to photograph the flowers with givers' names instead, not only to save time and ensure accuracy, but also to show the relative size (and expense) of the floral arrangement. These became guideposts to the web of obligations present at this event.

Part of my understanding of the web of obligations included my participation within it. I came with a meager bouquet; I left not only having dined upon an elaborate, expensive meal, but with a staggering armload of gifts as well. First there was the bag of goods given me upon signing the guest register. It contained the singer's debut cassette (retail price one thousand yen), a commemorative towel (five hundred yen), and a twenty-centimeter, two-panel clock with the singer's name and debut date inscribed (estimated cost, five thousand yen), which sits on my desk to this day. Then there was the *o-rei* (honorarium) envelope, given by the singer's mother to me and other honored guests at party's end. I was astonished to find myself a recipient, though I had done virtually nothing to deserve this gift. (Later in the train returning home, I was flabbergasted to open the envelope and find twenty thousand yen.) Finally, just as I was walking out the door, the singer's mother thrust into my arms a huge, hasty bouquet culled from hundreds of leftover flowers from the event. I bowed repeatedly, murmured my thank yous profusely, and wandered, dazed, back to the train station. The gifts I received were obviously not meant for me as an individual, but as a category of person, a guest of my teacher/composer. I was the beneficiary by association of deep, long-standing obligation.

There were other advantages to taking singing lessons besides debut parties and access to the commercial *enka* world. My second teacher was an *enka* composer known throughout Japan for his series of books on singing *enka*. I was able to become a student of his through an extended series of connections that began with my teacher in Hawai'i. Once every two months, the students of this well-known teacher gathered as members of a *karaoke* "circle" to eat, drink, socialize, and sing. This put me in direct contact with fans of *enka* in a classic example of participant observation.

Singing became my legitimation in the field. At these *karaoke* gatherings I furthered my understanding of *enka*'s practices in several important ways. First, I observed hierarchy in the social organization of the group and the practices of its leader, an older man who was the most senior student and, thankfully, a fair singer. He had both the ascribed (age, gender, seniority as a student) and achieved (singing) requirements for a leader. Second, I learned systems of evaluation of performance. In general, people avoided saying anything negative about a singer at this kind of friendly gathering. However, the range of positive comments was wide, from a simple *"Umai!"* (Well done!) to "That's a difficult song to sing" to "You put a lot of feeling into that." Oftentimes, a singer who in my mind had performed outstandingly well received the same accolades as a singer whose performance fell far short. Effort overrode the quality of singing amid this ethos of participation that sought to level the reception of individual performances, even under the glare of the spotlight. Third, I discovered my own (American) puritanism compared to those around me. I blushed at the soft porn projected on the video screen, a part of the visual accompaniment to song. Writhing bodies became the backdrop for the singer, a prim, pink-suited housewife performing with unblinking earnestness. I blushed alone; everyone else seemed to take the lust-filled video in stride. Fourth, and most significant, I got to talk with people about singing, *enka*, and their lives. This kind of conversation took place only in the context of my direct participation in performance of the songs that meant so much to them. Singing as a pathway to interaction took on particular significance within the context of *karaoke*, which focuses on performance not only as skill, but more important, as participation.

Working through *Amae*

As any fieldworker knows, one's experiences are molded in part by people's responses to you as a conglomeration of categories of persons. Besides the categories of wife and mother I mentioned earlier, I belong to that liminal category, *Nikkeijin* (Japanese American). Both Kondo (1990) and Hamabata (1990) have written about researching Japan as Japanese Americans, and I share some of their experiences. Like others, I have been praised for my English and sworn at for my stupidity (e.g., wearing toilet slippers out of the bathroom). In some ways, it was not so much how people mistreated or insulted me, but the kinds of things that people did *not* do that mattered most. In other words, as a *Nikkeijin* I lost out on the *gaijin* (foreigner; specifically, Caucasian foreigner) advantage. This was brought home to me when I spoke with a British female journalist who recounted the ease with which she entered the *enka* world. I marveled at her tale of walking one day into the offices of a top singer knowing virtually no Japanese, but pointing to the poster of the singer she had seen on television. Doors opened magically for her in ways I could only dream of. She is now a close friend and quasi-staff member of that singer, with personal backstage access. No one explicitly said that these doors were opened to her because she is blond and may therefore lend exotic prestige to the *enka* enterprise. And perhaps there are other valid reasons for her welcome reception. Yet I cannot help but contrast her experiences in the *enka* world with mine. To this end, I was not *gaijin* enough.

As a *Nikkeijin,* I occupied a liminal position exactly because I was a *gaijin,* but did not look like one. No matter how many times I explained to people that I was American, not Japanese, the phenotype held sway in people's minds. This took place even when I was surrounded by my Caucasian husband and mixed-race children, interacting in English. The notion remained stubbornly embedded in people's minds that a Japanese face presupposes a

Japanese mind. When these assumptions veered to my disadvantage, I made a point of asserting my difference.

The quickest method of asserting difference was to speak English, although as I indicate above, even that did not always work. Moreover, I used this method only out of desperation, since it ran the risk of alienating those with whom I needed to cultivate a close relationship. Another method was to apologize at the outset for any lack of Japanese-language skills. In fact, I turned this into an excuse to gain permission to utilize a tape recorder: recording conversations would allow me to listen repeatedly to fully grasp people's meanings. A third method was to bring the United States (or Hawai'i, in my case) into the conversation as a reminder of my place of origin.

My main cultural weapon for taking advantage of categories of identity— *Nikkeijin* and otherwise—was *amae* (dependency). Using *amae* astutely (as many Japanese do within their own cultural positionings), I could gain favors to advance my research. By occupying and asserting a lower status in a hierarchy, one may *amaeru* (to depend upon; act or be dependent) without compunction. Within *amae* I could be seen not as an aggressor, but as victim of my circumstances, seeking assistance to ameliorate my situation. I could *amaeru* within my position as inept Japanese (i.e., *Nikkeijin*) and ask the "dumb" questions by which anthropologists gather people's basic conceptualizations. I could talk about my relatives in Hawai'i who enjoy *enka* (not mentioning, of course, those who do not), and *amaeru* as a female far from home. Within the *karaoke* circle, I was always careful not to upstage any other singer, being very much junior to everyone else there both in chronological age but, more important, as a student of our teacher. By maintaining a "junior performance" that matched my junior (and foreigner) status, I could *amaeru* doubly as a newcomer and as a *Nikkeijin*. I could be simultaneously foreign and familiar, playing off both sides within my liminality. Unlike other foreigners, I (as a *Nikkeijin*) held out the possibility that with enough effort, I could actually overcome my foreignness. *Amaeru* played exactly into this: I could depend upon those around me to guide my efforts. I asked other members of the *karaoke* circle to correct my pronunciation in singing; it was one area in which they held indisputable expertise. Their efforts to help me proffered the rewards of "restoring" my Japaneseness. It was an interlocking situation built upon *amaeru*, capitalizing on the neediness of a *Nikkeijin*. In many ways, the *amaeru* was no act, since I was entirely dependent upon the good graces of those around me. I could show my sincerity (not feigned) as a prodigal daughter and orphan, positioning myself as available for adoption.

Conclusion

In many ways, this notion of playing situations—even frustrating ones—to your advantage is basic to all fieldwork. As other authors of this volume make clear, serendipity does not just happen, but is partly bestowed, partly earned, and partly exploited. It is really only in the combination of all three aspects that fieldwork in Japan can proceed. One turns closed doors into insights, catches conversations on the run, leaps from one's seat into the aisles or on stage as the situation requires. These in turn lead to other doors, conversations, and interactions. Multi-sited fieldwork forces one to proceed willy-nilly, balancing overarching research goals with happenstance. Our laboratory is not closed and controlled (or controllable), but open-ended, forcing us, too, to be open to unforeseen opportunities. As field researchers, we walk a tightrope of human interaction, balancing our needs with those around us. If we forget others' needs, then we cut off some of the most basic pathways to serendipity.

One other aspect remains critical: humor. Being able to laugh is crucial to surviving and enjoying the fieldwork endeavor. Amid the hierarchy and formality so often embedded in public interactions in Japan, laughter can be essential in keeping one's bearings. Laughter arises from and molds our own subject positions as students of culture, individuals interacting with other individuals, and ethnographers making sense of daily situations. Human beings are funny creatures, and this includes ourselves as researchers, as well as those whom we research. Humor not only helps us cope, but gives us insight as well. If we can laugh with those we study, then they become not objects of study, but subjects within our lives. Moreover, learning the humor of others gives us important lessons in cultural assumptions and practices. Humor can be one of the most culturally embedded aspects of social life. Oddly enough, I think it also important to retain the ability to laugh at those we study, if behind closed doors. This kind of laughter becomes our retreat from fieldwork while in the field, preserving some distance from the subject, maintaining our stance as observers. In fact, we want both—intimacy and distance—and humor helps us achieve them. Laughter becomes an invaluable tool for fieldwork in Japan as elsewhere, arising amid cultural difference as well as bonding us within our common foibles.

Notes

I am most grateful to the following programs for support I received for field-work and writing: Crown Prince Akihito Scholarship; Japan Foundation Dissertation Fellowship; the Center for Japanese Studies at the University of Hawai'i; the Northeast Asia Council of the Association for Asian Studies; and the Reischauer Institute for Japanese Studies at Harvard University.

1. *Hanamichi,* "flower way," refers to the runway to the stage in a traditional Japanese theater and also implies the fantasy world of the performing arts.

2. At the time of my initial fieldwork, the then-current exchange rate was about 110 yen to one U.S. dollar, so a 5,000-yen concert ticket cost roughly $45 and a 10,000-yen gift cost roughly $90. (Editor's note: exchange rates have fluctuated widely in the past generation, from roughly 230 yen to about 90 yen to the dollar.)

Related Readings

Yano, Christine R. 1997. "Charisma's Realm: Fandom in Japan." *Ethnology* 36(4):335–349.

———. 1999. "Distant Homelands: Nation as Place in Japanese Popular Song." In Kosaku Yoshino, ed., *Consuming Ethnicity and Nationalism: Asian Experiences.* London: Curzon Press, 158–176.

———. 2000a. "Dream Girl: Imagining the Girl-Next-Door within the Heart/Soul of Japan." *U.S.-Japan Women's Journal (English Supplement)* 19:122–141.

———. 2000b. "Marketing of Tears." In Timothy Craig, ed., *Japan Pop!* Armonk, N.Y.: M. E. Sharpe, 60–74.

———. 2001. "Torching the Stage: Korean Singers in a Japanese Popular Music World." *Hybridity: Journal of Cultures, Texts and Identities* 1(2):45–63.

———. 2002. *Tears of Longing: Nostalgia and the Nation in Japanese Popular Song.* Cambridge: Harvard University Asia Center, Harvard University Press.

Glenda S. Roberts
interviewing leaders of
the Zentoitsu Workers'
Union, 1997.

GLENDA S. ROBERTS

Bottom Up, Top Down, and Sideways: Studying Corporations, Government Programs, and NPOs

I study working people's lives and people's working lives. This overarching theme has engrossed me ever since I began my first research in 1983. It consumes my curiosity and pushes me to ask new questions to this day. My main areas of interest are gender and labor in contemporary society. These interests have expanded to include migration and population issues as I began to see the impacts of new trends in those areas on people's working lives.

Through studying people's working lives I also came to realize the importance of policy as a force in shaping opportunity. One could say I like to engage in both "studying up," that is, looking at work from the situation of the worker, and "studying down" (see Schwartzman, 1993), critically viewing the policy frameworks, both corporate and governmental, to attempt to obtain as broad as possible an understanding of the status quo and where it may be headed. Although I had not planned it that way, looking back on my career to date I can see how long relationships with a number of Japanese scholars and professionals in fields other than mine, especially law, economics, and labor sociology, led me to develop a kind of bifocal research perspective. I learned to focus at the microlevel, but then try to situate those microcontexts into the wider frameworks of corporate, governmental, and even global trends.

I was trained as an anthropologist; when I say trained, mostly that consisted of reading vast numbers of books on theory and the history of the discipline as well as ethnographies and listening to my professors' stories of life in "the field." Language training was also a very important part of the graduate school experience, and without it I could never have functioned convincingly or effectively. At Cornell's anthropology department in the early 1980s, though, there were no formal methods courses; one was to pick this up eclectically, in a context-appropriate manner, by way of the sink-or-swim method.

To date I have done major research in two corporations, one a lingerie firm that I will call "Azumi," the other a foreign multinational financial services corporation that I will call "MNF." I have also studied two government programs: Silver Talent Centers, a program that gives senior citizens opportunities to work on a part-time basis in their communities, and programs within the Angel Plan, a policy program that is shared among several government ministries with the aim of creating a Japan (in terms of child rearing, work, education, and environment) that is more amenable to family life. In an increasingly ethnically diverse Japan, I have also studied support groups for undocumented migrants. In these last cases, I have been focused on nonprofit organizations (written as "NPO," pronounced *enu-pii-oo* in Japanese), sometimes also called nongovernmental organizations (NGO, or *enu-jii-oo*). All these research projects share some similar challenges; each also had its peculiarities. Each is also connected to the others in interesting ways—that is, knowledge gained from each is cumulative and helps me to illuminate the diversity in working lives in Japan. In this chapter I will first discuss aspects of access to each field site, then I shall talk about methodologies I have used. Next I consider the importance of awareness of emotion as an aspect of research. From there I discuss some of my other identities, as a mother and as an "embedded researcher" who resides in "the field." I shall close with a bit of a "cautionary tale." Let me first turn to access.

Access

My first study resulted in my doctoral dissertation and later my book, *Staying on the Line, Blue-Collar Women in Contemporary Japan* (Roberts 1994). I had done a lot of reading about professional housewives and their salaryman counterpart husbands, but I did not understand what life was like for women who remained at work throughout childbearing and rearing. What were their motivations to work? How did they manage home and work in a culture that so lauded the professional homemaker? I thought the most likely place to find such women would be in a blue-collar work setting, the rationale being that those women would be more likely to need to work. The first problem I came upon was access: how to find a company willing to allow me to do participant observation?

In the case of the factory, which I call Azumi, an introduction while I was at Cornell to a well-known Japanese legal scholar was instrumental in eventually getting me placed. This introduction went through a circuitous route: the legal scholar introduced me to a nationally renowned occupational health and safety scholar. This scholar of occupational health and safety then introduced me to a doctor who oversaw occupational health and safety in Kyoto. It was ultimately through this doctor and the occupational health scholar that I gained an introduction to the large lingerie firm that agreed to host my research. They were quite impressed that such a famous scholar was introducing me, and in fact his latest book graced the shelves of their health section. Keep in mind, I myself had no direct connection with the occupational health and safety scholar, nor had I even met him before all this had taken place! So the power of the first introduction from the legal scholar paved the way.

In the end, I was introduced to a firm that allowed me to work part-time at the factory as well as interview personnel managers and union representatives. I was very surprised that ultimately it was via a kind of backdoor route—that of occupational health and safety—that I gained entry to this corporation. In my mind at the time, my dissertation topic had nothing to do with medical anthropology, health, or safety per se, but with women's motivations to stay on at work and gender norms governing their situations in the factory. Yet the networks that were activated on my behalf certainly proved to be just what I needed to gain entry as well as insight into the world of work in Japan. The introductions alone, however, were not enough to quite clinch the deal. The formal acceptance came through a meeting that took place among the company president, my mentor at the University of Kyoto, and me. As it turned out, my mentor and the company president were already acquainted with each other, and this, too, surely smoothed my way.

I should mention that the same legal scholar introduced me to a labor lawyer in Kobe who also attempted (unsuccessfully) to place me at a shoe factory. Citing poor financial conditions, this company turned me down, but the introduction to this labor lawyer proved pivotal in my research. He later introduced me to other factories where I was allowed to interview, he let me use his considerable library and his copy machine, he explained the legal frameworks for workers in Japan, opened to me his network of labor lawyers, and generally became a wonderful mentor and friend. Without his considerable advice and active intervention on my behalf, I would never have gained a critical perspective. From my coworkers and the factory and corporate managers alone I could not have understood the larger social and legal contexts of the system, nor would I have had the comparative perspective that his introductions to smaller factories in the region eventually gave me.

For instance, this labor lawyer opened my eyes to the vastly inferior working conditions enjoyed by women workers who, other than by virtue of their job titles as *pāto,* or "irregular employees," performed the same tasks as regular employees for the same number of hours per week, but for a fraction of the latter's wages and no benefits. Although there were a few *pāto* employees at Azumi, at the time I was there, Azumi did not rely on *pāto* to get much of its work done, as many smaller firms do. Interviewing *pāto* at smaller firms allowed me to understand why Azumi workers were so reluctant to quit their regular jobs and how much was at stake for them. These interviews also brought home to me how low-wage, largely female labor props up a great deal of the manufacturing sector in Japan. This attorney also introduced me to another lawyer who was in charge of a suit brought by *pāto* against their firm for reasons of unfair dismissal, the *Shinshirasuna* case. When I learned the details of this case and the difficulties the women had in pursuing it in court, I realized how much these women's jobs meant to them, a fact hidden by corporate rhetoric about the casual attitudes of women in irregular jobs. In a sense, then, this first research began from a "studying up" perspective, but through the tutelage of my lawyer mentor, it grew to embrace a kind of sideways grasp on the system, where I could see legal experts deploying their skills to try to give workers access to rights in the employment system and to push that system toward change. One might call this "studying sideways," or viewing the system from the perspective of actors such as lawyers or health professionals who have comprehensive knowledge of the larger system and the way it operates and who use this knowledge to connect workers to levels of power beyond their reach.

Several years later, the same Kawasaki-based occupational health and safety scholar who introduced me to Azumi urged me to do a study of the government's work program for the elderly, Silver Talent Centers. The relevant government officials were all well known to him, and he sang my praises enough to open the doors of local communities in Tokyo, Kyoto, and Osaka, where I carried out intensive interviews with senior citizens and the bureaucrats involved. This was my first extensive encounter with the bureaucracy and my first experience in fully incorporating the "studying down" perspective. I interviewed many bureaucrats at both national and local levels. Without their cooperation, the study would have been impossible. I found this research differed in interesting ways from that in the private sector. I will discuss this further later in the paper.

I began research on the Angel Plan in 1996, and I am still following it. I became interested in this issue when I saw the government advertising seminars for women who desire to return to work after child rearing. From my previous research, I knew how disadvantageous a career interruption can be; it can often mean forfeiting one's opportunity for a regular job with benefits. I was curious to see how the government was framing this return to work, how they were preparing women for it, and what sorts of new programs they were offering in terms of infrastructural support. As it turned out, the Angel Plan is the government's response to much more than women's desire to return to work. Through the plan, several ministries are attempting to address the "problems of the low-birth-rate society." Interestingly, the ministries do not always agree on the solutions. Furthermore, the policy frameworks they are putting in place to address some of the "problems" have to be negotiated through a number of institutions, such as day-care center unions and corporations, which may have different agendas. Finally, the public, too, has their own ideas about what should be done to improve families' lives, and several NPOs have been vocal throughout the Angel Plan campaigns.

I found access to the public programs in the plan itself to be quite straightforward: I simply contacted the appropriate ministry or affiliate and asked for permission to audit the public seminar. I found government officials quite willing to be interviewed about their programs, and I received several introductions from the officials to their affiliated institutions. I also made contact with the NPOs, such as the Parents Group Considering Day-care Centers, by directly contacting the head office and had several fruitful conversations with their representatives.

The difficulty came when I wanted to personally interview women who had participated in some of the government-sponsored seminars, such as the seminar supporting women's reentrance to work life. In the course of my research, I had gained permission to sit in on several seminars, which proved very useful in understanding the overall thrust of the programs. Still, I wanted to meet and talk with some of these women outside the program, and I could not figure out a way to do this. The reemployment support program published a newsmagazine for women who joined the seminar, with quite an extensive mailing list. Finally I got my courage up and requested the office in charge, which was a subcontractor for one of the government ministries, to allow me to insert a return-mail postcard in the magazine explaining my research and asking for volunteers to interview. I fully expected to be turned down flat, but actually the response was a "maybe"; it needed to be fielded with higher authorities. I was then informed a few days later in an unofficial phone call that the response was going to be favorable and that I should visit the office on a certain date to discuss the details.

The night before the auspicious day, I received another phone call from a distraught office staff member. In great embarrassment but with no full explanation, she informed me that it had all fallen through but that I should still appear at the office the next day to be told the bad news! I never did receive a convincing explanation for the sudden withdrawal of permission; perhaps someone at an even higher level simply thought it was imprudent to allow a foreign researcher such (I believe, unprecedented) access. I have since had something equally abrupt happen in regard to permission to do research at an American multinational corporation in China, so chances are that the more levels of bureaucracy there are, the more at risk researchers may be in gaining permission for access. I also think that personal connections are very important in these matters, and in neither case did I have really solid personal connections upon which a relationship of trust could be nurtured.

My research on the Angel Plan confirmed my understanding from the lingerie factory research years before that the definition of a regular employee centers on a gendered model whereby the regular employee must have access to someone else taking care of the home, if a home is to be kept. By 1998, the White Paper of the Ministry of Health and Welfare was itself bemoaning the gendered division of labor in Japanese society and blaming it for the low birth rate.

This interpretation created an opening for a variety of government policies encouraging gender equality. At the same time, the Ministry of Labour also began talking about work/life balance and the importance of corporations to assist employees to attain it. I knew that some corporations in the United States and other OECD countries had instituted flexible work arrangements for their employees (in fact, so did the Ministry of Labour; they went on fact-finding missions to companies in other OECD countries). I hoped to find a corporation that was introducing such policies to workers in Japan. As it so happened, a major U.S. financial services multinational corporation where a friend worked was just about to introduce new initiatives regarding work/life flexibility. I asked for an introduction, and after meeting key people in the personnel department, I began a two-year exploratory study of pregnancy leave, child-care leave, and reduced hours for regular workers, among other flexible work arrangements. The research opened up for me a window on globalization at the upper end as well as on work/life balance in the firm.

The last research project I would like to introduce is my work on support groups for undocumented migrant workers. I became interested in the topic because, when I was in Japan doing the Silver Talent Centers research at the peak of the economic bubble, I could see that migrant workers from other parts of Asia as well as from Brazil and Peru were taking on many of the jobs in manufacturing and construction that hitherto had been held by Japanese themselves. I wanted to understand how the society was responding to increasing ethnic diversity, and I wondered what this trend would mean for the society as a whole. To gain a foothold on what was taking place, in 1993 I organized an international conference at the University of Hawai'i to explore the issues surrounding the new migration to Japan. One of the conference members brought with him the head of the Zentōitsu Foreign Worker's Union. The then-director of HELP (House of Emergency, Love and Peace), a shelter for foreign women, also attended. It was through them that I was able to begin my own research in 1994 on support groups for foreign workers. I continued this research intermittently in 1996, after I came to Japan to work.

Methods

At Azumi

My first study, at Azumi, was probably the most satisfying for me in some ways. I had a full two years with nothing else on my plate, I had good access to company personnel records, and I was able to build up solid working relationships with my coworkers. When I later interviewed some of them individually, I already knew their circumstances to an extent, not just from work but also from outside of work. It was easier to get nuanced and detailed information, and I had a good grasp of the context as I was working at the very same factory and understood, at least to an extent, the atmosphere and key players being described to me. While interviewing is not always part of an anthropologist's method, I found that when studying the workplace, I needed to have some time to address explicit issues, one-on-one, with my coworkers, and this was the best way to do it.

To explain more clearly, when I entered the factory, I found, much to my chagrin, that workers were not allowed to chat with each other except during breaks. This presented some difficulties in getting to know people on the floor. How was I to find out my coworkers' personal situations and attitudes toward gender roles, the Equal Employment Opportunity Law, and so on, when I couldn't even talk to them during work? At the end of the day, everyone immediately rushed off to their homes, so opportunities for heart-to-heart conversations were sorely limited. Lunchtime was free, but I soon found that no one lingered over her bowl of noodles, but rather, food was consumed at an amazing pace, without much in the way of discussion, and people literally ran to purchase bags of snacks, divide into established cliques of friends, and make a bit of conversation before the bell rang again.

Literally the only good time to get to know people was at the lunch break, but I was such an oddball that it took quite a lot of time to break the ice. No one in my work group had ever known a foreigner, nor had they traveled abroad, nor had most of them attained more than a junior high school education. My knowledge of the local dialect was nil, and surely my standard dialect was off-putting. We had so many communication gulfs to cross, thinking back on it, it is a wonder that my coworkers ever befriended me. Eventually I brought in pictures of my family and my home and tried to somehow contextualize myself for them. I began attending company-sponsored events after work or on the weekends, and people also began inviting me to join them in the occasional weekend party or get-together. At the same time, I decided to be a less frequent visitor at the corporation's main office, where I had been offered a desk to study in the afternoons. I came to recognize that these frequent parlays into corporate headquarters only distanced me from the factory workers, who certainly lacked such direct access to the power center.

After several months the comfort level with my coworkers rose as I became accustomed to the routines and they became accustomed to my presence. I still realized, however, that I did not have the detailed information on the lives of my coworkers that I needed to understand their strategies to manage work and home life. I simply could not insinuate such topics into our short lunchtime conversations.

It was at this point that I decided to ask each coworker if she would let me interview her on topics related to work and home life in her home or at a coffee shop of her choice. With some apprehension, I drew up a list of open-ended questions that I hoped each person would answer, I explained that I needed the information for my thesis, and I promised not to divulge the responses to anyone, except in the thesis, with pseudonyms. The response was very positive, and I learned a great deal from these interviews. My questioning focused on individual education and employment histories, as well as the worker's attitudes toward her job, her home life and strategies for household management, her husband's involvement in the household, her hopes and plans for the future, and her opinions on national developments in labor, such as the Equal Employment Opportunity Law. I also interviewed the company's health-section nurses, who ended up giving me a great deal of insight into workers' stress and the nurses' role as intermediaries between workers and the company. There again the sideways perspective proved to be so illuminating. I hadn't anticipated those interviews would be so fruitful.

I am not blessed with a great short-term memory, so the tape recorder has proved my friend for years. I do always take notes as well, though, since occasionally there is some technical disaster that renders the tape useless. My notes are in English, interspersed with some Japanese. Especially if I want to remember the flavor of a particular expression, I jot it down in Japanese so that I don't forget just how it was put. I have learned much Japanese vocabulary simply from going over these interviews. Transcriptions also allow one to directly quote one's interviewees. There is always the possibility, however, that the person being interviewed may censor herself more when a recorder is present. In the case of the factory research this was obviated to a certain extent by the fact that we knew each other quite well by the time the interview took place. Interviews also afforded me the chance to meet people outside the factory and spend time relaxing with them. I often met their families and ended up spending hours with them, of which the interview was just a small part.

With Silver Talent Centers

In the research on Silver Talent Centers, I had the full cooperation of government officials at the top of the program. This meant I was able to study five different centers. Because time was limited to nine months and because I had decided to cover a number of centers from Tokyo to Kyoto to Osaka, however, this time I did not do participant observation and limited my study to interviewing and collecting documents.

As with the Azumi research, I conducted many of the interviews at people's homes, which I found much more fruitful than interviewing at the workplace. The time constraints were less, and the person being interviewed was usually more relaxed. Moreover, I could get an idea of the person's lifestyle outside work. In general I found these retirees to be very willing to talk about their experiences. I had few interviews where I felt that I could not connect well. I was interested in understanding people's motivations for joining Silver Talent Centers. I also wanted to hear their assessments of the centers. Were the centers offering people a new lease on life? Did they feel more connected to their communities as a result of participation? I took a brief educational and employment history of each person I interviewed and also asked questions about their current lives as retirees, their family situations, and their economic circumstances. I dealt with the question about finances by asking the person to identify the range that most fit him, and I also asked about his type of housing. While I had anticipated questions about finances might be sensitive, actually people were quite willing to respond, and the answers enabled me to see clearly the range of financial circumstances of the retirees in the program.

This was also the first time I worked extensively with government officials as I was studying a government-operated program, and I found they were very anxious that I publish something that would put their program in a good light. In other words, they wanted me to do PR for the program. They were not looking for any critical evaluation or assessment, as they felt their continued funding rested on a positive public perception of the program. Since that time, I have come across this issue on other occasions as well, when dealing with the bureaucracy. If I published more in Japanese I might well find my access to government programs impaired. It is not that I am trying to muckrake, but informants' accounts of programs are not always positive.

Among Angel Plan Promoters

The methods I employed in studying Angel Plan programs were similar to those in the other studies: I interviewed as many players at as many levels as possible. I also sat in on government-sponsored seminars and read widely in newspapers and popular media about the plan and analyzed government poster campaigns. Eventually I was able to interview some women who were seeking to return to work, although as I explained above, I could not gain access through the program's magazine. Instead, I met these women by way of introduction through several individuals who were connected in some way to one of my colleagues at the University of Tokyo. The problem with this method was that the women thereby accessed were almost universally well educated and solidly middle class or upper middle class. I had hoped to also meet working-class women, but this just did not happen with the snow-ball approach. At least in urban areas, the social circles do not overlap much, except perhaps at the public elementary school.

Non-Profit Organization (NPO) Research

Another type of organization I have studied is the support group, women's shelters and local unions for undocumented workers and Japanese workers in nonunion shops. I wanted to understand how these groups framed their understandings of the problems of foreign workers in Japanese society. I also hoped to figure out the relationship between support groups and the government services sector, and whether the support groups had any influence on government policy for foreign workers at the national level. I interviewed staff and sifted through piles of intake interviews at a women's shelter, followed union protests at government ministries and companies, and attended migrant workers' network meetings. I also took modified life histories of some union and shelter staff, thereby discovering that not a few of the movers and shakers had been involved in the student movement of the 1960s.

NPOs and corporations seem almost 180 degrees apart from each other. The shelters, local unions, and other support groups are much more free-wheeling and loosely organized. Many members are volunteers who do other things for income, so much of the work of the support groups, especially the organizational meetings and public educational programs, takes place during evenings and weekends. My impression was that support group staff live for their support groups. Though most have families, they must see very little of them. My study was more participatory, following events as well as interviewing.

Another aspect of the research on support groups for foreign workers is that it demands multilingual talents if one is to do the research to rigorous anthropological standards. Alas, I have never studied Thai, nor Tagalog, Korean, Portuguese, Bengali, Farsi, or any of the other languages that migrants here speak, save for English, Japanese, and a bit of Mandarin Chinese. For that reason I decided to concentrate on the Japanese support groups themselves rather than on the migrants' situations. A few of the most recent generation of Japan scholars have girded themselves with multilingual talents, performed transnational research, and given us some finely contextualized knowledge of migrants in Japan. I hope this continues. Japan is increasingly global, and Japanese alone is insufficient as a research tool for many important topics.

At MNF

The research that I did on the American multinational corporation, from 1999, consisted of interviews as well as a few focus groups. These were held mostly at the corporation itself, during lunch breaks in private meeting rooms. This was my first time to do research on people in a U.S.-based firm, and it was different from my previous experience in several ways.

First of all, information security was tight, and I had to draw up a formal security agreement with the corporation. I also had to set up an ombudsman at my university to whom interviewees could complain if they were unhappy with the manner in which the interview was conducted. I informed the person interviewed of this at the beginning of each interview, and as usual I assured each person that I would maintain his or her privacy and would use pseudonyms when I publish the study. The people who transcribed my interviews also had to sign security agreements. This was unprecedented for me.

Time, too, was very tight. These people were busy, and I was highly conscious that I was taking their time. I was extra careful to be prompt for meetings and interviews and to end them within the time specified, making another appointment if we did not have time to finish. I felt very much as if I myself were working in this high-pressured corporate environment. Unlike my research in the factory, here I did not meet people after work to spend leisure time together. In that sense, the information gained is less rich.

The research topic was fairly tightly demarcated. I was studying work/life balance and the company's introduction of flexible work arrangements. I had to be careful to structure the interview so as to get the information I needed in a short period of time. My lack of personal knowledge of the people I was interviewing was frustrating, but it was eased to an extent because I had a research assistant who was getting her Ph.D. in human development who had worked for this corporation for many years. She was also the vice president in charge of the implementation of work/life policy. Through e-mail correspondence, in coordination with this vice president, I was able to set up the interviews with those employees who volunteered to be a part of the study. We also did some of the interviewing together, and my research assistant's knowledge of the company and players was highly useful in clarifying issues. On the other hand, her presence may have biased some interviews, since she was after all in the employ of the company in a high-level position.

All in all I felt that the people we talked with were frank in their discussions of balancing work and life, as they wanted their environments to improve and they saw my research as a voice for them and an avenue for both praise and complaint. I informed them in advance that I would only relate to the company what they specifically asked me to convey, and many people did ask me to mention certain issues of importance to them. In this sense, the research at MNF was "action research," although not as intense as Leslie Perlow's (1997) work in *Finding Time*.

Another issue with the multinational corporation was that in order to understand it more fully, I needed to understand the place of the union. That was a very sensitive issue, because the union had shrunk by attrition since the 1970s, when the company began instituting merit-based incentives. By the time I began studying the union, only a handful of members were left. The company perceived these employees as losers who could not cut the competition in the fast-paced, self-driven environment. While I was not trying to study the union in detail, I did need to understand the broader context of labor-management relations over the years in order to understand current policy initiatives and the politics of implementation. The company, to their credit, did grant my request to be informed about the history and current status of the union, but I felt that the request was initially met with surprise on their part, as they perceived it as outside the bounds of my topic, which was flexible work policy implementation. The corporate vantage of research is more narrow; mine is much more broad. Developing trust over many months went a long way in opening this kind of access. I doubt if I could have gained this trust had I just come in and made demands for privileged information all at once without knowing people well.

Research and Emotional Engagement

Sometimes I need to step back from my research and see how it is affecting me as well as those I am studying. I discovered that talking with retirees about their past employment lives, their current lifestyles, and their future plans, while compelling and rich, could also be very depressing, and that was a factor I had not anticipated. That is, in some cases, these senior citizens were not happy with the way their lives had turned out, and at this point there was not a lot of time left. A few people had been at a series of small companies during their working years, all of which had gone bankrupt, leaving them with only a very small pension. Others had been disappointed in personal relationships with their children and had tried to live together but had ended up moving out and living alone. Poor health or fears of it kept some of the people I interviewed from enjoying life. While I certainly heard many pleasant reminiscences as well, I found my own high spirits sinking when I encountered those who were unhappy with where life had brought them.

This was something for which I was unprepared. I simply had not anticipated being personally affected by my research interviews. We don't usually mention this as a possible hazard of research, though I am sure that people in the health and social service professions are expressly taught to set up emotional barriers between themselves and their clients. It actually was a good lesson for me, albeit one that caught me off guard.

It was through interviews with mothers who wished to return to work that I learned how sensitive a method interviewing really is—to the informant. Most of my questions in these interviews dealt with family history, employment history, the person's current daily life, and reasons for wanting to return to work. I remember one person in particular who, when I asked her to tell me about why she wanted to go back to work, broke down in tears and cried for a few minutes. I told her we could stop right then and that there was no need to go on, but she wanted to continue. She proceeded to tell me how hard it was to raise three little ones by herself. She really wanted to get a job, any job, just to get out of the house. She really wanted to tell me what her life was like, and I felt privileged to listen. The problem is, and I have reflected on this many times since then, how much does the experience of being interviewed affect the informant? After all, I am asking personal questions and giving the informant ample time to think about things and discuss things with me that she may not ordinarily think of at all. My questions may point up contradictions in her life that she would rather not acknowledge.

My only "solution" to this dilemma, other than an awareness of this as an issue in interviewing, is not to push hard for information when the person with whom I am talking seems reluctant to divulge it. I also let her know she is free to decline answering. Furthermore, I tell people they are welcome to ask me whatever suits them, since they have given me so much knowledge of themselves.

Sometimes people ask advice, such as "Should I go on to pursue a high school diploma?" In that case, I have no qualms about saying, "Yes, I think that'd be a great idea." But when a person asks me, "Should I quit my job and just stay home with my baby? " I have a harder time giving a definitive reply. I also feel uneasy sometimes when people ask me what my own home life is like, since it has probably offered a lot more leeway and has given me a lot more time to myself than is the case for many women. A woman whose spouse comes home at midnight every night can hardly appreciate my description of a spouse who will assume the entire parenting load while I go off to do research. That is, even if she wanted a more involved spouse (and she might not), the operative constraints on our spouses are very different, so much so that it just emphasizes a different world in terms of lifestyle and life choices. Nevertheless, if someone asks me, I feel obliged to reply. I guess the upshot of this is that, while we probably cannot help but influence the people we meet, sincerity, mutuality, respect, and good will go some way in tempering the result.

Being a Mom in the Trenches

What's it like to be a mom in the field? During the Silver Talent Center project, I had my one-and-a-half-year-old daughter in tow, and her father was not with us for most of the nine months. I was a first-time parent and a youngest child myself, to boot. I had no clear idea of the pitfalls ahead. I discovered that tots get chicken pox and all manner of other ailments from being in day care, and these sudden events wreaked havoc on my research engagements. I did end up discovering a (very expensive) professional baby-sitter dispatch firm and relied on the occasional close friend or day-care center *pāto* personnel to watch my daughter when she was ill. I had clearly not factored Julia into the research design that had us moving to Kyoto after three months and back again to Tokyo in another three months. That was definitely overly ambitious and probably was very hard on Julia, who had to adjust to two very different settings at that tender age.

On the other hand, having a toddler in tow made me experience firsthand the frustrations of working parents. I observed the gamut of child care available for toddlers, from a nonlicensed, private, in-home arrangement that had what looked like over twenty runny-nosed toddlers running all over the place with only one person "in charge," to a public center with spacious yard, plenty of expert personnel, and an orderly schedule. I was fortunate to find spaces in a licensed private center in Tokyo and a public center in Kyoto, but the difficulty in making these arrangements made me realize why some parents were forced to place their babies into really inadequate facilities. I was also the recipient of much tongue clicking when my Silver Talent Center interviewees found out I was leaving my toddler in day care. These and later experiences with private and public educational institutions in Japan, while tangential to the central purpose of my research, greatly expanded my understanding of gender, work, family, and social class in Japan.

The Embedded Researcher

In June of 1996 I moved to Tokyo, where for two years I worked as a visiting associate professor at the University of Tokyo before taking my current tenured post at Waseda. This has meant that my days of seeing Japan as my research site alone are over. Now I live and work in Japan, and I am on a modified Japanese university schedule that gives me five or six weeks of unclaimed time during the summer and perhaps two weeks in the spring.

I spend any protracted time off returning to the United States to visit family and to browse bookstores and libraries for English-language research materials. While I have "the field" at my feet, I have to be very careful to protect my time so that I can actually *do* something. Never mind writing it up. Another aspect of living long-term in Japan is that the information never ceases coming in. There will always be a new account in the newspaper the next morning, another opportunity to interview, or one more event that is crucial to cover. I have had to learn to draw a line and force myself to deal with a defined body of information.

There were many small and surprising pitfalls that came with this new status as a regular Tokyoite. For instance, have you ever speculated on the importance of your address for your research? The import never really hit home for me until I ended up living in the Shiroganedai District of Tokyo, the location of the University of Tokyo lodge for foreign scholars. Never mind that it was the cheapest housing in all of Tokyo since the university heavily subsidized it. During my research on support groups for foreign workers, I suffered no end of snide comments about my upper-class lifestyle when I passed out my name card with the Shiroganedai address printed on it. Shopping bags from National Azabu or Meidi-ya (the local supermarkets stocking mostly foreign brands) also garnered comments. In retrospect I should not have printed my home address on the card, nor should I have used those nice brown paper bags to carry around materials! I eventually answered "near Meguro" or "not far from Shinagawa" or even "in Minato Ward" when asked my home address, but even that was not enough to suit people, who would inevitably go on to speculate how nice it must be to be able to live within the city proper (that is, how nice it must be to be able to *afford* to live within the city and not have to suffer the horrendous commute that most ordinary folk put up with). Several people encouraged me to relocate to Edogawa Ward, a working-class part of town, but the low rent at the lodge, plus our daughter's increasing attachments to her school friends and the neighborhood, precluded us from moving to a more neutral territory.

A major reason that I have curtailed further research on support groups is that until my daughter is in college, I simply do not have the time to work full-time as well as follow their activities. I maintain occasional contact, though, subscribe to their newsletters, and help them out with editing once in a while. I have also placed students as interns at these NPOs, and a staff member from one of the NPOs has even given a lecture to my "Studying the Workplace" class. One could say that my long-term presence in Japan offers a possibility for ongoing relationships, though it is difficult to find time for it all. I suppose this would be generally true of those who live long-term in "the field."

All in all, I have found that being a part of "the scene" rather than an occasional bystander offers both challenges as well as advantages. I am often made aware that my positions in academia here open many avenues to research.

Repayment of Debts

Time and again, other people are instrumental in getting in and getting the work of research done. Reciprocity goes hand in hand with the process of getting along. We are asked to do things for those who do for us: whether it is teaching English, editing manuscripts, giving lectures, or doing newspaper interviews, there is always something one is asked to do. As long as I do not feel that such activity compromises my research, I always try to be obliging. Over the years, a great number of people have gone out of their way to help me in my research, and there is really very little I can do in the way of recompense other than to assist them with whatever useful talents I can muster. In this vein, I should note that on more than one occasion I have been asked to lecture on some aspect of the situation of women in the United States or migration to the United States, and while my research field has never been my own country, over the years the U.S. section of my bookshelf has certainly grown in response to these inquiries. I have indeed found myself boning up on the legal and policy frameworks regarding gender, labor, and migration in the United States. Actually, this enforced expertise on the United States is very useful when trying to put Japan in a comparative framework. I have learned more about my own country and other OECD nations—advanced, industrial societies—from being in Japan than I ever knew while living in the United States, where I was always asked to lecture on Japan! By way of forewarning, then, it might behoove researchers going to Japan to carry with them some recent works from their home countries on topics similar to their research areas, in order to oblige these sorts of (really, very reasonable) requests.

And a Cautionary Tale

In my reflections above, I have attempted to give the reader some of my personal insights on how I encounter research, stumble through research, and what it has taught me along the way. There is one more story to relate, not a story of breakthrough and success, but one of naïveté, shock, and retreat.

Ordinarily one avenue of research opens up many other related areas, but at one time in my career I deliberately cut off an important avenue of inquiry because the key person holding information access in that area suddenly made it clear that cooperation from him would require more than sincere inquiry on my part.

Allow me to back up a bit. I was in Japan for a short-term stay; my daughter was with me but my husband had stayed home. Over the course of some weeks, people important to the research topic had introduced me to this senior scholar, who was himself involved in this topic and who had already published several articles on it, though in a different field from mine. I met him for coffee, we exchanged some publications, and he asked if he could be present at one of my interviews in order to better understand my technique. Later on, he invited me and my daughter to a party at his home, where he and his wife entertained a group of his students.

One day soon after that, I needed to have him return one of the books I had lent him. He suggested a coffee shop in the late afternoon, but I was constrained by needing to pick up my daughter from day-care and take her home, so I explained this and asked him to have coffee at my place instead. This apparently was my big mistake. He showed up at the apartment with a bottle of wine in hand, along with the book. I was totally mystified as to why he should bring wine when I had only mentioned a quick cup of coffee. Indeed, the coffee was on.

Instead of remaining seated in the chair I had proffered him, he got up and opened the door to the bedroom, inquiring of me how much rent I paid, by the way. I felt very uncomfortable. He then started talking about how we could collaborate on research, finally coming over behind where I sat. At this point he started massaging my shoulders. My little girl was on my lap with her picture book open. It was all I could do not to put her down and express my utter rage, but I was afraid he might get violent, and I did not want to risk it. I swiftly shrugged my shoulders a few times to get him to let go and asked him to sit down. He did, but then he wanted to know if I would be interested in going on a drive with him to someplace nice and peaceful in the country-side, maybe to a hot springs resort! By this time I was centered on just trying to get him out of the apartment. I held my temper and told him I had to run Julia's bath and make her supper, so perhaps it was time for him to be getting home. He did not take the hint. After a bit I repeated this and took her with me to start the bathwater. He finally decided to leave. I called my Japanese girlfriend, who, equally outraged and sympathetic, eventually offered me her husband's culturally specific translation of that event: never invite a man to your place for business. In fact, her husband thought it was hilarious.

Perhaps I should have known better, but my cultural blinders were on. Other men, friends of mine, had visited Julia and me at the apartment with no problem. One time a Japanese newspaper reporter came to my place to interview me in the very same dining room, with no problem whatsoever. I had been a passenger on Japan's notoriously groper-ridden trains for years without a single incident, perhaps because my height and fierce train demeanor discouraged the lot. Train drunks had presented an occasional problem, but I was always able to circumvent them by moving to another car. It simply never occurred to me that this senior scholar would make a move on me, in my own dining room, with my little girl on my lap. To him, though, a friendly female researcher whose husband was abroad and who needed access to research that he controlled must have seemed eminently available.

I never contacted him again, nor did I follow up on any of the promising avenues he offered me for further research. In fact, in this field, all roads led to Rome, and he was Rome. I was virtually unable to expand the research without collaboration with him. I hate to say it, but I guess the lesson is that if a woman asks a man over to her place on business, her intent may be totally misconstrued. Of course the invitation to a hot springs resort may as well have occurred at a coffee shop as at my place, but at least I would have felt safer in reacting to it. The result, though, would no doubt have been the same. I cut off that research and have never gone back to it.

So, research has its ups and downs, surprises and disappointments, as well as exhilarating highs when I put things together and it all starts making sense. Although there is no end to the "work" that is research, and the line between week and weekend is mostly in the imagination, I still keep going back to it. It is immensely rewarding. It is well worth waiting for the next "Aha!" I can't believe they pay me to have so much fun!

Note

This chapter discusses learning experiences from a number of research projects over the past twenty years. I would like to thank the Fulbright Commission, the Social Science Research Council, the Japan Foundation, the Center for Japanese Studies at the University of Hawai'i, the East-West Center, and all other agencies and organizations who have generously funded and supported my research.

Related Readings

In this chapter I have commented on five different research projects: my field-work at Azumi (Roberts 1994, 1996a), at Silver Talent Centers (1996b), among support groups for migrant workers (2000), on the Angel Plan (2002), and at Multinational Finance (MNF) (2003).

Roberts, Glenda S. 1994. *Staying on the Line: Blue-Collar Women in Contemporary Japan.* Honolulu: University of Hawai'i Press.

———. 1996a. "Careers and Commitment: Azumi's Blue-Collar Women." In Anne Imamura, ed., *Re-Imaging Japanese Women.* Stanford: Stanford University Press, 221–243.

———. 1996b. "Between Policy and Practice: Silver Human Resource Centers as Viewed from the Inside." *Journal of Aging and Social Policy* 8(2/3):115–132.

———. 2000. "NGO Support for Migrant Workers in Japan." In Mike Douglass and Glenda S. Roberts, eds., *Japan and Global Migration: Foreign Workers and the Advent of a Multicultural Society.* London: Routledge, 275–300.

———. 2002. "Pinning Hopes on Angels: Reflections from an Aging Japan's Urban Landscape." In Roger Goodman, ed., *Family and Social Policy in Japan: Anthropological Approaches.* Cambridge: Cambridge University Press.

———. 2003. "Balancing Work and Life: Whose Work? Whose Life? Whose Balance?" In Gil Latz, ed., *Challenges for Japan: Democracy, Finance, International Relations, Gender.* Tokyo: International House of Japan, for the Shibusawa Eiichi Memorial Foundation.

Theodore C. Bestor
talking with a tuna
wholesaler at Tsukiji,
ca. 1995.

THEODORE C. BESTOR

Inquisitive Observation: Following Networks in Urban Fieldwork

Finding and Following Networks

Finding my first field site was a daunting task. The second time, my site eventually found me, but it took me quite a while to realize it.

At the start of dissertation fieldwork in 1979, I spent several frustrating weeks searching for the perfect Tokyo neighborhood in which to study community institutions and local social networks. Finally, a fellow graduate student, Christena Turner, suggested I should "choose a network, not a neighborhood."[1] Her excellent advice was right on target: determine where my contacts are strongest and where introductions from existing contacts could be most effective, and go there; don't try to find an "ideal" place and *then* try to find a connection into it. I realize now that networks choose me (or choose to accept me) much more than I can possibly select them. The trick to fieldwork is figuring out how to harness networks that present themselves, as well as how to expand upon (and sometimes escape from) them.

During my research on Miyamoto-chō in 1979–1981 and in many return visits over the years since, my networks have snowballed because I more or less put myself in the path of contacts. I had the good sense (or good luck) to follow up what serendipity offered at the start. I "found" Miyamoto-chō because Dr. Machida, a friend with whose family my wife and I were staying during our search for a field site, suggested that we look at the place where he himself grew up. Through a chain of introductions—starting from Mrs. Machida, through a PTA friend of hers who was a real estate agent, finally to a local shopkeeper, Mr. Fukuda, who was himself close to Dr. Machida's father and brother (but *not* to the Mrs. Machida we knew)—we ended up renting an apartment above the Fukudas' shop in Miyamoto-chō.

So we started with a handful of contacts, but these quickly expanded as we encountered people in varied settings: sometimes spontaneously, sometimes by design. A week or so after we moved into the Fukudas' apartment, the neighborhood association held its annual *Bon Odori* festival, a midsummer outdoor dance at the local elementary school. The Fukuda family took us along and introduced us to a dozen local leaders, but the formal greetings were stiff and, no doubt, so was I.

I started to make informal contacts the next morning when I ventured up to the schoolyard early in the morning to photograph the festival lanterns on which donations by local residents were listed. While I was there, three guys arrived to take down the stage and lanterns. Feeling somewhat shy about my own presence taking pictures of an empty schoolyard, I went over and said hello. They started pulling the stage apart, and I lent a hand. A couple of hours later we were done, and they invited me along for lunch and a beer back at the neighborhood association hall. This chance to get to meet people came not from any conscious planning on my part but from being willing to pitch in unasked and stick out a morning of manual labor. Two of the guys I met that morning became extremely close friends over the years and introduced me in many ways into their own circles of family, friends, and contacts. (Twenty years later, my closest friend of the three is dead—a sad reminder that fieldwork takes place in real life, grief included. Andō Yoshi-fumi, to whom this volume is dedicated, died in early 2001. Nothing I can say can express my feeling of loss at his death.)

Another casual encounter brought me into contact with someone else who has remained a close friend ever since: Mr. Kuroda, a shopkeeper who had married into a local family (as a *mukoyōshi,* or adopted son-in-law). We met because I went to almost every local event to take pictures, and he was a camera buff. At the elementary school's athletic field day in October of my first year of fieldwork, he came over to chat casually about my camera equipment (which didn't hold a candle to his own). He mentioned that his three kids talked about the young foreign couple in the neighborhood. At that point I didn't have a clue who his kids were, but he invited Vickey and me to share the picnic lunch his wife had prepared. When we saw his wife, we immediately recognized her and their kids from many other neighborhood outings. Thereafter, Mrs. Kuroda frequently invited us to join her family for casual dinners, and Mr. Kuroda and I became regular drinking buddies. He was a friendly guy and would always help out with local events if asked, but he kept to himself and figured the business of the neighborhood association was really in the hands of local big shots, not him. The Kurodas became our informal sponsors into local circles quite distinct from the neighborhood association, those centered on the elementary school and Mrs. Kuroda's networks of childhood friends.

Increasingly, I met people through casual local interactions as well as through actively participating in any event or activity to which I could legitimately get access. Anthropologists often describe the fruits of this kind of connectedness as "participant observation," but the term is too vague to convey much about what actually takes place during ethnographic research. In reality, I cannot simply decide to participate and observe. It takes a long time to develop the access to be a "real" participant in local social life. Most fieldworkers legitimately cannot assume the social obligations or relationships required of "real" participants. Furthermore, "real" participants in most settings do not systematically compile information on the passing scene. Finally, observation is too passive a term to describe the activity of constantly asking questions about what's going on. So I prefer to think of what I do as "inquisitive observation."[2]

When I started my research in Miyamoto-chō, I had a topic in mind and found networks (and they found me). In a later research project, networks led me to the site, the Tsukiji wholesale seafood market in central Tokyo—the world's largest market for fresh seafood—and only then to the realization that I had found an ideal project.

I first visited Tsukiji to interview a few wholesalers about their connections with retailers and to ask them questions about supply and demand and market access, in connection with research I planned on the distribution system. Earlier, I had done research on distribution channels for whale meat, examining the routes along which this now controversial delicacy travels from small coastal whaling communities, like Ayukawa in Miyagi Prefecture and

Abashiri in Hokkaido, to regional markets for local consumers, and to metropolitan markets for the restaurant trade.[3] From these local markets I began to understand how a national network of markets was integrated through daily business ties. And people in the whale business introduced me to a few Tsukiji traders whom I could interview about the structure of the market at the top of the heap. I began to look around for more information about Tsukiji from a wider perspective.

An official I knew at the Tokyo Metropolitan Government suggested I meet a colleague, Mr. Shimizu, who was a senior administrator at the marketplace. Mr. Shimizu was a career bureaucrat who had rotated through dozens of positions, landing in the marketplace only a year or so before my visit to his office. He was a newcomer himself and appeared to be still fascinated by the world in which he found himself a powerful figure. Even more, he seemed happy to find me sitting before him, a younger foreign researcher asking him to explain the market.

What began as background inquiry for my research on shopkeepers along dozens of shopping streets dotted across Tokyo's landscape abruptly shifted —foreground and background reversing irreversibly—as I sat in Shimizu's office. He outlined for me a brief history of Tsukiji and explained the basic patterns of transactions that ebb and flow among the market's seven large auction houses and its hundreds of small-scale wholesalers, and among these small wholesalers and their clients, the fishmongers and sushi chefs scattered across the city who were typical of the shopkeepers I had been studying.

Gradually, his matter-of-fact recital caught my full attention. Details snapped into place, and Tsukiji came into sharp focus. What particularly struck me was the interplay he described between a complex economic system (in this case the market's auction system) and the market's small-scale wholesalers—*nakaoroshi gyōsha,* or intermediate wholesalers—and the ways in which the development of market institutions had affected and modified the balance of power over time between large corporations and family enterprises. Mr. Shimizu's explanations suddenly anchored my still-unfocused ideas about the social embeddedness of the distribution system into a tangible social world that I could explore.

Excitedly, I accepted his offer of introductions, and within a week I met officials of a major trade federation that represents the 1,677 stalls occupied by intermediate wholesalers. Federation officials were polite and helpful and showed me around the marketplace. I doubt they expected me to show up again and again, but when I did they rewarded my enthusiasm. Extraordinarily, they gave me access to documents, showed me around the marketplace, arranged interviews for me, and introduced me to many of their members. However, I was aware from the outset that the market was an enormously large and complex institution—market administrators estimate that some sixty thousand people work or do business there each day—and I wanted to avoid being somehow boxed in by reliance on a single source of access.

My desire to find other points of entry was not motivated by an attempt to try to cover everything in this vast place. Even in the early months of fieldwork, I realized that the intermediate wholesalers occupy a particularly pivotal role in the day-to-day operations of the marketplace, both buying and selling within the space of a few hours. Any anthropological research necessarily takes a group or groups of actors as occupying center stage; the stage set by immediate wholesalers frames the "point of view" of my work at Tsukiji. Another researcher approaching Tsukiji with different questions could just as easily focus on the role of workers in the marketplace, the structure of the Japanese fishing industry, the political influence of fishing interests in affecting policy-making, or the impact of consumers' and environmental movements on food distribution. I started—and continue—with the attempt to understand the market as it appears to those who show up each morning at the auctions with money to spend.

My networks of contacts in Miyamoto-chō expanded in part by playing the role of participant-observer. As a bona fide resident of the neighborhood I had both ample opportunities and a certain legitimate standing to play just that role. Guys in Miyamoto-chō were happy to let me share in the drudgery of cleaning up after festivals. In contrast, however, in a busy marketplace there is no legitimate participant-observer role for a wannabe researcher. No one at the Tsukiji market was going to let me carve a tuna or cast a casual bid into the auctions just so I could experience it myself. (At Tsukiji I first realized that the accurate label for my ethnographic technique is "inquisitive observation," since opportunities for "real" participation were limited.) So my networks had to be created through more formal introductions. And although many of my networks at Tsukiji expanded in snowballing fashion just as in Miyamoto-chō, I self-consciously worked on a technique for gaining access to people at Tsukiji by what I call "parachuting," dropping into the midst of things from multiple entry points.

In addition to my introductions from Mr. Shimizu to the wholesalers' federation, I went back to my whaling connections and followed out a couple of lines of contacts through that avenue. I sought out help from people in Miyamoto-chō. Mrs. Machida, my early guide to Miyamoto-chō, knew a woman (through the PTA for their daughters' exclusive private school) whose husband owned a Tsukiji stall that dealt in dried fish. The owner of the sushi bar where I went drinking with Miyamoto-chō's leaders introduced me to some of his suppliers. The vegetable dealer around the corner from my apartment took me through Tsukiji's vegetable auctions one morning. I sought out multiple entry points from as many angles as I could muster. Some led me only short distances, others proved to be gold mines. And I could never predict which would lead me where.

My entry into these networks was based on introductions from outsiders who only knew intermediaries or one or two possible entry points into Tsukiji. Nonetheless, I was able to follow these leads to a social space where the connections among people were overlapping, diffuse, multidirectional, and multistranded. In other words, at the outset, the people who were providing me with introductions really had no idea where those introductions would lead me, nor did I. Of networks there can be no end, certainly no single end, but I realized I had made it to a sufficiently *inside* place when I found myself in the midst of a highly interconnected social world in which most of my contacts all knew each other in many different contexts. Because each was closely and complexly interconnected to others in this tight social nexus, once I began to circulate in these circles, it ceased to matter very much the order in which I was introduced to them or by whom. And, through these chains of introductions I also gained access to several locations where I could hang out more or less on a daily basis—the offices of a social club run by a talkative old woman, Mrs. Yamazaki, who was visited every day by a couple of dozen traders, and several stalls in the market place where I could sit asking questions, sipping tea, and watching what people were doing. In settings like these, vouched for by the networks that had led me there, I could hang out, inquisitively participating, engaging in apparently casual, apparently unstructured interviews with whomever showed up. (I also found places "offstage"—a couple of coffee shops in the outer market—where I could retreat to write notes, think about questions, or just get out of the way when my presence obviously was not wanted.)

I worked hard to expand my networks among intermediate wholesalers and discovered that the face-to-face business they were in—with its strong orientation toward introductions based on prior interactions—made it easy to approach them, easy to establish connections. I cultivated more and more focused networks as my research led me to understand the position of intermediate wholesalers, and as these networks picked me up and passed me along, the centrality of this particular stratum became more self-evident to me. Thus following one sort of network determined that my research project would see the marketplace from the perspective of intermediate wholesalers. This is not to say that I necessarily accept or agree with their own interpretations of what goes on, but that I take their place in the market as a starting point for understanding the whole structure. If I had expanded my networks among supermarket buyers or sushi chefs, auctioneers or truck drivers, provincial fisheries cooperatives or day laborers, government bureaucrats or executives in large fisheries corporations, undoubtedly the point of view of the study would have been different.

These network choices do not result in ethnography that is incomplete, in the sense of lacking something that additional fieldwork could have provided. On the contrary, both my study of Miyamoto-chō and my study of Tsukiji—like any ethnography—are necessarily partial.

Reading the Labels

Exploring a research setting—figuring out what its social dimensions and boundaries are—is always a challenge. I often start out with the feeling that I am standing on a tiny outcropping of known territory, surrounded by huge white spaces. Fortunately, I can take advantage of the fact that Japan is a well-labeled society. Signs are everywhere and often on almost everyone. From these, I can collect rough-and-ready information on the local social environment, a sort of ethnoscience of categories. What kinds (categories) of people are here? What are the jobs or social roles they fill? What sorts of organizations exist? What are the social, political, or geographic boundaries where one institution leaves off and another picks up? A lot of this information is written on the surface of social life.

Take doorways, for example. Walking slowly down a side street in many neighborhoods, glancing at doorways and shop entries, I can pick up a lot about the character of local social life. Family names on small tablets by the door give me clues about multiple-generation families. If several households of the same surname live directly adjacent to one another, it's a reasonable starting assumption that the land has been in the same family for some time, perhaps subdivided several times with the passing of generations. Some doorpost plaques announce almost universal things like the payment of NHK fees; others tip off political party membership. Some announce that the occupants hold some local leadership position; others reveal that a death has occurred within the last year. The amulets or charms that decorate doorposts may demonstrate affinities for particular shrines or membership in specific religious groups.

Other streetscape hints can be equally telling. Before an election campaign officially begins, posters for local candidates may suggest the rough outlines of political support networks. Where styles of decorative street lamps or cheap, seasonal plastic decorations along a shopping street change abruptly, a neighborhood's economic boundary may run. Where the lanterns hung to celebrate a festival end, there may be a shrine parish boundary.

I pay attention to little things: styles of dress, uniforms, company badges, signs, logos, decorative motifs, even spatial orientations. At Tsukiji, I gradually learned that I can tell what people's jobs are and what organizations they belong to by the hats they wear. Literally, the colors and styles of baseball caps distinguish their wearers as auctioneers, buyers, or regulators, and also differentiate them by company and commodity specialization. In Miyamoto-chō, I could recognize at a glance local school uniforms. In other settings, I memorize company lapel pins to keep track of who's who in large meetings. And almost automatically, I count the people in a meeting and try to figure out whether their seating arrangements and demeanor toward one another indicate anything about relative social status (usually, it does).

Of course, learning to attach the proper significance to such indicators takes a long time, and these data are not ends in themselves. Looking for signs is a good way to gather material for later questions. The labels of Japanese daily life are not always self-explanatory, and it requires a great deal of patient ethnographic research—including interviews and local inquisitive observation—to decode and then contextualize the signs, labels, and other visual cues that present themselves. But once their significance becomes clear, a lot of social data are out there in the open, and I can roughly map a social setting with quick visual inspections.

In Miyamoto-chō, I spent many afternoons studying the inscriptions on various monuments at the local Shinto shrine, such as the stone guardian lions donated by the local volunteer fire department in the 1920s inscribed with the names of all its leaders and members at the time. I pored over several dozen stone fence posts carved with the names of local residents who donated money for the shrine's rebuilding in the 1970s. These inscriptions, along with other data from interviews, helped me put together a broad generation-to-generation picture of families' involvement in community institutions—a who's who carved in stone.

Information is on public display in many other settings as well. In many sushi bars, for example, large, wooden frames (called *senjagaku*) hold sets of decorative plaques given by people close to the shop's proprietor. Some of the individual plaques are contributed by long-time patrons of the sushi bar; others—marked with the distinctive calligraphic swirl of *uogashi* (fish quay), the traditional logo of the Tsukiji marketplace—are donated by a chef's suppliers. For people in the trade, the chef's professional and personal affiliations are splashed prominently across the wall for anyone to read and interpret if they care to pay attention.

In both Miyamoto-chō and Tsukiji I found that bulletin boards and *kairanban* (circulating message boards, passed from household to household or stall to stall) contain enormous amounts of local institutional information, often quite detailed. (In Miyamoto-chō, the local photo shop owner benignly regarded me as a nondemanding profit center for all the rolls of film I "wasted" on bulletin boards; now that I have a pocket digital camera, I regularly take snapshots of every local bulletin board I see.)

Sometimes learning to read relevant orthography requires special effort. At Tsukiji, to figure out what companies people were talking about, I had to learn rebus-like logos (known as *yagō* or *kigō*) that wholesalers use both as trademarks and as company names. Many people are familiar with corporate names like Mitsubishi (literally, "three diamonds") and its trademark of three diamonds, or Mitsui (three wells) represented by the character for "three" surrounded by the character for "well." In the fishing and food industries, these kinds of symbols are everywhere: one of Tsukiji's large auction houses is known universally as Marunaka because its logo is a circle *(maru)* surrounding the character for middle *(naka);* a stall known as Akiwa symbolizes itself with the elegantly simple logo of an *almost* complete circle (an "open" *[aki]* "circle" *[wa]*); a broker whose logo consists of three triangles does business as "Mitsuuoroku" ("three scales," the triangle being the conventional icon for a fish scale *[uoroku]*). Learning this specialized iconography of business symbols was an aspect of the market's visual cues that was essential for me to decipher Tsukiji's social world. And once I began to master it, the understanding provided me information, conversational fodder, and a degree of insider knowledge I could parlay into still further information.

Mapping the Scene

Just as looking for labels has helped me to figure out the categories of actors, institutions, and experiences in various social settings, so, too, understanding the spatial layout of ordinary events helps me grasp the significant activities, their organization, and their relationship to one another and to particular groups of actors.

At the start of my research in Miyamoto-chō, an important clue to the structure of neighborhood institutions and their boundaries came on the very first day my wife and I walked through the area, looking for an apartment. I was paying careful attention to street addresses and knew that we were walking around Yanagi 4-chōme, but within the space of three blocks, we came across two separate buildings labeled *"chōkai kaikan"* (neighborhood association hall), one bearing the name Yanagi 4-chōme Chōkai Kaikan, the other bearing the name Yanagi Miyamoto Chōkai Kaikan. I was intrigued, and once we had settled into the Fukudas' apartment building, I set out to find out the significance of what appeared to be overlapping institutions. The answer to the question eventually led me to understand the conflict between government definitions of communities (the larger Yanagi 4-chōme being the creation of the government) and local residents' definitions of community as expressed through their local institutions, including the separate and non-overlapping territories represented by the Yanagi 4-chōme chōkai and the Yanagi Miyamoto chōkai.

At Tsukiji, signs identifying shops and businesses as members of particular trade federations provided me with some of my first clues about the organization of the marketplace into dozens of trade communities, each with its own rules of business, its own specializations, and its own organizational infrastructure. During the first several months of fieldwork at the market, I constantly was on the lookout for organizational names on signs, bulletin boards, doors, and posters. This inventory of associational names (which eventually totaled more than fifty) then became the basis for innumerable interview questions as I sought to identify each of the groups and their particular niches within the marketplace as a whole. And as this inventory became more detailed, I quite quickly was able to identify the organizations most crucial to my own goals of understanding the key institutions that governed the transactional structures of the auction system and that coordinated the interactions of different sets of economic actors as they moved from place to place around the market. Tracing the spatial layout of the dozens of auction pits in the Tsukiji market and being able to connect each of them to different constellations of organizations was a set of steps in understanding the institutional structure of the market.

Along with a thousand other as yet unasked questions about details of Tsukiji's operations, I wondered about the arrangements of the stalls. For the time being, I loosely surmised that the visible jumble of specialties was probably the result of little more than historical accident, the random outcome of hundreds and hundreds of individual businesses, each evolving along its own trajectory over generations.

Then one day, a few weeks into my research, Mr. Kurosaki, a wholesaler in dried squid who had been introduced to me by Mrs. Machida from Miyamoto-chō, took my wife, Mrs. Machida, and me on a tour of the marketplace. After an hour's stroll and conversations about dozens of topics, I casually asked, "Why aren't there separate sections for, say, tuna or dried fish? How can anyone find what they are looking for? Why are the stalls all jumbled up like this?"

"Everyone asks that," he smiled. "We used to be divided like that, but now we're all mixed together."

"So, how long have all these stalls been where they are now?"

"For about four years," he answered.

Startled by this response, which neatly demolished my tentative hypotheses about collective continuities amid historical trajectories of individual change, I asked the obvious next question. "What happened four years ago?"

"Oh, that's when we held the lottery to reassign stall locations. We do it every four or five years."

I was stunned by this totally unexpected piece of information. Kurosaki outlined briefly a complex system of lotteries that shift wholesalers from good to bad or from bad to better places in the market, regardless of their specialties, size, or social influence. I was staggered that 1,677 stalls could change places without a total breakdown of trade, and even more skeptical that the system could possibly work as evenhandedly as he described it. Surely, in a society where connections accomplish almost everything and where there is a public face and an inner reality—a *tatemae* and a *honne*—to every level of social interaction, highly competitive wholesalers would not voluntarily let their fortunes ride on a lottery that might assign them a stall next door to bankruptcy.

Kurosaki's comment put me on the trail of a critically important aspect of the market's social structure. It took many months of research, including extensive interviews with market officials and wholesalers, as well as a great deal of digging through marketplace records on stall locations over the past generation, to understand how this system works and its relationship to the social structure of the marketplace. In a nutshell, the periodic relocation of stalls through the lottery system smoothes out inequalities among traders as one element in a complex system of equalization that is at the heart of the collective governance of the marketplace as a form of socially constructed "common property." My attention to the geography of the market's layout led me to the first steps toward figuring this out.

Cueing up Conversations

Another key to my research is that most people are pretty comfortable talking about their own lives. But they don't generally volunteer information about their own social environments if they don't have reason to think that I also find it particularly interesting or significant. Successful fieldwork, therefore, requires me to explore a social environment on my own—through mapping, studying labels, and so forth—to become familiar with the features of the local scene that may turn out to be significant once I get people talking about them. My job as an ethnographic researcher is to get them talking by being interested, but, even more important, by asking questions that prod people to think about (and to talk about) the mundane aspects of their lives. If I have explored the local social environment on my own, it helps me to pose better questions, to convey to my informants why I think the place or the activity is significant, and to prompt them to tell me about what they think about the subject at hand.

Dr. Machida didn't think his own "hometown" neighborhood was worth my attention until I had explained several times that I was looking for a very "ordinary" urban place; it was my fault that I didn't understand beforehand how hard it would be to explain the sort of research setting I was looking for. By the time I met Mr. Kurosaki a decade or more later, I had learned that a constant flow of questions from me could usually elicit some interesting leads. Mr. Kurosaki would never have mentioned the lottery system for stall locations—why would a foreigner (or any outsider to the market) want to know about that?—unless I had pressed him to explain what seemed to me to be the inexplicably random distribution of stalls in the market.

Once they are cued to the fact that I am interested in the mundane, day-to-day patterns of life, often people will talk about them at great length. After all, their own lives are generally interesting to them, and my interest is generally welcomed, if sometimes puzzling. One of the virtues of ethnographic "inquisitive observation" (in contrast to more structured interviews) is that I can turn on the spot to someone beside me and ask, "Why are we doing this?" For example, I learned a lot about community boundaries, the dynamics of leadership, and the sense of obligation to neighbors by asking such simple questions while helping a pesticide-spraying crew in Miyamoto-chō during many smelly Sundays spread over several summers.[4] Since much of people's own experience of daily life, social activities, local institutions, and so forth, is shared by many if not most of their family members, coworkers, neighbors, or whomever, there really aren't a lot of people with whom they talk who don't already understand the ins and outs of their lives. So, as a foreign researcher and patient—if slightly prodding—listener, I often find that interviewees are almost eager to tell me about their lives since everyone *else* they know either has heard the stories already or doesn't care much about them anyway.

This is especially true at Tsukiji. People at Tsukiji are very proud of their occupations, their market, their way of life, but since it is a socially isolated place (isolated in part by the hours of their jobs, which get many people up at 2:00 A.M. and in bed by 6:00 P.M.), they don't interact a lot with people from other walks of life. They can't tell each other how interesting the place is, since all their buddies already know (and do) the same things. Along I come, and with some gentle prompting, people are happy to explain even the simplest things. Part of this, of course, is the time-tested advantage of being an ethnographer in a culture other than one's own. I can ask about the simplest things, things that even a six-year-old child ought to know, and very rarely does any one think it odd that I am asking.

Never hesitate to ask trivial questions, even sometimes in very formal settings. They can lead to interesting discoveries. Several years ago I interviewed officials of a tuna producers' federation to discuss international environmental regulations. In the federation's board room was a large poster with a colorful cartoon of a tuna. The poster caught my eye and I commented on it, whereupon my hosts called up the marketing office, which sent someone over with a copy of the poster for me, along with a set of souvenir postcards, all of which were produced to promote Maguro no Hi—Tuna Day—on October 10. As the woman who delivered the poster and postcards started to leave, I asked—with no particular intent, but simply amused at the whole idea of Tuna Day—"Is there some special significance to October 10?" It turned out that October 10th was the date of the first reference to tuna in Japanese literature, in the *Man'yōshu,* the eighth-century collection of classical poetry. This answer itself provided me with a trivial, but unexpectedly useful, factoid that sustained a general idea at the heart of much of my research: the uses of "tradition" as a discursive space within which to situate contemporary social, political, and economic practices. My question and interest in their campaign also broke the ice and stimulated the marketing people to provide me with still another set of materials on their advertising strategies, something I had not come to ask about but was very happy to gain access to.

Often, seemingly unlikely people will turn out to have incredible amounts of information. Once on a dock a manager with whom I was talking casually introduced me to a hanger-on, a guy who looked like the most down-on-his-luck day laborer I had ever seen. I would never have even bothered to ask who he was or what he did there until we were introduced. After a moment's conversation, however, I discovered that the guy was a researcher culling genetic material from tuna. The lab he worked for was developing DNA tests to determine the intermingling of tuna stocks in the Atlantic Ocean (which is actually a very hot topic, with major political ramifications), and he gave me a quick explanation of how the magnetic patterns in tuna otoliths (bony structures in the inner ear) can be used to trace migration paths. Another time at Tsukiji, I struck up a casual conversation with a sweeper who called out *"Haroo"* as I passed by him one morning. A few days later, I ran into him again, not with a broom in his hand but cutting up fish to load into the back of the tiny, open-sided van that he drove around the Tokyo suburbs in the late afternoon, after finishing a full day's work at the marketplace. Meeting him a second time in this new light gave me the chance (because I had said hello to him the first time) to learn much more from him about peddlers and about the chancy occupational perch between manual labor and entrepreneurship.

My ability to take advantage of chance encounters or the opportunities to pursue a trivial question in the midst of a formal interview depends on my capacity to create a framework in which it is both logical and legitimate that I ask questions. This seems like a simple (or simpleminded) point, but presentation of self is tricky. Especially at the beginning of a research project, when I am uncertain about where the project will go, about the reception I will receive, and about whether there are explosive issues or trip wires I don't know about yet, introducing myself and my interests is usually difficult. Part of the problem is to create a persona as a researcher (not a typical social role in most people's lives) that is authentic in the eyes of those around me and comfortable to me, as well. It is a real effort to overcome my own shyness when I begin research.

Convincing myself that I can legitimately ask questions is always the first step. After that, being seen interviewing, taking notes, taking photos, hanging around, and so forth, begins to construct the social role of researcher as an expected one for those around me.

The other closely related aspect of establishing myself as a bona fide researcher is to be able to explain what I am interested in and to offer some plausible reason why. Given my general focus on mundane practices and relationships of daily life, I am used to getting incredulous responses when I explain my research: "You can't be interested in *that!*" I try to work out a couple of sound bites that sum up the gist of any project that I am working on, and since my fieldwork per se rarely involves lots of discussions with other academics, I try to keep my explanations rather straightforward and nontechnical. Usually, the observation that whatever it is I am looking at is different from the situation in the United States or some other foreign country is sufficient rationale for a project to most people, at least in a casual, observational context. I can watch auctions at Tsukiji for days on end with the simple explanation (frequently repeated) that there are not auctions like them in the United States. Few people need more explanation than that.

More intensive interaction, either through participation or focused interviews, requires more detailed explanation, but not always a lot more. In my research on neighborhood social organization, I generally explained to people that I was interested in community associations that brought people together for common, local purposes, and the social networks that residents formed in, through, and around these organizations, because (a) they seemed to be important in daily life, and (b) in American urban society, neighborhoods did not often have such active and intense local activities and interpersonal ties.

Since most of the people among whom I was doing research also believed that local groups and activities were important in their own lives, they were willing to accept my interest as understandable, although perhaps a bit overblown. I was frequently kidded by people in the neighborhood about whether I could really be writing a doctoral dissertation about such a mundane subject as their community. (Years later some of them take a perverse pleasure in introducing me as the *chōnaikai hakase,* the neighborhood association Ph.D.)

Interestingly, up the social and intellectual ladder, I sometimes encounter greater difficulty getting people to understand the social reality of my research. I once was introduced to an eminent Japanese economist who, upon learning that my research was about neighborhood associations, flatly declared that they were extinct. They had disappeared after World War II, and everyone was delighted they were gone, he told me. I have learned over the years that people (both in Japan and in the United States) are often eager to offer definitive statements about social and cultural phenomena about which they know little or nothing. University professors, intellectuals, and government bureaucrats are often the happiest to provide (mis)guided tours of social reality. So it is important to be able to smile politely, change the subject, and note down as an important piece of social and cultural data that "experts" sometimes portray the world quite apart from the lived experiences of other members of their own society.

At Tsukiji, a fairly simple explanation that the place is—as market denizens already know—the world's largest fish market and that there were no markets like it in the United States was often sufficient rationale. The fact that the place has a long and colorful history, a complicated social structure that many outsiders do not fathom, a massive niche in Japan's economy, and a product line—seafood—that is richly saturated with culinary folklore made it simple to explain why the place was interesting to me and why it was worthy of study. Other than one trader who remembered reading *Argonauts of the Western Pacific* (Malinowski 1922) in college, no one at Tsukiji has ever asked me to explain my research in terms of theoretical rationales or hypotheses based in economic anthropology.

In the case of Tsukiji, however, misinterpretations of my role and motives caused occasional problems. It was hard to explain why an anthropologist would be doing research on a market, since most Japanese, like most Americans, think of anthropologists—if they think of us at all—as studying isolated, "primitive" societies. Many people at Tsukiji assume that I am an economist or a market researcher. This isn't usually a big problem, although one interviewee once was rather irritated by some questions about institutional history and food culture since—as he chided me—it was not directly relevant to understanding contemporary supply and demand curves, which was the topic I had come to talk to him about. From then on, I learned to introduce my interests and topics of questioning with somewhat broader—perhaps vaguer—definitions.

In retrospect, I realize I had defined my interests to him narrowly out of a misguided sense of insecurity. In setting up that interview, I was anxious not to appear too naive about the topic and so had quickly focused on a very specific issue that interested me (but it wasn't the only thing I was interested in). This is a fundamental dilemma in conducting fieldwork, especially when my research brings me in contact with many people I have not previously met.

Almost every day I have to explain myself to someone new, and with each person I start off as something of a blank slate. Even when I have been introduced by a mutual acquaintance, the person I am just meeting will not know much about me and often may fall back on the comfortable assumption that as a *gaijin* (foreigner) I simply don't know anything.

This is tricky to play out in an interview. On the one hand, I am quite comfortable listening to interviewees explain to me something that I think I already understand quite well. Often, in fact, in the course of hearing something for the umpteenth time, I will pick up some new fragment of information, and particularly will get to see it from the point of view of a different actor in the setting. So, it is valuable to travel over familiar terrain from time to time, and I sometimes play rather dumb while doing it, to draw out my interviewee further. Also, playing a little dumb can be a ploy, so that as the discussion moves to a central issue that I am interested in, I can sometimes pose a provocative question or elicit a frank comment that I might not get if I started out sounding extremely knowledgeable.

The other side of the coin, however, is that one eventually does want to cut to the chase, and I am always anxious to cut through the inevitable framing of the *gaijin* experience. It is always a balancing act to know how much of my own knowledge I want to display; too much knowledge can turn off the discussion or make the interviewee defensive; too little knowledge may relegate me to the *gaijin* visitor role.

At Tsukiji other misinterpretations of my role came up as well. Because the international seafood industry is highly competitive and Tsukiji is a major world market, a few people assumed that I was working for (or at least on behalf of) trade negotiators. Others, seeing me as a bearded American college professor, assumed that my interest in the market was motivated by sympathies for Greenpeace or other environmentalist groups that have attacked the Japanese fishing industry (most notably the whaling industry, of course) for what these groups regard as unconscionable activities against the environment.[5]

In such cases, I have often been able to avoid misunderstandings by referring back to the networks of introductions that have led me to the present interview, activity, or interaction. Throughout my research, the social sponsorship of people who have befriended me along the way has been critical repeatedly, to get me started, to pass me along to others, and, occasionally, to vouch for me when questions arise.

Conclusions

Ethnographic research is inherently open-ended and multifaceted. Given its avowed goals of enabling a researcher to participate in, record, convey, and analyze something of the complexity and coherence of ongoing social and cultural life, how could it be otherwise? Any set of ethnographic research techniques is therefore necessarily partial, just as the results of ethnography necessarily reflect a point of view developed in the course of research. One important difference between my research in Miyamoto-chō and at the Tsukiji market was, of course, that one is a residential community and the other is a workplace. The opportunities for participation, for observation, for inquisitiveness are necessarily different. Another, equally important difference in the research I could do in both places is that in Miyamoto-chō, I had my family with me on many occasions, and my wife—Victoria Lyon Bestor—contributed her observations and insights, had her own experiences and networks of contacts in local social life, critiqued my ideas, and frequently pointed out things I had overlooked. During a later stay in Miyamoto-chō, in 1988–1989, when our son Nick was a toddler, we experienced very different aspects of neighborhood life because we saw it for the first time through the eyes of parents, and, equally importantly, our friends and neighbors saw us for the first time as a complete family. At Tsukiji, however, the social facts of "participant observation" could not accommodate a family or involve them in my research. In the end, fieldwork and ethnography are shaped, for better or for worse, by many factors irreducibly connected to both the research setting and the researcher's personal circumstance. No two projects can ever be the same.

I have outlined some of the techniques or perspectives that help me make the most of informal interactions and casual opportunities to collect information about life in urban settings. In some ways, these techniques are ideally suited to urban contexts in that they mimic (or use as protective coloration) some common characteristics of urban social life: fleeting, fragmentary, quasi-anonymous, and fast paced. It would be a mistake, however, to suggest that my research relies solely on these techniques. I see these as a means of getting started and keeping going, getting information on the move. And, in the final analysis, momentum is the key to starting and finishing a piece of research.

Notes

The research discussed in this chapter spans more than twenty years, from 1979 to 2001, during which time I have incurred innumerable debts, most importantly to the many residents of Miyamoto-chō and the many proprietors, officials, and workers at Tsukiji who have graciously endured my questions, have tolerated my presence, and have made me feel welcome far beyond reasonable expectation. I am also grateful to numerous institutions for supporting and facilitating my research, including the Japan Foundation, the Fulbright Commission, the Social Science Research Council, the National Science Foundation, the Abe Fellowship Program of the Center for Global Partnership, the New York Sea Grant Institute, the Wenner-Gren Foundation, the Geirui Kenkyūjo, Tokyo Tōritsu University, and Japan research funds from Columbia and Cornell Universities.

1. See Turner (1995) for an excellent account of her own fieldwork among Tokyo labor activists. I describe my initial criteria for selecting a neighborhood in T. Bestor 1989a, 1–11.

2. Whether one calls this participant observation, inquisitive observation, or hanging out, it is important to remember this is only one aspect of doing ethnography. Inquisitive observation is the necessary prelude and cross-check for many other types of intensive research, including systematic formal interviewing, administering questionnaires, digging through public archives and statistical data, charting organizational structures, and carrying out detailed historical research (both oral and documentary).

3. In 1988 I was part of a team of anthropologists that conducted research on Japanese coastal whaling villages to assess the social impact of the moratorium on "small-type coastal whaling" imposed by the International Whaling Commission, and in 1989 I made short research trips to several whaling ports in Hokkaido; see Akimichi et al. (1988) and Takahashi et al. (1989).

4. My evident enthusiasm for this toxic activity prompts neighborhood leaders to invite me to participate in spraying whenever I am in Tokyo during the summer, even many years after my first fieldwork.

5. For the record, my research at Tsukiji is not (and has never been) connected with, supported by, nor sponsored by environmental activists, trade negotiators,

or commercial fishing interests. The research project in 1988–1989 on coastal whaling was commissioned by the Japanese Institute of Cetacean Research (Nihon Geirui Kenkyūjo) to generate data for reports submitted to the International Whaling Commission on the community-level impact of the cessation of Japanese local whaling.

Related Readings

I have written extensively about Miyamoto-chō (including T. Bestor 1989a, 1989b, 1996), and there is also a video documentary about my research in the community (Media Production Group 1992a). Research at Tsukiji appears in T. Bestor (2001, 2004). My web site lists other research and publications: www.fas.harvard.edu/rijs/Bestor.

Bestor, Theodore C. 1989a. *Neighborhood Tokyo*. Stanford: Stanford University Press.

———. 1989b. "Tōkyō no aru machi ni okeru Kattō, Dentō, Seitōsei" [Conflict, legitimacy, and tradition in a Tokyo neighborhood]. *Minzoku-gaku kenkyū* [Japanese journal of ethnology] 54(3):257–274.

———. 1996. "Forging Tradition: Social Life and Identity in a Tokyo Neighborhood." In George Gmelch and Walter P. Zenner, eds., *Urban Life: Readings in Urban Anthropology* (3d ed.). Prospect Heights, Ill.: Waveland Press, 524–547.

———. 2001a. "Supply-Side Sushi: Commodity, Market, and the Global City." *American Anthropologist* 102(1):76–95.

———. 2004. *Tokyo's Marketplace*. Berkeley: University of California Press.

Media Production Group. 1992a. *Neighborhood Tokyo*. Documentary video produced by David W. Plath, distributed by DER, Watertown, Mass. [www.der.org]

Joshua Hotaka Roth
(on the right) on the
assembly line.

J O S H U A   H O T A K A   R O T H

Responsibility and the Limits of Identification: Fieldwork among Japanese and Japanese Brazilian Workers in Japan

I went to Japan in 1994 to investigate interactions between *Nikkeijin* (overseas Japanese) migrants, most of whom were from Brazil, and the Japanese with whom they came into contact in workplaces and in neighborhoods (Roth 2002). I had made one preliminary trip to Japan in 1993 and selected the city of Hamamatsu as my primary field site. Several other industrial cities such as Nagoya and Toyota in Aichi Prefecture and the town of Ōizumi and city of Ōta in Gunma Prefecture had large *Nikkeijin* populations. Many *Nikkeijin* in Japan were concentrated in a short string of highly industrialized prefectures running from Aichi through Shizuoka, Gunma, Nagano, Kanagawa, to Tokyo. Others lived scattered in different regions from Hiroshima in the southwest, to Toyama on the Japanese Sea, up to Hokkaido in the north. I chose to do research in Hamamatsu because of the relatively high concentration of *Nikkeijin* there and the intermediate size of the city. Its size made it a more manageable research site than were larger cities such as

Nagoya and Tokyo, where *Nikkeijin* were relatively scattered over much larger areas. *Nikkeijin* were more visible in Hamamatsu and the subject of much public discourse, yet their presence had not transformed Hamamatsu as it had smaller cities such as Ōta or the town of Ōizumi, where *Nikkeijin* had come to comprise as much as 10 percent of the total population.

The majority of *Nikkeijin* in Hamamatsu were working in auto-parts factories, and I was determined to spend part of my time in Japan conducting research in such factories. Participant observation while working on an assembly line involves considerable physical and logistical challenges. Throughout this process I had to sort through ethical issues involved in conducting research under the conditions that I had arranged.

My introduction to Yusumi Motors, where I worked for three months on the assembly line, came through a friend of a friend of a friend, a middle-aged Japanese man who had grown up in Hamamatsu and had a number of childhood friends in administrative positions at several of the major manufacturers in town. He ran a small English-language school, which provided language training to employees of various firms, and was generous enough to arrange an interview for me with Yusumi managers. During this interview, I requested permission to conduct participant observation in their factory. I explained my position as a student of anthropology and Japanese workplace organization. They hired me for an initial three-month contract on the condition that I pulled my weight and worked like everyone else. One of my interviewers said that the work would be hard and that I would not receive any special privileges as a researcher. He reassured me, however, that I would probably be able to handle it since I was still young (I was twenty-nine at the time). The average age of Brazilians working on the line at their plant was twenty-six, the average for all line workers including both Japanese and foreigners was about thirty, and the average for the plant as a whole including line and office workers and administrators was thirty-six.

Participant Observation in an Auto Factory

Conducting participant observation in a Japanese automobile factory, I had limited opportunities to communicate with people during working hours. Nine and a half hours a day I was focused on my work installing air filters and tubing as pickup trucks and minivans streamed relentlessly down the assembly line. Most workers used earplugs, and the workstations were all several yards apart from each other, making conversation during work practically impossible. Sometimes when I was falling behind and working desperately on a truck that had already passed into the next workstation, Alex, the Japanese Peruvian into whose workstation I had encroached would shout questions at me in Spanish: "What's America like?" "Have you been to California?" "How much does a car cost in America?" All I could do most times was smile nervously and rush back to my area to start work on the next truck moving by overhead.

My most extended conversations were really just brief snippets with my section chief or others who responded to my calls when I fell behind. I would pull on a yellow cord, which set off an alarm and flashed my workstation number on a screen overhead. A red cord hung beside the yellow one. It would bring the entire assembly line, with more than one hundred workstations, to a halt, and I was told not to pull it except under life-threatening circumstances. Usually my section chief, Kimata, would rush over when I yanked the yellow cord and my number flashed. Several years previously, he had spent eight months helping start up a Yusumi joint venture factory in Canada. After he had helped me, he would often linger at my section longer than was necessary reminiscing about how good life had been there. Houses in Canada were much larger and cheaper than in Japan, he recollected. Golf was so inexpensive he had played practically every week that snow did not cover the ground. He remembered losing golf balls in the dandelions in the spring and in the maple leaves in the autumn.

Participant observation serves several research goals. Participation is often essential in order to access certain research sites. In my case, participation was crucial for access, but at the same time it placed severe restrictions on the amount of observation I could undertake. Working full-time on the assembly line, I could speak only to those who came to my aid and observe at a distance the two stations on either side of mine. Every two hours the line would come to a halt for a five-minute break, and most of the workers clustered in a small, smoke-filled rest area staring at the TV in one corner. We would have forty-five minutes for mealtime, and I tried to make the best use of it as possible. I often sat with Japanese workers for the first fifteen minutes because they generally ate the fastest and then retired to the rest areas by their work sections. When they left, I would move to a table of Japanese Brazilians or Peruvians. Most of the Peruvians had picked up a significant amount of Portuguese working with Brazilians for several years in Japan, and I could communicate with them in a mixture of Japanese and Portuguese. Sometimes I would eat with a group of Indian trainees, some of whom spoke some English. I had no way of communicating with the Chinese or Korean trainees and just gave them a friendly nod or smile when they passed. In the factory there were about 2,000 Japanese employees, 250 *Nikkeijin* (mostly from Brazil but including a handful of Peruvians) hired on temporary contracts or through employment brokers, and about 200 trainees *(kenshūsei)* from various Asian joint ventures.

Not only was time for discussion limited during working hours, but time for reflection and writing was limited both during and after work. I worked the late shift my first week. I had to be at my post when the line started moving at 5:15 P.M. until my shift ended at 3:40 A.M., with a break for dinner and three five-minute breaks at roughly two-hour intervals. It took me just five minutes to walk back to the dormitory when I got off work. I would get out of my work clothes, wash off and soak in the communal bath, then go to bed. The first couple of weeks I was too exhausted to spend substantial time writing observations and reflections in my diary. The alternating shifts required me to devise two different schedules for writing. After the night shift, I would leave my diary entry for the next morning. After the day shift, which was from 7:00 A.M. until 5:15 P.M., I would write before going to bed. When I was particularly tired, I found speaking into a tape recorder much faster and less strenuous than writing in my notebook or laptop. I tried not to fall back on tape recording excessively, however, because of the time it takes to transcribe tape later on. Still, if time is limited in the field and one foresees having a more leisurely period for write-up, tape recording diary entries can be very useful.

Throughout my few months at Yusumi I grappled with the dilemma of how to present myself to my fellow workers. I had been honest about my research interests during my job interview, but my official status in the firm was as a contract worker. I did not have any special privileges as a researcher. I told people in my work section and those with whom I spoke during lunch or dinner about my research, but my ambiguous status meant that many other in the factory probably had no idea that I was conducting research. This ethical dilemma may face researchers not just in workplaces, but in any context that is hierarchically organized and where access is granted by those at the upper levels without the consultation of all of the other members of the group. Under those circumstances, I felt constrained and pulled by multiple obligations. I was responsible for working according to the terms of the agreement made during my job interview. I also felt a responsibility toward the people with whom I worked and lived, who had no say in granting me entry into their spaces, to be as unobtrusive as possible.

With regard to the agreement I had made with those managers who hired me, there was at least one instance in which I unconsciously allowed my research interests to affect my work responsibilities. The cafeteria could not accommodate the entire workforce at the same time, so workers on different assembly lines got their lunch breaks at staggered, partially overlapping intervals. One day I was sitting with an Indian trainee discussing the origins of Yusumi's Indian joint venture. His lunch break started twenty minutes after mine. We were so engrossed in conversation that I did not notice that the people from my line had all left their tables. By the time I made it back to my workstation, four trucks and one minivan had already gone by without having their air filters installed. I pulled frantically on the yellow cord and sent my section chief scurrying down the line to install them. In four out of the five vehicles, he was able to get the filters in before other parts added at subsequent workstations made it impossible. The one minivan had to be partially disassembled later on in order to install the filter. My section chief looked exhausted during the next five-minute break and asked in an irritated manner whether I had a watch. I should buy a good watch, he scolded, a Japanese watch with an alarm, not one made in Korea or China.

Needless to say, I was mortified that I had lost track of time and caused my section chief so much unnecessary work. Not only did it diminish my stature in the eyes of one of my most valuable informants, I was conscious that I may have reinforced common Japanese stereotypes of foreign workers. In other contexts, Japanese have often noted that Brazilians (*Burajirujin*—a term that included those of Japanese ancestry as well as their non-*Nikkeijin* spouses) had a very loose notion of time and that this caused Japanese managers many headaches. Brazilians and other foreigners supposedly lacked a sense of responsibility toward the group. My section chief considered the Korean trainees to be the hardest workers among the foreigners—they were young and most had been in the military several years. He ranked Indians and Chinese at the bottom as workers. As a whole, Japanese thought foreigners to be less capable and less responsible workers, and I regretted that my own lapse might have contributed to this impression.

I was also somewhat peeved, however, that the Japanese who manned the workstation immediately prior to mine hadn't called our section chief over when the line started up after lunch. It would have been very difficult for him not to notice that I was missing. Why hadn't he notified the section chief? If my forgetfulness had indicated insufficient sense of responsibility toward the group, my Japanese neighbor, concerned only with his direct responsibilities at his workstation, also suffered from this deficiency. While acknowledging my lapse, I was unwilling to accept generalized characterizations of foreigners as irresponsible. The issue of responsibility in relation to representations of ethnicity eventually became one of the focuses of my research.

Official Identity Categories

Approval for my research probably came from just one higher-level Yusumi manager—a close friend of the director of the English-language school. Such expedited approval for my research was possible because they could hire me on the same short-term contract that they issued to Japanese Brazilians and Peruvians. This, in turn, was possible since I had been able to get the same kind of visas as other *Nikkeijin*. Initially, I had been issued the standard "cultural activities" *(bunka katsudō)* visa for foreign researchers, which did not allow me to work.

The Japanese immigration bureau allowed only one group of foreigners—overseas Japanese—to work without restrictions. Foreign students and trainees were both issued visas that allowed them to work a limited number of hours per week, but *Nikkeijin* were the only category of foreigner that was allowed to perform so-called unskilled labor full-time. Prior to my experience at Yusumi, I had visited a number of factories and interviewed managers and *Nikkeijin* workers, but these visits were of limited duration, and I was not able to establish any longer-term relationships. If I were to gain long-term access to a factory setting, I needed to get a job in one, and this required me to obtain the same visa as did second- and third-generation *Nikkeijin*.

Nikkeijin were issued two types of visa—one for the status of "spouse (or child) of Japanese national" *(Nihonjin no haigūsha nado),* another for "long-term resident" *(teijūsha)*—for periods of between six months and three years, which carried no restrictions on the work they could perform in Japan. Since 1990 the immigration bureau has facilitated the processing of these visas for *Nikkeijin,* but it did not issue them automatically. It retained the discretion to deny visa applications or to deny renewals after visas expired.

I needed to present the immigration bureau with copies of my birth certificate and my mother's household registry *(koseki)* in order to prove Japanese ancestry. The ward in Tokyo where my mother had been born provided the necessary documents upon request. It was the first time I had seen my Japanese family's household registry, and I was surprised to learn that my grandmother had been born in Nagoya, not far away from Hamamatsu. This made it possible for me to claim roots in the Chubu region of Japan, within which Hamamatsu fell. I also noted that my grandmother had been adopted into another family prior to getting married. I asked my mother about this and learned that my grandmother came from a common family without any money. My grandfather's family in Tokyo, on the other hand, had been relatively wealthy sake makers who also claimed samurai status. My grandmother's future father-in-law had identified her as an attractive and capable woman, but decided that she was not of appropriate rank to marry his son. He resolved this problem, however, by having a family with samurai status distantly related to his own nominally adopt before having her marry in.

The process of applying for a visa taught me a little about the status concerns of my Japanese family and also about my grandmother—a figure I had known only briefly as a small child. I had lived in Japan between the ages of two and four with my brother and parents. I have a few vague images of visiting *Kunitachi obāsan* (grandmother in Kunitachi) at her house and remember visiting her in the hospital and later attending an intolerably long Buddhist funeral service. Learning more about her made me more curious to ask my mother about her family. Similarly, the process of applying for visas may have stimulated some second- and third-generation *Nikkeijin* from Brazil to discover more about their Japanese heritage, a heritage toward which many of them had previously been indifferent. Several I knew had indeed looked up their Japanese relatives, but most avoided such contact, sensing that they would not be welcomed.

In addition to learning about my own family when I applied for a visa, I learned a lot about the ways in which the immigration bureau categorized foreigners and got a sense of how these categories could impact the ways in which migrants identified themselves in relation to Japan. The immigration bureau generally issued second-generation *Nikkeijin* three-year visas, while they issued those of the third generation one-year visas. *Nikkeijin* leaders have petitioned the Japanese government not to make any distinctions between second- and third-generation *Nikkeijin*—to issue all of them three-year visas. The Japanese immigration bureau seemed to consider both generational (thus cultural) and racial criteria when issuing visas. Those who were separated by less generational and racial distance from Japanese nationals in Japan were accorded longer visas. Since my mother was a Japanese national at the time I was born, I was second-generation Japanese American, yet the immigration bureau issued me a "spouse or child of Japanese national" visa for a one-year period, the length usually given to third-generation *Nikkeijin*. My father does not have any Japanese ancestry, and I suspect that immigration officials were more likely to give "mixed bloods" *(konketsuji)* of both second or third generation shorter visas especially when the Japanese parent was the mother and the applicant did not have a Japanese surname. Until the Nationality Law was revised in 1985, children of mixed marriages had the option of taking Japanese citizenship only in cases where the father was Japanese.

In 1991 and 1992, leading Japanese newspapers such as *Mainichi Shinbun* and *Asahi Shinbun* ran stories about Peruvians without any Japanese ancestry who had bought or forged documents necessary to apply for visas as Japanese Peruvians. Since then, minor discrepancies in the way Japanese names were transliterated on different Peruvian documents have led Japanese officials to reject many applications from Japanese Peruvians (Fuchigami 1995, 49–54). While I waited for approval of my own visa application, I could sympathize with the position of those *Nikkeijin* whose "authenticity" had to be validated by the immigration bureau. In the case of *Nikkeijin* of Okinawan ancestry, who comprise an even greater proportion of Japanese Peruvians than of Japanese Brazilians, many family registries were lost during World War II, making it even more difficult for some of them to prove their ancestry.

Cultural Brokers

Getting the proper visa was a time-consuming process that significantly delayed my entry into the factory. My new visa application took three months to be approved. Even after I obtained my visa, it was another three months before I was able to arrange to work in a factory. Production was down during the summer months, and it wasn't until autumn that my acquaintance at the language school was able to arrange an interview for me at Yusumi. These six months were not wasted, however, as I got involved in several other groups that later became important parts of my overall research. I enrolled in Portuguese-language classes at two different community centers and got to know a group of Japanese whose interactions with Brazilians at the workplace and in neighborhoods had motivated them to learn the language. In April and May, I participated in the Hamamatsu Kite Festival, an activity I initially thought may not have anything to do with my primary research but that later provided an interesting perspective on how newcomer residents, including *Nikkeijin,* could be ritually incorporated into the community. I also got involved with a local nongovernmental organization (NGO) dedicated to helping foreigners with legal or medical problems. Finally, I joined a local samba group comprised primarily of Japanese but that included several Brazilians as well.

Journalists were particularly helpful in making contacts with these and other groups early on in my research. Some journalists were knowledgeable about important issues confronting *Nikkeijin* in Hamamatsu such as the lack of health insurance, withholding of wages, and juvenile delinquency. They helped me think about how to focus my research. In the pastry corner of a Brazilian supermarket, I first became acquainted with a *Nikkeijin* journalist working for one of the four Portuguese-language weeklies published in Japan. He took me to the few Brazilian restaurants in town and the Brazilian disco that had opened in a converted warehouse near the highway exit. Before long, I met the other *Nikkeijin* journalists in town. Within a newly established migrant community, there seemed to be an insatiable appetite for articles about Japanese culture and the *Nikkeijin* migrant experience. As an anthropologist researching relations between Japanese and *Nikkeijin,* journalists constantly asked for my opinions. Although I agreed to be interviewed on several occasions, my reluctance to reinforce preconceptions about the coldness of Japanese, rigidity of Japanese culture, and the struggles of *Nikkeijin* meant that only one such interview was published in very abridged form. Japanese university professors and students frequently passed through Hamamatsu doing research about *Nikkeijin* and supplied plenty of material for the *Nikkeijin* journalists. I submitted an op-ed piece to one journal about the pressing health insurance issue for foreigners in Hamamatsu when I felt my statements could actually serve a positive purpose.

Early in my fieldwork, I also made the rounds of the municipal-, prefectural-, and national-level government offices that dealt with foreigners in various capacities. Many of them were very generous with their time and seemed eager to share data their offices had collected. I got to know the interpreters in the city's foreigners' registration desk and those Japanese who were given special responsibility for dealing with foreigners. By talking to as many of these writers, bureaucrats, and other intermediary cultural brokers as I could early on in my research, I was able to get my bearings in the field site more quickly than I could have on my own.

Situational Identities during Research

Depending on the person and the context, Japanese friends and acquaintances referred to me as *Amerikajin* (American), *gaijin* (foreigner), *hāfu* ("half" Japanese), *Nikkeijin* (overseas Japanese), and *daigakuinsei* (graduate student). These could be used in both inclusive and exclusive ways. At times my section chief perceived me as a North American with whom he could reminisce about his time in Canada. When I lost track of time, however, he perceived me as more generically foreign.

In some circumstances, it is possible for one to shape the perceptions others have of oneself. Matthews Hamabata, a single, male, third-generation Japanese American of Okinawan descent who conducted research among a very elite set of Japanese business families in Tokyo (Hamabata 1990, chap. 1), was able to successfully establish relationships only after learning to calibrate his presentation of self. Takeyuki Tsuda, a second-generation Japanese American who conducted research among Japanese and Japanese Brazilians in an electronics factory, was ambivalent about his efforts to emphasize shared identities with both groups, a strategy of self-presentation he termed "identity prostitution" (Tsuda 1998).

When I was initially trying to gain access to a workplace setting, my identities as a student, as an American, and as the friend of an associate of the firm were all important. Unlike Brazilians, for whom the anthropologist was a relatively familiar figure, few Japanese had any idea of what an anthropologist was when I identified myself as one. *"Daigakuinsei"* was a culturally recognizable category that placed me within an academic environment, but in a position of immaturity in relation to university professors who were often accorded more respectful, but also more cautious, treatment. I could heighten my status if I so chose by specifying that I was completing a doctoral program *(hakase katei)*. My association with a prestigious American university may have given me a certain cachet, and the fact that I was from the United States and thus probably would publish results in English also may have reduced any anxieties on their part.

When *Nikkeijin* heard that my mother was Japanese, they would refer to me as a *decendente* (descendant of Japanese), constructing a shared identity with me. They used other terms such as "mestizo" (mixed Japanese and other ancestry) and *"Americano"* in more exclusive ways. "Mestizo" simultaneously referred to my Japanese and non-Japanese ancestry, thus signifying both my identity and difference. *"Americano"* indicated that I shared the condition of being a foreigner in Japan at the same time it distinguished me from *Brasileiros.* Some Brazilians were sensitive to the fact that whereas most Japanese often viewed Americans as role models, political leaders, and pop cultural innovators, they dismissed Brazilians as members of a poor Third World country. But others had a similarly high regard for things American and would frequently request English lessons and information about travel and study opportunities to the United States. I would try to comply with such requests when these relationships appeared to be useful for my research.

I tried to present myself to people using terms that emphasized a shared identity or experience. With *Nikkeijin,* I favored the term *"descendente."* With Japanese I rarely failed to mention that my mother was Japanese. These shared identities may have sometimes helped establish relationships, but they never assured me of them. To a great extent, these terms of affiliation had to be proved and earned over time through my actions. It was through reciprocating gifts, sending cards, or even just relishing Japanese food when dining together that some Japanese would note appreciatively that "after all your mother is Japanese" *(yappari okāsan wa Nihonjin).* With *Nikkeijin* it was more my increasingly successful effort to improve my Portuguese as well as my regular interactions over a long period of time that assured my relationships with them.

I quickly developed an expanding circle of *Nikkeijin* friends and acquaintances who enjoyed what they saw as my heroic efforts at gaining some fluency in Portuguese. I would go out with them to barbecues, discos, restaurants, amusement parks, but I was initially limited to interviewing people who spoke either Japanese or English fairly well. By the end of my fieldwork, however, most Brazilians had enough confidence in my Portuguese that they did not resort to Japanese except when describing interactions or conversations they had had in Japanese. Many peppered their speech with creolized expressions of Japanese and Portuguese.

Among some groups of people I encountered during the period of my fieldwork I was initially somewhat circumspect about my role as a researcher. I had been reluctant to engage in those activities that defined what most researchers did: distributing survey questionnaires and conducting interviews. I was not interested in questionnaires. And I did not assume interviews were a recognizable or comfortable form of metacommentary about experience within Japanese or *Nikkeijin* cultures (see Briggs 1986). But I also led myself to believe that I undertook certain activities, such as participation in the kite festival and samba group, more for social reasons than as a part of my research project. Eventually, I recognized these activities to be part of my research, and in retrospect, it would have been more honest if I had engaged people in all contexts from the start by describing my research project and asking them if they wouldn't mind being a part of it. Some may not have been interested in speaking to me, but I do not think this would have had an adverse impact on my research. In those contexts in which I was formally introduced as a researcher, I was able to establish productive relations with people. I came to realize that many *Nikkeijin* were very eager to talk about their experiences in Japan, whether in formal or informal contexts.

Contextualizing the Limits of Identification

At times I found that I had achieved more intimacy or informality in relationships than I was comfortable with. In addition to referring to me as *Americano,* mestizo, and *descendente,* some *Nikkeijin* also called me *antropólogo* or *antropólogo picareta* (phony anthropologist)—the latter term applied to me by certain friends of mine who did not understand how going out with them to bowling lanes, discos, and barbecues constituted anthropological research. Although said in jest, I did not appreciate it when these friends occasionally introduced me as such to people I did not know. Among certain male friends, the constant sexual jokes involving accusations of homosexuality and masturbation that they flung at each other and at me at times tried my patience. Some of them tested the limits of my identification with them when they joked about my Jewish heritage. On several occasions when out to eat with a group of five or six, one of them would suggest that I treat everyone. Any hesitation on my part elicited a mutter of *"Judeu"* followed by laughter and a closed fist indicating my unwillingness to part with money.

I would return their accusations of stinginess in kind, but their use of the Jewish stereotype hurt me and threatened the relationships that I had worked to develop. At such times it was important for me to distance myself from the immediacy of these relationships and to think about how larger contexts may have influenced specific actions or postures.[1] When the first *Nikkeijin* started migrating to Japan in the late 1980s, their primary goal was to save as much money in as little time as possible in Japan and take it back to buy a house or start a business in Brazil. In later years, migrants thought more about how to enjoy their time in Japan and became conspicuous consumers. *Nikkeijin* in Japan made enough to travel both within Japan and to other parts of Asia. They purchased cars, expensive clothes, computers, Game Boys, and a host of other electronic appliances on the wages they made in factories. Some Japanese managers commented to me that *Nikkeijin* had been very hard working early on but later became less motivated, and connected it to their changed attitudes toward savings and consumption in Japan. Many *Nikkeijin*, on the other hand, evaluated the newfound attitudes in a more positive light and defended their right to live life fully in Japan instead of working three hours of overtime six days per week. Viewed from such a perspective, I could start to understand my acquaintances' jabs at stinginess, although I was still unhappy about their use of the Jewish stereotype.

Many *Nikkeijin* were white-collar and professional workers for much of their careers in Brazil. By taking blue-collar jobs in Japan, they were able to make much more than they had in Brazil, especially given the inflation of the late 1980s, but many felt this shift as a serious drop in status. Some complained strongly about the treatment they encountered in Japanese workplaces, being ordered about roughly and shouted at when they misunderstood instructions. These kinds of interactions may have been especially difficult for someone who had been accustomed to a degree of respect in their former careers. In their search for value and meaning in their lives in Japan, *Nikkeijin* often had no choice but to turn away from the workplace. Many found it in conspicuous consumption, others in performances of masculinity, some in religious practice, and others in celebrations of their Brazilian identities.

Conflicting Responsibilities

I continued investigating workplace issues after leaving my job at the factory. I had come across many cases of work-related injury among *Nikkeijin* and decided to undertake a more systematic investigation of this issue. One of my friends, Edivaldo Kishimoto, said the condition of Japanese factories and the safety standards in them were an embarrassment. In my own experience working in the auto factory, I developed repetitive stress injury, which I learned was very common among workers on the assembly line. I would wake up in the morning and my fingers would be frozen in a curled position. They would not open even after running warm water over them, and they felt as if they would snap if I tried to force them straight. Eventually I took to rubbing Tiger Balm over the joints of my fingers just before going to bed and sleeping with gloves on. This helped a little, but did not cure me.

I went to the factory's clinic during lunch break and the doctor gave me a painkilling cream that worked to loosen the joints of my fingers. One middle-aged Japanese seasonal worker from Hokkaido told me that his hands hurt so badly he would wake up at night. He said he did not use the cream so much because it only helped temporarily and apparently had bad side effects if used too often. A young Japanese worker told me it took almost a full year from the time he started working before the pain in his hands subsided.

The state of my fingers made me worry whether I would be able to do my job, especially working in the unheated factory during December and January. Usually, my fingers were stiff when I got to the factory at the start of the day, but once the line started moving, my fingers warmed up quickly enough for me to keep up with the line. It was strange that precisely that which had produced my condition in the first place—working on the line—was what brought my fingers back to life each morning, as if they had signed a contract only to function for the benefit of Yusumi. My condition persisted for the duration of my three-month contract and disappeared shortly after I stopped working.

I did not know of any more serious injuries at Yusumi in the months that I worked there. Some Japanese outside the firm told me that there had been a few serious cases in the past, but it seemed that the firm made a dedicated effort to comply with the government's workplace safety standards. "Safety first" (*Anzen dai'ichi*) banners and stickers covered the factory walls and machinery. I was given earplugs from the very start. I was not issued goggles, however, until a metal shaving flew into my eye while attaching a metal plate to the underside of a minivan.

Smaller firms, where the majority of *Nikkeijin* were employed in Hamamatsu, were much more lax than Yusumi about safety procedures. The first time I met one of my closer friends, Gilberto Honda, I noticed as he extended his arm to shake my hand that the top joint of his thumb was missing. I did not have the nerve to ask him about it right away, but later I found out that he had lost it working in a tire factory. His managers hadn't installed legally required safety sensors on the machinery he used. Another of my *Nikkeijin* friends was hospitalized for two weeks after a leak of toxic fumes at his work-station. Another had a long scar running up the full length of his forearm. It had been sliced open when he worked in an old sawmill and one of the circular saws had spun off its mount.

In the months before starting work in the factory I had already joined a Japanese NGO called Hamamatsu Overseas Laborers Solidarity, which had been formed several years previously by an eclectic group of people including a labor organizer, social worker, schoolteacher, postal worker, French Catholic priest, and Japanese Protestant pastor who had lived over ten years in Brazil. I attended their monthly meetings and learned about a variety of issues facing foreign workers, among which compensation for workplace accidents was one of the most serious. Later, I conducted interviews with several *Nikkeijin* who had lost fingers working at metal presses and referred them to the NGO and the appropriate government offices that could further their cases.

I pursued the issue of accidents and compensation because I felt that it was in part my responsibility as an anthropologist to direct my research in ways that would contribute to solving or alleviating social problems (see Greenwood 1993). I discovered later on that accident and compensation cases could also provide a revealing perspective on the way in which workplace communities were constructed and negotiated by Japanese and *Nikkeijin*. Japanese managers often maligned Brazilians' sense of responsibility toward the firm, suggesting that *Nikkeijin* considered important only their personal economic interests. By examining accident cases, I learned that *Nikkeijin* often desired a stronger sense of community in the workplace, one that they felt was denied to them. *Nikkeijin* may not have desired to identify as exclusively with the workplace community in the way some Japanese employees did, but they did desire membership in what I term "just communities"—communities in which they were treated with respect, where some minimum standard of human interaction was acknowledged and upheld.

While Japanese and *Nikkeijin* discussed the issue of responsibility in relation to punctuality, job hopping, accidents, and compensation, I had to reflect on my role as an anthropologist and the responsibility that I had toward the people whom I had interviewed and the institutions within which I had conducted research. Most fieldwork situations require researchers to balance multiple responsibilities to various groups or people. At times for me these responsibilities came in conflict with each other and I had to choose sides. This was difficult to do after having spent months ingratiating myself with anyone who had anything to do with my research. After a certain amount of time in the field, however, to have maintained a neutral position in the name of academic objectivity would have meant forgoing my responsibilities to all parties. I supported the NGO in its critique of the segmented labor market and the city's exclusionary policy on health insurance, a stance that hurt my relationship with bureaucrats in the city government who had been helpful to me earlier. I supported accident victims in their efforts to get compensation from employers. I supported one faction of *Nikkeijin* against another in their struggle for control over a Brazilian culture center.

As I reflect back upon the relationships I developed during the course of my fieldwork, I realize that I may have been able to avoid some conflicts of interest by trying to maintain a professional distance within certain kinds of relationships rather than always striving for the intimacy that is set up as the hallmark of successful participant observation. Conflicting responsibilities may have been more acute in my fieldwork context in which two distinct groups—Japanese and *Nikkeijin*—were often interacting in tense relations with each other, but all research contexts are to some extent riven by conflicting interests. Researchers should be aware of the possibility of such conflict and be willing to choose sides if necessary, depending on the responsibilities they have incurred within research relationships. We should also be aware of the danger that our findings can be co-opted for political interests we may not support.

Researchers in Japan as elsewhere must build into their research design a significant amount of flexibility. Access to research settings such as workplaces can require a great deal of negotiation and time before it is granted. I would encourage researchers initially to cast their net widely, even as they pursue their most central research goals. During the months before entering the factory setting, I made contacts with a variety of groups and people who eventually became at least as important for me as the factory context itself. I regret not having been as up-front about my research as possible, even when engaging in activities that initially did not appear to be directly related to my research. Once I successfully enmeshed myself within a network of social relationships, I found it useful occasionally to distance myself from these relationships, to recognize the limits of identification, and to try to understand the dynamics of the relationships within a larger context. Finally, I struggled constantly to balance the multiple responsibilities I incurred while conducting research.

Notes

This research was made possible by a dissertation research grant from the Japan Foundation. I wish to thank Maeyama Takashi at Shizuoka University for sponsoring my research. Thanks also go to Beth Notar and the editors of this volume for reading drafts of this chapter.

1. See José Limón's analysis of jokes and dances among Mexican-American men as expressions of virtuoso masculinity (Limón 1994, chaps. 6 and 7). He suggests these are important ways in which these working-class men create value within race/ethnic and socioeconomic circumstances that marginalize and stigmatize them.

Related Readings

Roth, Joshua Hotaka. 2002. *Brokered Homeland: Japanese Brazilian Migrants in Japan.* Ithaca, N.Y.: Cornell University Press.
———. 2003. "Urashima Taro's Ambiguating Practices: The Significance of Overseas Voting Rights for Elderly Japanese Migrants to Brazil." In Jeffrey Lesser, ed., *Searching for Home Abroad.* Durham, N.C.: Duke University Press.

Robert J. Smith at
the bridge entering
Kurusu, 1951.

ROBERT J. SMITH

Time and Ethnology: Long-Term Field Research

Discussions of field research ordinarily take a short-term view on how to effect entry, establish and maintain relationships, and exit gracefully. I have chosen instead to write about the experience of conducting research in a single community over more than a half century and some of its implications for the ethnological enterprise. I first came to know the community in 1951–1952 and visited it many times before and after my wife Kazuko and I conducted a restudy in 1975 (R. J. Smith 1976, 1978). We have revisited the place many times since. The implications for ethnology have to do with not only social and cultural change, but also how one's view of that process in a single place is affected by the inevitable process of growing older.

By way of background let me say that in many ways I count myself a "typical American," born and raised in the United States and resident here for almost all my life. Since 1944, when I entered the U. S. Army Japanese Language and Area Program, I have been engaged in the study of Japan. When I first went there as an eighteen-year-old, everything I saw and experienced was new to me. Since then I have often been asked by Japanese of all ages, "Aren't you amazed at how much Japan has changed since you first came here so many years ago?" Indeed I am, but in fact, I am even more struck by the rapid pace of change in the United States. Fifty years ago, Japanese society, American society, and I were all very different. As a consequence, my perspective on research problems has been influenced at least as much by the changes that have taken place in American society in my lifetime as by those that have occurred in Japan. And above all, it has been influenced by the changes in myself—a researcher no longer in his twenties, now well past seventy.

A twenty-something American embarking on the study of Japanese society and culture today brings to the commitment experience of an American society so different, and takes it into a country so changed, that I find it difficult to conceive of what the relationship might be like. For the United States of today is at least as different from that of my youth as the Japan of today is from the country I first encountered in 1946. That Japan was burned out, devastated, and prostrate in defeat—a different world. But it is too easily forgotten that the United States I had come from had only recently recovered from the disastrous effects of the Great Depression of the 1930s. Neither country was a stranger to economic hardship, and, as time passed, both achieved quite remarkable degrees of prosperity.

Contrary to my students' assumptions about the relationship between conqueror and conquered, I made many friends during my military service in 1946 and still see some of them every time I visit Japan. Our get-togethers almost always turn to the subject of how greatly our two countries and our personal relationships have changed since we first met. When the yen was trading at 360 to the dollar, it was my habit to treat friends to the theater (tickets were practically free by my standards) and dinner. I even had the occasional use of a car, so rare in 1946 that I actually knew only one individual who owned a private automobile. But after the dollar began its dramatic slide, the "rich American" who might have been mistaken for an indolent colonialist in the early days, but really was just a poorly paid American academic, was transformed into a foreign visitor who could ill afford a cup of coffee. As our societies have changed, so has our relationship. And, of course, we have all grown older. A consequence of this inevitability is that I find it increasingly difficult to remember the Japan I first encountered and virtually impossible to convey to my students a sense of what life was like there in those days.

Doing Fieldwork Fifty Years Ago

When I was in graduate school, the reigning style of ethnological research was the "community study." One of the very first such studies, undertaken by John Embree and his wife Ella in 1935–1936, was of an agricultural community in Kyushu. In 1939, Embree published his classic *Suye Mura: A Japanese Village* (Embree 1939). It had been used as a textbook in my army courses, for it was one of the very few English-language books on Japanese society then available. Every anthropologist who went to Japan to conduct research in the 1950s knew Embree's book well. Our intent was not to replicate his study, but rather to see what had happened to the Japanese rural community as a result of the war and subsequent occupation. In my case, pursuing a line of research then heavily promoted at Cornell University, the project was to try to understand the social effects of technological change.

I found "my" community in Kagawa Prefecture on the island of Shikoku in 1951, well before the peace treaty was signed. In those days, a researcher looking for a site had no choice but to start at the top, for the country was still under military occupation. I enjoy telling my students who are preparing to conduct research in Japan that when I first arrived in Kagawa Prefecture as a very young Ph.D. candidate, the only thing anybody could think to do was to take me directly to the office of the governor.[1] So I found myself sitting there, wondering what to say to this jovial man, who asked me what I was there for. When I told him, he was incredulous. "You mean you want to live in a village?" I said I did, and he asked, "But why would you do that if you don't have to?" I explained as best I could, to discover only later that in many ways it was a very good question.

In any event, I first saw Kurusu from the window of an automobile (with driver) provided by the governor himself. There could be no better evidence for the scope of the outrageous privileges accorded Americans in Japan just as the Occupation was about to end. There were almost no American civilians on the island of Shikoku, and in those days all military personnel were required to wear uniforms. It must have been obvious that I was not a missionary, the only reasonable alternative assumption the people of Kurusu might have made about me. So I was a real anomaly, but my initial contact with them was of such a character that they could not refuse to deal with me. After all, the governor's car had stopped first at the village office just across the river, and it was immediately clear that they were expected to be helpful. At the very outset of my year there, then, we were cast in our respective roles by relations of power. It is not the way I would have chosen to select a community for study, but circumstances in Japan at that time offered no alternative. So, people were forthcoming enough, but I worked very hard at ingratiating myself, and soon it became apparent that at least some of them were being far more helpful than their perception of the situation really required.

Life in the villages of Japan in those days was very hard. It was not as hard on me as on the people of Kurusu, of course, but it was a difficult time for everyone. Most of them were very kind and certainly puzzled about why I was there. Some entertained vague suspicions about my true intentions and some, like the local socialists and communists, thought they knew precisely what my business was. The rest, who dealt with me in a slightly bemused way, conveyed the distinct impression that they concurred in the governor's grave doubts about my judgment.

I had at least three things to recommend me. One was the entertainment value of my fractured Japanese, serviceable enough but deeply flawed. Another was my typewriter, a machine that none of them had ever seen, which proved to be a source of endless fascination to those who came to watch me use it. I also had a camera, and to suggest just how long ago that was, it was the only functioning one in Kurusu. Consequently, I soon found myself designated the official photographer.

Once, early in my stay, the head of a family I often visited came running in and said, "Come quickly. There's a funeral up the river." This man, one of the first people I met in Kurusu, had listened to my account of my reasons for being there (phrased along the lines of "in order to find out how things were done," as I recall) and taken it upon himself to help me do just that. He had instructed me in the festival calendar, indicating clearly that I must attend them all, and whenever there was to be an event or occasion of a kind I had not yet witnessed, he often let me know. He was reasonably certain that I had not yet attended a funeral, and off we went. When we reached the house, he introduced me to the husband of the deceased, who took one look and asked, "Where's his camera?" Now, in my version of American culture, one does not take pictures at funerals, so it had never crossed my mind to bring the thing with me. Indeed, I had deliberately left it behind. I was sent back to get it, took pictures of the funeral ceremony from start to finish, and started to leave. After all, we had been taught in the little training we had in fieldwork techniques not to offend by intruding into truly private occasions, lest we arouse quite understandable resentment. As I soon discovered, however, the end of the funeral service itself was not the end of my assignment.

I was told to follow the procession up to the cremation ground, where I took more pictures of the lighting of the pyre, the billowing smoke, and the knot of mourners gathered to the edge of the pit. Later I took the rolls of film to the shop in the city of Takamatsu, where I had all my photographic work done, and when I went back to pick up the prints, the owner shook his head and said, "Even cremations!" He had printed my photographs of weddings, memorial services, and agricultural activities, but this time it was clear that he thought I had gone beyond the pale. I thought so, too, and had the prints delivered to the family through an intermediary because I could not over-come my misgivings about what I had done.

I settled in, aiming to find out what I could about how the war had affected the place. Among other discoveries, I learned that Kurusu and the neighbor-ing communities had lost a lot of men, yet even at drinking parties no one ever confronted me as a former enemy. Indeed, I was constantly being asked questions about the United States that sometimes caught me unprepared. What had been the monthly production of military aircraft in the closing months of the war? With the emphasis on individualism, wasn't it true that children didn't have to obey their parents? What did Americans think of MacArthur? Surely it was not true that in some areas of the United States the rice fields were sown from airplanes? How much land did the average farm family cultivate? I did fairly well with the agricultural questions, aided by having spent the summers of my youth on my grandmother's farm in south-eastern Missouri. The end of the war had brought real hardship, and these farmers were being urged by the government to produce as much rice as possible to feed the malnourished population. Food shortages were so severe that they were actually clearing new land and constructing new rice paddies. All of this was done without the aid of a single internal combustion engine—all the work done by hand. I had the strong feeling that for most villagers the future seemed to hold little promise of anything more than a long, slow grind toward a life that might, with luck, be slightly better. None of us could pos-sibly have imagined how things would turn out.

After spending nearly a year there, I prepared to leave the village. Our parting was touching in many respects, for many people came down to the bus stop to see me off with gifts of vegetables, eggs, rice cakes, noodles, and pickles. I am not sure that I have it right, but in retrospect it seems to me that we must have assumed that we would never see one another again.

I returned to Cornell in the fall of 1952 and tried to catch up on the current literature on "community studies," the most influential model of research at the time. I found that it was assumed that because places like Kurusu worked, because they really did function and people really did cooperate, community life must be harmonious as well. It was further assumed that because it was harmonious, people must like each other, but I had observed that there were long-standing enmities and rivalries, and some people actively detested some of their neighbors, as only those who know one another really well can. They tolerated one another, however, much as members of the extended family in Japan may do, because there were virtually no options to getting along together over the long haul. It seemed clear to me that just because people lived in apparent harmony, they were not necessarily well disposed toward one another.

Back in the Field, Twenty-Five Years Later

This modest insight subsequently helped me understand the most dramatic single event during my long association with the community, for Kurusu very nearly came apart over an issue that brought to the fore long-festering antagonism, resentment, jealousy, and suspicion. The crisis had occurred just before the restudy of the place my wife and I carried out in the summer of 1975, twenty years after our marriage. In those intervening years, we had made occasional short visits there, and the villagers had always made her feel as welcome as they had me. Because she is a city girl, they found it amusing that I could explain some things about Japanese rural life to her and a relief that they could tell her things they feared I might not understand. Some of the women took obvious delight in regaling her with stories of my early days in Kurusu, for the most part highlighting misadventures with the language and etiquette. In the role of listener to their conversations, I was provided an unexpected lesson in how usage depends on the speaker's solution to the necessity of combining efficiency of communication with propriety. Not quite realizing what I was hearing, it was only gradually borne in on me that very few honorifics came into play when the women and I conversed. Upon reflection, it occurred to me that I did not handle levels of politeness all that well and they were not only unused to doing so, but apparently had decided to keep it simple for the foreigner. This behavior was in sharp contrast to their only moderately successful efforts to produce the kind of speech my urban wife routinely employed. She quickly sensed their discomfort and, in the best fieldwork tradition, adjusted her behavior accordingly.

A word about spouses in the field is in order. There appears to be a widespread assumption that in the course of field research those of us who are married to Japanese either exploit them shamelessly or are thoroughly dependent on them by virtue of their superior language ability and familiarity with the culture. Both charges strike me as revealing a heavy degree of condescension, for one assumes that they are naturally exploitable, lacking any degree of autonomy, and the other assumes that they have nothing better to do than act as handlers for their ineffective spouse. By the end of the summer, the warm reception given Kazuko, coupled with the assiduity with which the women let her know just how much amusement my slips and faux pas had afforded them, allayed my initial fears that they might find it more difficult to deal with me in my role of spouse-of-one-of-them than with the foreigner on his own.

These fears were based on experiences during my first year in Kurusu involving visiting Japanese friends and academics—all urbanites who barely concealed their disdain for the villagers. One particularly egregious example involved a young salaryman's contribution to my conversation with a Kurusu woman about her new house. She had been explaining how it had been laid out on geomantic principles after consultation with a local specialist. Out of the blue the young man asked her if many people still believed in such superstitions (he used the word *meishin*). Bristling with indignation, she said she had to get back to work. I was appalled, and it took me some time and several subsequent visits to persuade her to complete the account of how the house had been built. Finally, after other examples of such insensitivity, I adopted a "no visitors" policy that greatly simplified my life in the role of interested observer of everything these patient people allowed me to see. Kazuko's extended stay was the only time that I had ever violated that policy.

The title of the restudy, *Kurusu: The Price of Progress in a Japanese Village* (R. J. Smith 1978), was meant to sum up my feelings about what we had found. Now in the course of thinking back over one's past it is easy to become nostalgic, and I will admit to some feeling of loss at discovering what had happened to Kurusu. But during that summer an incident occurred that will always epitomize for me the transformations that have occurred in the place and my relationship to it. Up to 1952 one of the most memorable days in the lives of Kurusu kids, I was later told, was when I arrived in a borrowed Jeep station wagon and gave them rides up and down the valley all day long. Most had been on a bus, but none had ever ridden in a private automobile before. One hot afternoon twenty-five years later, I was standing at a bus stop in a pouring rain without an umbrella. I had been there a while when a shiny, new pickup truck slowed and stopped. The driver rolled down his window and called out, "Can I give you a lift?" He turned out to be the grandson of a man I had known quite well twenty-five years before. I thanked him and hopped in, feeling as the British surely felt at their surrender to Washington at Yorktown, where it is said a military band played "The World Turned Upside Down."

The pickup truck incident marked a shift in our relationship that I welcome wholeheartedly. Nowadays almost every family has at least one automobile, their cameras are far superior in quality to any I have ever owned, most houses have been completely rebuilt and enlarged, the level of education of Kurusu's young has outpaced the wildest dreams of even the richest local households of an earlier day, and people's health is immeasurably better. Virtually no one farms more than they want to, and other sources of income have so swamped agriculture that it accounts for no more than 5 or 10 percent of the total. Many people who work in offices and factories in nearby towns and the city of Takamatsu commute by automobile five or six days a week, leaving early and returning late.

All of these developments were accompanied by steady erosion of most of the institutions and practices that once defined Kurusu as a place. For the most part, the festivals for its tutelary deity are in abeyance; weddings are now held in wedding halls or Shinto shrines in towns down the river; the communal cremation grounds have been replaced by an oil-powered crematorium built by the town. The notion of shared fate, symbolized by the name by which the place is known locally, has weakened greatly over the decades.

Nonetheless, most of the twenty-five households I knew in 1951 were still there in 1975, lending an air of continuity that is belied by the circumstances of their lives. Kurusu still exists, then, albeit much reduced in salience in the lives of its inhabitants. These institutional changes are less striking in many ways, however, than changes of another kind. If you were to arrive about midday on your first visit to Kurusu today, you would probably fail to notice a phenomenon that epitomizes what has happened. There is almost no one about on the paths or in the fields. The place seems deserted, in sharp contrast to the scene you would have encountered until the early 1970s. If you call at a house, you are likely to find an elderly man or woman, perhaps a very small child or two (too young to be in school, left in the care of a grandparent). One of the ubiquitous sounds coming from those houses where anyone is home is the low murmur of the television. The thick texture of community life has thinned dramatically over the years, leaving the shell of what once was, only fitfully animated by sparks of its once vibrant life. It struck me that conducting field research in such a place would be immeasurably more difficult than it had been twenty-five years before.

Almost all ethnologists who began field research in many parts of the world in the early 1950s and kept track of the place and its people as I have done tell much the same story. Indeed, the literature abounds with stories of the displacement of community values, the decline of cooperative enterprise, the mechanization of agriculture or its disappearance, and the slow, apparently inexorable, eradication of a way of life that had existed for a very long time.

Are there particular advantages to conducting long-term research in one place rather than the more common practice of conducting comparative research in many different ones? It is obvious that I have found the former style both congenial and productive, and I value both the extent and depth of familiarity with that one place. New problems arise constantly because no situation is ever stable, and it is in the context of the long-term study that it becomes clearest that change and not stability is the norm. Tracking change in a single place over time does require close attention to the relevant developments in the larger society that affect the small community in which one works. In the intervals between research trips there may be major shifts in government policies and large-scale economic changes that may well have an impact on the local situation. It is both possible and advisable, then, to try to stay current with respect to such matters. Keeping up with the purely local scene during one's absence is more difficult. At least in the case of Kurusu, correspondence is very spotty, so that on every visit it is necessary to begin by updating information about people and events.

I have found it particularly useful to return with old photographs, which are a remarkably effective way of getting reentry conversation started. In my experience, discussing the events depicted and the people in photographs taken on past visits has multiple advantageous outcomes. Often one learns a great deal more about what was going on than had been apparent at the time; even more often there are stories about what followed the event or what has happened to individuals in the picture; occasionally what is shown in the photograph unexpectedly proves a corrective to false or imperfect memories. In this last case, it may come as a surprise to people to find that, contrary to what they believed, such and such a family had not yet left the village, "for there they are at the dedication of the day-care center," or that a certain kind of food was served at weddings "as early as that," or even that a given building had already been put up "before the bridge was repaired." The photographs also serve to validate one's position in the community as an occasional guest, a particularly useful device when it comes to establishing relationships with the few newcomers in a place like Kurusu or local people one did not know very well earlier.

Not all return trips to Kurusu have been devoted solely to catching up on developments, getting to know grandchildren, lighting incense at the ancestral altar for former acquaintances, and the like. I have found it particularly useful to take advantage of the density of the earlier contacts to move on to topics more specialized than "finding out how things are done." One of the themes of my later research, in fact, emerged directly from being asked to pay respects at the ancestral altars of Kurusu. I had been struck by many aspects of behavior toward the ancestors, not least of which was to treat them as though they were still active members of the household. And occasionally they were dealt with as though they were still alive. A particularly poignant example involved my visit to the house of an elderly man I had a drinking-buddy relationship with, where I learned that he had died the year before. When his daughter led me to the altar and handed me the incense, she said in a very loud voice, "Grandpa, Mr. Smith is here!" I was puzzled why she had shouted until I remembered that in the last years of his life he had been very deaf.

And so it was in the summer of 1962, in a conversation with two other Americans it suddenly occurred to me to wonder if anybody had ever asked whom the memorial tablets in those altars represented. That is, I had learned a great deal about how they were treated, but I had failed to ask what range of individuals were venerated. The study that ended with the publication of *Ancestor Worship in Contemporary Japan* (R. J. Smith 1974) began one summer in Kurusu, where I felt I could ask a question that as far as I know had never been asked before: "Who are the people in your ancestral altar?" The villagers, prepared to believe that I might actually ask anything, were amused and intrigued. What surprises they found there is an important aspect of the findings of the study, which I then extended into several more widely scattered communities, both urban and rural.

All of which has to do with serendipity and the absolutely crucial part it plays in field research of all kinds. "Hanging out" remains my favored field-work technique, at least in the early stages of every visit, for it permits the researcher to catch hints and passing references to people and events that no amount of preparatory work could elicit. Perhaps the most dramatic example of this from my own experience is what I have called "the Clover affair"—a seismic event that came very close to shattering the community and that some villagers would have much preferred I had never found out about. It was by sheer chance that I stopped by a particular house one afternoon, intending only to tell them I was back. Instead, after a long, unsolicited account of events that I did not fully understand, I came away with the realization that something momentous had happened and took it as my task for the rest of that visit to try to unravel the complexities of a serious dispute (R. J. Smith 1978, 229–250).

I did manage to understand at least the basic outlines of the event, but at the cost of being a great deal more persistent in some lines of questioning than was my habit. For a time, I worried about overstaying my welcome and even wondered if I would find as generous and open a reception on my next visit as I had become accustomed to. There appear to have been no such long-term negative effects, in part, perhaps, because the whole sad affair has receded in the memories of the elderly and was never so important to the young who are now securely middle-aged.

Briefly, here is the substance of the first version of the story as it was told to me. In the drive to attempt to stabilize small, rural communities like Kurusu, various levels of government were endeavoring to encourage the establishment of light industries in the countryside. The Clover Company, taking advantage of the offer of facilitation, proposed to build a broiler-processing plant in the very heart of Kurusu. The local government offered to help in securing the land needed, and the Kurusu council appointed four representatives to handle the details. They signed an agreement giving the project the go-ahead. Without warning, a group of families that claimed to have opposed construction of the plant went public with placards and petitions. The press got wind of the story, with the result that everything came out and Kurusu, a community that had always prided itself on its solidarity, was revealed to be riven by bitter dissension. Heated exchanges involving accusations of bad faith, underhanded dealing, and worse ensued, and ultimately the agreement with Clover was canceled. The local jobs that would have been created were lost, one side complained; the other pointed out that such a plant produces severe environmental pollution that the community had been spared.

Not surprisingly, we were to hear several versions of this sad story, but only after considerable soul-searching on my part that finally led me to conclude that I really had to pursue it. The problem was that I was well acquainted with almost all of the major players in the drama, including some in the local government office, and feared the likelihood of alienating some or all of them by pushing too hard for details on what had happened. Once it was known that I had been given a general idea of what had happened, I did not foresee that virtually everyone involved wanted to make sure that I got the story right. I never felt the slightest pressure to take sides, although it was clear enough that some of the people I knew best simply assumed that I had taken theirs. Happily, the language and normal demeanor make it possible for a person to suggest interest without involvement, maintaining a kind of surface neutrality that seemed to satisfy most.

With only one major exception, people who had been at the center of the controversy were anxious to explain themselves because, as it turned out, most of them were embarrassed by Kurusu's failure to live up to the reputation for solidarity that they had always assured me was so well deserved. The major exception was the local government people, whose role in the whole matter remains ambiguous to me and, I think, to the villagers as well. By far the most important result of my effort to understand a series of events of unprecedented intensity, I submit, is that the vindication of my early argument that a solidary community need not be harmonious was amply confirmed. But why the rancor? One answer was supplied by an astute local observer. I quote it because it puts the issue so succinctly:

> They say that they've started to patch things up in Kurusu, but in my opinion it will take a long time before they can restore the kind of unity the place used to be famous for. I wonder if they'll ever recover. You see, what really got people upset was that the whole thing was fought out right in the open. Everyone hates that to happen. Places like Kurusu are a bit like a stage where most of the action goes on with the curtain down. But the Clover affair tore the curtain to shreds, so that everyone could look in and see exactly what was going on. (R. J. Smith 1978, 233)

On the basis of my success in securing much of the story, I would argue that rapport endures, once it is established and properly nurtured. Would a newcomer have been startled by the earliest mentions of the affair? I think not, and if they had, surely they'd have been hard pressed to secure so many versions of it. Because everyone was well aware of whom my closest acquaintances were, they could guess with reasonable certainty what I'd hear from whom. As a consequence, I know for a fact that two or three people actually sought me out, primarily to justify their actions in the affair.

By now there are in Kurusu multiple copies of my book about the place, scores of photographs spanning almost fifty years, and even some recent videotapes of television programs dealing with village life since the end of World War II. Part of the pleasure of returning to the same place over and over again is the maintaining of ties with members of one's own generation and following them and their offspring as their world changes in ways that no one could possibly have imagined when their grandparents and I were young.

The Long-Term Rewards

It is obvious that I view the rewards of long-term involvement with a community to be manifold—personally, emotionally, and professionally. Those residents of Kurusu of my generation are essentially relics of a bygone era in whose lives their children and grandchildren express little interest. It is clear that the old-timers are so glad to see me because we share something they do not share with their own children and grandchildren. But there is good reason to believe that such long-term associations provide more than simple mutual satisfaction. These days it appears to be taken for granted that the relationship between the people and the ethnographer is asymmetrical, and therefore exploitative. I believe this to be a profound misrepresentation of that relationship, and offer a case in point.

It concerns the first study of a Japanese rural community by the American anthropologists referred to above. The place is called Suye-mura, the study was carried out in 1935–1936 by John and Ella Embree, and the results of John's and Ella's work were published decades apart (Embree 1939; R. J. Smith and Wiswell 1982). In 1950, after he had joined the Yale faculty, John Embree and their daughter Claire were killed by a drunken driver. In 1951, Ella Embree returned to Suye to visit old friends there and attend a memorial service for her husband and only child. She returned again in 1968 with her second husband Frederick Wiswell, and both were warmly welcomed. In the meantime, any number of ethnologists, both Japanese and American, had visited the place, keeping alive the connection between the community and the discipline of ethnology. This was so much the case that when the government initiated a program to amalgamate the *mura* into larger administrative units, Suye refused to give up the name by which it was so widely known. And for some years there was a signboard on a road leading into Suye, one of the few official *mura* left in Japan, announcing its special status as "The village studied by John Embree."[2]

The Wiswells retired in Honolulu, and Ella's contacts with Suye thinned out, but without warning in 1994, she received an invitation to come to the village the following year with her husband to take part in the fiftieth anniversary observances of the start of the Embree study. The village office sent air tickets and the Wiswells were met at the nearest airport by a delegation with a minibus to take them to their hotel. (The banner on the side of the bus read: Welcome, Mr. and Mrs. Ella Wiswell.) The elaborate program included an appearance by then Governor Hosokawa of Kumamoto Prefecture, who later became prime minister (Wiswell 1988; R. J. Smith 1988). The Japan Broadcasting Corporation produced a two-hour television program on Suye, and the villagers made an hour-long one of their own.[3]

What the Suye events strongly suggest is that a great deal of current soul-searching by ethnologists, having to do with feelings of guilt for exploiting the objects of their study, is misplaced. Of course, the relationship of ethnologist and the people studied is essentially an exploitative one, but it has been my experience that the uses to which we put one another are mutual and reciprocal. I have been helpful to some Kurusu people, of course, and occasionally used them for my own purposes. It is equally important to point out that, for their part, they have been not at all shy about using me for theirs.

Suye, as one of its young politicians wrote to me some years ago, had been put on the map by the Embree study and become well known as the first Japanese community to be studied by a foreigner. Viewing the television footage of the fiftieth-anniversary celebration, one cannot help but be struck by the way in which the elderly in Suye, those who knew the Embrees, blossom under the lights of the camera crew. They comment on their initial impression of the Embrees, confess that they were deeply suspicious of them at first, and then reminisce about this and that encounter they remember from their childhood.

And finally, a closing thought about the implications of long-term research in a single place for thinking about the nature of ethnographic authority, responsibility, and guilt. A valuable legacy of the Japanese community studies done so long ago is that, taken together, they afford us cross-sectional views of the process of a society's becoming something other than it had been. They now represent an archive, a record of a kind that otherwise would not exist. It is a large claim, but I think a defensible one because at the time almost no one else had the slightest interest in learning about, much less making a record of, that way of life. The residents of those communities have been given a kind of immortality. That surely is some compensation for whatever small shock waves our presence may have caused in the very brief time we spent among them.

Notes

My original research received crucial logistical support from the University of Michigan, Center for Japanese Studies. Funding was provided by the Social Science Research Council.

1. Anthropologists have tended to move in less exalted circles since; he is the only prefectural governor I ever met.

2. Recent word has it that the place-name is scheduled to disappear at last, with the amalgamation of several contiguous small communities.

3. I seriously doubt that it has ever occurred to anyone to celebrate my arrival in Kurusu, although Okayama Television did film a visit that Kazuko and I made there in 1993.

Related Readings

Three video documentaries, *Ella's Journal, The Language of My Teachers,* and *Times of Witness,* produced by David W. Plath (Media Production Group 1996a, 1996b, 1996c), focus on Ella Lury Wiswell's research with John Embree in Suye Mura in the 1930s and Robert J. Smith's career in Japanese studies from language training during World War II to field research into the late 1990s.

Smith, Robert J. 1952. "Cooperative Forms in a Japanese Agricultural Community." *Occasional Papers, Center for Japanese Studies, University of Michigan,* no. 3:59–70.
———. 1957. "Community Interrelations with the Outside World: The Case of the Japanese Agricultural Community." *American Anthropologist* 59(3):463–472.
———. 1961. "The Japanese Rural Community: Norms, Sanctions, and Ostracism." *American Anthropologist* 63(3):522–533.
———. 1976. "A Japanese Community and Its Anthropologist, 1951–1975." *Journal of Japanese Studies* 2(2):209–223.
———. 1978. *Kurusu: The Price of Progress in a Japanese Village, 1951–1975.* Stanford, Calif.: Stanford University Press.
Smith, Robert J., and Ella Lury Wiswell. 1982. *The Women of Suye Mura.* Chicago: University of Chicago Press.

Victoria Lyon Bestor and her son, Nick, 1988, introducing Halloween to Miyamoto-chō, with children and grandchildren of Andō Yoshifumi, to whom this book is dedicated.

VICTORIA LYON BESTOR

Appendix: Digital Resources and Fieldwork

The environment for research is constantly evolving, and the rapid expansion of electronic media is transforming both fieldwork and preparation for fieldwork before arriving in Japan. Although only a few of the chapters in this volume specifically mention digital resources, several of the authors have been involved in creating on-line resources for teaching and research, and web-based material is increasingly becoming available on a vast array of topics (e.g., Steinhoff 2001).

The range of possible sources of digital information about Japan is staggering. Many of the sources mentioned below are listed in the following on-line guides that provide advice about which sites are best for specific kinds of searches and a wide range of other supplementary bibliographic aids for research and teaching.

- Duke University's site, maintained by Kristina Troost, is organized around disciplines and topics for research and looks both at print and electronic resources: www.lib.duke.edu/ias/eac/japanesestudies.html.
- "Online Resources for Japanese Studies" at the University of Massachu-

setts, Amherst, maintained by Sharon Domier, is categorized by types of resources: www.library.umass.edu/subject/easian/eajpn.html.

• The University of Wisconsin's Digital Asia Library, maintained by Rebecca Payne, provides a searchable catalog of web resources originating in Asia: http://digitalasia.library.wisc.edu/about.html.

All the major Japanese newspapers and media organizations maintain extensive web sites. Several major sites include:

• *Asahi Shinbun:* www.asahi.com/home.html
• Kyodo News Service: www.kyodo.co.jp/
• *Mainichi Shinbun:* www.mainichi.co.jp/
• NHK: www.nhk.or.jp/
• *Yomiuri Shinbun:* www.yomiuri.co.jp/index-j.htm

Current stories are kept on-line only for a limited period of time; older stories are sometimes retrievable through archival searches, but often a fee or subscription is required. An excellent compilation to newspaper sites is provided by Jissen Joshi University (www.jissen.ac.jp/library/frame/janews.htm). Most newspapers maintain English-language sites in parallel to their Japanese-language sites, but the coverage of the English sites is much less extensive than the Japanese sites. Researchers should also search for keywords related to their projects in the LEXIS-NEXIS Academic Universe World News using Asia/Pacific news sources, which provide extensive coverage of English-language news on Japan.

Several news organizations have extensive on-line photo archives. Mainichi Photo Bank (http://photobank.mainichi.co.jp/), for example, allows free searches of their photo collection; downloads and reproduction rights are available for a fee. A guide to digital images on-line has been written by Kazuko Sakaguchi at the Documentation Center on Contemporary Japan at Harvard's Reischauer Institute of Japanese Studies. This guide and several others on topics such as databases of antique maps, electronic journals, and so forth (all of which have been published in the Reischauer Institute's newsletter, *Tsūshin*) can be accessed through the Reischauer web site: www.fas.harvard.edu/~rijs.

Major national and local Japanese government agencies also maintain extensive sites. (As is true of news sites, the English-language versions of these government sites are far less comprehensive than the Japanese versions). A few random examples include:

- Hokkaido Prefectural Government: www.pref.hokkaido.jp/menu.html
- Ministry of Agriculture, Forestry and Fisheries:
  www.maff.go.jp/index.html
- Ministry of Health, Labour and Welfare: www.mhlw.go.jp/index.html
- Tokyo Metropolitan Government: www.metro.tokyo.jp/index.htm

In addition, religious organizations, labor unions, political parties, trade groups, journals, social movements, schools, artistic groups, theatres, museums, fisheries cooperatives, consumers groups, peace activists, and virtually every other kind of group, organization, movement, or institution you can imagine has some kind of presence on the web, as you can find through a quick search on the Japanese versions of Google and Yahoo (www.google.co.jp/; www.yahoo.co.jp/). The vast majority of these sites are solely in Japanese. A systematically organized approach to Japanese-language Internet resources is a site at the University of Tokyo Library (http://resource.lib.u-tokyo.ac.jp/iri/url_search.cgi), which includes brief annotations and is an excellent way to look at a well-vetted set of links.

In my own research on the reimagination of civil society in Japan (V. Bestor 2002), I have found that on-line discussion groups create opportunities for new interest groups and discourse unmediated by conservative Japanese publishers, business leaders, and government agencies, as well as by physical, cultural, and political boundaries worldwide. Locating the appropriate discussion groups and subscribing to them is a great way both to begin one's research while still at home and to keep in touch with the individuals and the discourse after you are back from the field.

As Steinhoff notes in her chapter, the first step for anyone seeking to tap these resources is to make sure that one's e-mail and web browser systems are Japanese-language capable. Although the technological standards change rapidly, one source of frequently updated information on Japanese-language-capable systems is the AskEASL web site: (http://askvrd.org/askeasl). AskEASL (short for "Ask an East Asian Studies Librarian") is a free scholarly reference service that includes a series of downloadable guides written by expert librarians that cover topics ranging from setting up Japanese-language e-mail and downloading Asian fonts, to how to get access to major on-line public access catalogs (OPACs) in Japan and how to navigate some of the comprehensive commercial electronic databases available in Japanese. The information posted on AskEASL is kept up-to-date by Sharon Domier at the University of Massachusetts, Amherst, and many other reference librarians who volunteer their services to this. (More on AskEASL in a moment.)

Anyone starting a research project, whether based outside Japan or already in the country, should begin by talking to researchers already knowledgeable about the topic *and* to librarians familiar with Japanese studies about published materials (both print and digital) and identifiable archival resources. Consulting both researchers and librarians early in the process of thinking through a research project is important because their approaches to a topic begin from different starting points (topical and methodological, on the one hand, and source based, on the other hand). These are not necessarily mutually exclusive perspectives, but without consultations on both aspects, the feasibility (and potential pitfalls) of relying on particular print, archival, and digital resources may not be readily apparent. For researchers who are based at an institution with a Japanese-studies library and professional librarians, this advice may seem obvious. But even for scholars who do not have immediate access to expert librarians, there are some extraordinarily good resources available.

Most major North American academic libraries with Japanese-language collections and universities with East Asian Studies centers maintain web sites with extensive links to major on-line public access catalogs and Japanese organizational web sites. Since the 1980s, the Japan-United States Friendship Commission has provided generous support for building and maintaining collaborative links among North American libraries and between North American and Japanese libraries, and many of these sites and the reference tools they include are the results of this support and collaboration. An easy way to get an excellent overview of the resources available in North American collections—to get an idea of both their size and special strengths—is to visit the "Finding Materials" section contained on the Duke University site at (www.lib.duke.edu/ias/eac/japanesestudies.html).

Of course, web resources are constantly shifting, but major sites at university and other libraries tend to be relatively up-to-date and to remain in operation because of their institutional bases. The following web pages include extensive links to on-line resources on Japan and also have some distinctive resources reflecting ongoing research interests at the sponsoring institution (e.g., links on photography and maps at Columbia; the on-line catalog of the Takazawa Collection on Japanese Social Movements at Hawai'i; Asian theater and performing arts at Cornell; Japanese-Canadian studies on the Toronto site; etc.):

- Columbia University's C.V. Starr Library:
  www.columbia.edu/cu/lweb/indiv/eastasian/Japan/J-subjects/
  J-bibresource.html
- Cornell University's Wason Collection:
  www.library.cornell.edu/wason
- The Harvard-Yenching Library: http://hcl.harvard.edu/
  harvard-yenching/japandatabase.html#database
- The University of Hawai'i, Manoa:
  www.hawaii.edu/asiaref/japan/main/main.html
- International House of Japan's library:
  www.i-house.or.jp/ihj_e/lbrar_e/index.html
- The University of Michigan: www.lib.umich.edu/asia
- Ohio State University: http://pears.lib.ohio-state.edu/
- The University of Pittsburgh, Japan Information Center:
  www.library.pitt.edu/libraries/jic/jic.html
- University of Toronto: http://ots.utoronto.ca/users/japanguide

Two web sites with "PURLs" (persistent or permanent URLs) that maintain extensive links to major North American, European, and Japanese libraries and that include extensive information on library and information exchange issues in addition to reference resources, are:

- Council on East Asian Libraries (CEAL) of the Association for Asian
  Studies: http://purl.oclc.org/net/ceal
- North American Coordinating Council for Japanese Library Resources
  (NCC): http://purl.oclc.org/NET/ncc/index.html

Many universities (particularly those with U.S. Department of Education Title VI Grants) offer small travel grants for researchers who wish to use their library collections, especially for researchers who are based at institutions without major Asian library collections. (General information on travel support for use of North American collections is also contained on the Duke University site, mentioned above.) And for researchers without ready access to a Japanese-studies library or librarian, AskEASL also offers invaluable reference tools. Users may submit bibliographic inquiries on-line in English, Japanese, Korean, or Chinese, and the questions will be answered by volunteer reference librarians. On AskEASL, a researcher has several options, including public inquiry, asking questions anonymously, or labeling a series of questions and answers as "private," in order to refine and modify questions in the same way one would in a face-to-face discussion with a librarian or archivist. The AskEASL site is also building an archive of the "public" scholarly questions and answers about specific research tools and topics that have been handled on AskEASL.

The library web sites mentioned above include many links to the on-line public access catalogs of major Japanese libraries. The Global Interlibrary Loan Framework (GIF), www.arl.org/collect/grp/japan/GIF.html, established in May 2002, includes a growing number of North American and Japanese research libraries using a newly developed international interlibrary loan system, which now enables affiliated North American users to access materials contained in the collections of participating Japanese libraries.

Japan's National Diet Library (NDL) is also a leader in developing electronic resources. With the completion of NDL's Kansai-based facility (Kansaikan) in October 2002, a range of materials became more readily available free of charge over the Internet (www.ndl.go.jp). A particularly important resource is NDL's Zasshi Kiji Sakuin (Japanese scholarly periodical index; Zassaku for short), which indexes over 14,000 periodicals in Japan and held by NDL. A complete list of periodicals indexed in Zassaku between 1975 and 1995 is accessible via the NDL home page at www.ndl.go.jp/jp/data/sakuin/sakuin_index.html. NDL's home page is available in both Japanese- and English-language versions.

As the chapters in this volume make clear, doing good fieldwork and getting access to documents are often inseparable activities. Although electronic access to documents is an enormous boon, it does not take the place of fieldwork. The *machikomi* (street-corner information) that White records, the *mini-komi* (small-circulation publications) that Steinhoff collects, the *kairanban* (circulating message boards) that Ted Bestor reads are all kinds of documentation that the web will not likely make available. And even among conventional documentary collections—some tiny portion of which eventually might be available on-line—the process of *hakkutsu* (excavation) is, as Gordon points out, what enables the historian to piece together the tale. All this is to say that documents—whether on-line or not—exist in a social context. Good fieldwork both explores that context to get access to documents and pays attention to that context in order to understand and interpret what the documents mean.

Electronic resources may be enormously useful in getting aggregate statistical data on the national or prefectural level, public policy statements, reports that appear in the mass media, and the published scholarship on a subject, but only fieldwork on site and visits to libraries, archives, and document rooms will get the researcher in touch with the grey literature, the public but not widely disseminated reports, and the private though not necessarily secret opinions and interpretations of those whose lives are (only partially) recorded in documents on-line. Nothing will substitute for the on-the-ground reality of fieldwork or the on-site combing of libraries and archives for the vast amounts of illuminating material that is not and never will be available in digital form.

And on this score, it is important to remember that most Japanese libraries require visiting researchers to make arrangements to use their collections in advance and often want letters of introduction. The home pages of individual Japanese universities generally contain information about their requirements for library use by outside scholars and outline the procedures for application and the terms under which those privileges are granted. It is wise to negotiate such privileges in advance through the Japanese-studies library staff at the researcher's home institution. The AskEASL web site has developed a quick reference guide to the process.

GLOSSARY OF JAPANESE TERMS AND ABBREVIATIONS

amae	甘え	psychological or interpersonal dependency
amaeru	甘える	to act or be dependent upon another
Amerikajin	アメリカ人	an American (person)
anaunsā	アナウンサー	"announcer," a news reader
Anpo	安保	U.S.-Japan Security Treaty
Anzen dai'ichi	安全第一	"Safety first!"
arerugii	アレルギー	allergy; (political) antipathy
Aum Shinrikyō	オウム真理教	name of a religious sect; perpetrators of subway gas attacks
benkyōkai	勉強会	study group
bōchōken	傍聴券	an observer's pass (to view a trial session)
Bon Odori	盆踊リ	summer festival for the ancestral dead
buchō	部長	division head
bunka katsudō	文化活動	cultural activities, cultural affairs
Burajirujin	ブラジル人	a Brazilian (person)
chiimu	チーム	team, working group
chōkai	町会	neighborhood association

chōnaikai	町内会	neighborhood association
daigakuinsei	大学院生	graduate student
dasai	ダサい	gauche
dokyumento	ドキュメント	eyewitness accounts or primary documents, a term often used by journalists
enka	演歌	old-fashioned popular song genre, usually very sentimental
enko shūshoku	縁故就職	getting a job through connections or social ties
fusuma	襖	sliding doors, usually covered in opaque paper
gaijin	外人	foreigner
gaijin tokken	外人特権	"special foreigners' privileges"
gaikaku dantai	外郭団体	organization affiliated with a government agency or program; an extragovernmental body
ganbatte	頑張って	"Hang in there!" (verb: *ganbaru*—to persevere)
geisha	芸者	traditional female entertainers
gikai	議会	legislative assembly
gun	軍	military
gunjin	軍人	military personnel
Gyōsei kikan no hoyū suru jōhō no kōkai ni kansuru hō	行政機関の保有する情報の公開に関する法	Information Disclosure Law (2001)—for English translation of the law, see www.soumu.go.jp/gyoukan/kanri/translation3.htm
hāfu	ハーフ	half [Japanese]; person with "mixed" parentage
haigūsha	配偶者	a spouse
hakase	博士	a doctor (Ph.D. or M.D.)
hakase katei	博士課程	doctoral program
hakkutsu	発掘	literally "to excavate," finding documents
hanmen kyōshi	反面教師	negative role model
heiwa-shugi	平和主義	pacifism
hitorikko	一人っ子	an "only" child
honne	本音	the real intention, essence, or private truth; bottom-line interest (cf. *tatemae*)
hyōronka	評論家	commentator, critic

ikizumari	行き詰まり	dead-end experiments
JET Program	JET プログラム	Japan Exchange and Teaching Program, an English-teaching program sponsored by the Japanese government
jieikan	自衛艦	self-defense ship; destroyer
jieiken	自衛権	right of self-defense
Jieitai	自衛隊	Self Defense Force (SDF)
jigyō	事業	activity, program (work, enterprise, undertaking)
jiyū sakubun	自由作文	a "free" composition, a free-form essay
juku	塾	a test preparation school, a cram school
kachō	課長	section chief
kaigo hoken	介護保険	long-term care insurance
Kaijo Jieitai	海上自衛隊	Maritime Self Defense Force (MSDF)
kaikan	会館	a meeting hall or building
kairanban	回覧板	circulating message board
kaiseki ryōri	懐石料理	elegant, Kyoto-style cuisine
kakko-ii	かっこいい	cool, trendy, "in"
kakuron	各論	specialized articles on particular topics
kamikaze	神風	suicide pilots during World War II
kanji	漢字	written characters, ideographs
karaoke	カラオケ	singing to a prerecorded accompaniment
Keidanren	経団連	Federation of Economic Organizations
keigo	敬語	polite, honorific language
kenji	検事	prosecutor
kenjisei	検事正	chief prosecutor
kenkyū jugyō	研究授業	demonstration class
kenkyūin	研究員	research fellow
kenkyūjo	研究所	research institute
kenkyūkai	研究会	study group, research circle
kenkyūsei	研究生	research student
kenmin	県民	prefectural citizen or resident
kenshūsei	研修生	trainee
kessai	決裁	consultation and approval
kigō	企号	a company name or trademark
kō	講	pilgrimage group; a group of religious devotees
kobetsuteki jieiken	個別的自衛権	right of individual self-defense
kodomo	子供	child
kōeki	公益	public interest
kōenkai	後援会	a support group or fan club

kōhan kenji	公判検事	trial prosecutor
kōkan nikki	交換日記	a diary exchanged with a friend
kokoro	心	heart, soul
Kōkū Jieitai	航空自衛隊	Air Self Defense Force (ASDF)
kokueki	国益	national interest
kōmoku	項目	a budget item, a program
kondankai	懇談会	discussion group
kone	コネ	connections or influence
konketsuji	混血児	biracial person (literally, mixed-blood person)
koseki	戸籍	family registers; legal records of genealogy
kuyakusho	区役所	ward office
kyasutā	キャスター	"caster," a newscaster, a news anchor
kyōiku iinkai	教育委員会	board of education
kyūenkai	救援会	a support group, for example, for a person on trial
LDP	自民党	Liberal Democratic Party; Japan's leading conservative party (LDP is an abbreviation for the English name. The Japanese name for the organization is Jimintō.)
machikomi	街コミ	street-corner communication
maguro	鮪	bluefin tuna
manga	漫画	comics; a cartoon magazine or book
Man'yōshu	万葉集	eighth-century poetry collection
meishi	名刺	a business card, a name card
meishin	迷信	superstition
miai	見合い	arranged marriage; also a formal meeting for marriage arrangements
mini-komi	ミニコミ	small-circulation publications
MITI	通産省	Ministry of International Trade and Industry (MITI is an abbreviation for the English name. The Japanese name for the organization is Tsūsanshō.)
MOF	大蔵省	Ministry of Finance (MOF is an abbreviation for the English name. The Japanese name for the organization is Ōkurashō.)
mukoyōshi	婿養子	an adopted son-in-law
mura	村	village
murahachibu	村八分	ostracism, "ejection from the village"

nakaoroshi gyōsha	中卸業者	a wholesaler, a middleman
naki-bushi	泣き節	"crying song," *enka*
nakōdo	仲人	a go-between, an intermediary
NHK	日本放送協会 (NHK)	pronounced as "enu-echi-kei" in Japanese; an abbreviation for Nippon Hōsō Kyōkai, the national public-broadcasting system
Nichibei bōei kyōryoku	日米防衛協力	U.S.-Japan defense cooperation
Nihon no shūhen jitai	日本の周辺事態	area surrounding Japan [defensive zone]
Nihonjin	日本人	a Japanese (person)
nijikai	二次会	an after-party, a second round of drinking
Nikkeijin	日系人	overseas Japanese; person of Japanese descent
nisei	二世	second-generation overseas Japanese
NGO		pronounced "enu-jii-o" in Japanese, nongovernmental organization; voluntary organization
NPO		pronounced "enu-pii-o" in Japanese; NPO, nonprofit organization
obāsan	お婆さん	grandmother
Obon	お盆	summer holiday that celebrates ancestral spirits
oisogashii toki ni	お忙しいときに	[Pardon me for bothering you] at such a busy time …
okāsan	お母さん	mother
OL		pronounced "ō-eru" in Japanese; literally, "Office Ladies," a term for female clerical employees, usually young and unmarried
omiyage	お土産	gifts, souvenirs
omoiyari yosan	思いやり予算	"generosity" or "sympathy budget"
omote	表	the outward appearance, the public face of things; (cf. *ura*); front stage
o-rei	お礼	honorarium
osamefuda	納め札	prayer slips
pāto	パート	"part-time" or irregular worker not covered by regular employment benefits (regardless of number of hours actually worked)

purikura	プリクラ	photo stickers available from coin machines that are popular among teenagers [shortened form of "print club"]
puroguramu	プログラム	program, activity
purojekuto	プロジェクト	project
purojekuto chiimu	プロジェクトチーム	project team
ranma	欄間	carved wooden panels above doors
Reiyūkai kyōdan	霊友会教団	name of a religious sect
riji	理事	director of a company or an organization; a board member
Rikujo Jieitai	陸上自衛隊	Ground Self Defense Force (GDSF)
rōjin	老人	an old person, the elderly
rōnin	浪人	"masterless samurai"—a student preparing for entrance exams; someone without regular affiliations; a "floater"
sakaki	榊	a sacred tree in Shinto (*Cleyera ochanacea / Cleyera japonica*)
sakubun	作文	a school essay, usually in a set form and length
sansei	三世	third-generation overseas Japanese
sebiro kontorōru	背広コントロール	"control by those wearing suits"; civilian control
Seifu Kankōbutsu Ryūtsū Sentā	政府刊行物流通センター	retail outlets for Japanese government publications
seisaku	政策	policy, program
seiza	正座	formal sitting position, kneeling position
sendatsu	先達	leader of a pilgrimage group
senjagaku	千社額	a frame holding celebratory tablets presented to a shrine or person
senkyonin meibo	選挙人名簿	voter registration rolls
senmon gakkō	専門学校	vocational school
senpai	先輩	a senior to oneself, someone who was ahead of you in school or on the job
sensei	先生	teacher, professor, political leader; often used as honorific direct form of address
senshu bōeiron	専守防衛論	exclusively defensive policy
shakai hoshō	社会保障	social security
shibu-kaji	渋カジ	"Shibuya-casual," a clothing style popular in Tokyo's Shibuya district in the 1990s
shidō gakari kenji	指導係検事	instructing prosecutor training legal apprentices

shienkai	支援会	a support group, for example, for a person on trial
shihō shūshūsei	司法修習生	legal apprentices
shingikai	審議会	"expert" advisory body to a government agency or program
shinkansen	新幹線	high-speed "Bullet Trains"
shinro shidōbu	進路指導部	career planning and guidance office (of a school)
shiryō	資料	documents
shiryōkan	資料館	archive
shiryōshitsu	資料室	archive or specialized reference library (for internal use)
shittenshugi	失点主義	demerit system of evaluation; "demeritocracy"
shiyakusho	市役所	municipal office
shōji	障子	translucent paper screen
shūdan ryokō	集団旅行	group trip, excursion
shūdanteki jieiken	集団的自衛権	right of collective self-defense
shūkai	集会	public meeting or rally
shukusatsuban	縮刷版	a bound, small-print archival reprint edition of a publication such as a newspaper
sōsa kenji	捜査検事	investigative prosecutor
soto	外	outside (an organization or group) (cf. *uchi*)
sunakku	スナック	a bar, a drinking establishment
taisaku	対策	policy
tamagushi	玉串	a decorated branch of a sacred tree offered at a Shinto altar (*tamagushi ryō* = a monetary contribution)
tatami	畳	straw floor mats
tatemae	建前	the official intention or public truth; rhetorical rationale (cf. *honne*)
teijūsha	定住者	long-term resident
tobikomi	飛び込み	popping in unannounced
tsūshi	通史	chronological history from remote past to the present
uchi	内	inside, within one's own organization (cf. *soto*)
ukeirekata	受け入れ方	structures for receiving outsiders
umai	うまい	good (tasty), "bravo!"
uogashi	魚河岸	fish quay, fish market

ura	裏	behind the scenes, the seamy side of things; backstage (cf. *omote*)
wāpuro	ワープロ	word processor
yagō	屋号	"house name," a company name or trademark
yosan	予算	budget
yūji kenkyū	有事研究	emergency planning
zadankai	座談会	a group discussion, often written up as a magazine article
zatsuyō	雑用	nonresearch tasks, miscellaneous tasks
zoku	族	"tribe," members of a social set or scene

BIBLIOGRAPHY

Akimichi, Tomoyo et al. 1988. *Small-Type Coastal Whaling in Japan: Report of an International Workshop.* Occasional Publication no. 27. Edmonton: Boreal Institute for Northern Studies, University of Alberta.

Allison, Anne. 1994. *Nightwork.* Chicago: University of Chicago Press.

Ames, Walter L. 1981. *Police and Community in Japan.* Berkeley: University of California Press.

Anton, Thomas J. 1980. *Moving Money: An Empirical Analysis of Federal Expenditure Patterns.* Cambridge, Mass.: Oelgeschlager, Gunn, and Hain.

Arase, David M. 1994. "Public-Private Sector Interest Coordination in Japan's ODA." *Pacific Affairs* 67(2):171–199.

———. 1995. *Buying Power: The Political Economy of Japan's Foreign Aid.* Boulder, Colo.: Lynne Rienner.

Ashkenazi, Michael. 1997. "Informant Networks and Their Anthropologists." *Human Organization* 56(4):471–478.

Bayley, David H. 1991. *Forces of Order: Policing Modern Japan.* Berkeley: University of California Press.

Befu, Harumi, and Josef Kreiner, eds. 1992. *Othernesses of Japan: Historical and Cultural Influences on Japanese Studies in Ten Countries.* Munich: Iudicium Verlag.

Berger, Peter L. 1963. *Invitation to Sociology.* New York: Anchor Books.

Bernstein, Gail Lee. 1985. *Haruko's World: A Japanese Farm Woman and Her Community.* Stanford, Calif.: Stanford University Press.

Bestor, Theodore C. 1989a. *Neighborhood Tokyo*. Stanford, Calif.: Stanford University Press.

———. 1989b. "Tōkyō no aru machi ni okeru Kattō, Dentō, Seitōsei" [Conflict, legitimacy, and tradition in a Tokyo neighborhood]. *Minzokugaku Kenkyū* [Japanese journal of ethnology] 54(3):257–274.

———. 1990. "Tokyo Mom-and-Pop." *The Wilson Quarterly* 14(4):27–33.

———. 1992a. "Conflict, Legitimacy, and Tradition in a Tokyo Neighborhood." In Takie S. Lebra, ed., *Japanese Social Organization*. Honolulu: University of Hawai'i Press, 23–47.

———. 1992b. "Rediscovering *Shitamachi*: Subculture, Class, and Tokyo's 'Traditional' Urbanism." In Gary McDonogh and Robert Rotenberg, eds., *The Cultural Meaning of Urban Space*. North Hadley, Mass.: Bergen and Garvey, 47–60.

———. 1996. "Forging Tradition: Social Life and Identity in a Tokyo Neighborhood." In George Gmelch and Walter P. Zenner, eds., *Urban Life: Readings in Urban Anthropology*. 3d ed. Prospect Heights, Ill.: Waveland Press, 524–547.

———. 1998. "Making Things Clique: Cartels, Coalitions, and Institutional Structure in the Tsukiji Wholesale Seafood Market." In W. Mark Fruin, ed., *Networks, Markets, and the Pacific Rim: Studies in Strategy*. Oxford and New York: Oxford University Press, 154–180.

———. 1999. "Wholesale Sushi: Culture and Commodity in Tokyo's Tsukiji Market." In Setha Low, ed., *Theorizing the City: The New Urban Anthropology Reader*. New Brunswick, N.J.: Rutgers University Press, 201–242.

———. 2000. "How Sushi Went Global." *Foreign Policy* (November–December):52–64. [www.foreignpolicy.com/issue_novdec_2000/essay-bestor.html]

———. 2001a. "Supply-Side Sushi: Commodity, Market, and The Global City." *American Anthropologist* 102(1):76–95.

———. 2001b. "Tsukiji: Tokyo's Marketplace." *The Japan Quarterly* (January): 31–41.

———. 2004. *Tokyo's Marketplace*. Berkeley: University of California Press.

Bestor, Victoria Lyon. 2002. "Toward a Cultural Biography of Civil Society in Japan." In Roger Goodman, ed., *Family and Social Policy in Japan: Anthropological Approaches*. Cambridge: Cambridge University Press, 29–53.

Bestor, Victoria Lyon, and Reiko Maekawa. 2003. "The Philanthropic Roots of the Voluntary and Nonprofit Sector in Japan: The Rockefeller Legacy." In Stephen P. Osborne, ed., *The Voluntary and Nonprofit Sector in Japan: An Emerging Response to a Changing Society*. London: Routledge.

Bloch, Maurice. 1991. "Language, Anthropology and Cognitive Science." *Man* (n.s.) 26(2):183–198.

Booth, Alan. 1997. *The Roads to Sata: A 2000-Mile Walk through Japan*. Tokyo and New York: Kodansha International.

Bosk, Charles L. 1979. *Forgive and Remember*. Chicago: University of Chicago Press.

Briggs, Charles. 1986. *Learning How to Ask: A Sociolinguistic Appraisal of the Role of the Interview in Social Science Research.* Cambridge: Cambridge University Press.

Brinton, Mary C. 1988. "The Social-Institutional Bases of Gender Stratification: Japan as an Illustrative Case." *American Journal of Sociology* 94(2):300–334.

———. 1989. "Gender Stratification in Contemporary Urban Japan." *American Sociological Review* 54(4):549–564.

———. 1991. "Sex Differences in On-the-Job Training and Job Rotation in Japanese Firms." *Research in Social Stratification and Mobility* 10:3–25.

———. 1993. *Women and the Economic Miracle: Gender and Work in Postwar Japan.* Berkeley: University of California Press.

———. 1998a. "Manufacturing Class: Urban Japanese High Schools at Work." *Hitotsubashi Journal of Social Studies* 30:49 -60.

———. 1998b. "From High School to Work in Japan: Lessons for the United States?" *Social Service Review* (December):442–451.

———. 2000. "Social Capital in the Japanese Youth Labor Market: Labor Market Policy, Schools, and Norms." *Policy Sciences* 33(4):289–306. (Reprinted in John D. Montgomery and Alex Inkeles, eds., *Social Capital as a Policy Resource.* Boston: Kluwer Academic Publishers, 2001.)

———. 2001. "Married Women's Labor in East Asian Economies." In Mary C. Brinton, ed., *Women's Working Lives in East Asia.* Stanford, Calif.: Stanford University Press, 1–37.

Brinton, Mary C., Hang-Yue Ngo, and Kumiko Shibuya. 1991. "Gendered Mobility Patterns in Industrial Economies: The Case of Japan." *Social Science Quarterly* 72(4):807–816.

Budner, Stanley, and Ellis S. Krauss. 1995. "Balance and Objectivity in Newspaper Coverage of U.S.-Japan Frictions." *Asian Survey* 35(4):336–356.

Campbell, John Creighton. 1977. *Contemporary Japanese Budget Politics.* Berkeley: University of California Press. (Translated version: 1984. *Yosan bundori: Nihongata yosan seiji no kenkyū.* Tokyo: Saimaru.)

———. 1984. "Policy Conflict and Its Resolution within the Governmental System." In Ellis S. Krauss, Thomas P. Rohlen, and Patricia G. Steinhoff, eds., *Conflict in Japan.* Honolulu: University of Hawai'i Press, 294–334.

———. 1992. *How Policies Change: The Japanese Government and the Aging Society.* Princeton, N.J.: Princeton University Press. (Translated version: 1995. *Nihon seifu to kōreika shakai: Seisaku tenkan no riron to kenshō.* Tokyo: Chūō Hōki Shuppansha.)

———. 1993a. "Japan and the United States: Games That Work." In Gerald Curtis, ed., *Japan's Foreign Policy: After the Cold War.* New York: M. E. Sharpe, 43–61.

———. 1993b. "Managing Organizational Conflict in Japan: Implications for International Relations." In William Zimmerman and Harold K. Jacobson, eds., *Behavior, Culture and Conflict in World Politics.* Ann Arbor: University of Michigan Press, 291–311.

————. 1996. "Media and Policy Change in Japan." In Susan J. Pharr and Ellis S. Krauss, eds., *Media and Politics in Japan*. Honolulu: University of Hawai'i Press, 187–212.

————. 1999. "Administrative Reform as Policy Change and Policy Non-change." *Social Science Japan Journal* 2(2):157–176. (Reprinted 2001 in Friederike Bosse and Patrick Köllner, eds., *Reformen in Japan*. Hamburg: Mitteilungen des Instituts für Aseinkunde, 111–135.)

————. 2000. "Changing Meanings of Frail Old People and the Japanese Welfare State." In Susan O. Long, ed., *Caring for the Elderly in Japan and the U.S.: Practices and Policies*. London: Routledge, 84–99.

Campbell, John Creighton, and Naoki Ikegami. 1998. *The Art of Balance in Health Policy: Maintaining Japan's Low-Cost, Egalitarian System*. New York: Cambridge University Press. (Translated version: 1996. *Nihon no iryō: Seido to kōzō*. Tokyo: Chūō Kōron Shinsho.)

————. 2000. "Long-Term-Care Insurance Comes to Japan." *Health Affairs* 19(3):26–39.

Choate, Pat. 1990. *Agents of Influence*. New York: Knopf.

Choy, Jon. 1999. "New Law Provides Ax to Fell Bureaucracy's Bamboo Veil," *Japan Economic Institute Report* 20B (May 21):3–5.

Cohn, Bernard S. 1980. "History and Anthropology: The State of Play." *Comparative Studies in Society and History* 22(2):198–220.

Coleman, Samuel. 1983 (1991). *Family Planning in Japanese Society: Traditional Birth Control in a Modern Urban Culture*. Princeton, N.J.: Princeton University Press. (Expanded ed. 1991.)

————. 1996. "Obstacles and Opportunities in Access to Professional Work Organizations for Long-Term Fieldwork: The Case of Japanese Laboratories." *Human Organization* 55(3):334–343.

————. 1999. *Japanese Science: From the Inside*. London: Routledge. (Translated version: 2002. *Kenshō: Naze Nihon no kagakusha wa mukuwarenai no ka?* Tokyo: Bun-ichi Sōgō Shuppan.)

Csikszentmihalyi, Mihaly, and Reed Larson. 1984. *Being Adolescent: Conflict and Growth in the Teenage Years*. New York: Basic Books.

Culter, Suzanne. 1992. "Coal Industry Decline in Japan: Community and Household Response." In Dan A. Chekki, ed., *Research in Community Sociology*. Vol. 2. Greenwich, Conn.: JAI Press.

————. 1994. "Industry Restructuring and Family Migration Decisions: A Community Study in Japan." In Lee-Jay Cho and Moto Yada, eds., *Tradition and Change in the Asian Family*. Honolulu and Tokyo: East-West Center and University Research Center, Nihon University, 247–270.

————. 1997. "Reflections on Being a Foreigner Doing Research on Foreigners in Japan" (Part I). *Hikaku Bunka* 44(1):20–24.

————. 1998. "Reflections on Being a Foreigner Doing Research on Foreigners in Japan" (Part II). *Hikaku Bunka* 44(2):16–20.

————. 1999. *Managing Decline: Japan's Coal Industry Restructuring and Community Response.* Honolulu: University of Hawai'i Press.

Dalby, Liza. 1983. *Geisha.* Berkeley: University of California Press.

Dore, R. P. 1958. *City Life in Japan.* Berkeley: University of California Press.

Embree, John F. 1939. *Suye Mura: A Japanese Village.* Chicago: University of Chicago Press.

Epstein, Edward J. 1973. *News from Nowhere: Television and the News.* New York: Vintage Books.

Feiler, Bruce S. 1991. *Learning to Bow: An American Teacher in a Japanese School.* New York: Ticknor and Fields.

Fowler, Edward. 1997. *San'ya Blues.* Ithaca, N.Y.: Cornell University Press.

Fuchigami, Eiji. 1995. *Nikkeijin shōmei: Nanbei imin, Nihon e no dekasegi no kōzu.* Tokyo: Shinhyōron.

Geertz, Clifford. 1977. *Interpretation of Cultures.* New York: Basic Books.

————. 1988. *Works and Lives.* Stanford, Calif.: Stanford University Press.

Gerber, Jurg, and Susan L. Weeks. 1992. "Some Reflections on Doing Cross-Cultural Research: Interviewing Japanese Prison Inmates. *The Criminologist* (Nov–Dec):7–13.

Goffman, Erving. 1963. *Stigma.* New York: Simon and Schuster.

Gordon, Andrew. 1985. *The Evolution of Labor Relations in Japan.* Cambridge, Mass.: Harvard Council on East Asian Studies Monographs.

————. 1991. *Imperial Democracy in Japan.* Berkeley: University of California Press.

————. 1996. "The Disappearance of the Japanese Working Class Movement." In Elizabeth J. Perry, ed., *Putting Class in Its Place: Worker Identities in East Asia.* Berkeley: Institute of East Asian Studies, 11–52.

————. 1997. "Managing the Japanese Household: The New Life Movement in Postwar Japan." *Social Politics* (Summer):245–283.

————. 1998a. *Wages of Affluence.* Cambridge, Mass.: Harvard University Press.

————. 1998b. "Taking Japanese Studies Seriously." In Helen Hardacre, ed., *The Postwar Development of Japanese Studies in the United States.* Leiden: E. J. Brill, 387–405.

————. 2003. *A Modern History of Japan.* Oxford and New York: Oxford University Press.

Greenwood, Davydd. 1993. "Participatory Action Research as a Process and a Goal." *Human Relations* 46(2):173–192.

Hall, Ivan P. 1998. *Cartels of the Mind: Japan's Intellectual Closed Shop.* New York: W. W. Norton and Company.

Hamabata, Matthews Masayuki. 1990. *Crested Kimono: Power and Love in the Japanese Business Family.* Ithaca, N.Y.: Cornell University Press.

Hardacre, Helen. 1984a. *The Religion of Japan's Korean Minority.* Berkeley: Center for Korean Studies, Institute of East Asian Studies, University of California.

————. 1984b. *Lay Buddhism in Contemporary Japan: Reiyūkai Kyōdan.*
Princeton, N.J.: Princeton University Press.

————. 1986. *Kurozumikyō and the New Religions of Japan.* Princeton, N.J.:
Princeton University Press.

————. 1989. *Shinto and the State, 1868–1988.* Princeton, N.J.: Princeton University Press.

————. 1997. *Marketing the Menacing Fetus in Japan.* Berkeley: University of
California Press.

————, ed. 1998. *The Postwar Development of Japanese Studies in the United
States.* Leiden: E. J. Brill.

Hendry, Joy. 1979–1980. "Is Science Maintaining Tradition in Japan?" *Bulletin
of the British Association of Orientalists* NS11:24–34.

————. 1981a. *Marriage in Changing Japan: Community and Society.* London
and New York: Croom-Helm and St. Martins Press. (Tokyo and Rutland,
Vt.: Charles Tuttle, 1986.)

————. 1981b. "*Tomodachi ko:* Age-Mate Groups in Northern Kyushu."
Proceedings of the British Association for Japanese Studies 6(2):43–56.

————. 1981c. "The Modification of Tradition in Modern Japanese Weddings
and Some Implications for the Social Structure." In P. G. O'Neill, ed., *Tradition in Modern Japan.* Tenterden, Kent, U.K.: Paul Norbury Publications.

————. 1987. *Understanding Japanese Society.* London and New York: Routledge.

————. 1999a. *An Anthropologist in Japan: Glimpses of Life in the Field.* London and New York: Routledge.

————. 1999b. *Other People's Worlds: An Introduction to Social Anthropology.*
London and New York: Macmillan and New York University Press.

————. 2000. *The Orient Strikes Back: A Global View of Cultural Display.*
Oxford and New York: Berg.

Johnson, Chalmers. 1982. *MITI and the Japanese Miracle.* Stanford, Calif.:
Stanford University Press.

Johnson, David T. 1998. "The Organization of Prosecution and the Possibility
of Order." *Law and Society Review* 32:247–308.

————. 1999. "Kumo no su ni shōchō sareru Nihonhō no tokushoku."
Jurisuto 1148 (January 1–15):185–189.

————. 2002. *The Japanese Way of Justice: Prosecuting Crime in Japan.* New
York: Oxford University Press.

Kelly, William W. 1991. "Directions in the Anthropology of Contemporary
Japan." *Annual Review of Anthropology* 20:395–431.

————. 1999. "Caught in the Spin Cycle: An Anthropological Observer at the
Sites of Japanese Professional Baseball." In Susan O. Long, ed., *Lives in
Motion: Composing Circles of Self and Community in Japan.* Ithaca, N.Y.:
Cornell East Asia Series, 137–149.

Kondo, Dorinne K. 1990. *Crafting Selves: Power, Gender and Discourses of
Identity in a Japanese Workplace.* Chicago: University of Chicago Press.

Krauss, Ellis S. 1995. "Varieties of Television News: Explaining Japanese and American Coverage of the Other." *Studies of Broadcasting* 31:47–67.

———. 1996. "Portraying the State in Japan: NHK Television News and Politics." In Susan J. Pharr and Ellis S. Krauss, eds., *Media and Politics in Japan.* Honolulu: University of Hawai'i Press, 89–129.

———. 1998. "Changing Television News and Politics in Japan." *Journal of Asian Studies* 57(3):663–692.

———. 2000. *Broadcasting Politics in Japan: NHK and Television News.* Ithaca, N.Y.: Cornell University Press.

Krauss, Ellis S., and Priscilla Lambert. 2002. "The Press and Reform in Japan." *The Harvard International Journal of Press/Politics* 7(1):57–78.

Kubo, Hiroshi. 1989. *Nihon no kensatsu.* Tokyo: Kodansha.

Kuhaulua, Jesse, with John Wheeler. 1973. *Takamiyama: The World of Sumo.* Tokyo and New York: Kodansha International.

Kuwayama, Takami. 2000. "'Native Anthropologists': With Special Reference to Japanese Studies Inside and Outside Japan." *Ritsumeikan Journal of Asia Pacific Studies* 6:7–33.

Kyūen Shukusatsuban Kankō Iinkai, comp. 1977. *Kyūen shukusatsuban 1968/12–1977/8, sōkangō-100 gō* [Kyūen, reduced print edition 12/1968–8/1977, first issue-#100]. Tokyo: Kyūen Renraku Sentā.

———. 1984. *Kyūen shukusatsuban dai 2 shū, 1977/9–1983/12, dai 101gō–dai 176 gō* [Kyūen reduced print edition #2, 9/1977–12/1983, #101–#176]. Tokyo: Kyūen Renraku Sentā.

LeBlanc, Robin M. 1999. *Bicycle Citizens: The Political World of the Japanese Housewife.* Berkeley: University of California Press.

Limón, José Eduardo. 1994. *Dancing with the Devil: Society and Cultural Poetics in Mexican-American South Texas.* Madison: University of Wisconsin Press.

Lofland, John, and Lyn H. Lofland. 1984. *Analyzing Social Settings.* Belmont, Calif.: Wadsworth.

Maclachlan, Patricia L. 2002. *Consumer Politics in Postwar Japan: The Institutional Boundaries of Citizen Activism.* New York: Columbia University Press.

Malinowski, Bronislaw. 1922. *Argonauts of the Western Pacific.* London: G. Routledge.

———. 1967. *A Diary in the Strict Sense of the Term.* London: Routledge and Kegan Paul. (Reprinted 1989. Stanford, Calif.: Stanford University Press.)

Marcus, George E. 1998. *Ethnography through Thick and Thin.* Princeton, N.J.: Princeton University Press.

Markowitz, Fran, and Michael Ashkenazi, eds. 1999. *Sex, Sexuality, and the Anthropologist.* Urbana: University of Illinois Press.

Mason, Karen. 1989. "The Impact of Women's Social Position on Fertility in Developing Countries." *Sociological Forum* 2:718–745.

McConnell, David L. 1996. "Education for Global Integration in Japan: A Case Study of the JET Program." *Human Organization* 55(4):446–457.

———. 1999. "Coping with Diversity: The 'Achilles Heel' of Japanese Education?" In Gerald LeTendre, ed., *Competitor or Ally? Japan's Role in American Educational Debates.* New York: Falmer Press, 47–64.

———. 2000. *Importing Diversity: Inside Japan's JET Program.* Berkeley: University of California Press.

———. 2002. "It's Glacial: Incrementalism and Japan's Reform of Foreign Language Education." In Gary DeCoker, ed., *National Standards and School Reform in Japan and the United States.* New York: Teachers College Press, 123–140.

McConnell, David L., and Jackson P. Bailey. 1999. "Power in Ambiguity: The Shido Shuji and Japanese Educational Innovation." In Susan O. Long, ed., *Lives in Motion: Composing Circles of Self and Community in Japan.* Ithaca, N.Y.: Cornell East Asia Series, 63–88.

McSweeney, Elizabeth. 1999. "Towards a Universal Sociology." Paper presented at the Annual Meeting of the Association for Asian Studies, Washington D.C.

Mead, Margaret. 1928. *Coming of Age in Samoa.* New York: Morrow.

———. 1977. *Letters from the Field, 1925–1975.* New York: Harper and Row.

Media Production Group. 1992a. *Neighborhood Tokyo.* Documentary video produced by David W. Plath, distributed by DER, Watertown, Mass.

———. 1992b. *What's an Anthropologist Doing in Japan?* Documentary video produced by David W. Plath, distributed by Asian Educational Media Services, Urbana, Ill.

———. 1996a. *Ella's Journal.* Documentary video produced by David W. Plath, distributed by Asian Educational Media Services, Urbana, Ill.

———. 1996b. *The Language of My Teachers.* Documentary video produced by David W. Plath, distributed by Asian Educational Media Services, Urbana, Ill.

———. 1996c. *Times of Witness: Fieldwork in Japan.* Documentary video produced by David W. Plath, distributed by Asian Educational Media Services, Urbana, Ill.

Miller, Alan S., and Satoshi Kanazawa. 2000. *Order by Accident: The Origins and Consequences of Conformity in Japan.* Boulder, Colo.: Westview Press.

Miyamoto, Masao. 1994. *Straitjacket Society.* Tokyo: Kodansha International.

Moeran, Brian. 1985. *Okubo Diary.* Stanford, Calif.: Stanford University Press. (Reprinted as *A Far Valley: Four Years in a Japanese Village.* Tokyo: Kodansha, 1998.)

Moffatt, Michael. 1989. *Coming of Age in New Jersey: College and American Culture.* Rutgers, N.J.: Rutgers University Press.

National Science Foundation. 2002. *NSF Grant Policy Manual.* Arlington, Va.: National Science Foundation.

Ogasawara, Yuko. 1998. *Office Ladies and Salaried Men: Power, Gender, and Work in Japanese Companies.* Berkeley: University of California Press.

———. 2001. "Women's Solidarity: Company Policies and Japanese Office

Ladies." In Mary C. Brinton, ed., *Women's Working Lives in East Asia.* Stanford, Calif.: Stanford University Press, 151–179.

Ogawa, Naohiro, and Robert L. Clark. 1995. "Earnings Patterns of Japanese Women: 1976–1988." *Economic Development and Cultural Change* 3:295–313.

Okimoto, Daniel I. 1971. *American in Disguise.* Tokyo and New York: Walker/Weatherhill.

Perlow, Leslie. 1997. *Finding Time.* Ithaca, N.Y.: Cornell University Press.

Pharr, Susan J. 1990. *Losing Face.* Berkeley: University of California Press.

Pharr, Susan J., and Ellis S. Krauss, eds. 1996. *Media and Politics in Japan.* Honolulu: University of Hawai'i Press.

Plath, David W. 1990. "Field Notes, the Filing of Notes, and Conferring of Note." In Roger Sanjek, ed., *Fieldnotes: The Making of Anthropology.* Ithaca, N.Y.: Cornell University Press.

Plath, David W., and Robert J. Smith. 1992. "How 'American' Are Studies of Modern Japan Done in the United States?" In Harumi Befu and Josef Kreiner, eds., *Othernesses of Japan: Historical and Cultural Influences on Japanese Studies in Ten Countries.* Munich: Iudicium Verlag, 201–229.

Rauch, Jonathan. 1992. *The Outnation.* Boston: Little, Brown, and Company.

Reader, Ian. 1987. "From Asceticism to the Package Tour: The Pilgrim's Progress in Japan." *Religion* 17(2):133–148.

———. 1991. *Religion in Contemporary Japan.* Basingstoke and Honolulu: Macmillan and University of Hawai'i Press.

———. 1993a. "Dead to the World: Pilgrims in Shikoku." In Ian Reader and Tony Walter, eds., *Pilgrimage in Popular Culture.* Basingstoke: Macmillan, 107–136. (Republished 2001, London: Palgrave.)

———. 1993b. *Sendatsu and the Development of Contemporary Japanese Pilgrimage.* Nissan Occasional Papers on Japan no. 17, Nissan Institute for Japanese Studies, University of Oxford.

———. 1996a. "Creating Pilgrimages: Buddhist Priests and Popular Religion in Contemporary Japan." *Proceedings of the Kyoto Conference on Japanese Studies.* Vol. 3. International Research Center for Japanese Studies, Kyoto, 311–324.

———. 1996b. "Pilgrimage as Cult: The Shikoku Pilgrimage as a Window on Japanese Religion." In P. F. Kornicki and I. J. McMullen, eds., *Religion in Japan: Arrows to Heaven and Earth.* Cambridge: Cambridge University Press, 267–286.

———. 2000. *Religious Violence in Contemporary Japan: The Case of Aum Shinrikyo.* Richmond, England, and Honolulu: Curzon Press and University of Hawai'i Press.

Reader, Ian, and George J. Tanabe Jr. 1998. *Practically Religious: Worldly Benefits and the Common Religion of Japan.* Honolulu: University of Hawai'i Press.

Repeta, Lawrence, et al. 1991. *Memo ga torenai.* Tokyo: Yūhikaku.

Roberts, Glenda S. 1994. *Staying on the Line: Blue-Collar Women in Contemporary Japan.* Honolulu: University of Hawai'i Press.

———. 1996a. "Careers and Commitment: Azumi's Blue-Collar Women." In Anne Imamura, ed., *Reimaging Japanese Women.* Berkeley: University of California Press, 221–243.

———. 1996b. "Between Policy and Practice: Silver Human Resource Centers as Viewed from the Inside." *Journal of Aging and Social Policy* 8(2/3):115–132.

———. 2000. "NGO Support for Migrant Workers in Japan." In Mike Douglass and Glenda S. Roberts, eds., *Japan and Global Migration: Foreign Workers and the Advent of a Multicultural Society.* London: Routledge, 275–300.

———. 2002. "Pinning Hopes on Angels: Reflections from an Aging Japan's Urban Landscape." In Roger Goodman, ed., *Family and Social Policy in Japan: Anthropological Approaches.* Cambridge: Cambridge University Press, 54–91.

———. 2003. "Balancing Work and Life: Whose Work? Whose Life? Whose Balance?" In Gil Latz, ed., *Challenges for Japan: Democracy, Finance, International Relations, Gender.* Tokyo: International House of Japan for the Shibusawa Eiichi Memorial Foundation.

Robertson, Jennifer. 1998. "When and Where Japan Enters: American Anthropology since 1945." In Helen Hardacre, ed., *The Postwar Development of Japanese Studies in the United States.* Leiden: E. J. Brill, 294–335.

Rohlen, Thomas P. 1974. *For Harmony and Strength.* Berkeley: University of California Press.

———. 1983. *Japan's High Schools.* Berkeley: University of California Press.

———. 1984. "Conflict in Institutional Environments: Politics in Education." In Ellis S. Krauss, Thomas P. Rohlen, and Patricia G. Steinhoff, eds., *Conflict in Japan.* Honolulu: University of Hawai'i Press, 136–173.

Roth, Joshua Hotaka. 2002. *Brokered Homeland: Japanese Brazilian Migrants in Japan.* Ithaca, N.Y.: Cornell University Press.

———. 2003. "Urashima Taro's Ambiguating Practices: The Significance of Overseas Voting Rights for Elderly Japanese Migrants to Brazil." In Jeffrey Lesser, ed., *Searching for Home Abroad.* Durham, N.C.: Duke University Press.

Samuels, Richard J. 1992. "Japanese Political Studies and the Myth of the Independent Intellectual." In Richard J. Samuels and Myron Weiner, eds., *The Political Culture of Foreign Area and International Studies: Essays in Honor of Lucian W. Pye.* Washington, D.C.: Brassey, 17–55.

———. 1994. *Rich Nation, Strong Army: National Security and the Technological Transformation of Japan.* Ithaca, N.Y.: Cornell University Press.

Schwartzman, Helen B. 1993. *Ethnography in Organizations.* Newbury Park, London, and New Delhi: Sage Publications, Qualitative Research Methods Series, vol. 27.

Small, Cathy. 1997. *Voyages: From Tongan Villages to American Suburbs.* Ithaca, N.Y.: Cornell University Press.

Smith, Robert J. 1952. "Cooperative Forms in a Japanese Agricultural Community." *Occasional Papers, Center for Japanese Studies, University of Michigan* no. 3:59–70.

———. 1957. "Community Interrelations with the Outside World: The Case of the Japanese Agricultural Community." *American Anthropologist* 59(3):463–472.

———. 1961. "The Japanese Rural Community: Norms, Sanctions, and Ostracism." *American Anthropologist* 63(3):522–533.

———. 1974. *Ancestor Worship in Contemporary Japan.* Stanford, Calif.: Stanford University Press.

———. 1976. "A Japanese Community and Its Anthropologist, 1951–1975." *Journal of Japanese Studies* 2(2):209–223.

———. 1978. *Kurusu: The Price of Progress in a Japanese Village, 1951–1975.* Stanford, Calif.: Stanford University Press.

———. 1980. *Japanese Society.* Cambridge and New York: Cambridge University Press.

———. 1981. "Japanese Village Women: Suye-mura, 1935–1936." *Journal of Japanese Studies* 7(2):259–284.

———. 1983. "Making Village Women into 'Good Wives and Wise Mothers' in Prewar Japan." *Journal of Family History* 8(1):70–84.

———. 1988. "Postscript: Ella L. Wiswell 'Suye mura fifty years later.'" *American Ethnologist* 15(2):380-384.

———. 1990. "Hearing Voices, Joining the Chorus: Appropriating Someone Else's Fieldnotes." In Roger Sanjek, ed., *Fieldnotes: The Making of Anthropology.* Ithaca, N.Y.: Cornell University Press, 356–370.

———. 1997. "Intermittent Field Research in a Japanese Community: 1951–1996." *The Hong Kong Anthropologist* 10:2–10.

Smith, Robert J., and Ella Lury Wiswell. 1982. *The Women of Suye Mura.* Chicago: University of Chicago Press.

Smith, Sheila A. 1990. *"Henyō suru nichibei anpo." Kokusai Mondai* 369:15–28.

———. 1997. "The Wider Implications of the Bilateral Alliance." *Japan Quarterly* 44 (October–December):4–11.

———. 1998. "Representing the Citizens of Okinawa." *Social Science Japan* (Special issue on Okinawa) 14:8–10.

———. 1999. "The Evolution of Military Cooperation in the US-Japan Alliance." In Michael J. Green and Patrick Cronin, eds., *The US-Japan Alliance: Past, Present and Future.* New York: Council on Foreign Relations, 69–93. (Japanese version: 1999. *"Nichibei Dōmei ni okeru Boeikyōryoku no Shinten." In Nichibei Dōmei—Beikoku no Senryaku.* Tokyo: Keiso Shobō, 20–41.)

———. 2000. "Challenging National Authority: Okinawa Prefecture and the US Military Bases." In Sheila A. Smith, ed., *Local Voices, National Issues: The Impact of Local Initiative in Japanese Policymaking.* Ann Arbor: Center for Japanese Studies, University of Michigan, 75–114.

————. 2001. "A Place Apart: Okinawa in Japan's Postwar Peace." In Akira Iriye and Robert Wampler, eds., *Partnership: The United States and Japan, 1951–2001.* Tokyo: Kōdansha International, 179–200. (Japanese version: 2001. *"Hedaterareta basho—Okinawa to sengo Nihon no Heiwa."* In Iriye Akira and Robert Wampler, eds., *Nichibei sengo kankeishi.* Tokyo: Kōdansha International, 212–232. [Translation ed. Hosoya Chihiro and Aruga Tadashi.])

————. In preparation. *Borrowed Power: The Japanese State in the Cold War.*

Social Science Japan Data Archive. 2002. [http://ssjda.iss.u-tokyo.ac.jp/]

Spilerman, Seymour, and Takeshi Ishida. 1996. "Stratification and Attainment in a Large Japanese Firm." In Alan C. Kerckhoff, ed., *Generating Social Stratification.* Boulder, Colo.: Westview, 317–342.

SSM Chōsa Kenkyūkai. 1998. *Genda Nihon no shakai kaisō ni kansuru zenkoku Chōsa Kenkyūkai Seika Hōkokusho.* Tokyo: SSM Chōsa Kenkyūkai.

Steinhoff, Patricia G. 1976. "Portrait of a Terrorist: An Interview with Kozo Okamoto." *Asian Survey* 16 (September):830–845.

————. 1989. "Hijackers, Bombers and Bank Robbers: Managerial Style in the Japanese Red Army." *Journal of Asian Studies* 48(4):724–740.

————. 1991. *Nihon Sekigunha: Sono shakaigakuteki monogatari* [Japan Red Army faction: A sociological tale]. Tokyo: Kawade Shobō Shinsha.

————. 1992. "Death by Defeatism and Other Fables: The Social Dynamics of the Rengo Sekigun Purge."In Takie S. Lebra, ed., *Japanese Social Organization.* Honolulu: University of Hawai'i Press, 195–224.

————. 1996. "Three Women Who Loved the Left: Radical Woman Leaders in the Japanese Red Army Movement." In Anne E. Imamura, ed., *Re-Imaging Japanese Women.* Berkeley: University of California Press, 301–323.

————. 1999. "Doing the Defendant's Laundry: Support Groups as Social Movement Organizations in Contemporary Japan." *Japanstudien, Jährbuch des Deutschen Instituts für Japanstudien* 11:55–78.

————. 2001. The Takazawa Collection of Social Movement Materials at the University of Hawai'i. [www.takazawa.hawaii.edu]

Steinhoff, Patricia G., and Yoshinori Itoh. 1996. *Rengo Sekigun to Aum Shinrikyo: Nihon shakai o kataru* [The United Red Army and Aum Shinrikyo: A discussion of Japanese society]. Tokyo: Sairyusha.

Takahashi, Jun'ichi, et al. 1989. "Japanese Whaling Culture: Continuities and Diversities." *Maritime Anthropological Studies* 2(2):125–133.

Takemae, Eiji. 1994. *Shiryō: Nihon no rōdō.* Tokyo: Yūshisha.

Tamanoi, Mariko. 1990. "Women's Voices: Their Critique of the Anthropology of Japan." *Annual Review of Anthropology* 19:17–37.

Tanabe, George J., Jr., ed. 1998. *Religions of Japan in Practice.* Princeton, N.J.: Princeton University Press.

Tokunaga Masaki. 1981. *NHK fushoku kenkyū.* Tokyo: Chūmonsha.

Tsuda, Takeyuki. 1998. "Ethnicity and the Anthropologist: Negotiating Identities in the Field." *Anthropological Quarterly* 71(3):107–124.

Turner, Christena. 1995. *Japanese Workers in Protest: An Ethnography of Consciousness and Experience.* Berkeley: University of California Press.

White, Merry Isaacs. 1986. *The Japanese Educational Challenge: A Commitment to Children.* New York: Free Press.

———. 1993. *The Material Child: Coming of Age in Japan and America.* New York: Free Press. (Paperback ed.: 1995. Berkeley: University of California Press.)

———. 1995a. "The Marketing of Adolescence in Japan: Buying and Dreaming." In Brian Moeran and Lise Skov, eds., *Women, Media and Consumption in Japan.* London: Curzon Press.

———. 1995b. "Virtual Friendship: The New Media and the Material Child." In *Media of the Twentieth Century.* Tokyo: Justsystem.

———. 2002. *Perfectly Japanese: Making Family in an Age of Upheaval.* Berkeley: University of California Press.

White, Merry Isaacs, and Robert A. LeVine. 1986. "What Is an *Ii Ko?*" In Harold W. Stevenson, Hiroshi Azuma, and Kenji Hakuta, eds., *Child Development and Education in Japan.* New York: W. H. Freeman.

Wildavsky, Aaron. 1964. *The Politics of the Budgetary Process.* Boston: Little, Brown.

Wiswell, Ella Lury. 1988. "Suye Mura Fifty Years Later." *American Ethnologist* 15(2):369–380.

Yano, Christine R. 1997. "Charisma's Realm: Fandom in Japan." *Ethnology* 36(4):335–349.

———. 1999. "Distant Homelands: Nation as Place in Japanese Popular Song." In Kosaku Yoshino, ed., *Consuming Ethnicity and Nationalism: Asian Experiences.* London: Curzon Press, 158–176.

———. 2000a. "Dream Girl: Imagining the Girl-Next-Door within the Heart/Soul of Japan." *U.S.-Japan Women's Journal (English Supplement)* 19:122–141.

———. 2000b. "Marketing of Tears." In Timothy Craig, ed., *Japan Pop!* Armonk, N.Y.: M. E. Sharpe, 60–74.

———. 2001. "Torching the Stage: Korean Singers in a Japanese Popular Music World." *Hybridity: Journal of Cultures, Texts and Identities* 1(2):45–63.

———. 2002. *Tears of Longing.* Cambridge, Mass.: Harvard University Asia Center, Harvard University Press.

Yoshida, Teigo. 1981. "The Stranger as God: The Place of the Outsider in Japanese Folk Religion." *Ethnology* 20(2):87–99.

Zwerman, Gilda, Patricia G. Steinhoff, and Donatella della Porta. 2000. "Disappearing Social Movements: Clandestinity in the Cycle of New Left Protest in the United States, Japan, Germany, and Italy." *Mobilization* 5(1):85–104.

ABOUT THE CONTRIBUTORS

David M. Arase is associate professor of political science at Pomona College and the Claremont Graduate School. He holds a Ph.D. from the University of California, Berkeley. He has been affiliated with Tokyo University, and most recently with the Institute of Social Science at Tsukuba University, working on his current project on economic cooperation around the Sea of Japan. Arase is the author of *Buying Power: The Political Economy of Japan's Foreign Aid* (Lynne Rienner, 1995).

Theodore C. Bestor is professor of anthropology and Japanese studies, Harvard University. He received his Ph.D. from Stanford University and has been affiliated with Tokyo Tōritsu University. His latest book, *Tokyo's Marketplace* (University of California Press, 2004), is an ethnographic study of the massive Tsukiji seafood market, and he is working on a companion project, tentatively titled *Global Sushi*, which examines the economic, cultural, and environmental impacts of the worldwide reach of Japanese seafood markets. His web site is: www.fas.harvard.edu/rijs/Bestor.

Victoria Lyon Bestor is the executive director of the North American Coordinating Council on Japanese Library Resources. She holds a master's degree from the University of California, Berkeley, in Asian Studies and divides her career between nonprofit administration and research and writing on philanthropy and civil society in Japan. She has been a Fulbright Scholar at Dōshisha University and is currently completing research for *The Rockefeller Legacy in Japan*.

Mary C. Brinton is professor of sociology at Harvard University. Her Ph.D. is from the University of Washington. Her principal research areas are gender inequality, education, and labor markets. She has been affiliated with Keio, Hitotsubashi, and Tokyo Universities and the Japan Institute of Labour and has also done research in South Korea. Most recently, she was the editor of *Women's Working Lives in East Asia* (Stanford University Press, 2001).

John Creighton Campbell is professor of political science at the University of Michigan. His Ph.D. is from Columbia University. An expert on decision making and public policy in Japan, he has written extensively on social policy, including *How Policies Change: The Japanese Government and the Aging Society* (Princeton University Press, 1992). His web site is: http://polisci.lsa.umich.edu/faculty/jcampbell.html.

Samuel Coleman recently completed the master's degree program in social work at California State University, Long Beach, preparing for clinical social work and research addressing poverty and oppression. He received his Ph.D. in anthropology from Columbia University and has been affiliated with the University of Tokyo, the Osaka Bioscience Institute, and the Japanese National Institute of Science and Technology Policy. He is currently writing *Who's Doing What to Whom, and Why? Emics and Etics for Social Workers*.

Suzanne Culter, Ph.D., R.N., is currently working for the American Red Cross. Her Ph.D. in sociology is from the University of Hawaiʻi, Manoa, and in Japan she was affiliated with Nihon and Tokyo Women's Universities. She is the author of *Managing Decline: Japan's Coal Industry Restructuring and Community Response* (University of Hawaiʻi Press, 1999) and is currently working on institutional care for homeless women and children in Japan and the United States.

Andrew Gordon is the Folger Professor of History and director of the Reischauer Institute for Japanese Studies, Harvard University, from which he also holds a Ph.D. in history and East Asian languages. He has been affiliated with Tokyo and Hōsei Universities and is the author of *A Modern History of Japan* (Oxford University Press, 2003). His web site is: www.oxfordjapan.org.

Helen Hardacre is Reischauer Institute Professor of Japanese Religions and Society at Harvard University. Hardacre received her Ph.D. from the University of Chicago. A specialist on new religions in Japan, she has written recently on Aum Shinrikyo and is the author of *Marketing the Menacing Fetus in Japan* (University of California Press, 1997) and the editor of *The Postwar Development of Japanese Studies in the United States* (E. J. Brill, 1998).

Joy Hendry is professor of social anthropology and director of the Europe Japan Research Centre, Oxford Brookes University. Her D.Phil. is from Oxford University, and she has been affiliated with Tokyo, Hitotsubashi, and Keio Universities. She is the author of *The Orient Strikes Back: A Global View of Cultural*

Display (Berg, 2000) and is continuing research on cultural display in a global context by examining indigenous alternatives to European-style museums. Her web site is: http://ssl.brookes.ac.uk/JIG/ejrc/staff/Hendry.htm.

David T. Johnson is associate professor of sociology at the University of Hawai'i. He received his Ph.D. from the University of California at Berkeley. He has done research at Kobe and Waseda Universities and is the author of *The Japanese Way of Justice: Prosecuting Crime in Japan* (Oxford University Press, 2002).

Ellis S. Krauss is professor at the Graduate School of International Relations and Pacific Studies, University of California, San Diego. His Ph.D. in political science is from Stanford University. During his research on NHK he was affiliated with Tokyo and Keio Universities and the Japan Center for Michigan Universities. He has published widely on Japanese media and is the author (with Priscilla Lambert) of "The Press and Reform in Japan," *The Harvard International Journal of Press/Politics* (Winter 2002). His web site is: www-irps.ucsd.edu/irps/faculty/ekrauss/index.html.

David L. McConnell is associate professor and chair of the Department of Sociology and Anthropology at the College of Wooster. He received his doctorate in the anthropology of education from Stanford University and has been affiliated with Kyoto University. He is the author of *Importing Diversity: Inside Japan's JET Program* (University of California Press, 2000).

Ian Reader holds a Ph.D. from the University of Leeds and is professor of religious studies at Lancaster University. His major works include *Religious Violence in Contemporary Japan: The Case of Aum Shinrikyo* (Curzon Press and University of Hawai'i Press, 2000), and he is completing a book on pilgrimage in Shikoku.

Glenda S. Roberts is professor at the Graduate School of Asia-Pacific Studies, Waseda University. Her Ph.D. in anthropology is from Cornell University. She has held research appointments with Kyoto and Tokyo Universities. She is continuing research on gender and work/life balance among married working couples and is also examining the migration experiences of women workers in Japanese multinational electronics firms in South China.

Joshua Hotaka Roth is an assistant professor of anthropology, Mount Holyoke College. He received his Ph.D. from Cornell University and is the author of *Brokered Homeland: Japanese Brazilian Migrants in Japan* (Cornell University Press, 2002). Currently, he is working on sports and aging among elderly Japanese Brazilians in Sao Paulo, Brazil. His web site is: www.mtholyoke.edu/acad/soci/faculty/jr/facroth.html.

Robert J. Smith is Goldwin Smith professor of anthropology and Asian studies emeritus at Cornell University, from which he received his Ph.D. in anthropology. He is the author of numerous books on Japanese society and culture, including *Ancestor Worship in Contemporary Japan* (Stanford University Press, 1974) and *Japanese Society* (Cambridge University Press, 1980). In 1992, he was awarded the Order of the Rising Sun by the government of Japan for his contributions to scholarship on Japan.

Sheila A. Smith is a research fellow in politics, governance, and security at the East-West Center in Honolulu. She received her Ph.D. in political science from Columbia University and has been a visiting research scholar at the Japan Institute for International Affairs, the University of Tokyo, the Research Institute on Peace and Security, and the University of the Ryukyus. Her research has focused on U.S.-Japan security relations, most recently on the Okinawa base controversy, and on regional security in the Asia-Pacific region. She is currently examining the social impact of U.S. bases in Asia. She is the editor of *Local Voices, National Issues: The Impact of Local Initiative in Japanese Policymaking* (Center for Japanese Studies, University of Michigan, 2000). Her web site is: www.eastwestcenter.org/about-dy-detail.asp?staff_ID=384.

Patricia G. Steinhoff is professor of sociology at the University of Hawai'i. She received a Ph.D. in sociology from the Social Relations Department, Harvard University, and has been affiliated with the Institute of Social Science, Tokyo University. She is the author of *Nihon Sekigunha: Sono shakaigakuteki monogatari* (Kawade Shobō Shinsha, 1991). She is currently editing *Going to Court to Change Japan: Social Movements and the Law* and is studying the influence of late 1960s protest movements on contemporary Japanese civil society. Her web site is: www2.hawaii.edu/~steinhof.

Merry Isaacs White received her Ph.D. from Harvard University and is professor of anthropology at Boston University. She has written on Japanese internationalization, education, adolescence, popular culture, and aspects of food, culture, and social change. Her most recent book is *Perfectly Japanese: Making Family in an Age of Upheaval* (University of California Press, 2002).

Christine R. Yano is associate professor of anthropology, University of Hawai'i, from which she received her Ph.D. She has been affiliated with Keio University and Tokyo University of Fine Arts. Her recent book is *Tears of Longing: Nostalgia and the Nation in Japanese Popular Song* (Harvard University Asia Center/Harvard University Press, 2002). Currently she is studying fans and fandom of deceased postwar diva Misora Hibari and the global consumption of Sanrio/Hello Kitty products.

appointments, 57, 60, 130, 140, 179, 181–183, 235, 237, 245, 283, 305. *See also* access; introductions; entry points; interviews

Arase, David M., 12, 248, 260

archival resources, 10, 82, 262, 263, 264, 370. *See also* archives; data archives

archives, 1, 12, 79, 98, 167, 185–187, 258–264, 272, 373; newspaper, 266; photo, 368, 370

area studies, 4–8, 198. *See also* cultural context; interdisciplinary research and training; Japanese studies

Ashkenazi, Michael, 4

AskEASL (Ask an East Asian Studies Librarian), 369–373

Association for Asian Studies (AAS), 7, 88, 137, 293, 371

associations: business, 256; industry, 258; trade federations, 318, 324, 369

auctions, 321–322, 325

Aum Shinrikyō, 103–104. *See also* religion

automobile, 336, 353–354, 358–359

Ayukawa, 317

Bailey, Jackson H., 3, 374

Bayley, David, 145

Befu, Harumi, 4

Bernstein, Gail Lee, 3

Bestor, Theodore C., 1, 6, 12, 315, 333

Bestor, Victoria Lyon, 1, 7, 13, 332, 367

bias, 45, 122, 206, 251. *See also* loyalty; neutrality; research, objectivity

birth control, 109–111, 114–115, 117–119, 123

board of education, 60, 126, 130–134

books, 42, 43, 46, 233, 242–244, 250, 259, 261, 289; in Japanese, 104; nonacademic, 44

bookstores, 44, 242; specialized, 43–44, 46

boundaries, 149, 262, 272, 284, 321, 324, 327

Brazil, 300, 335, 338, 341, 347, 349

Brinton, Mary C., 7, 11, 211

buchō (division head), 130. *See also* section chief

Buddhism, 74, 78, 82, 341

Bureau of Labor Statistics (U.S.), 199

bureaucracy, 1, 5, 10–12, 16, 68, 114, 127, 140, 142, 151, 160, 162, 229, 232, 235, 239, 240–243, 248–254, 258–260, 298–299, 304. *See also* government offices; local government; local government offices; Ministry of . . .

bureaucrats, 11–12, 121, 126–129, 136, 143, 156, 158, 161, 164–166, 171–173, 231, 238, 251, 253, 264, 298, 321, 330, 344, 350. *See also* interviewing; interviews

business card *(meishi)*, 111, 114, 122, 159, 182, 235, 236. *See also* etiquette; introductions

business firms, 2, 202, 204, 206, 253, 256, 258, 260, 262, 283, 298. *See also* family, business; multinational corporations; private sector

camera, 316–317, 323, 355, 359, 365. *See also* photographs

Campbell, John Creighton, 12, 128, 229, 246

case studies, 65, 201, 204–205, 230, 259. *See also* research; research methods

CD recordings, 259, 278, 286, 287

cell phones, 33, 51

census data, 197, 241; Census Bureau, 199, 200

chance, 11, 22, 49, 61, 89–90, 97–104, 142, 169, 284, 287, 316, 328, 362. *See also* serendipity

child care, 81, 298, 360

children, 23, 25–26, 29–30, 34–35, 78,

203, 227, 280–282, 307, 342, 364; of
researcher, 279–281, 290, 312. *See
also* teenagers
Chitose, 167
Christian, 42, 43, 75
citizens, Japanese, 44, 166, 170–173,
184, 298. *See also* civil society
civil society, 7, 252, 256, 299, 304, 369.
See also associations; social movements
CLAIR (Council of Local Authorities
for International Relations),
125–129, 133, 136. *See also* JET
Program
coal miners, 216–217, 221
coffee shops, 21, 29, 35, 131, 162, 182,
237, 269, 302, 320
Cold War, 156, 160, 171–172
Coleman, Samuel, 11, 109, 123
collaboration, 7, 110, 112, 208, 241, 313,
370. *See also* Japanese scholars,
working with
commercial interests, 91–94, 97–100,
103, 121, 185–188, 191, 254, 256, 258,
282–283, 286, 288–289, 369
communication, 21–22, 31–34, 47, 59,
70, 121, 217, 231, 301, 357
communities, 2–3, 12–13, 24, 35,
58–59, 64–66, 69, 112, 158 -159, 164,
166, 169, 170, 204, 206, 215, 217,
218–221, 279, 281, 285, 298, 315,
323–324, 327–332, 342–343, 349,
352–357, 360–365; informal, 253
community studies, 354, 356, 365
comparative research, 2, 11, 142, 187,
198, 209, 230–311, 360
Constitution of Japan, 161
consumers, 171, 286, 318–319, 347, 369.
See also popular culture
content analysis, 11, 185–189
cooperation, 48, 66–68, 109–112, 115,
117, 122, 125, 128, 170, 201, 226–227,
240, 253, 298, 303, 312
cooperatives, 321, 369

corporations. *See* business firms
criminal justice system, 40, 139,
145–149, 155. *See also* prisons; trials
Csikszentmihalyi, Mihaly, 34
Culter, Suzanne, 7, 11, 214, 228
cultural context, 2, 4, 6–8, 13–14, 68,
82–83, 209, 215–216, 227, 255, 264,
313, 372. *See also* demeanor;
etiquette; factions; favors; gesture;
gifts; harmony; *honne;* honorific
language; introductions; Japanese
language; loyalty; networks; *omote;*
personal connections; posture;
reciprocity; sincerity; *soto;* sponsorship; *tatemae;* trust; *uchi; ura*
Cummings, William, 136

data, 9, 11, 26, 74, 77, 92, 115, 134–137,
143, 154, 176, 185, 196, 199–200, 223,
240, 250, 322, 343, 372; access,
199–201, 207–211, 241, 301, 319;
from fieldwork, 2, 4, 24; individual
level, 196–202, 207–211 (*See also*
data archives; data sets) protection
of, 53; quantitative, 101, 161, 196,
201, 209–210, 241, 251; raw, 187, 195,
206, 208, 241; social and cultural,
10, 27, 330; unpublished, 240–241.
See also data sets; statistics
data archives, 200, 210–211
data collection techniques, 31, 118,
201; appointment calendars, 265;
chronologies, 267; essays, 33;
exchange diaries, 22, 31; interactive,
34; organizing, 282; participatory,
278, 287, 289; visual, 12, 278,
321–326, 360, 372
data sets, 11, 196, 200–201, 207, 210,
241; public use, 200, 204
day laborers, 321, 328
defense, 143, 162–164, 168, 171–173,
238; policy, 11, 171–173. *See also*
military; security policy; Self-
Defense Force

demeanor, 73, 77, 313, 322, 363. *See also* etiquette

demonstrations, 11, 37, 43, 48–49, 53, 78

dependency. See *amae*

diaries, 31–32, 97, 280

Diet, 61, 160–166, 171–172, 178, 234, 239, 257. *See also* politics

dissertation, 38, 72, 114, 124, 135, 141, 156, 195, 214, 230, 244–246, 251, 296, 315, 330. *See also* dissertation research

dissertation research, 38, 109, 123, 162, 195, 214–215, 248, 260, 264, 277, 351

division head. See *būchō*

documents, 128, 227, 230–231, 238–239, 258–265, 303, 319; historical, 185; legal, 50. *See also* archives; gray literature; publications

Domier, Sharon, 368–369

Dore, Ronald, 136

drinking, 49, 66, 102, 130, 132, 151–154, 317, 320, 356, 361. *See also* participant observation; socializing

Economic Planning Agency, 250, 253

economics, 3, 8, 195–196, 243–244, 295

editors, 7, 42, 44, 181, 259; visual, 180. *See also* English language editing; publishers

education, 196, 208–209, 226. *See also* entrance exams; high schools; JET Program; schools

elderly, 95, 97, 111, 230–232, 235, 284, 295, 298, 307, 359, 361–362, 365

electronic resources, 7, 13, 266, 367–373; databases, 369; digital images, 368; discussion groups, 159; e-mail, 47, 369; journals, 368; public access catalogs, 367, 369; search engines, 369; web browsers, 47, 369; web sites, 13, 34–35, 47, 243, 279, 368–372

Embree, John, 354, 364–365

emotion, 73, 133, 147, 151, 277, 295, 307; in interviews, 307

English language, 4, 119, 218. *See also* English language editing

English language editing, 116, 159, 252, 311

enka, 12, 277–282, 286–291. See also *karaoke;* popular culture; music

entrance exams, 130–131, 134. *See also* education

entry points, 219, 319–320; unannounced visits, 93, 127, 131, 235. *See also* access

environmental pollution, 170, 362

Equal Employment Opportunity Law, 301–302. *See also* women

Etajima, 167

ethnicity, 83–84, 199, 340, 342. *See also* foreign workers; foreigners; Japanese Americans; Japanese Brazilians; Japanese Peruvians; Korean residents in Japan; *Nikkeijin*

etiquette, 75–76, 85, 102, 269–270, 357. *See also* demeanor; gifts; honorific language; obligations; reciprocity; thank-you notes

executives, 140, 142, 179, 181, 192, 282, 286, 321

factions, 143, 144, 181, 255, 270

factories, 3, 4, 12, 28, 296–297, 299–303, 306, 336–344, 347–350, 359; assembly line, 336–339, 347; workstations, 336–339

family, 3–4, 23–32, 38–39, 60–61, 68, 78, 83, 91, 97, 100, 140, 169, 184, 202, 208–209, 216, 255, 288, 295, 298, 303–309, 316–317, 321, 323, 327, 344, 355–362; business, 197, 202, 318; of researcher, 75, 126, 233, 279–281, 301, 309, 332, 341, 357–358

family register. *See* household registry

fan clubs, 279, 283–285, 288. *See also* popular culture

farmers, 64, 217, 221, 356. *See also* rural Japan; villagers

favors, 117, 120, 129, 130, 144, 221, 224, 232, 242, 252, 287, 291. *See also* obligations; reciprocity

Federation of Economic Organizations (Keidanren), 257

feminism, 77, 81

festivals, 68, 168, 262, 316, 322, 343, 346, 355

fiction, 32, 45

field notes, 4, 49, 75, 144, 151; of interviews, 38, 237; organizing, 135, 238. *See also* participant observation

focus groups, 27, 29, 225, 305

foreign aid, 12, 249–253, 256–258

foreign policy, 49, 157, 172, 229, 249–250

foreign workers, 4, 206, 215, 218, 223, 300, 304–305, 310, 339, 349; undocumented, 111, 206, 295, 300. *See also* Japanese Brazilians; Japanese Peruvians; *Nikkeijin*

foreigners, 94, 131, 133, 146, 154, 180, 183, 217–220, 224, 226, 253, 255, 269, 270–271, 290–301, 326, 331, 340, 344–345, 357–358, 365. *See also* outsiders

Fowler, Edward, 3

Fulbright Program, 54, 88, 125, 127–128, 137, 141, 150, 192, 214, 219, 228, 246, 313, 333

gatherings, 36, 47, 49, 52, 289. *See also* rally

Geertz, Clifford, 10

gender, 3, 4, 11, 78, 82–83, 152, 196, 198, 202–203, 208, 226, 289, 294, 296, 309, 311; discrimination, 81, 114, 198, 207; division of labor, 299–300; equality, 300; inequality, 199; of researcher, 78–79, 215,

225–226; roles, 301; stratification, 199; wage gap, 197–198, 204

gesture, 77, 285

gifts, 38, 85, 269, 287, 345; to researcher, 86–87, 150, 288–289, 356. *See also* obligations; reciprocity

globalization, 24, 124, 128–129, 131, 135, 279

Gluck, Carol, 136

go-between, 14, 57, 141, 224, 235. *See also* introductions; personal connections

Gordon, Andrew, 4, 8, 12, 261, 272

government agencies, 45, 179, 199, 204, 210, 240, 252–253, 259, 368–369. *See also* Ministry of . . .

government employees, 202, 217–218, 221, 263

government offices, 343, 349; education office, 60, 68; prefectural, 60, 235. *See also* CLAIR; local government offices

government officials, 173, 219, 227, 250–252, 256, 298, 303

government publications, 45, 229, 239, 258. *See also* bookstores, specialized; publications

government regulations, 225

gray literature, 241–242, 259, 373. *See also* bookstores, specialized; government publications; *minikomi*; newsletters; publications

guest register, 47, 288

Hall, Ivan, 121

Hamabata, Matthews, 4, 290, 344

Hamamatsu, 12, 335–336, 341, 343, 348–349

Hardacre, Helen, 4, 11, 71, 88

harmony, 26, 83, 144, 357, 363

Hawai'i, 47, 219, 300

Hendry, Joy, 3, 11, 55

hierarchy, 114, 122, 165, 226, 253, 284, 289–292, 338. *See also* status

high schools, 21, 24, 29–30, 33, 124, 126, 130, 133, 205, 210, 214, 216, 301, 308; junior, 9, 26, 125, 133, 301

Hiroshima, 29–31, 34, 235, 334

histories: agency, 259, 262; business, 259, 262; local area, 262–263; memoirs, 243, 259, 263; organizational, 262, 264; union, 262

history, 3, 6, 8, 12, 72, 85, 87, 103, 169, 185, 189, 261–262, 263, 267, 330; of labor, 265, 270, 272

Hokkaido, 6, 9, 167, 168, 214, 216–221, 318, 335, 348, 369

honne (true feelings or position), 130, 143, 153, 255–256, 325. See also *tatemae*

honorific language, 71, 76–77, 216, 218, 357. *See also* Japanese language, gendered speech patterns

Honshu, 6

household registry *(koseki)*, 68, 340, 341–342

households, 202, 215, 221–222, 241, 321, 359

housewives, 280, 285, 289, 296

humor, 78, 165, 292. *See also* laughter

identity, 22, 31, 148, 159, 340, 344–345, 347; Japanese, 277; of research subjects, 28, 34–35; of researcher, 3, 12, 77, 291, 284, 295, 344; shared, 344–345

ideology, 24–25, 37, 46, 48

immigration bureau, 340–342. *See also* visa

Indonesia, 256, 257–259

inequality, 145, 196, 198–201, 209, 326

informants, 3, 16, 21–22, 24, 27–28, 32–34, 53, 64, 67, 70, 94, 110–111, 238, 304, 326, 339. *See also* interview subjects

information disclosure law, 121, 171, 242

informed consent, 13–15, 41, 110, 116, 118, 183, 237, 302, 305, 346. *See also* research ethics; responsibility, of researcher

inquisitive observation, 12, 317, 319, 322, 327. *See also* participant observation

Institute for Social Science, University of Tokyo, 210, 266

institutions, 2, 5–6, 10–13, 22–27, 33, 35, 93, 121, 157, 171, 298–299, 318, 323–327, 349, 359

interdisciplinary research and training, 7–8. *See also* area studies; Japanese studies

International House of Japan, 7, 233, 371

international relations, 6, 157, 159, 249

internationalization. *See* globalization

interpreter, use of, 133, 218, 223–225

interpreting, by researcher, 150

Inter-University Center for Japanese Language Studies (IUC), 280, 283

interview subjects, 38, 94, 101, 116, 267–271, 330–331. *See also* informants

interviewing, 11–14, 22, 27, 38, 93, 117, 125, 128, 182–183, 215, 218–220, 223, 229, 234–235, 279, 301, 303, 305–308, 329, 345; employment history, 303, 307; life histories, 3, 267, 304. *See also* interviews; oral history

interviews, 10, 14–16, 25, 28–33, 36–41, 49–51, 81, 94–99, 102, 104, 113, 116–119, 126–128, 131–136, 140, 157, 162, 165, 180–184, 196, 201, 205–206, 210, 214–227, 231–239, 242–243, 246–251, 254, 257–258, 267–272, 278–283, 286, 296–299, 302–307, 310–313, 317–319, 322–336,

Koreans, 305, 338–339

koseki. See household registry

Krauss, Ellis S., 11, 176, 192

Kreiner, Josef, 4

Kumamoto prefecture, 365

Kure, 167

Kurusu, 354, 355–365

Kyoto, 6, 31, 92, 125–126, 133–134, 137, 235, 296–298, 303, 309

kyūenkai. See support groups

Kyushu, 3, 6, 26, 59–63, 68, 70, 97, 167, 216, 354

labor unions, 132, 261–262, 264, 271–272, 298, 300, 306, 369; local area, 304

labor-management relations, 261, 306

language. *See* honorific language; interpreter, use of; interpreting, by researcher; Japanese language; Japanese language proficiency, importance of; Portuguese; research, multilingual; translation

laughter, 217, 254, 292, 346. *See also* humor

lawyers, 42, 48, 50–52, 144–146, 297. *See also* criminal justice system; prosecutors

LeBlanc, Robin, 3

Lebra, Takie S., 4, 7, 54, 374

letters of introduction, 115, 140, 219, 223, 232, 246, 265, 373. *See also* introductions

Liberal Democratic Party, 156, 257

librarians, 220–222, 225, 243, 266, 369–373

libraries, 7, 185, 220–221, 233, 242, 252, 261, 265–266, 297, 368, 370–373; coordinating bodies, 371; Library of Congress, 243; National Diet Library, 82, 232, 372; special collections, 47, 243, 370

local government, 126, 128, 170, 206, 215, 218, 223, 231, 234–235, 241, 263, 362–363. *See also* local government offices

local government offices, 121, 202–203, 216–217, 220–222, 280, 318, 363, 369. *See also* local government

long-term-care insurance, 230–232. *See also* social issues; social welfare

lottery, 51, 325–326

loyalty, 81, 144, 195

lunchtime, 116, 256, 301–302, 305, 337, 339, 348. *See also* interviewing; interviews; participant observation; socializing

magazine articles, 217, 243

maps, 6, 32, 60, 65–66, 68, 283, 322, 365, 368, 370

market research, 26, 29, 30, 34, 330. *See also* commercial interests

marketplace, 9, 318–330. *See also* Tsukiji

Markowitz, Fran, 4

marriage, 56–59, 62, 64, 67, 69, 70, 81, 199, 202, 357; arranged, 57, 62. *See also* married couples; weddings

married couples, 109, 115, 117

mass media, 11, 45, 118, 176, 373. *See also* media organizations; newspapers; television

McConnell, David L., 11, 124, 137

media organizations, 191, 278, 282–283, 286, 288, 368. *See also* mass media; newspapers; television

meishi. See business card

men, 82, 100, 116, 123, 196–198, 202–203, 217, 313; subordination to, 76; working, 198

mentors, 125–128, 130, 140–141, 180–181, 230–232, 235, 297. *See also* introductions; personal connections; *senpai*

migration, 61, 216, 294, 300, 311. *See also* foreign workers; foreigners

military, 157, 160–172, 354, 359; civilian control, 165–166; weapons, 162–163, 168. *See also* defense; security policy; Self-Defense Force

minikomi (small circulation publications), 43, 46, 372. *See also* bookstores, specialized; newsletters; social movements

ministers, 42, 349

Ministry of Economy, Trade and Industry (METI). *See* Ministry of International Trade and Industry

Ministry of Education, 11, 121, 127–129, 136, 200, 208, 211

Ministry of Education, Culture, Sports, Science, and Technology (MEXT). *See* Ministry of Education

Ministry of Finance, 253

Ministry of Foreign Affairs, 127, 135, 157, 158–159, 161, 249–251, 253–254, 260

Ministry of Health, Labour, and Welfare, 200, 207, 210, 232, 235, 243, 265, 300, 369

Ministry of Home Affairs, 125, 128–129

Ministry of International Trade and Industry, 242, 248, 250, 252

Ministry of Justice, 140–142

Misawa, 167, 169

Moeran, Brian, 3

mothers, 26, 199, 218, 281–282, 288–289, 307, 342, 344; of researcher, 340, 345; researchers as, 280–281, 295, 308; working, 296

multinational corporations, 299–300, 305–306

municipal government. *See* local government

municipal government offices. *See* local government offices

music, 21, 31, 277–278, 282–283, 287. See also *enka; karaoke;* popular culture

Nakane, Chie, 4

name card. *See* business card

National Science Foundation, 113, 122–123, 199–200, 208, 333

neighborhood associations, 316–317, 324, 330

neighborhoods, 12, 24, 44, 64, 187, 219, 269, 280, 310, 315–333, 335, 342

networks, 3, 10–14, 31, 36, 41–42, 49, 52, 114, 145, 253, 257, 296, 315–322, 329, 332. *See also* interviews, snowball; introductions; personal connections

neutrality, 132, 270–271, 350, 363. *See also* bias; factions; loyalty; sincerity

New Year's cards, 268. *See also* obligations; reciprocity

news: broadcasts, 11, 185, 186; process, 178–184

newsletters, 43, 46, 48–52, 92–93, 97, 242, 245, 284–285, 310, 368. See also *minikomi*

newspapers, 37–40, 43, 45–46, 49, 61, 86, 92, 135, 177, 180, 184–186, 217, 233–234, 240, 242–243, 249, 259, 266, 279, 287, 304, 310, 313, 342, 368; archival edition, 40, 185, 233; *Asahi Shinbun,* 185, 234, 259, 342, 368; *Mainichi Shinbun,* 185, 342, 368; *Nihon Keizai Shinbun,* 185; *Yomiuri Shinbun,* 97, 185, 234, 368

NGO. *See* nongovernmental organizations

NHK, 9, 11, 176–192, 232, 322, 368

Nikkeijin, 12, 290–291, 335–350. *See also* Japanese Americans; Japanese Brazilians; Japanese Peruvians

nongovernmental organizations (NGO), 205–206, 257, 295, 343, 349–350

nonprofit organizations (NPO), 294–295, 298–299, 304, 310
nonverbal communication. *See* demeanor; gesture; posture; silence
NPO. *See* nonprofit organizations

obligations, 14, 16, 86, 117, 141, 149, 289, 327, 333, 338. *See also* gifts; reciprocity
occupations. *See* coal miners; day laborers; editors; housewives; journalists; lawyers; ministers; police; priests; prosecutors; publishers; scientists; shopkeepers; wholesalers. *See also* work
Ogasawara, Yuko, 3
Ohnuki-Tierney, Emiko, 4
Okimoto, Daniel I., 3
Okinawa, 6, 9, 26, 167, 169, 170, 173
Okinawans, 170, 342, 344
omote (outward appearance), 255. See also *ura*
oral history, 264–265, 267–272. *See also* interviewing; interviews
organizations, 16, 24, 37, 43, 46–48, 53, 85–87, 92–93, 112, 119, 121–123, 144, 204–205, 209, 219, 227, 259, 262–264, 295, 321–322, 324–325, 329, 369; company-led, 283; umbrella, 43. *See also* aid agencies; business firms; civil society; government agencies; social movements, organizations
Osaka, 6, 30–31, 74, 79–80, 83–84, 92, 98, 102, 112, 133, 298, 303
outsiders, 5, 22, 42, 64, 120–121, 143–145, 148, 209, 218, 253, 255, 270–272, 320, 326, 330; researchers as, 103. *See also* foreigners

Parliament. *See* Diet
participant observation, 7, 14–16, 36, 57, 82, 112, 116, 125, 127, 134, 140,

284–285, 287, 289, 296, 305, 316–317, 332, 336–337, 346, 350. *See also* inquisitive observation
pāto. See work, part-time
peace, 167–172, 369
personal connections, 207, 241, 257, 265, 279, 282, 298–299, 318. *See also* go-between; introductions; networks
photographs, 33, 85, 100, 129, 187–188, 238, 262, 268–269, 279, 281, 285, 301, 323, 329, 356, 360–361, 364, 368
pilgrimage, 90–104
Plath, David W., 3–4
police, 36–37, 45, 47–48, 53, 65–68, 140, 144–147, 280. *See also* criminal justice system
policy issues, 120, 161, 164–165, 171–173, 198, 229–230, 233–235, 243–245, 373. *See also* defense policy; foreign aid; social issues
policy research, 171, 173, 229–231, 243, 252–253, 294, 298, 311. *See also* policy-making
policy-making, 6, 159–160, 165, 170–173, 248–253, 319; advisory committees, 241–242, 246. *See also* policy issues; policy research
political science, 3, 6, 185, 195, 231, 243–244, 254
politics, 3, 6, 12, 53, 157, 160, 166, 171, 176–177, 185, 233, 245, 248–249, 260–261, 306; opposition, 177–178; political parties, 158, 205, 369; political process, 172, 229. *See also* policy-making; Diet
popular culture, 11, 283; artifacts, 168; fan magazines, 278, 282; fans, 12, 279, 283–285, 289; *manga*, 32, 118; media, 27, 82, 259, 304; music, 278; stars, 26
Portuguese, 305, 337, 342–343, 345. *See also* research, multilingual
postcards, 41, 119, 203, 238, 299,

327–328. *See also* New Year's cards; thank-you notes

posters, 277, 290, 304, 322, 324, 327–328

posture, 71, 77, 286. *See also* demeanor

prayer, 98, 100–103

presentation of self, 50, 144, 329, 338, 344. *See also* researcher, characteristics of; role

priests, 42, 91, 98, 102

prisons, 11, 38–41, 50–51, 151; prisoners, 13, 15, 37, 40–41. *See also* criminal justice system

private sector, 128, 253, 259, 298. *See also* business firms; commercial interests; multinational corporations

prosecutors, 9, 11, 139, 140–154. *See also* criminal justice system; lawyers

protest, 9, 36, 37, 39, 40, 168, 170, 304. *See also* demonstrations; rally

pseudonyms, 140, 302, 305. *See also* anonymity; informed consent; research ethics

publications, 36, 43, 44, 46–47, 53–54, 86, 111, 119–120, 191, 227, 242–243, 259, 262, 370, 372; academic, 44, 91; business firm reports, 258; industry association reports, 258; of researcher in Japanese, 53, 119–120, 231–232, 236, 245; think tank reports, 242, 258. *See also* books; gray literature; magazine articles; *minikomi;* newsletters

publishers, 42–45, 119, 244, 369. *See also* editors

rally *(shūkai),* 47–48, 53. *See also* demonstrations; protest

Reader, Ian, 11, 89, 105

reading, 1, 41, 46, 56, 76, 162, 216, 330; background, 39, 126, 233, 244, 304; in English, 244

reciprocity, 16, 32, 64, 133, 311. *See also* gifts; obligations

Red Army, 39–41, 50, 54

Reiyūkai Kyōdan, 74–82. *See also* religion

reliability, of sources, 15, 45, 185

religion, 3, 6, 11, 71–96, 98, 103, 104; rituals, 72, 75, 83, 85, 89, 100, 102, 341, 355, 361; sacred sites, 90. *See also* Aum Shinrikyō; ministers; priests; Reiyūkai Kyōdan; shrines

reports. *See* documents; government publications; gray literature; publications

research: ethnographic, 113, 139, 317, 322, 326, 332, 352, 354, 364; getting started, 10, 230, 333; hazards of, 312; library, 249, 258; long-term, 136, 190–191, 207, 357, 364–365; multilingual, 305, 345; multi-site, 30, 36, 205, 286, 287; objectivity, 15–16, 49, 53, 154, 350; research questions, 188, 206, 209; sites, 6, 10, 15, 110, 117, 155, 196, 204, 337

research assistants, use of, 33, 182–183, 189–192, 203, 306

research ethics, 13, 52–53, 338, 346, 355–356, 365. *See also* gifts; informed consent; responsibility, of researcher; trust

research fellow. See *kenkyūin*

research methods, 7–8, 189, 240, 295; qualitative, 204, 209, 227. *See also* case studies; data collection techniques; inquisitive observation; interviewing; participant observation; research; survey research; videotape

research resources, 263; primary materials, 45, 284; secondary sources, 45, 47, 181; yearbooks, 283. *See also* archival resources; electronic resources; government publications; gray literature;

social welfare, 12, 227, 230, 232, 243–244. *See also* long-term care insurance; policy research; social issues

socializing, 49, 133, 136, 252, 256. *See also* drinking

sociology, 2, 6, 8, 23, 144, 195–196, 201, 203, 214, 295

soto (outside), 254. See also *uchi*

sponsorship: informal, 317, 332; institutional, 39–40, 58, 206, 219; professors, 54, 61, 82, 227–228, 231. *See also* academic affiliation

state, the, 36–37, 157, 161, 165–166, 265. *See also* government . . .

statistical analysis, 197, 210, 223

statistics, 10, 12, 65, 68, 74, 111, 121, 204, 207, 210, 218–220, 224–227, 240–242, 373; reliability, 240; tables, 197, 207, 239, 241, 243, 262. *See also* data; data, individuallevel; survey research

status, 4, 31, 68, 96, 101, 111, 114, 130, 145, 148, 159, 180–181, 227, 235–236, 270, 284, 291, 310, 322, 340–341, 344, 347, 365; of researcher, 78, 215, 225–226, 269, 281, 338. *See also* age; hierarchy; role

Steinhoff, Patricia G., 1, 6, 11, 36, 54

stereotypes, 5, 27, 84, 263, 339, 346, 347. *See also* foreign workers; harmony

Steslicke, William, 232

study groups, 241, 253–254

support groups, 43, 48–52, 295, 300, 304–305, 310, 349

survey research, 10–11, 33, 74, 79–80, 112, 116, 119, 196–208, 215–216, 219, 222–223, 241, 345; mail surveys, 80, 203, 223–224; questionnaires, 115, 201, 206, 217, 223–224, 250, 254; representative sample, 15, 199, 201–202, 204, 279; response rate, 201–205, 224; Social Science Japan

Data Archive, 210–211; Social Stratification and Mobility Survey, 208–210

sushi, 146, 318, 320–323

Suye-mura, 354, 364–365, 374

Takamatsu, 356, 359

Tamanoi, Mariko, 4

tape recorder, 38–39, 132, 182–183, 217, 222–225, 268, 291, 302, 338. *See also* interviews, tape recording; video-tape

tatemae (formal position), 127, 143–145, 152, 255–256, 258, 325. See also *honne*

teachers, 5, 11, 22, 28, 31, 60, 67–68, 72, 82, 124, 126, 129–137, 148–149, 154, 210, 217, 266, 278, 282, 287–291, 349. *See also* education; high schools; JET Program; schools

teenagers, 10, 21–22, 29, 34, 343. *See also* children

television, 9, 82, 112, 177–178, 184, 187, 282, 290, 359, 364–365; documentaries, 217; news, 11, 177–178, 185–188, 191; stations, 282

Thailand, 256, 257, 305

thank-you notes, 238, 268. *See also* etiquette; New Year's cards; postcards

theory, 8, 82, 137, 198, 245, 272, 295

think tanks, 25–27, 159, 251, 253, 258; reports, 242

Third World, 120, 345

Tohoku, 26, 216

Tokyo, 3, 5–7, 21–22, 27–31, 34, 37–39, 43, 51, 54–55, 58–59, 70, 74, 79–80, 103, 111, 118, 122, 126–129, 133, 136, 153, 156, 158–159, 162, 166–171, 202, 204–205, 214–233, 240, 246, 251, 258, 260, 262, 277, 279–280, 288, 298, 303, 309–310, 315, 317–318, 328, 335–336, 340–341, 344, 369

tradition, 31, 71, 328